D1029692

ALFRED CALDWELL

EDITED BY **DENNIS DOMER** ■

ALFRED CALDWELL

The Life and Work of a Prairie School Landscape Architect

The Johns Hopkins University Press

BALTIMORE AND LONDON

Published in cooperation with the Center for American Places,
Harrisonburg, Virginia

© 1997 The Johns Hopkins University Press
All rights reserved. Published 1997
Printed in the United States of America on acid-free paper

06   05   04   03   02   01   00   99   98   97   5   4   3   2   1

The Johns Hopkins University Press
2715 North Charles Street
Baltimore, Maryland 21218-4319
The Johns Hopkins Press Ltd., London

Library of Congress Cataloging-in-Publication data will be found
at the end of this book.
A catalog record for this book is available from the British
Library.

Frontispiece: Alfred Caldwell at the council ring, Eagle Point
Park, Dubuque, Iowa, 1991. (Photo by Dennis Domer)

ISBN 0-8018-5551-9

To Geda
Close to the hand were you, close to the heart—A. C.

CONTENTS

Like a Roman soldier rereading Epictetus before every battle, I have studied Alfred Caldwell's life and grasped endlessly for every meaning. Embedded in "Atlantis and Return," his autobiography of prose and poetry, one finds the major thoughts and deeds of his many years. The people of his life are all there too, however hidden by symbol or allusion. It is impossible, though, to miss the passion in his writing, even as it would be impossible to avoid his passion were he sitting beside you as you read his book. In these lines his burning heart lives on. For the courage of his life and the inspiration I have derived from his counsel, I gratefully acknowledge Alfred Caldwell.

The years I spent with Caldwell, the days I lingered in archives before collections of his spectacular drawings, and the hours I searched through every scrap of paper in every closet would not have been possible without a grant from the Graham Foundation for the Advancement of the Fine Arts. My colleague Professor Gerald McSheffrey, who received the grant jointly with me and administered it and who participated in many of the travels, always brought with his Irish wit a crisp perspective on our subject. Early on he collaborated with me and wrote essays that gave me important directions to follow, but most important, he unflaggingly pressed me to finish this volume of Caldwell's work.

To Carol Caldwell Dooley, who helped me make many complicated connections with Caldwell, I owe my heartfelt thanks. From her I received countless interpretations of his life. She knows this man best. To George Schipporeit, formerly dean of the College of Architecture at Illinois Institute of Technology and a student and longtime friend of Caldwell's, I give praise, for he worked tirelessly on my behalf and cheerfully drove me hundreds of miles from place to place. Dan Lawrence of Los Angeles spent many hours planning Caldwell's return to southern California in 1994, and for three days he took us from appointment to appointment over the freeways of that warm Siberia. He also provided a long interview and copies of all his student work at the University of Southern California. Likewise, Dennis DePietro of Los Angeles sent audiotapes of lectures Caldwell gave at USC as well as photographs of his student work.

John Hail and his staff at the Dubuque, Iowa, Park and Recreation Department provided many documents and spent two days showing us Eagle Point Park when Alfred made his fiery return in 1991. Mrs. Helen Henschel, who was secretary to the chairman of the Dubuque Park Board when Caldwell built Eagle Point Park, sent me her "Memories of Alfred Caldwell" and photos of the park and gave me vivid descriptions of the man she deemed a "poet-artist." The staff at the Dubuque Historical Society was helpful and responsive. To all these people I am much indebted.

Julia Sniderman of the Chicago Park District reviewed the original volume and urged me to take it beyond Caldwell's early life. Bart H. Ryckbosch, at that time archivist and curator of Special Collections at the Chicago Park Distrist and now with the Art Institute of Chicago, assisted me with the reproduction of Caldwell's large drawings for Chicago's parks. Carol Doty, exhibit and interpretation specialist of the Morton Arboretum, spent most of an afternoon copying Caldwell's letters to Jens Jensen. Howard Shubert and Jean-François Bédard of the Canadian Centre for Architecture helped me through the large collection of Caldwell's drawings in Montreal, and Phyllis Lambert, founder of the CCA, engaged me in a long, spirited conversation about Caldwell deep in the vaults of her fantastic center. I also appreciate the efforts of Luigi Mumford of the Art Institute of Chicago and the librarians at the Ryerson and Burnham Archives of the Art Institute of Chicago. Kathleen C. McDonough, manuscript reference librarian at the Library of Congress, assisted me with the papers of Ludwig Mies van der Rohe. Susan Hikida, assistant archivist at the University of Southern California Library, copied a stack of student correspondence about Caldwell's teaching days at USC. Anita Anderson, librarian of the IIT College of Architecture, gave her time graciously in my cause. George Danforth, Mies van der Rohe's successor as dean of IIT, provided helpful comments and corrections to the text.

For information, interviews, meetings, and assistance of many kinds, I also wish to thank the following individuals: Eli Bornstein, editor of the *Structurist*, Gerald Estes, David Swan, Paul Thomas, Myron Goldsmith, John Vinci, Luke Cosme, Robert Grese, William Tishler, Susanne Askinoza, James Tyler, Crombie and Hope Taylor, Gene Sommers, Louis Johnson, David Sharpe, James DeStefano, Gertrude Kerbis, Indira Berndtson of the Frank Lloyd Wright Archives, Ceci Rusnak, George F. Thompson, president of the Center for American Places and my editor for this project, Carol Mishler, associate editor of the Center for American Places, Alice M. Bennett, senior manuscript editor at the University of Chicago Press, Geraldine Stey of the State Historical Society of Wisconsin, David Hiebert and Laura F. Triplett at Arnold Air Force Base, Tennessee, Mary Ann Latham, David Spaeth, John R. Kuefel of the Picture Works, R. Thomas Schorer, James Porter, Ron Altoon, Jim Kehr, Eric Katzmaier, Sonja Olson, John Dooley, Mark Alfred Buchman, John Sugden, William Tuttle, James Mayo, John Gaunt, Lois Clark, Kent Spreckelmeyer, Barbara Watkins, Richard Holland, Cynthia Bryant, and Richard Gwin. To others not mentioned here, whom I have met in this work over the past four years, please accept my gratitude.

Cynthia Muckey of the School of Architecture and Urban Design at the University of Kansas entered the manuscript on the computer and reproduced it tirelessly in its several manifestations. I continuously appreciate her help and the help of Julie Rea and Heather Suggs, who typed in early drafts. Professor Michael Johnson, a poet and the chair of the Department of English at the University of Kansas, gave me good advice about the quality of Caldwell's compelling work.

And finally, to Shirley Domer, my partner and guide through life, I am grateful for helping me with editing decisions, grammar issues, spelling problems, and questions of layout and meaning, and for supporting me through thick and thin.

Letters from Caldwell are quoted as written except that obvious misspellings have been silently corrected; variant spellings are left as is, and *sic* is added only where there might be confusion.

Caldwell's published works are reproduced as they appeared in print, but with obvious typographical errors silently corrected and punctuation, spelling, and capitalization regularized. Prose works by Caldwell that have never before been published have been lightly edited to correct any misspellings and grammatical errors or infelicities as well as typographical errors. Punctuation, spelling, and capitalization have been minimally adjusted, and numbers have been spelled out where appropriate. Poems are for the most part reproduced as written in both wording and format.

The footnotes to "Atlantis and Return" are the editor's, and those to the essay "The Living Landscape" are Caldwell's.

Birth

    St. Louis, Missouri, May 26, 1903

Family

    Wife, Virginia (April 9, 1905, to September 2, 1988)
    Daughter, Carol Caldwell Dooley (born January 25, 1931)
    Son, James Allen Caldwell (born December 12, 1933)

Education

    Master of science in city planning, Illinois Institute of Technology, 1948
    Thesis, "The City in the Landscape: A Preface for Planning"

Honors

    Distinguished Educator Award, Chicago chapter of the AIA, 1980
    ACSA Distinguished Professor, 1985
    Doctor of Humane Letters, Illinois Institute of Technology, 1988

Experience

    1924–31, assistant to Jens Jensen
    1931–34, private practice as landscape architect, Chicago
    1934–36, superintendent of parks, Eagle Point Park, Dubuque, Iowa
    1936–39, landscape designer, Chicago Park District
    1940–45, civil engineer, United States War Department

1945–60, professor of architecture, Illinois Institute of Technology

1960–64, city planner, Department of City Planning, Chicago

1965, visiting professor, Virginia Polytechnic Institute, Blacksburg, Virginia

1965–74, professor of architecture, University of Southern California, Los Angeles

1973–81, private landscape architecture practice, Los Angeles and Bristol, Wisconsin

1981–96, Ludwig Mies van der Rohe Professor of Architecture, Illinois Institute of Technology

ALFRED CALDWELL

THE LIFE OF ALFRED CALDWELL

Dear life be good and let me worship you;
Black as the night, I say, and strewn with jewels
Is this forlorn desire that is your due.
                    Alfred Caldwell, The sonnets of "Atlantis and Return"

In spite of Alfred Caldwell's reputation in Chicago as a professor at Illinois Institute of Technology and as a landscape architect in the Chicago Park District, scholars are only beginning to understand the significant role he played in modern architecture—particularly his contributions to the prairie school as a landscape architect.[1] There are many reasons for this delay. For years historians worshiped only a few of the modern masters, creating a narrow picture of modern architecture and leaving many important individuals from the prairie school and other schools of modernism forgotten in the background.[2] Within this background Caldwell was a shadow figure who worked quietly with Ludwig Mies van der Rohe, Ludwig Hilberseimer, and Jens Jensen.[3] During his California years he was the éminence gris behind Craig Ellwood's office. In the legacies of all these famous men, Caldwell's essential contribution still lies hidden. They simply absorbed his ideas and often failed to credit him. Even Chicago scholars such as Carl Condit, whose job it was to unearth the real makers of the Chicago school of architecture, misattributed Caldwell's Lily Pool in Lincoln Park to the "landscape architect's staff of the Chicago Park District," though Caldwell's name was clearly on the drawing.[4] Further, Caldwell's drawings have been scattered among his friends and among several archives, making them difficult to understand in a coherent way.[5]

As a deeply philosophical man under the influence of Friedrich Nietzsche, Oswald Spengler, José Ortega y Gasset, and poets such as Algernon Swinburne, Caldwell disdained mass culture and considered it demeaning to seek notoriety.[6] And though he has published many articles in *Landscape Architecture*, the *Structurist*, and *Encyclopaedia Britannica*, they remain largely unknown. A major manuscript, "The Living Landscape," was lost for years and has never been published.[7] His autobiography for the years 1903 to 1936, "Atlantis and Return," is only now coming to light. Finally, his earthy appearance, with ever present pipe, his sense of humor, and his modest demeanor belie a genius that is almost always explosive. Today this genius is closed off from many people because it is expressed in powerful jeremiads that tend to leave them stunned. Though Caldwell is not religious in a traditional sense, "there is something of the Old Testament prophet in his manner of speaking and listening and in his penetrating gaze."[8] And though these qualities are also those of a great teacher, they leave one searching for words to explain an ineffable nature. With the publication of this book, Caldwell speaks for himself as poet, landscape architect, architect, civil engineer, city planner, philosopher, and teacher.

Born in St. Louis, Missouri, on May 26, 1903, the third of six children, in 1909 Alfred Caldwell moved to Chicago, where he met hardship early on.[9] His father had squandered the family fortune, and Caldwell grew up in poverty listening to the incessant battles between his beloved mother and his unsuccessful father. Caldwell was often on his own in the city, and he became both streetwise and an astute, inquiring observer of society. "Pervasive in all his childhood experiences was the burgeoning industrial city of Chicago, with its ethnic neighborhoods, its stench and poverty, its grime and graft, wedged between the great blue lake on the east and the expansive green prairies to the west."[10] In street games he acted out the legends of Homer and King Arthur and dreamed of lost cities. He found ways to watch the Chicago Cubs play at Wrigley Field without a ticket. But his days of play with friends such as Louie Haller were short. He never had any money, and as a young entrepreneur he sold farm and nursery produce door-to-door and thus expanded his knowledge of the world. He loved to grow things, including mushrooms that he raised in the basement and sold to augment the produce he picked up at the farmers' market. His business interests also included a newspaper stand: the stories of wars, millionaires, and gangsters on the front page fueled his young imagination. Caldwell was a dreamer, and his dreams of a city eventually turned into a dream as big as life, "Atlantis and Return." On a clear day Caldwell could see civic pride emanating from tall buildings and new parks in Chicago, but behind them lurked the dark satanic mills described by

William Blake. His boyish dream was to dredge up a lost city from the bottom of a murky sea, set it right, and create an advanced civilization. It was a thoroughly modern dream.

Caldwell was a thinker and philosopher early on. "Highly intelligent and sensitive, and urged on by his French American mother, in his teenage years he acquired reading habits that lasted a lifetime."[11] He tells how one summer his mother made him read Wells's *Short History of the World* and commit it to memory. He memorized poetry as well, poetry that he has quoted passionately throughout his life. He borrowed books of poems from school and carried them around until they wore out his pockets. Though school itself was not his main interest, he did well at Ravenswood Primary School and at Lakeview High School, where he encountered several memorable teachers of Latin (and fell in love with one of them). He also learned Latin while studying botany with Dr. Pepoon. Poetry and Latin and English literature fired his passion. Science and technology shaped an analytical mind, particularly through his high school science teacher, the noted botanist Dr. Hermann Silas Pepoon, who inspired him with the wonders of nature. Pepoon had published a book on the flora of Chicago, and for his young student "he made nature romance . . . and like others in the class, I wanted to be like him."[12] Caldwell later used his Latin and his science together in the landscape drawings: all the plants carried their Latin names alongside technical illustrations of pools, walkways, and pavilions.

He was a determined young man and ambitious to make a difference. In response to advice from Charles Terrel, a family friend, that he continue his studies, in 1921, at age eighteen, he took his small savings and headed for the University of Illinois at Champaign-Urbana to study landscape architecture.[13] Both of Caldwell's periods of study at the university were short-lived. His studies bored him. Like Sullivan and Wright, he was impatient to build and found the university tedious. He was also poor. Somehow he managed to make a living by doing odd jobs and by selling trees and shrubs for a national catalog company, which earned him small commissions. He even became a member of a fraternity, waiting on tables to pay his way. But he left disappointed, for whatever he was seeking was to be found not in school but at work, and though he would later teach at universities for more than forty-five years he always disdained them. He loved to teach because he was good at it, but from the very beginning he hated institutional humdrum like faculty meetings and despised intellectual laziness or mediocrity. He often tells how Frank Lloyd Wright recommended in a lecture to students at Lawrence College that instead of studying they go home and find a job that would teach them something.[14] Of his own experience as a student Caldwell said, "No lifted word, no beautiful infallible phrase ever disturbed the pedagogical cemetery."[15]

Alfred Caldwell, 1920. (Courtesy of Carol Caldwell Dooley)

Shortly after leaving the university Caldwell eloped "in childlike inno-cence" with his seventeen-year-old cousin, Virginia, who was called Geda.[16] "Geda," he said, "was only a slip of a girl" with a ready smile and an outgoing personality. After they married in Cleveland in 1923, they returned to Chicago, where Caldwell began a business relationship with George Donoghue, an engi-neer and businessman who later became superintendent of the South Chicago Park District. Caldwell wanted to be an architect like his heroes Louis Sullivan and Frank Lloyd Wright, and his experience at the university had only made him more determined to start in business for himself. He introduced himself to Donoghue, who was amused by the young man's request for sponsorship of an architectural practice in which Caldwell would provide the experience while he, as the major shareholder, would provide the capital. "He laughed at me," Cald-well remembered, "and he said, 'Al, you're really laughable but I love you. You come to my office, and I'll talk to you.' So I went to his office in downtown Chicago and he said, 'You know, I talked about this with my wife and she said I shouldn't do it, and other people said I shouldn't do it, but you know, there's an old saying: Two people go into business, one of them has money and the other has the experience. When they go out of business, the man who had the experience has the money and the man who had the money has the experience.' And he laughed over that and said, 'But I'll do it!'" This new venture, with offices in the Wrigley Building, met with some financial success, and for about two years the

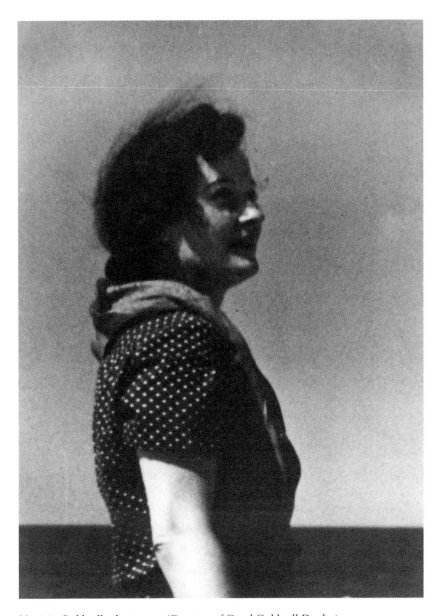

Virginia Caldwell, about 1935. (Courtesy of Carol Caldwell Dooley)

young entrepreneur made a living on small building and landscape projects. He even bought his first automobile. But his dreams of reaching the Olympian heights of the great Sullivan and Wright seemed even further out of reach. He became aware of how little he knew and surmised that he had "only been trading dollars, and needed to learn something first."

At this juncture, in about 1924, his old mentor Charles Terrel suggested that Caldwell work with Jens Jensen.[17] Terrel himself had worked for Jensen and had frequently spoken to Caldwell about him. In 1884, at age twenty-four, Jensen had arrived in Florida as an immigrant from Denmark. In 1885 he and his wife moved to Iowa, where he worked as a farm laborer. The following year they moved to Chicago and Jensen was employed as a gardener by the West Park Commission. By 1895 he had become superintendent of Union Park, and a year later he was superintendent of Humboldt Park. Jensen made significant contributions to the landscape design tradition of Andrew Jackson Downing, Frederick Law Olmsted, H. W. S. Cleveland, and William Le Baron Jenney, who made the natural environment a metaphor for their landscape design. In this tradition Jensen became a "primary practitioner of the 'Prairie style' of landscape gardening" in Chicago along with Ossian Cole Simonds.[18]

Recognizing Simonds and Jensen as leaders of the movement, Wilhelm Miller wrote an early article about the prairie style, which he said could be "characterized by preservation of typical western scenery, by restoration of local color and by repetition of the horizontal line of land or sky, which is the strongest feature of prairie scenery."[19] With these three principles in mind, Jensen created parks with broad prairie vistas formed by meadows edged with native plants, shrubs, and trees. He used stratified rock formations, especially the council ring, to emphasize the horizontality of the region and to provide places for democratic discussion.[20] As a member of the urban reform movement in Chicago, Jensen believed the park system should help relieve the manifold ills of the city. He was also an ecologist who recognized that the prairie was vanishing under the pavement of Chicago, and in 1913 he founded an early preservation organization, the Friends of Our Native Landscape. In addition to his work for the Park District, Jensen had many Chicago landscape clients from 1900 to 1935, including wealthy owners of the great suburban estates surrounding Chicago in Illinois and Wisconsin. Henry Ford of Dearborn, Michigan, was the most famous. By 1924 Jens Jensen had already achieved great distinction as a landscape architect and civic leader. As a man who had both knowledge and causes, he perfectly fit the needs of the idealistic Caldwell.[21]

Besides his being newlywed, impoverished, and idealistic, Caldwell's big trouble as he saw it in 1924 was that "I didn't know anything. I was a phenomenal boy of twenty-one, but I didn't know anything and I hated universities, and there was only one answer. There was one man who was the greatest man in the world, named Jens Jensen." With the help of Charles Terrel, Caldwell was able to get an appointment with Jensen, but it took all his courage to go to Jensen's office in Ravinia, Illinois. A secretary showed him into the studio, and he found Jensen sitting by the fireplace. He was "six feet two inches tall, red-haired, eager" as Caldwell recalls. "Are you any good?" asked Jensen, and without waiting for a reply he continued, "I've been watching the sunshine on the hazelnut tree." He talked about waste in America, about how technology gives but also destroys,

Jens Jensen. (Courtesy of Alfred Caldwell)

about the need to save the wetlands, the Everglades, and the prairies, and about how water was being poisoned with our own waste. "He was such a splendid talker. I didn't say a word, you know," Caldwell remembers. The secretary asked him to stay for lunch in the studio, and Jensen continued talking. "It made a tremendous impression on me," Caldwell notes. "He became the great symbol of my life."

Jensen was a symbol, but he was also an explicit guide for Caldwell's conduct of his own life. Caldwell adopted many of Jensen's characteristic values and employed his modes of expressing them, values and modes that he no doubt heard about at their first meeting. Jensen's ecological lecture turned into a jeremiad, a rhetorical device that Caldwell himself would later be remembered for.[22] "He screamed from excitement," Caldwell remarked. "He was in his peak and very emotional. Tears would come down from his eyes, streams, hot tears." Jensen "had a bad temper," according to Caldwell, and wasn't afraid to use it. Nor was Caldwell, who never hesitated to raise his voice about the hideousness of cities and cry over the loss of the prairie. Caldwell frequently used his temper to make a point, just as Jensen did. Caldwell was mesmerized by Jensen, and Jensen was in a sense mesmerized by Caldwell. At least he recognized the boy's great potential as that September morning stretched into afternoon. At the end of the session he told Caldwell to see his engineer the next day for a job. Except for his wife, throughout his life there was nothing Caldwell found more important and more exciting than a job, and this was a job with the greatest man in the world! From Jensen he could learn something.

Between 1924 and 1929 Caldwell completed a large number of landscape jobs with Jensen and eventually became superintendent on many of Jensen's projects. "I did small jobs for him. But I did one job that he considered a great masterpiece. The Clarke house in Evanston. I was one year working there, and that was the best thing I did in my lifetime."[23] Caldwell's work at the Harley Clarke house in 1925 included "landscape work, planting, walks, drives and gardens," according to a list of his executed work he drew up in 1939 to accompany a discussion of his "experiential qualifications."[24] Caldwell worked on other notable landscape projects for Jensen, including the O. C. Barber house (1924) in Akron, Ohio; the Norman Perry house (1926) in Culver, Indiana; the Harold Florsheim house in Ravinia, Illinois (1927); the Edsel B. Ford house (1926–32), designed by Albert Kahn in Grosse Pointe Shores, Michigan; stone garden seats for Jens Jensen's garden in Ravinia, Illinois, in 1928; and a fountain and stonework for the Mrs. Julius Rosenwald Memorial (1928) in Ravinia.[25] The hours were long and the pay meager at sixty dollars a week, but Caldwell was so inspired by Jensen that he concentrated all his energies on the enterprise. Jensen would visit the sites occasionally, not so much to give orders as to consult on the subtleties of the enterprise. Dressed immaculately, "looking not unlike Mark Twain," he viewed the landscape as a painter would, advising on the shape of a lake or the exact positioning of a group of trees. "I never drew a line for Jensen. We did it all out on the landscapes. It all had to be done out of the air as he talked about it. Then he went away and I wouldn't see him for two or three weeks, and then I would show him what I had done."[26] The six years Caldwell spent with Jensen were seminal in his career because he was given responsibilities that taught him all aspects of

Harley L. Clarke grounds, Evanston, Illinois, 1926. Jens Jensen, landscape architect; Alfred Caldwell, superintendent. (Photo by Richard Nickel; courtesy of Alfred Caldwell)

landscape design from philosophy to process. Although landscape design was art to the master, for his young superintendent it was backbreaking work; but the most difficult work was the most important. "Stonework—that's how he got to me," Caldwell confesses. "I became sophisticated enough that I really was good at it. It came naturally."

But the exhilaration of learning from a master was halted by the stock market crash of 1929. For Jensen the day was about lost fortunes, fortunes that had fed the growth of building in the Chicago area throughout his career.[27] At sixty-nine Jensen had been continuously busy for forty-five years, either in the Park District or with a relatively large private practice, but after the crash not even he had enough work to keep his best people. Jensen's business would never recover its vitality, and Caldwell lost his job. It was not the first job he had lost, nor would it be the last. The shock of not having work, followed by days of desperation and

eventually hunger, happened frequently in Caldwell's career. Deprivation became a central theme of his life, emerging not only in interviews but also in
"Atlantis and Return." "Unless you lived through it, no one could imagine just
how bad things were," Caldwell remembers. He was barely able to keep the
family alive with whatever small jobs he could garner.

During the long days between jobs Caldwell drew imaginary projects and
read voraciously. He had plenty of time to study, a habit he had picked up to fill
his days when Jensen's work halted in cold weather. He would gladly have studied
with Frank Lloyd Wright, whom he had met while working for Jens Jensen. He
had carefully observed Wright's work in Oak Park since the day in about 1925
when he bought his first flivver and took Geda for a ride to see Wright houses. In
spite of his passionate need to study the work of the prairie school master,
however, a search for books on Wright in Chicago libraries during the early 1930s
was in vain. Wright had been an outcast since the scandal that broke in 1910 when
he left Oak Park with Mrs. Cheney to go to Berlin to prepare the Wasmuth
exhibition drawings. Although books and articles on Wright existed, most were
published in Europe, and many libraries probably would not have purchased
them even had they been available.[28] Caldwell's thirst eventually was quenched
in the studio of the master himself at Spring Green, Wisconsin.

Caldwell might never have taken the first of four trips to Taliesin had he not
been working for Jensen. Jensen and Wright knew and respected each other, but
they were not friends, though they collaborated uneasily on a number of projects.
Both men had big egos, and each claimed to know more than the other. Jensen
did not like Wright's prairie style architecture, with its flat roofs. He recommended the pitched roof, a more vernacular expression that responded better to
the midwestern climate. And Wright did not like Jensen's landscape proposals for
his prairie residences.[29] When Wright's name came up in conversation with
Caldwell, Jensen pronounced Wright "an actor."[30] Jensen's criticisms, however,
did not dissuade Caldwell from his interest in Wright. Wright's name came up
again between Caldwell and Bob Priest, who worked for Jensen as a day laborer.
Caldwell and Priest were "close as thieves," and Priest emboldened Caldwell,
who was otherwise shy. Together they drove to Spring Green in Caldwell's flivver
for the first meeting, in about 1927. They found Wright indignantly chasing pigs
out of his cornfield. Caldwell recalls that he introduced Priest as an eccentric
with degrees from Harvard and Oxford, and Wright asked if he was carrying any
bombs. The only bombs Priest brought were his naive questions about new
photographs Wright showed them of the Imperial Hotel in Tokyo. Priest thought
the building looked heavy, but Wright assured him it was not. Things must have
improved, because at their departure, Caldwell remembers, Wright said, "I'm
glad you boys came. We artists have to stick together." "Not architects, artists,"

Caldwell proclaimed with a smile, touching his first finger to his thumb. It was the beginning of a significant yet problematic relationship.

Approximately a year and a half later, Caldwell became bored while moving stone on one of Jensen's projects near La Valle, Wisconsin. He was thinking a lot about Wright, and over the lunch break he called him from a pay telephone in this small town about twenty miles north of Spring Green. "I want to talk to you very much," Caldwell said, and Wright replied that he could come "if you promise not to talk too much." So Caldwell drove up that afternoon, and he remembers that Wright was wonderful and wanted to talk mostly about him. "He asked me what I did. I told him all the details about myself. Then he said, What do you do for yourself, anything? I said, I write poetry. He replied that it's good to write a poem but better to live one." From then on Caldwell tried to incorporate his poetry into his life, and he later called his poetry his Rosetta stone. Wright and Caldwell also talked about Sullivan's firing Wright for doing outside work. According to Caldwell, Wright was furious with Sullivan yet believed his *lieber Meister* was right to fire him. As they parted Wright asked Caldwell to bring Geda to Spring Green on his next trip. He said that Mrs. Wright was all alone, and if the Caldwells were to stay awhile, the women could grow flowers together like the Japanese.

This was Wright's invitation to join what would become the fellowship, an invitation Caldwell would have gladly accepted except that Geda wanted nothing to do with it. She understood Wright's importance and was not against her husband's spending time in Spring Green, but she did not want to live in someone else's home. She told him she would go back to Cleveland until he returned for her. Caldwell's third trip to Taliesin in about 1930 was difficult because he had to turn down Wright's invitation. Caldwell apparently spent several days there on this visit. Part of the time he joined in the chores, and the rest he spent carefully studying Taliesin's buildings, talking to Wright, and reading books in Wright's studio. Caldwell liked to get up early, and one morning he decided to go down to Wright's studio to read.

> So I came in about seven o'clock and walked briskly into the room, and there was Frank Lloyd Wright sitting over there writing the Princeton lectures. And he looked up at me with early morning sourness in his face, and I thought, well, I stepped right into this like a brass funnel and I might as well stay here. So I just turned the pages a little bit, gently. I kept looking over at Wright. The books were fabulous. They were the new books. Oh, they were the books I had been waiting for. They were the new books by new young writers, and they talked about Wright incessantly. I was in absolute paradise. Finally, I thought to relieve this terrible uncertainty I would say something. So I said, "Mr. Wright, they sure talk a lot about you, don't they." And he looked up,

sour for these many years of neglect. He said, "I wish to hell they would give me some buildings and stop talking about me."[31]

Caldwell remembers that Wright was in bad shape at that time. Early one morning Caldwell was standing out on the terrace at Taliesin. "It was one of the most beautiful terraces I ever saw in my life, facing the farm fields. Suddenly I felt a hand on my shoulder, and I looked up and it was Wright." Wright always called him by his first name. "He was a wonderful guy that way and not at all the devil on wheels he's depicted as." Caldwell recalls their poignant conversation of over sixty years ago.

> Mr. Wright said, "Alfred, I haven't had a building for eight years. It is impossible for a genuine architect to operate in America. So what I'm going to do, I'm going to be a farmer. You see this land over there? That's real good soil. It belongs to my uncles. It's two hundred acres. It could be mine if I want it. I'm going to farm it. You stay, and we'll farm it together. How's that? Stay with me."[32]

"Geda won't come," Caldwell replied. Wright assumed that Virginia wouldn't come because of his reputation as a ladies' man. He explained to Caldwell that at sixty-seven he would not be falling in love with her. Caldwell replied that Geda was too innocent to worry about that; she wanted to live in her own house. Wright told Caldwell to go home to her.

Caldwell did go back to Chicago, but for some time he obsessed about his parting with Wright. On March 27, 1932, he wrote Wright a letter of explanation.

> Dear Frank Lloyd Wright—
>
> May I come up to see you at Taliesin some time next month? My request is meager. I only wish to spend one day and to talk to you a short time or as long as you are inclined.
>
> Silence is strong:
>
> I left Taliesin because you were greater than I supposed. I say this without ornament but it is in my heart. It is clean and true.
>
> It is the gap that creates; a species of ignorance that creates. Let me have only a quick look at the giant. Let me observe only roughly the shape of his club. I shall go away to the next mountain and try my strength. I shall curse myself perhaps for not remembering in which hand he held his club. But my ignorance shall be my salvation. I shall end up holding my club in my best hand—the hand most natural to me. Did Horace Trumbel write another Leaves of Grass?
>
> So much for the incident of my leaving—
>
> I must hold myself in. But listen oh cube-maker, form-finder, trail-driver! I do not praise you half-measure. I do not first tip my hat to Louis Sullivan before I pay you a pretty compliment. I have calculated close and I know where you stand. I know your significance. Let Oswald Spengler go to Oak

Park, to Tokio and California and then come back and write his book over again.[33]

Caldwell did not receive a reply from Wright, but apparently this meant nothing negative, because he and Geda visited Taliesin again between 1934 and 1936 while Caldwell was working on Eagle Point Park in Dubuque, Iowa, a project Wright admired. This time Caldwell found Wright in a Taliesin field planting trees with his apprentices. Wright was tossing the trees randomly here and there, and the apprentices planted them wherever they landed. During their discussions Wright asked if Caldwell was writing any poetry, and he replied that he was so busy constructing the park that he didn't have time. Wright insisted that construction was poetry. Apparently Caldwell had brought some poems with him, because he remembers reading them to Wright, who laughed because they were so serious. This response did not offend Caldwell at all because, as Caldwell said later, "Wright was really my alter ego." This was particularly true at that time; visitors to Eagle Point Park would forever mistake Caldwell's work for Wright's. Certainly Caldwell had Wright and Jens Jensen in mind when he designed it. He believed that both men had brought the ideas of Jefferson, Whitman, Emerson, and Thoreau into a visible, modern form in which "the concept of motion was embodied in a powerful symbol: the prairie."[34] For the rest of his life Caldwell used the dynamic principles of the prairie he had learned from the two masters, and more than half a century later Caldwell confessed, "I am more influenced by Wright than by Jensen. People sometimes thought I was influenced by Mies or Sullivan. I was really only interested in Wright. I had a feeling of joy when I saw Wright's buildings."

Although both Jensen and Wright had a profound impact on Caldwell's career, neither could help him financially during the Great Depression. Jensen had nothing. Wright offered Taliesin several times, an impossible dream for Caldwell. Having left Jensen's employ in 1931, Caldwell was on the streets, finding only a few odd jobs here and there to support his wife and his baby daughter, Carol. "But lost in exile, I on midnight tours . . . ," Caldwell wrote forty years later in the first sonnet of "Atlantis and Return." These dreary days lasted until after the election of Franklin Delano Roosevelt and the establishment of the Civil Works Administration in the first year of the new president's administration. Caldwell became a direct beneficiary of Roosevelt's New Deal when he finally found a job in late 1933 through his old friend George Donoghue, who was by then the general superintendent of the South Parks in Chicago. Donoghue was able to help Caldwell get a position as a landscape superintendent on a CWA bridge and garden project for the South Park commissioners. Donoghue saved him several times throughout the depression.[35]

Caldwell had been working on this project for only about two months when

Gateway Pavilion, Eagle Point Park, Dubuque, Iowa, 1936. (Photo by Dennis Domer)

Donoghue called him into his office in January 1934. Through Vic K. Brown, superintendent of playgrounds and sports for the South Park commissioners, Donoghue had received notice of an opening for a WPA (Works Progress Administration) superintendent in Dubuque, Iowa, a job for which Caldwell was highly qualified. Donoghue wrote Charles T. Landon in Dubuque that Caldwell "has the faculty of transforming unsightly spaces into beautiful vistas. In making transformations of this kind he always takes the opportunity of using materials at hand rather than going to great expense to bring materials in from the outside." Donoghue went on to recount a luncheon conversation with Jens Jensen in which Jensen described Caldwell as "a genius and in his judgment . . . the outstanding prospect as a landscape gardener in this country."[36] Jensen's letter of recommendation was short but emphatic: "He who presents these lines to you has been my assistant for five years. Caldwell is an artist—a poet. He is going to try new pastures—I wish him joy and happiness. Alfred Caldwell is sincere and honest and well qualified."[37] In his own letter of application for the Eagle Point

Park position, Caldwell described both his experience, which by that time was comprehensive, and his dreams, which needed a place to be realized:

> I have a thorough knowledge of landscape and forestry engineering. I have designed and built roads, bridges, and several swimming pools, one house. I have a technical and working knowledge of re-inforced concrete construction. I can qualify as a quarryman and a stone mason. Aside from training, I have botanized over most of the Middle West. I am a student of plant ecology.
>
> Partly out of the Jensen stimulus, I resolved, several years past, to secure a superintendent's position in some smaller park system. I have certain ideas, long cherished, too difficult or impossible of achievement in a large system with its bureaucracies and affinities: In a small park, even with a little money to spend, relatively speaking, much might be done. It is out of the nature of things, that the cheapest and nearest to hand, properly understood, is the best and the most beautiful. All ugliness is expensive—certainly expensive to build.[38]

The Dubuque park board desperately needed the kind of experienced leadership Caldwell could provide in order to qualify for federal funds, and since so many Dubuque people needed work, the board was in a hurry to interview him. In early February 1934 Caldwell bought a train ticket to Dubuque, where he was met at the station by Glenn Brown, chairman of the board and senior member of the law firm of Brown, Lacy and Clewell, and Charles Landon, another board member and a furrier.[39] They drove Caldwell to the 160-acre park site and explained what they wanted, including pavilions to shelter people who would come to the park even in winter. Landon told Caldwell that the board would hire an architect to design the buildings and Caldwell would "boss the whole shebang." This whole shebang would have to be done within a $16,000 annual budget, they explained, and the superintendent's salary would be $2,100 a year. Would he take the job? Caldwell needed this job badly, but he would take it, he said, only if he could design the whole park, including the pavilions. Landon replied that it was impossible, since the board needed the drawings right away to get the engineer's approval so the project could proceed the following week. Caldwell insisted that he could give them the drawings by the next day, and he did—two sections, an elevation, details, and a perspective.

Brown and Landon were impressed with the drawings; they immediately took them to the city engineer, who approved them after a few questions about reinforcing bars. In a letter to Caldwell of February 22, 1934, Landon wrote that "in talking the matter over with Mr. Brown this morning, he feels, and I agree with him, that you should have complete say so, as to the type of building to be put up . . . and we are wondering if you would be willing to come to Dubuque again on next Sunday, and go over the plans for this building."[40] In the spring of 1934 Caldwell moved Virginia, Carol (three years old), and James (four months) to a house on North Grandview Avenue in Dubuque.[41]

Pavilion, Eagle Point Park, Dubuque, Iowa, 1936. (Photo by Dennis Domer)

Eagle Point Park, a project Caldwell described as "a city in a garden" was probably the most challenging job he ever had.[42] The site was a magnificent forested bluff high above the Mississippi River, but there were few roads and little other infrastructure. Basically Caldwell began from scratch, which was all to his liking. He designed everything and he built everything. He also produced most of the materials needed. He opened a stone quarry: "I didn't buy a stone." He cut the lumber from timber. He oversaw approximately two hundred WPA workers, few if any of them with design, landscaping, or building experience. He had to teach his workers how to cut stones and lay them up in buildings and gardens, how to build roads, trails, and bridges, how to grade different sites, and where and how to plant the natural vegetation that made this park a quintessential example of a prairie school landscape. Caldwell took his example for this teaching from Jens Jensen and certainly from Frank Lloyd Wright, according to a letter he wrote to Charles Landon in 1934:

On a high hill in the wilderness of Wisconsin there is a school. The students, working in gangs like laborers, blast the stone from the quarry, haul it and handle it. Some of it they burn into lime for mortar, and they lay up the walls of their own school building. They cut trees out of the woods and run the logs thru the saw mill to make joists and timbers for the roof. Each student must become a stone worker, a stone lover, a carpenter, a wood lover, a manufacturer before he becomes an architect. It is the school of Frank Lloyd Wright world famous architect. Such a school could teach landscape gardening.[43]

Caldwell remembers his experience in Dubuque as mostly work. "I worked like mad all the time. I performed a kind of miracle there." Clearly he did.

The city in a garden idea reveals not only the immensity and complexity of the project but also, as Richard Guy Wilson contends, Caldwell's "fundamental belief in the unity of nature and man."[44] He constructed three pavilions out of striated limestone that pulsates dynamically in and out from the vertical plane while enhancing the horizontality of the buildings with their low-slung hipped roofs and wide eaves. These pavilions, clustered near the highest point in the park, provided meeting rooms, dining rooms, and bathrooms around magnificent stone hearths. The gateway pavilion, which also functioned as a reservoir, stretched across the main road, creating a formal entry to the park. Caldwell connected these buildings with wide stone terraces, benches, and walls, and to further emphasize the unity of the complex he designed similar abstract wooden screens, cornice details, and stone hearths for all three buildings. He placed this cluster on the site so that it appears to be, in Wrightian terms, of the hill rather than on the hill. The organic quality of his designs and site plan were strengthened by the native plants he placed informally around the pavilions and throughout the park. Caldwell intended to blur the distinction between nature and built form, and he expressed this concept perfectly in his ledge garden, horticultural garden, lily pool, and numerous council rings that he set strategically in the park so they seem to grow out of the hills. Like nature, they have a scale that can be both monumental and intimate, delicate and rough, designed and serendipitous. Caldwell saw his job simply as "nature helping" with a "syntax of stone."[45] This syntax synthesizes Frank Lloyd Wright's ideas about the nature of materials, prairie horizontality, and the art of the machine age with Jens Jensen's philosophy of making clearings edged with native plants, using stratified stonework for ledges and waterfalls, establishing curving paths, and stimulating discussion and storytelling, perhaps even community, in the semicircular council rings.

Eagle Point Park is poetry, always the fiery force behind the unusual quality of Caldwell's work. Indeed, poetry is a key to his character and a source of his power, a power that often separated him from his generation and caused him to be misunderstood by so many. Although it is not literally true, Caldwell claims he was fired from every job he ever had. He was indeed fired many times in his life,

Ledge garden, Eagle Point Park, Dubuque, Iowa, 1936. (Photo by Dennis Domer)

including from his job as superintendent of Eagle Point Park. But what finally happened in Dubuque was particularly tragic, not only because his efforts there produced a work of art but also because it was the middle of the depression. During the 1936 campaign Franklin and Eleanor Roosevelt visited the park, which had won a national WPA design award. According to Caldwell, Roosevelt "stopped right at the nose of my bridge. Mrs. Roosevelt got out of the car and walked to the bridge. And she came back and sat down." Then President Roosevelt summed up their opinion of the park by saying, "This is my idea of a worthwhile boondoggle." But common people either could not understand it or envied it. Even Charles Landon of the park board questioned Caldwell's insistence on the high architectural quality of the work.

Eventually Dubuque citizens began to complain about Caldwell and his park. It was nitpicking. Mrs. Henschel, secretary to Glenn Brown, remembered some fifty years later only that some people criticized Caldwell for cutting down trees for the road at the entry gate. The *Dubuque Telegraph Herald* reported that Caldwell was discharged because he would not speed up the building to meet the park board's deadlines. Charles Landon told the newspaper that Caldwell had "given too much attention to details."[46] Trees, deadlines, and details, however, were only pretenses rather than the real problem. Caldwell was simply different—too different for Dubuque. He dressed differently, just as his mentors Frank Lloyd Wright and Jens Jensen did. He was too much for "the biggest small town in America," as Caldwell described it. Why a man from Chicago? In this small town in 1936, the park board eventually could no longer resist the pressure from the townspeople to put one of their own in charge.[47] In the end they telephoned Caldwell at 7:30 on Tuesday morning, January 14, 1936, and asked him to meet them at 8:00 in Landon's office, where Glenn Brown gave him the bad news that he was to collect his pay. When asked fifty-seven years later why he was fired, Caldwell took a deep breath, pointed his finger, and whispered, "because the bastards had no dreams." Then he added, "We didn't have a penny in the house, you know. We didn't have an automobile. We didn't have anything."

The train trip back to Chicago gave him and Geda time to lick their wounds, examine the dashed dream of Dubuque, and ponder how to support their small family in the middle of the depression when private landscape jobs were nearly impossible to find. Caldwell thought his life was over because he had lost the most important job he had ever had. But in Chicago he dragged himself back to his old friend George Donoghue, now general superintendent of the huge Chicago Park District, which had been consolidated in 1934 out of twenty-two separate districts.[48] This consolidation was necessary if Chicago was to receive the WPA program funding that eventually employed more than 10,000 Chicago workers by 1937. The federal government's WPA investment in Chicago amounted to an expenditure of $84 million for labor and park materials between 1935 and 1942.[49] These federal funds meant good fortune for the defeated family just home from Dubuque. Donoghue quickly gave Caldwell another WPA job as a senior draftsman in the Chicago Park District, where he worked from 1936 to 1941. Caldwell was extremely productive in those five years, producing over a hundred large and complicated drawings, but he suffered great indignities all the time he was there. He was fired three times, and each discharge led to a desperate period of hunger and privation. These depression experiences in the Park District, along with the loss at Dubuque, impressed on him forever the view that life is fundamentally tragic, unjust, and cockeyed, a theme later reflected in his poetry and prose.

The Chicago Park District, however, hired him for his knowledge of plants and his ability to rapidly draw intricate plans for park designs and plantings. Luke Cosme, a young engineer who sat next to Caldwell during his years in the Park District, said that everyone knew Caldwell was an uncompromising genius with a demanding personality who was best left alone to draw.[50] Caldwell turned out a landscape drawing a week, sometimes working seven days a week from 9:00 A.M. to 8:00 P.M. so that the WPA could have the drawings it needed to employ the destitute victims of an economic system run amok. Although Cosme believes

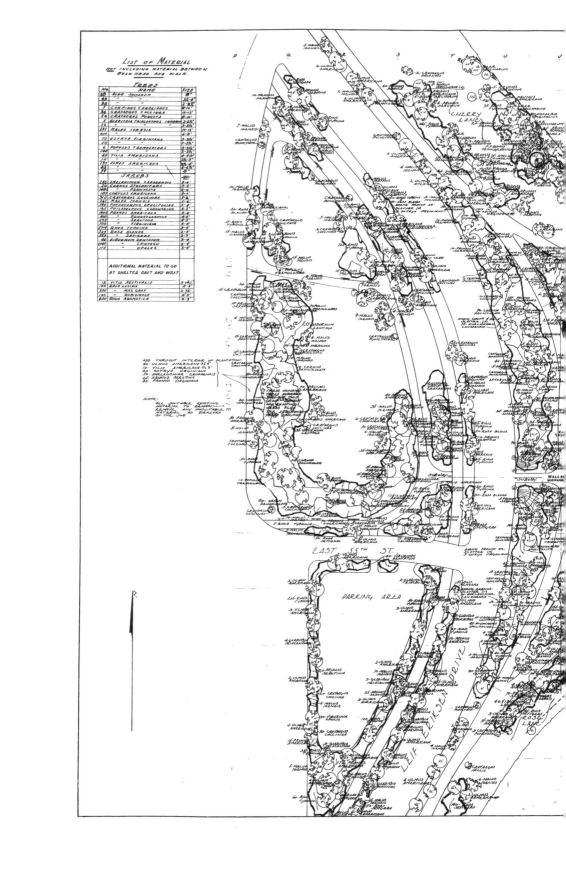

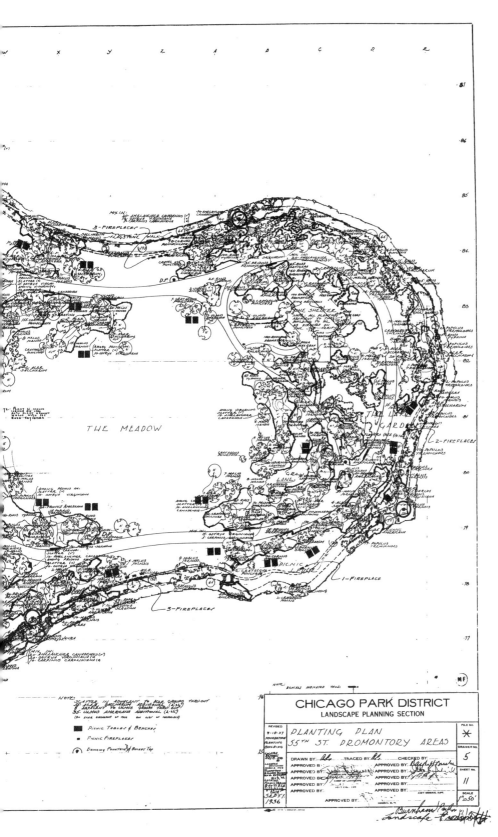

Planting plan for Promontory Point, Burnham Park, Chicago, Illinois, 1936. (Courtesy of Chicago Park District Special Collections)

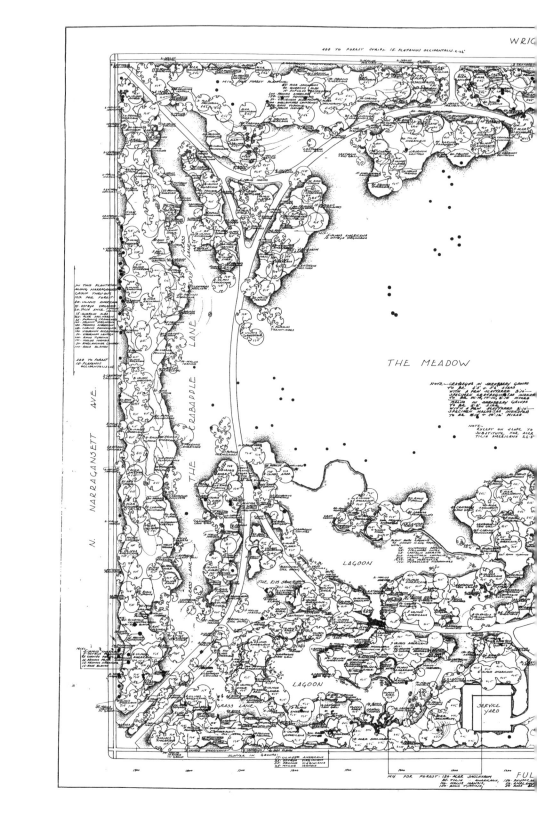

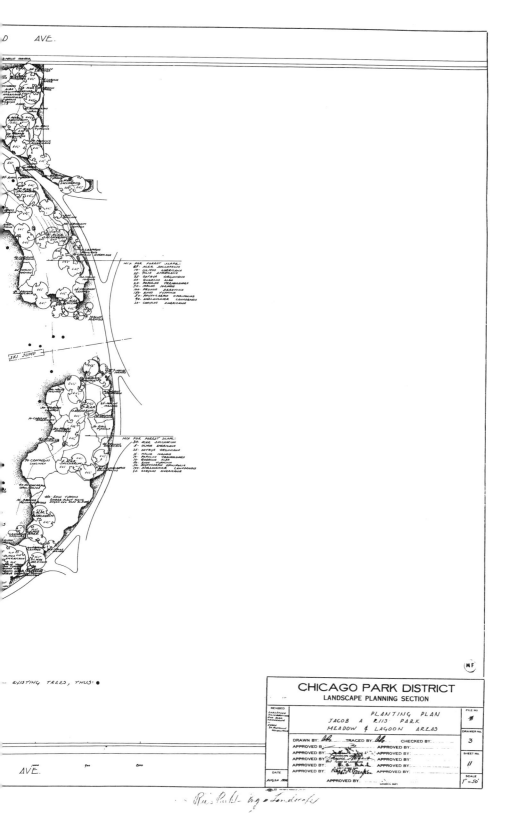

Planting plan for Riis Park, Chicago, Illinois, 1936. (Courtesy of Chicago Park District Special Collections)

Detail, planting plan for Riis Park, Chicago, Illinois, 1936. (Courtesy of Chicago Park District Special Collections)

Caldwell made well over a hundred drawings, the Chicago Park District Archives have only twenty-six. If he did all the drawings in the sets now only partially represented, he would have made well over two hundred. The drawings in the Chicago Park District Archives are mostly large—forty by thirty inches or larger—intricate planting plans done in ink on vellum that provide the rich and delicate details of prairie school park landscapes at Montrose Park, the Lily Pool at Lincoln Park, Northerly Island, Promontory Point at Burnham Park, Jackson Park, and Riis Park. These drawings show the placement of native plants and shrubs, prairie flowers, and trees around the edges of open meadows that create the vista of a prairie school park. The plant materials are called out in notes, lists, and symbols by their vernacular names and sometimes in Latin as well. The drawings are highly stylized in the unmistakable Caldwell hand, which was sure and precise. The plans and drawings for the Lily Pool, particularly the pavilions, have a Japanese quality, influenced by Frank Lloyd Wright. The use of native plants wherever possible, as well as council rings and meadows, restated Caldwell's philosophical connection to his mentor Jens Jensen. These drawings still stand as unique works of art, and at the time even his worst enemies recognized their value and wanted to sign them, according to Cosme. Sometimes the drawings carry the signatures of six approving officials.

Caldwell spent about 75 percent of the time at the Park District making his magnificent drawings. The other 25 percent of the time he consulted with his superiors, such as Robert Moore, Cushing Smith, May McAdams, Ray Haycamp, Bart Austin, Clair O'Neil, and Max Matts, about what plants could survive the stress of an urban setting, or he gave instructions at the sites themselves. His superiors really needed him, because they were all landscape designers who had university training but little experience. Since the city was hard on plants that did not belong to the ecology of the region, they feared expensive outlays for unsuitable choices. Caldwell was uniquely experienced, and no one other than Jens Jensen knew the botany of the Chicago area better, knowledge he had gained from Hermann Pepoon. He learned what native plants worked in Illinois from his continuing association with Jensen. According to Cosme everyone recognized Caldwell's ability, and though he was a loner and difficult to get along with, there was often a line of people leading to his desk.

Caldwell was such a powerful influence that, for a short time at least, his approach to landscape design became the philosophy of the Chicago Park District. In its 1937 annual report, the landscape design section is filled with prairie style ideas. Terms such as "naturalistic effects," "Illinois way of planting," the "prairie style," and "plant ecology" guide the unusually philosophical text. The report also emphasizes that using native plants, such as a ground cover of wildflowers, eliminates spading and maintenance and therefore makes good economic sense. The report even quotes Pepoon's *Flora of the Chicago Region*.[51] The next year this section of the report was dropped, however, as if to suggest that the Park District had, indirectly at least, repudiated Caldwell's influence. Still, Cosme says again and again that Caldwell "was the best we ever had."

Being the best and most sought after did not create a happy work life for Caldwell. "The depression made me belligerent, and I was in no mood for humility. I have been belligerent ever since." He revealed his discontent in an extraordinary correspondence with Jens Jensen during his Chicago Park District years.[52] Caldwell, who at the time always wore bell-bottom trousers to work, clearly had a different sensibility than did the university crowd. He was incapable of holding his tongue in the face of what he considered to be their stupidity and ignorance, and his forthrightness cost him a promotion and even his job. In a letter to Jensen dated August 6, 1938, Caldwell describes how he failed the exam for promotion to landscape designer:

Promontory Point, Burnham Park, Chicago, Illinois, 1946. (Courtesy of Chicago Park District Special Collections)

By the way the Prairie Landscape got repudiated in the recent Civil Service Examinations. What I designed for the examination was the best work I ever did. The problem was a 60 acre park: it made a Prairie and a Prairie river. My mark was 36 the lowest grade of 18 applicants, many of them terribly inferior people like florists and foremen and such like. F. A. C. Smith with a presumably French design was the highest grade: 89. Mr. Otto Shaffer of the University of Illinois and Mr. Robert Moore were the experts selected to grade the papers.

The day the results were made known I sent the following telegram to Donoghue: "Civil Service list posted today makes me ineligible. You fellows have been signing my plans for 2 years. Native plants and Beachscapes and Prairies. Lincoln Park Extension, 55th St, Promontory, your new boulevards, the Lily Pool, the Riis park meadow, the biggest and best things you have had. If I am incompetent a million dollars of landscape work is incompetent, most of it already planted, all of it approved. Do not fancy that Moore ever had anything to contribute to these plans but his name. Here is obvious fraud and sabotage of Civil Service and it happens to cast a very nasty slur indeed on my ability as a craftsman. If you are interested in investigating these antics I promise to come to you well heeled with evidence."

But no answer.

Why should a man have to stand such bastards just for the sake of doing a little work.

He did not tell Jensen in the letter what he had written at the end of the exam—that it was a stupid exam and that whoever created it didn't know what he was doing. In retaliation the graders, including Robert Moore, who was the landscape architect of the Park District, failed him.[53] Friends persuaded Caldwell just to take the exam again and make no comments, and in June 1940 he passed it at the head of his group with a mark of 86.7 percent.

But frequent confrontations with his superiors over specific plans and general philosophy increased Caldwell's unhappiness and frustration. In his letters to Jensen he consistently attacked the academics he worked with, the parks they were designing, the roads they were building, and the decay of the cities. He even asserted several times that capitalism would likely collapse under the burden of the depression and be replaced by a more just communist economic system. Such radical ideas, often coming from the "Bohemians" Caldwell associated with on Washington Square, were never appreciated at work. He and Geda fed their radical interests in those years at the Dill Pickle Club, established in 1917 at Washington Square to foster free speech and expression. The club's members were described variously in the press as "Bohemians, hobo intellectuals, poets, philosophers, and tale tellers." The Dill Pickle Club also met in Tooker Alley in a room entered through a wall on State Street.[54] Caldwell said he was a "little pink" at the time, although he was never a card-carrying communist as were some other Dill Pickle members. Given his mood, what he said to his superiors and fellow workers could not have been far from the content of his letters to Jensen. He also insisted on his own way, just as he had always done. When he was fired in June 1939, it did not take long for the money to run out, and he described his plight to his old mentor:

Dear Mr. Jensen,

Things are very bad with us. We have not food to eat and soon not even a place to sleep.

Can you suggest anyone who will give me work? Are all these years of earnestness and diligence worth nothing in the world? Please do not forsake me. If you have heard of anything, can suggest something—please do.

It is bad, very bad.

Alfred Caldwell

Caldwell eventually went back to the Park District, but in June 1940 he was fired again. In a letter to Jensen dated June 17, 1940, he admits that "speaking

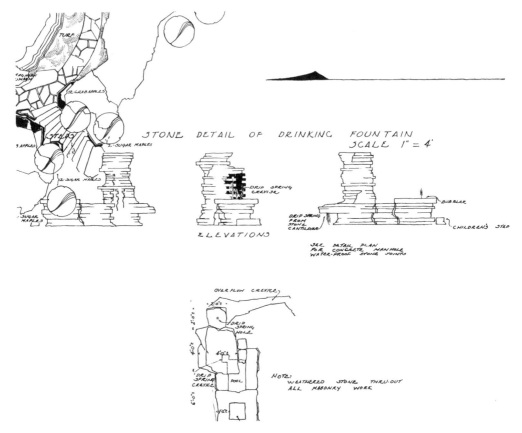

Detail, general landscape plan for Lincoln Park Lily Pool, Chicago, Illinois, 1936. (Courtesy of Chicago Park District Special Collections)

freely is one of my specialties: do you think I am disliked at the parks so much because my shoes aren't shined. Give the devil his due. I am much influenced by a certain man I worked with for 6 years who was very good at speaking freely. Perhaps you know him."

In spite of his problems at the Chicago Park District, something happened there that would prove a great turning point in his life. What happened was an unpredictable meeting brought on by circumstances in Germany. In 1938 Caldwell was frustrated as usual by the lack of support at the Park District for wildflowers, this time at the Lily Pool in Lincoln Park. To remedy this lack of commitment, after consulting with a reluctant Geda, he cashed in his insurance policy and for about $300 paid for the wildflowers himself. Several trucks and men accompanied him to northern Wisconsin to collect these native plants. On the day Caldwell was setting the wildflowers around the Lily Pool, three men in black coats paid a visit. "I'd never seen them before. They looked very foreign. They spoke German. The big guy was very interested in the pavilions. He liked their touch of Frank Lloyd Wright. The little guy and the middling guy were fascinated with the wildflowers that could be planted in rocks." The men were Ludwig Mies van der Rohe, Ludwig Hilberseimer, and Walter Peterhans, the architecture faculty from the Armour Institute, later renamed Illinois Institute of Technology. Caldwell had no idea what these people would mean to him.

He met these famous German émigrés again by chance in the spring of 1940. In late 1939 he had decided to use his evenings, and days when he could not find work after being let go at the Park District, preparing for the Illinois architects' examination. He took courses in strength of materials and reinforced concrete from November 1939 to May 1940 at the Armour Institute.[55] This was no trouble. He was a precise, neat, and careful mathematician who excelled in everything. In preparation for the design portion of the architects' exam, a friend persuaded Caldwell to take a three-part course in architectural design at the Art Institute of Chicago. His friend told him that "three Krauts who do awful architecture" would grade the drawings. Mies and his men gave the students briefs for small, medium, and large houses and asked them to bring in drawings of three designs to pin up. Mies was attracted to Caldwell's designs for the medium-sized house just as he had been to the Lily Pool because both were clear and reminded him of Frank Lloyd Wright's prairie style work in Oak Park. Through an interpreter, he asked Caldwell to study with Hilberseimer and Peterhans in preparation for the exam, which he passed without difficulty at the University of Illinois at Champaign-Urbana.

The Germans were so impressed with Caldwell's work that Mies also asked him to do some drawings for Hilberseimer, who was laboring on a book about planning new cities. Through frequent contact over these drawings, often with an interpreter in the early days, Caldwell and "Hilbs" became friends, and they stayed in frequent professional and personal contact from 1940 until 1960 when Caldwell resigned from IIT.[56] Caldwell considered Hilberseimer an intellectual, and they had passionate discussions about urban development in Chicago. Caldwell had worried about the city since his days with Jensen, and here was a famous transplanted European planner who placed great emphasis on environmental issues in his suggested plans and rationale for a newly conceived, decentralized city. Caldwell read early versions of Hilberseimer's book *The New City*, published in 1944, and he recognized ideas that paralleled his own philosophy of urban development. He had been writing about the ills of the industrial city in a manuscript he had been preparing since the early 1930s, but he had not finished it by the time he met Hilberseimer.[57] Not only did Hilberseimer agree with Caldwell on many issues and work with him on several projects including private architectural design (none of which were ever built), but he urged him on. Hilberseimer recognized Caldwell's knowledge of parks and cities, and he en-

Ludwig Mies van der Rohe and Alfred Caldwell, about 1950. (Courtesy of Alfred Caldwell)

couraged him to write about the "new conception of parks, their relation to industrial areas. Productive parks and their connection with gardens, farms and camps. The city in the landscape. You know all about it."[58]

But what Hilberseimer wanted most, and what caught the critical eyes of Mies and Peterhans, were the exquisite drawings Caldwell could produce to illustrate the new city. Full of idealism and commitment to Hilberseimer's urban vision, Caldwell did "a dozen or more" drawings for him between 1944 and 1960. Hilberseimer could not draw well—at least not in the eyes of Caldwell, who drew better than just about anyone. He described Hilberseimer's drawings as "rough like hell."[59] In contrast, Caldwell could present the most complex concepts clearly and with ease, and no one could successfully copy his delicate and artful pen-and-ink schemes. Although some of these drawings took days to complete, Caldwell did not charge for his work because he considered himself "a refugee from Chicago who could not charge a refugee from Germany."

Hilberseimer was so enthusiastic about Caldwell's drawings in 1941 that he talked to him about entering a competition and about teaching at the Armour

Alfred Caldwell and Ludwig Hilberseimer, about 1955. (Courtesy of Alfred Caldwell)

Institute when the war was over. "You know what I told you about teaching. Such a work may become the basis for it."[60] As usual, Caldwell responded with enthusiasm, and in 1942 he entered his drawing, "The City in the Landscape," in the *Herald American* competition soliciting ways to improve Chicago. "The City in the Landscape" was a three-point perspective, aerial view of a decentralized Chicago curving into infinity.[61] In this drawing the city and the landscape are woven tightly together so that the city almost disappears in a natural setting. Caldwell would later call this drawing "The Living Landscape."[62] As Alfred Willis noted, no aerial photograph could have covered such a vast area as clearly as Caldwell's drawing, whose crucial feature is "the penetration of nature into all zones."[63]

"The City in the Landscape," 1942. *(Courtesy of Centre Canadien d'Architecture/Canadian Centre for Architecture, Montreal)*

Hilberseimer published a version of this drawing in *The New City*, titled "Aerial View of the Replanned City of Chicago," without giving any credit to Caldwell. Other drawings that Hilberseimer published in that book without attribution to Caldwell include "View of Settlement Unit," "View of L-Shaped Houses," "View of a Commercial Area," a number of the wind diagrams, "City of Chicago," and several diagrams of the American and industrial city that are not dated. Ten years later he also used "L-Shaped Houses," "Commercial Area," and "Decentralized City around an Inlet" as well as several wind studies, in *The Nature of Cities*. In 1963, in *Entfaltung einer Planungsidee*, Hilberseimer republished "L-förmige Häuser," "Chicago Vogelschau," "Geschäftsgebiet Vogelschau," several wind studies including "Chicago, Plan mit Stadtaggregaten, umgeben von kleinen Gehöften," and two schemes of "Project Evergreen II." Hilberseimer neither paid Caldwell nor gave him specific credit for any of this work, although he did mention him in the prefaces of the latter two books. Drawing was not the only talent Caldwell gave to the men in dark coats, for in many ways they were helpless early on before their private and public tasks in the United States.

Both Hilberseimer and Mies were famous men by the time they met Caldwell, and they were frequently asked to deliver public lectures to various groups about their views on architecture and the city. Neither, however, had the confidence during the first several years to speak English before an American audience. They found Caldwell the perfect stand-in. He was poetic, he had a booming voice, and he gave short speeches. Exactly how many times he took to the podium for his German friends cannot be easily ascertained. Caldwell estimates about twenty.[64] Perhaps the most notable lecture during the war period was "Design to Fit the Human Spirit: The Evolution of City Plans," which Caldwell wrote with Hilberseimer and gave on November 7, 1944. It was a part of a series titled "The City: Organism and Artifact," held at the University of Chicago and led by Robert Maynard Hutchins. Other lecturers in that series included Meyer Schapiro, John Nef, Joseph Hudnut, and Mortimer J. Adler. Caldwell remembered that Mies stood up and clapped after Caldwell's lecture and shook hands with him in the aisle after he left the podium. Caldwell never spoke very long, but it took him little time to summarize Hilberseimer's views, which he soon knew by heart. The decentralized cities Caldwell promoted carefully exploited the environmental advantages of placing polluting industries downwind, gave residents ready access to healthful sunlight, separated traffic from pedestrians with green space, made walking to work possible, and formed neighborhoods into new settlement units, each "limited in size and containing within itself all the necessary parts."[65] The need to write lectures for these Germans sparked the zeal for writing and publishing that had begun with his poetry in the 1920s and an essay in 1931 in the newsletter of the Friends of Our Native Landscape titled "In Defense of Animals." From the outset Caldwell had a yen for provocative argument. This yen, along with the unusual fervor and showmanship he had learned from watching Jensen and Wright speak, was the basis for a brilliant teaching career.[66]

Caldwell had to put off beginning that teaching career during the war years, and his unpaid work with Hilberseimer was interrupted between 1940 and 1942 by brief stints of desperately needed paid work out of town. The nation was reluctantly preparing for war, and an architect with Caldwell's experience was well suited to oversee the construction of military bases. His first job of this sort was at Camp Forrest at Tullahoma, Tennessee, where he was a "building inspector for the government."[67] Tullahoma was a town of 4,500, and in October 1940 Caldwell and 19,000 other workers descended on the place. In spite of the chaos and under the leadership of men like Caldwell, these workers transformed a National Guard camp into one of the largest United States Army bases of World War II. This meant dozens of wooden structures of all sizes, including barracks, mess halls, guardhouses, warehouses, clubs, officers' quarters, and storage buildings for soldiers such as General Patton and his "Hell on Wheels" division when they rolled into town.[68] In correspondence with Hilberseimer, Caldwell brought up the quality of vernacular buildings and their appropriateness, contending that "you would find much in the structures to approve of. Perhaps they are not at all architecture—not studied at all as architecture—but at least they are clear and understandable."[69] In his laconic fashion, Hilberseimer wrote back to Caldwell at Tullahoma that it "may be a good experience to work sometimes on such buildings."[70] In a later letter Caldwell described a second advantage of this "camp of 1,400 buildings" that was "very much like a planned city and it is good and satisfying in a spatial sense. Many things are bad about it but it is better than any of the cities. Too monotonous—nothing high (I know now in a very real way how right your schemes are with the tall buildings spaced thruout."[71]

Building at night under lights was an experience Caldwell would never forget, and in early 1941 he was glad to get out of Tennessee and go on to the next job, this time at Camp McCoy near Sparta, Wisconsin, which the War Department was expanding to serve 35,000 troops.[72] He was put to work for several months estimating the cost of this expansion and says his estimates were close to the actual cost. From Camp McCoy he went to a camp in Nebraska for a short stint that he now recalls only as hot and dusty. But his complaint about Nebraska to Hilberseimer at the time was very different. "The work in Nebraska was very bad. I saw what was happening and left. No, you wouldn't believe it: a munitions dump by these architects designed in Colonial Architecture. War too can be pretty."[73] In August 1942 he was back in Chicago, and by that time the War Department had taken over the Merchandise Mart. This meant plenty of federal jobs for qualified builders, and through the encouragement of friends from his Chicago Park District days, he sat for the civil service examination to become a government civil engineer. With that exam successfully behind him, Geda, Carol, and James came from Pittsburgh to join him, and he settled in to design training aids in downtown Chicago for the rest of the war.

War has its expected destructive aspects, but wherever there is destruction creative forces are also at work, as Caldwell explained in an essay in 1967 called "A Job for Durga and Shiva." "Durga is part of life and Shiva is the other part."[74] For all the gloom of World War II, it changed the course of Caldwell's life and gave him many opportunities to live out his dream. For one thing, he had some money. Working for the War Department, he made more money than he ever had before, and in 1943 he used that money to purchase his beloved forty-acre farm near Bristol in southern Wisconsin. It was an emphatic statement about powerful influences on his life. Both of Caldwell's early mentors, Wright and Jensen, had houses in the country. Since 1936 Caldwell and Jensen had been writing about the evils of the city, particularly Chicago, in a volley of letters and debating the problems in numerous meetings in Chicago and Wisconsin. Caldwell also believed deeply that Jefferson's idea of a small farm for every family was the best

Alfred Caldwell house, Bristol, Wisconsin, 1948. (Photo by Richard Nickel; courtesy of Centre Canadien d'Architecture/Canadian Centre for Architecture, Montreal)

scheme for human survival in a dangerous age, and this scheme fit well with Hilberseimer's vision of the city as a decentralized suburb.

In 1940 Hilberseimer encouraged Caldwell to buy a farm near Chicago because "it may save your whole life." He added in uncertain English, "If I would not be too old I would like to do it for myself. I think it is the only solution in this unsecure time."[75] Intellectual reasons aside, Caldwell's own experience of harsh poverty in the depression drove him to the conclusion that "if I ever got any money I would buy a piece of land and be a farmer; that was my dream, I would be a farmer." He never actually lived off the land, and the farm was more of an experiment in living. It is Caldwell's clearing, a place to plant deep roots and to think clearly.

Building the house and planting the hundreds of trees developed into a test of his ideas about the living landscape, one that went on almost every weekend for years. It was a labor of love but also a long struggle for the whole Caldwell family. Like any struggle it would leave its scars, but over the next fifty years the farm evolved into a highly planned prairie style landscape with a modern stone house as the focal point. The house, a synthesis of ideas flowing from Wright, Jensen, and Mies van der Rohe, faces a meadow edged in trees and wildflowers. As a created prairie space, the meadow characteristically curves away out of sight. Caldwell explains why in "Columbus Park," an article he wrote for *Parks and Recreation* in 1942: "The prairie space between the freestanding forest and the forest background is like a broad pathway to a world unseen. It possesses a mystical quality of infinite space, like the premonition of some irrational dimension."[76]

In addition to the house Caldwell built a studio, garage, grape arbor, lily

Alfred Caldwell house, Bristol, Wisconsin, 1970. (Courtesy of Centre Canadien d'Architecture/Canadian Centre for Architecture)

pool, and council ring and planted an orchard and other trees including "Geda's 100." He is still making new clearings for meadows and new paths for contemplative walks with a master. Later in life, on a walk with Geda that he passionately remembers, Caldwell described the house as "melting right into the landscape, it's melting right into the landscape. I get such an exaltation, I can't stop it, I can't stop it, it's so beautiful, it's so beautiful, and that we have it. Nothing can take it away from us. Oh, how hard we worked, and Geda said, 'Don't talk about it.' I said, 'I'm not going to talk about it, but I just want to remind you.'"[77] The farm is his ultimate work of art, still in the making. Caldwell is not trying to duplicate nature; like Jensen at Columbus Park, he is searching for "the oneness of things and a sense of life and space. That sense of space rejects the tyranny of closure. It asserts the rights of man to the wide green earth."[78]

While working at the Merchandise Mart, setting up his farm, making drawings and speeches for Hilberseimer, working on a few houses, publishing his first articles, and making speeches for Mies, Caldwell was unknowingly building the foundation for a career in teaching. It was not the speeches he made that really counted for Mies. What counted was his ability to construct delightful buildings, such as the pavilions Mies admired in 1938 at the Lily Pool, to design and draw buildings, such as the plans he made for a medium-sized house Mies critiqued in 1940 at the Art Institute, and to illustrate landscapes, such as the numerous drawings he had been doing for Hilberseimer's book *The New City*. Hilberseimer's high opinion of Caldwell also counted, and he was clearly needed at the Armour Institute. During the war Mies, Hilberseimer, and Walter Peterhans taught the lion's share of the curriculum, along with George Danforth, who taught full time from 1941 to 1943, because there were only a few students.[79] They had part-time help from Edward Duckett, Elmer Forsberg, Alberta A. Krehbiel, Alfred Mell, Addis Osborn, William Priestley, and John Barney

Alfred Caldwell studio, Bristol, Wisconsin, 1970. (Courtesy of Centre Canadien d'Architec-ture/Canadian Centre for Architecture, Montreal)

Alfred Caldwell house seen from the meadow, Bristol, Wisconsin, 1991.
(Photo by Dennis Domer)

Rodgers.[80] When the war ended in 1945 and a flood of new students in khaki uniforms and battle ribbons stood at the door, financed by the GI Bill, Mies decided to sweep out the part-timers in favor of one individual. Caldwell had proved himself the kind of universal talent needed—landscape architect, architect, civil engineer, lecturer, and poet—to help make a fledgling wartime architecture department into the world-famous postwar program at Illinois Institute of Technology. Caldwell had no college degree, and this had eliminated him from teaching jobs before, even though Jensen called him "by far the most able and studious young man that has left my employ."[81] Mies didn't care. He had no college degree either, and on a rainy day he called Caldwell at home just after he had come storming back from Wisconsin because it was too wet to work on the farm. "I am Ludwig Mies van der Rohe. Would you be willing to teach our young architects?" his deep voice rang out. Mies was absolutely certain of his decision, even though Caldwell had no teaching experience, no philosophy of teaching, and no diplomacy, though he had charm.[82] He wanted Caldwell to play a pivotal role in the new school. In one of the early Chicago speeches Mies had to give in German, he called construction "that loyal safekeeper of an epoch's spirit" and proclaimed that "construction not only determines form but is form itself."[83] Mies was so certain of Caldwell that he entrusted him with the cornerstone of the modern curriculum—construction. As the essence of modern architecture, absolutely nothing was more important to teach in Mies's school than construction, and before 1945 Mies, Hilberseimer, and John Rodgers met often at Fred Harvey's

Alfred Caldwell about 1945. (Courtesy of Carol Caldwell Dooley)

restaurant in the 310 South Michigan Building to discuss it. But Mies, Hilberseimer, and Alfred Mell gave up teaching construction, architectural construction, and architectural history so that Caldwell could teach the courses. He covered the structure, function, and design and materials of buildings from wood to steel to concrete. He also carried the students "beyond individual buildings into groups of buildings and communities, demonstrating the interdependence of all buildings in relation to the city as an organic whole."[84] Mies reasoned that after students completed Caldwell's courses and the four visual training courses taught by Peterhans in the second and third years, they would be ready for his advanced courses in architecture and Hilberseimer's city planning courses in the fourth and fifth years. Caldwell accepted Mies's offer on the telephone, essentially an offer to take over the heart of the new school at IIT, and he would "emerge as a force in the school equivalent to Mies and Hilberseimer."[85] Caldwell was a great influence in the lives of hundreds of architecture students for the next fifty years, and he served as the loyal safekeeper of the Miesian curriculum not only at IIT but also at the University of Southern California. He taught basically the same material in the same way at both institutions, regardless of the difference in the teaching assignment, and it was recognized that "generations of students are indebted to him because of his teaching, principles, ideas, presence and humanity."[86] In Caldwell, Mies made one of the most significant teaching appointments in architectural education in the twentieth century.

In 1945 Caldwell had not the slightest idea what to teach or how to teach

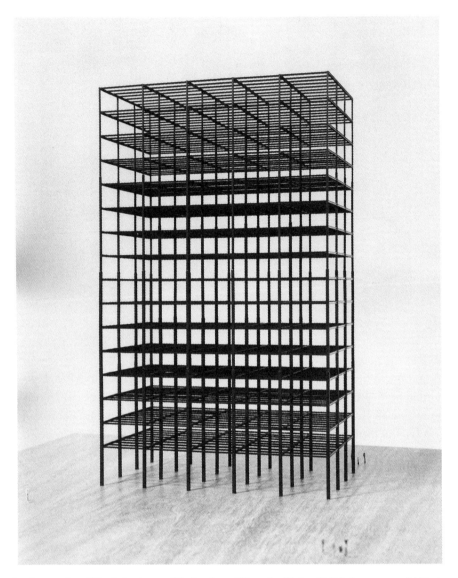

Student work at Illinois Institute of Technology. (Photo by Richard Nickel; courtesy of Alfred Caldwell)

sophomore and junior architecture students. He had gone to college less than a semester in the early 1920s; he had never gone to architecture school. He was a self-taught man. What was he supposed to do when he walked into his first class in materials and construction? He turned to his old friend Ludwig Hilberseimer, who showed him "in five minutes . . . in the faculty room" how to teach brick construction. "I had to be a fast learner," Caldwell recalled.[87] He also turned to Mies for advice about teaching construction and history. Mies told him to "show them factory buildings and piston houses, to show the genuine architecture

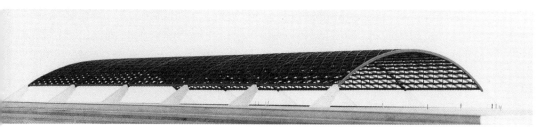

Student work at Illinois Institute of Technology. (Photo by Richard Nickel; courtesy of Alfred Caldwell)

where there's no fake, no show-off. It's all real, like a piston house is real, not a shape made up for the sake of a shape. Like you see in Ireland, the old houses."[88] Mies also stressed the need for students to demonstrate clarity and logic in their buildings. Caldwell accepted this advice and characteristically threw himself into his tasks. He studied and learned so much about brick and how to teach about brick that Hilberseimer's five-minute lesson eventually led to an article on brick-work in the *Encyclopaedia Britannica*.[89] He transformed the short demonstration on brick construction into a coherent formula, a series of exercises in building with brick that taught students a deep appreciation of the material and gave them a solid understanding of its construction qualities on a specific site. "He insisted on great technical proficiency and attention to detail in his courses in material and construction."[90] He was unrelenting. "Try it again," he would order a student; "do it over. Work on it."[91] Over the years Caldwell perfected these exercises of the brick house assignment, the first project of the sophomore year, and though his students worked with thousands upon thousands of bricks in models and drawings representing many careful lessons in clarity and discipline, they were never bored.[92]

Caldwell, like Wright and Jensen, was a showman. He was passionate, and he knew how to impress young people, how to get to the point, and how to make the simplest issue in architecture an issue for all humanity. He did not just talk about the facts of brick, although with meticulous calculation and careful illustrations his lecture notebooks thoroughly explain all these facts, from foundation requirements to loads on beams and structural moments in the overhangs. To be sure, he helped students find "reasonable solutions to reasonable problems," but he also talked about why bricks were "one of the great inventions of mankind."[93] Caldwell lectured to the sophomores and juniors on the importance of brick in architectural history starting with the Sumerians five thousand years ago and ending with the Monadnock Building in Chicago. Whether the topic was brick or Chartres, in the lecture or construction class, he "emphasized the broad cultural impact of architecture" and stressed the need for architects to act heroically in spite of the likelihood that they would be misunderstood.[94] He never missed a chance to bring in the Romans, or to point out how "goddamned" bad everything was in the third century A.D., what a "whorehouse" everything had become. All the while his finger would be punching the student's shoulder until it was black and blue. He was never talking only about bricks or any other material thing. He waxed poetic and philosophic about values and principles and whispered the truth in the students' ears while they furiously but painstakingly drew one brick after another.[95]

While the students were meeting these incessant demands—building the brick house, the wood and stone house, or the T-column house in models and on Strathmore boards—Caldwell was endlessly molding their minds, for he was fundamentally interested in the students themselves. "It was impossible to be in the class and not be aware that the teacher was absolutely involved with each guy."[96] Dan Lawrence, his student at USC and now a teacher of architecture himself, described his teaching method as "unconditional love."[97] "I gave blood," Caldwell insisted frequently, because "the students were the future. The future of America would not be any better than the students. I had nothing to invest but my life—and I put it in."[98] Since Caldwell obviously worked so hard for them, his students worked just as hard for him. His absorption in the students was genuine, and it was love, but he also based this philosophy of teaching on his knowledge of the Greeks, particularly on Greek ideas about education that he had gleaned from Werner Jaeger's three-volume *Paideia: The Ideals of Greek Culture*. Education meant more than bricks. To the Greeks and to Caldwell, education was supposed "to shape the living man as the potter moulds clay and the sculptor carves stone into preconceived form."[99] He considered his calling "the process of educating man into his true form, the real and genuine human nature."[100] By the time he was through with the brick project or any other project, students believed their brick houses were the most important things in the world—that the whole world depended on them and they were up to the challenge. "We got that feeling that we were artists. We were actually doing works of art. Our stuff was as good as there was in the world."[101] Throughout his teaching career, Caldwell taught confidence. "He had only known me for three seconds. And it didn't seem to matter and suddenly I was being lifted. Lifted to a beginning of a sense of confidence and self-empowerment and maybe I'm OK," remarked Dan Lawrence.[102] But Caldwell had other views of education that went beyond the importance of the individual, and he forged these ideas, particularly those drawn from Thomas Jefferson, into his repertoire of lectures. Nose-to-nose and in a thundering voice heard figuratively round the world and certainly from one end of Crown Hall to the other, students heard Caldwell make his point to some sophomore who had failed to give blood. "You see, this is not some little pretty thing about being educated. Education serves a very great and deep purpose. It gives us our freedom. Ignorance will always result in tyranny."

Choreographing every project into a teaching formula, demanding perfection in the model and on the Strathmore board, committing himself completely to his students and expecting complete commitment in return, building confidence, "screeching and screaming" about life beyond architecture, critiquing without juries, and requiring that each construction student keep a careful notebook of the lectures in construction, history, and landscape were all teaching methods that distinguished him from many other teachers of his generation.[103] After twenty years of teaching he added the coffee talk, in which he regularly invited his California students, one by one or two by two, to sit down with him at the student union and talk about themselves. In Chicago and Los Angeles and presumably also at Virginia Polytechnic Institute, where he was offered a contract after teaching for one semester in 1965, the students loved him.

But as might be expected, his dedication, intensity, and passion as well as his provocative ideas got him into trouble with the faculty and administration at IIT, including Hilberseimer and Walter Peterhans, the businessmen of Chicago, and later the administration and faculty at USC. In Chicago Mies protected Caldwell as much as he could, and in Los Angeles Crombie Taylor did so to the point of getting fired himself. Mies and Taylor knew what they were doing, and they were willing to accept controversy as part of the bargain. When Mies hired Caldwell in 1945, he knew all about the problems Caldwell had had in Dubuque and at the Chicago Park District. At the end of his first day at IIT, Caldwell drove Mies back to his office, which he often did for the next fifteen years, and in their conversation Mies gave him license to disagree. "Hilberseimer, Peterhans and I all believe the same thing about architecture. However, over the interpretation of architecture we fight like cats and dogs. That is perfectly all right."

Caldwell had not worked a year at IIT before he got into hot water with the president, Henry Townley Heald, over a provocative idea that had consequences well beyond the Department of Architecture.[104] On August 6, 1945, while driving back late from the farm, Caldwell passed a newsstand and was shocked by the huge headlines about Hiroshima. By the time he got home, he had worked out an essay about a decentralized city based on his 1942 drawing "The Living Landscape," and with the encouragement of Mies and Hilberseimer this idea was published in the *Journal of the American Institute of Architects* of December 1945.[105] The idea was not entirely his, since Wright, Hilberseimer, and others had proposed it before. But Caldwell's timing was perfect, and connecting the proposal with the devastation at Hiroshima and Nagasaki made it more compelling. To some, especially investors concerned about going ahead with projects in downtown Chicago and architects worried about losing money if these projects were halted, "Atomic Bombs and City Planning" was more powerful than the atomic bomb itself.[106] The logic was convincing, and no one at that time could misunderstand the eloquence of Caldwell's words:

> From today on, our city, and every large city, can be completely destroyed in a
> moment. . . .
>
> A few brief months ago Berlin was demolished by means we must soon
> consider needlessly laborious and primitive. . . .
>
> During the years of peace we could disperse our cities and decentralize
> our industries. Then the city would be agrarian and the countryside would be
> industrial. The city would be everywhere and yet nowhere. The enemy
> would have practically nothing to attack. . . . Through the years, our city has
> become unlivable. . . .
>
> One-third of our population has already moved to suburbs. . . .
>
> . . . a simple house in a safe place. If we lack the wisdom to provide for our
> own safety in the immediate tomorrow by performing the relatively easy task
> of replanning our cities. . . .
>
> Then perhaps, after all, we are men on a doomed planet, and destruction
> is our domicile at last.

Caldwell was never a man to make a point and walk away from it. He believed
then and believes now that "centralized cities are evil in themselves." In an
editorial titled "No Dodging the Bomb," the *Chicago Sun* rejected his idea as
"academic," which Caldwell denied in a fiery reply. He also attacked the idea of
urban renewal, at that time being considered by Chicago planners.

> We are determined, in the manner of the late Joe Chamberlain at Munich, to
> save the slums for our time. In order to accomplish this highly dubious
> objective we propose to rip down the old tenements and build new tene-
> ments (called "slum clearance projects") on the same ground; that is, in the
> smokiest, dirtiest and most congested and disordered section of our city, and,
> naturally, the most dangerous in time of war. We call this City Planning, and
> represent it as noble service to the poor and underprivileged.[107]

He continued this public correspondence with letters to editors that criticized as a
waste of money the powerful City Club's proposals to relieve parking problems in
the Loop. He contended that in the decentralized city one could walk to work.[108]
He always brought up Hiroshima and the bomb, war and peace. He argued in a
letter to the *Saturday Review of Literature* that war could not be banished, and
that given the atomic bomb, the only answer was to decentralize cities in defense.
He mentioned Ludwig Hilberseimer's *The New City* and proposed "that the
Saturday Review of Literature review this book, against that ominous day when
children may be burnt wisps of flesh in the philistine air or charred bone in
rubble and real estate."[109] On top of all this, Caldwell always began his lectures at
IIT with atomic bombs and babies. "Atomic bombs and babies do not go together," he bellowed to his students, many of whom were former GIs at that
moment creating the Baby Boom. The administration put pressure on Caldwell,
and Hilberseimer was afraid of the administration. He persuaded Caldwell not to

get involved publicly, to join the City Club, and to lie low.[110] Unfortunately, it was too late. He had stirred up so many powerful people that President Heald, as Caldwell remembers, eventually had to assemble his furious detractors and, with him in the room, dissociate IIT from any thought of decentralizing Chicago. Caldwell did not say a word, for as an untenured assistant professor he had committed the worst of academic sins — a show of idealism supported by powerful logic and the courage to speak out. Heald, although deeply involved in the development of downtown Chicago through his work with Fred Kramer of the Metropolitan Housing and Planning Council, did not fire Caldwell.[111] Dismissing him would have been easy for Heald and would have earned applause from his powerful development friends, but the incident luckily turned into just another close call in Caldwell's teaching career.

Caldwell did stay out of the public eye, but he did not give up his ideas about the need to change the city. Again Hilberseimer and Mies encouraged him. Against the wishes of a member of the committee from the business school who objected — Mies said because Caldwell's thesis was "leftist" — in 1948 Mies and Hilberseimer voted to award Caldwell an IIT master of science degree in city planning for his thesis "The City in the Landscape: A Preface for Planning."[112] It was based on ideas he had published in 1945 and on Hilberseimer's book of 1944, outlining how the decentralization of Chicago could be planned so that "city and landscape could be joined."[113] He left out the bombs and babies theme in the thesis, but he added this controversial element in his book manuscript titled "The Living Landscape," which was never published.[114]

Caldwell always stuck doggedly to his ideas and his teaching agenda and was unable to forge compromises with his old and new faculty colleagues at IIT. The biggest disagreement festered over the demands Caldwell placed on his students. Hilberseimer, along with Peterhans, James Speyer, and Daniel Brenner, complained to Mies that Caldwell required so much that his students had no time for other courses in the second and third years. "You make the whole school yours," Hilberseimer protested.[115] It was true. But as Caldwell argued, he required from them only what he required of himself: devotion to the creative task. How could one argue against this?

For Walter Peterhans the problem with Caldwell was more than time. Peterhans taught visual training in the second and third years, and though he complained that Caldwell kept students too long, the visual training boards from his fifteen years of teaching at IIT are exceptional in quality. The differences between Peterhans and Caldwell went deeper. Peterhans had the respect of his students and they produced for him, but Caldwell clearly had their hearts and minds. As a German intellectual, Peterhans could not compete with Caldwell's fire. Peterhans, who also taught architectural history, was critical, "remarking to students who asked about the difference between his and Caldwell's approach,

Walter Peterhans at the Blue Note, 1950. (Courtesy of Mary Ann Latham)

that his students would understand what he had been discussing in the future."[116]

This prediction did not come true. What counted in the long run among students was not knowledge but inspiration, and Caldwell created his teaching method to inspire, not just to appeal to the intellect. "Where Peterhans sought to discern the processes of history so that students could then have comprehension and possible effect on its future course, Caldwell assumed a more mythic structure in which the individual was necessarily opposed to the inevitable destructive forces of time."[117] To students, Caldwell was the most persuasive and entertaining teacher on the faculty, and Mies knew it.[118] When Hilberseimer and Peterhans complained too much, Caldwell always offered to resign, much to Mies's chagrin. Mies remarked that he could "always tell when it's springtime because Caldwell resigns."[119] On one occasion when it had gone too far, Mies said to him, "Look Caldwell, Hilbs is not the director, I am. Never mind Peterhans, just do what I ask you to do, that's all. Let's not talk any more about it. If they come to you, say talk to Mies." This kind of talk frequently ended up with martinis at Mies's apartment, where he would manage to persuade Caldwell to stay on. "You are irreplaceable," he told him; "one day the students will put you on a pedestal."[120] Mies was right, and he managed to keep Caldwell on the faculty even beyond his own tenure.[121] But when Mies left it was only a matter of time before Caldwell resigned from IIT for the last time on January 29, 1960.[122]

This resignation was precipitated by Ludwig Hilberseimer. He was angry about Mies's losing the design of the IIT campus to Skidmore, Owings and Merrill, and he egged Caldwell on at a dinner at the Chicago Athletic Club.[123] The atmosphere was especially charged because SOM's coup at IIT, right or wrong, had become a national scandal among architects. Hilberseimer knew that Caldwell was furious and in a mood to rant. After a few drinks the conversation turned into a row between Caldwell and Bill Dunlap, a partner at SOM.[124] Myron Goldsmith remembered that Caldwell gave a speech in which he argued that the architects at SOM, many of whom had studied under Mies, Hilberseimer, and Caldwell at IIT, should relinquish the campus design to Mies, who had worked on this project since 1939. In Caldwell's view, SOM owed it to their old and now arthritic teacher and friend. Hilberseimer suggested to Caldwell that they resign from IIT that night if SOM did not give up the project. Caldwell always acted on principles of friendship and loyalty, and he did not mind going first. He never objected to being a sacrificial lamb, for he had endured these tribulations many times before. "If he [Mies] goes, I go," he proclaimed at the end of his resignation speech. Never mind that Mies could never have gotten the project back no matter what SOM did. Never mind that Gordon Bunshaft had offered to put Mies in charge of the SOM project and Mies had turned down the offer.[125]

No resignation could have straightened out this tangle. Even though the profession considered SOM's behavior unethical, the leaders at SOM believed they were free to accept the job because the new president of IIT, J. T. Rettaliata, had decided to fire Mies. Rettaliata wanted Mies to come to meetings, and Mies sent his assistants. Rettaliata, a man of thirty-seven, wanted Mies, a man of seventy-two, to respond faster to IIT's requests.[126] In Rettaliata's view Mies could not do the job, and he promptly accepted Caldwell's formal resignation. Hilberseimer promised Caldwell that he too would resign, but then he backed down. When the dust had settled, the events of the evening sank in like a death in the family. George Danforth, who headed the school of architecture, and Hilberseimer tried to persuade Rettaliata to reconsider. He declined. This left Danforth with a difficult problem, because Caldwell had taught the heart of the IIT curriculum for fifteen years and did the work of three faculty members. The students, faculty, and Chicago professionals were in an uproar. With Mies, Peterhans, and now Caldwell gone, IIT would never be the same.[127] "I resigned to protect architecture, an idea," Caldwell explained to Ruth Roberg; "I protected it by protesting its destruction." Friends worried more about the destruction of Alfred Caldwell, and to Ruth he admitted some responsibility for creating a difficult situation. "You would have to be a saint to put up with me. I myself feel that if I ever met Alfred Caldwell I would dislike him very much. He is just the kind of person I can't abide."[128]

The summer and fall of 1960 were filled with anxiety. Brooding, yet spirited as usual, Caldwell approached a number of schools of architecture about a teaching position. Mies wrote effusive letters of recommendation to Carnegie Mellon and Notre Dame on Caldwell's behalf, testifying that his teaching was "based on clear principles, a fact I find important in this time of confusion in the fields of architecture and planning. His is a strong and uncompromising personality."[129] Mies testified that Caldwell was "one of the hardest workers I have ever met, and a man of unusual integrity, who possesses great practical knowledge."[130] Although many universities responded with interest, nothing was available at the time of Caldwell's unplanned departure from IIT. He had much to offer academia and the profession, but nobody was prepared for his sudden appearance on the market. Besides being a legendary teacher, philosopher, poet, and artist, Caldwell had thirty-five years of practical experience on large-scale urban landscape projects. In addition to his work with Jensen during the 1920s, at Dubuque and in the Chicago Park District in the 1930s, and in the War Department and at IIT with his landscape design for Mies's campus and the Farnsworth house in the late 1940s, he carried out a series of architectural and landscape projects in the 1950s that sealed his reputation as extremely competent, if uncompromising.[131] The Montreal zoo project (1954, not built), which Caldwell "planned as an educational and epic poem to nature, explaining and showing the creatures of

Design for Montreal zoo, 1954 (not built). (Photo by Richard Nickel; courtesy of Alfred Caldwell and Centre Canadien d'Architecture/Canadian Centre for Architecture, Montreal)

the planet," was an almost barless zoo of modern steel and glass structures set behind moats and stone walls so that visitors viewed the animals across natural, open landscapes.[132] The Omaha zoo project (1955, not built) used a "demountable-prefabricated system of construction" with hexagonal buildings of steel and glass that a crew of three persons could easily disassemble and reerect depending on the needs of the zoo. The Omaha project included an aviary dome (1956, not built) in a lamellar grid of aluminum joists supporting a greenhouse roof.[133] Caldwell also planned the lush prairie landscape of native flora for Lafayette Park in Detroit (1955–63), an urban renewal project he worked on with Mies, Hilberseimer, and the developer Herbert Greenwald. Caldwell took advantage of Hilberseimer's "settlement unit" plan for the seventy-eight-acre tract that prohibited through traffic, called for sunken parking to hide the automobiles from view, and gave pedestrians access to common space without their crossing busy streets.[134] The minuscule trees and shrubs Caldwell had planted in Lafayette Park are now a canopy of mature trees that shade dramatic clearings around Mies's serene modern architecture. David Spaeth praised the park, asserting that "what Hilberseimer, Mies, Caldwell, and Greenwald achieved is nothing less than a working model for future urbanization, predicated on human values and

Design for small zoological garden, Omaha, Nebraska, 1955 (not built). (Photo by Richard Nickel; courtesy of Alfred Caldwell and Centre Canadien d'Architecture/Canadian Centre for Architecture, Montreal)

needs, accommodating but not dominated by the automobile."[135] Other proposals such as the drawings and models for the ingenious indoor-outdoor pool project in Chicago in 1956 and 1957, drawings for a regional park in 1957, and plans and models for the Winnipeg zoo in 1958 were further proof of his design capabilities and technical skill as an architect, engineer, and landscape architect.[136] Caldwell also had numerous smaller landscape projects during the 1950s, such as the landscape for the Hall residence (1954) in Deerfield, Illinois, and the striking prairie school landscape for Roosevelt Park Elementary School (1957) in Gary, Indiana. But in spite of his extensive professional background he had no work, and the summer months dragged on into the late fall of 1960 until finally the unpredictable happened.

The Chicago Department of City Planning, under the direction of Commissioner Ira J. Bach and Assistant Commissioner for Planning and Research Larry Reich, snapped Caldwell up to spark a special projects department they created to provide ideas, drawings, models, and reports for extensive urban design projects in the city. Chicago politicians had always had their own ideas and pet design projects. This was especially true during the robust development period of the 1950s and 1960s, and city officials had to respond to Mayor Richard Daley, city commissioners, and developers as they worked on the complex, politically sensitive planning issues of an immense city. These issues, vast in scope and expensive to address, created equally vast urban planning opportunities that took the likes of a Daniel Burnham to consider and comprehend in physical terms. Reich, who was primarily responsible for this special projects department, needed a person who had extensive knowledge of Chicago and the city in history, someone with a penetrating imagination, a track record for developing visionary ideas on a large scale, the ability to inspire others, an extraordinary capacity to present these visionary ideas and make them convincing, and perhaps the ability to manage the construction of large-scale projects for the city should any be adopted. Caldwell fascinated Reich, who was compelled by his personality, intelligence, and

Design for aviary in small zoological garden, Omaha, Nebraska, 1956 (not built). (Photo by Richard Nickel; courtesy of Alfred Caldwell and Centre Canadien d'Architecture/Canadian Centre for Architecture, Montreal)

passion. He knew that his presence charged the atmosphere of a school or professional environment and inspired people to strive for perfection. Caldwell was called to be "the commissioner of faith," as his young coworkers fondly dubbed him.

The commissioner of faith and the special projects department occupied a floor in the YMCA building on Wacker Drive, along with other members of the Central Area Section of the General Plan Division. Caldwell's think tank was loosely organized so that no one really worked for anyone, but since most of Caldwell's group had been his students at IIT—he was fifty-seven and they were in their twenties and early thirties—Caldwell was obviously the most experienced, and they considered him their intellectual and design superior. His job was to bring historical understanding to projects and provide the visionary ideas for the special projects workforce to carry out. Caldwell called it "Job's job." Gerald Estes, Tom Bacouris, David Swan, Tom Murphy, Bob Gordon, Marshall Boskin, and Kyle Benkert, who at thirty-one was chief of the Central Area Section, listened with rapt attention as Caldwell inspired them to follow his planning

Lafayette Park, Detroit, Michigan, 1955–63. Ludwig Mies van der Rohe, architect; Alfred Caldwell, landscape architect. (Photo by Dennis Domer)

Lafayette Park, Detroit, Michigan, 1955–63. Ludwig Mies van der Rohe, architect; Alfred Caldwell, landscape architect. (Photo by Dennis Domer)

visions with lectures on history and quotations from poets and philosophers.[137] He met with them regularly at morning and afternoon coffee talks, a device he used to discuss the underlying theory and structure of his ideas.

Early in his tenure at the Department of City Planning he laid out a planning philosophy for colleagues to follow in an essay titled "Order and Beauty." Caldwell explained the disorderly flight to the suburbs as a flight from the city's ugliness: its slums, alleys, automobile parking, low and tall buildings packed together, lack of parks, gridiron street pattern, grime and filth, improper placement of factories, garish commercial areas, and urban renewal projects composed of "enormous boxes, tier on tier, ten stories high."[138] Caldwell described the city as a kind of prison and wrote, "Men confined in prisons have always felt the loss of nature more than anything else. This indeed is the psychology involved in escape to the suburbs, a psychic drive so powerful that it is breaking down the city."[139] Caldwell's remedies for this disorder drew heavily on Hilberseimer's planning theories, because he had helped him develop and test those theories at IIT. Hilberseimer had republished some of Caldwell's drawings

Design for indoor-outdoor swimming pool, Chicago, Illinois, 1956–57 (not built). (Photo by Richard Nickel; courtesy of Alfred Caldwell and Centre Canadien d'Architecture/Canadian Centre for Architecture, Montreal)

as recently as 1955 in *The Nature of Cities.* Caldwell, like Hilberseimer, wanted to decentralize the city into settlement units zoned as industrial, commercial, and residential districts based on environmental factors such as prevailing winds, orientation and sun penetration, and noise and air pollution. Caldwell wanted as much green space as possible for both high- and low-density residential areas. "Tall buildings should be placed far apart in the landscape with both parks and one-story houses in the space between."[140] Critical of Chicago's urban renewal projects, Caldwell believed "the intention of slum reclamation should be to achieve the motto of Chicago, '*Urbs in Horto*' — 'A City in a Garden.'"[141] He argued that all residential areas should have garden space and parks within walking distance, and he called for the elimination of the grid system throughout the city and especially through-traffic streets in residential areas. He wanted to get rid of on-street parking and alleys in replanned areas of the city. In short, Caldwell wanted a living landscape, for "if the city is to survive, it must conform to life. Life will not conform to it."[142] He ended his essay with his advice in Latin that these planning principles applied always, everywhere, and to everyone: "Quod semper; quod ubique; quod ab omnibus."[143] He was a prophet to his young colleagues and a thorn in the side of the bureaucrats and politicians who were responsible for many of the city's ills and who did not want to hear Caldwell's criticism.

Caldwell enchanted his younger colleagues and even his enemies with his exquisite drawings, many of which disappeared into the homes of planning department executives. He could draw in any medium, but at the planning department he often used Prismacolor pencils to express his imaginative ideas. Everyone waited impatiently for him to finish the next drawing, and "if you asked him what he was working on," Gerald Estes remarked thirty years later, "he asked you if you knew *Prometheus Bound* and *Prometheus Unbound*."[144] He could amaze them with the quick "desktop collage models" he created with aerial photo prints and "pieces of wood, plastic, colored paper, and ground-up green rubber sponge."[145] No one worked harder than Caldwell; he was always at his desk drawing by the time everyone else arrived in the morning. His total dedication to his work and the excitement of the creative moment drove his young colleagues to extend themselves on every project. Through his discussions, drawings, and models, Caldwell made them believe that what they were doing was the most important thing in the world, and consequently his tight little band of true believers mesmerized the commissioners and politicians by their ability to visualize and dramatize their proposals.

One of the earliest special projects Caldwell and his followers designed was a grand proposal for a Chicago world's fair to commemorate the bicentennial of the United States in 1976. The city planning department, along with a group of Chicago business and professional leaders called the Committee of Seventy-six, had been preparing a world's fair proposal since 1954, and by the time Caldwell came to the planning department in late 1960 the committee had secured resolutions of support from the city of Chicago, Cook County, the General Assembly of Illinois, and the Senate of the United States.[146] In 1961 Illinois passed a bill that created a bipartisan commission to "cooperate with any interested organizations in the planning and organization of a World Fair to be held in Chicago in 1976."[147] It was easy to get enthusiastic support for Chicago, especially from Chicago politicians who wanted the fair because both of Chicago's previous world fairs had made money, stimulated the city's economy, dazzled millions of

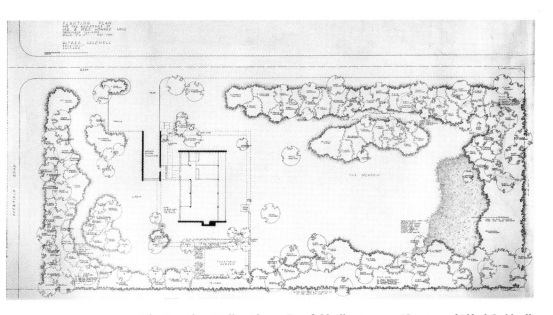

Planting plan, Hall residence, Deerfield, Illinois, 1954. (Courtesy of Alfred Caldwell)

visitors, and dramatized the city as one of the most influential economic, technological, and design centers in the United States. If Chicago got the invitation for
the 1976 fair, the Committee of Seventy-six expected to bring 50 million visitors to
the city, end up in the black, and leave behind a permanent investment in the
city.[148] What the committee and the city needed was "a preliminary but somewhat definitive concept of plans, designs, possible sites and the philosophy of
Chicago World's Fair—1976."[149]

Larry Reich knew Caldwell was perfectly suited for this intellectual challenge. He was arguably as capable of creating spectacular, monumental urban
design schemes backed by a convincing philosophy as Daniel Burnham, though
he did not possess Burnham's political and social skills. The nature of Caldwell's
task, as stated in the committee's objectives, was to create a design that would

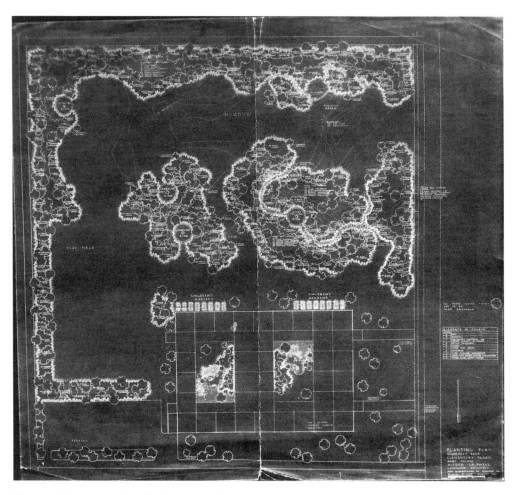

Planting plan, Roosevelt Park Elementary School, Gary, Indiana, 1957. (Courtesy of Alfred Caldwell)

Design for proposed bicentennial exposition, Chicago, Illinois, 1976. (Chicago Department of City Planning; courtesy of Gerald Estes)

"measure the state of technology, to give glimpses of the future and show how life might be lived if certain things come to pass. *Its purpose is to inspire hope, to give vision, to entertain.*" Further, the committee believed it had "a deep, serious responsibility: to speak for society as a whole and present a picture of the world's potentialities."[150] As a quintessential modernist, Caldwell considered any design's "cultural significance . . . [to be] related to the clarity of its statement. That statement is not a question of word or slogan but of deed. The Fair must demonstrate its proposition. If it fails, it loses itself in emptiness."[151]

After briefly analyzing the possibility of constructing five islands in Lake Michigan, Caldwell proposed a dispersed fair near the downtown with three sites that were connected by the Chicago River, itself an important part of the transportation system in his plan. A superbuilding, "2,000 feet square, constructed on the suspension principle like the suspension bridge, and hence free of interior supports" anchored this dispersed fair on the south. With a ceiling height of 180 feet and 4 million square feet of usable space, the building could stack "vast exhibition halls on a scale never before attempted."[152] When the fair was over, the superbuilding would house sports events such as football and baseball as well as theaters, bazaars, and industrial exhibitions, "simultaneously if desirable."[153] The superbuilding, like all parts of the fair, came out of Caldwell's experience, and in that sense this giant was not an entirely new idea. In fact Caldwell had already worked out the design for it in 1959 at IIT, and it had attracted national attention when *Progressive Architecture* published his design in 1961 as an example of "a daring use of suspension principles."[154] The Chicago fair proposal gave him the opportunity to use his stunning technological achievement, and as the journal noted, carry out Mies's dictum that "whenever technology reaches its real fulfillment, it transcends into architecture."[155] On the second site, near Goose

Design for suspension building 2,000 feet square, 1959. (Photo by Richard Nickel; courtesy of Alfred Caldwell)

Island, he planned an "in-town new-town" based partially on ideas he and Hilber-seimer had worked out at IIT for a modern dispersed city within a living land-scape designed according to Jensen's prairie school principles. The committee believed this part of the fair, a square mile of residential, industrial, and public space, would attract the most attention and have the most influence because after seeing it "people might no longer be content to have their cities be less than what cities should be: cities for *living,* wholesome and beautiful."[156] On the third site, near the mouth of the Chicago River, Caldwell and his team proposed a 150-story skyscraper for vertical exhibitions, surrounded by a pedestrian plaza that covered a large underground parking area. The bronze dome proposed for the plaza was just one of many domes Caldwell had worked out with students at IIT or in previous projects such as the Montreal zoo and the indoor-outdoor pool. Near this glamorous center Caldwell floated fair pavilions on pontoons. The sky-scraper and plaza would remain after the fair as a commercial building with luxury apartments, and the floating fair would be dismantled. These sites were to be connected by expressways, rapid transit, fixed railroads, and the Chicago River, which "was the transportation spine of the fair and slated to be landscaped and upgraded with walkways and other amenities."[157]

Adopting Daniel Burnham's often-quoted advice "Make no little plans" as their "CREDO for '76," the Committee of Seventy-six and the city officials enthusi-astically adopted Caldwell's fantastic scheme, which in their view offered three unusual features. First, each of the elements would become a permanent part of the city and, except for the structures on pontoons, would not be dismantled as in the case of Chicago's two previous world's fairs. The elements would act "as a bridge between the old city and the new." Second, it was "a moving fair" because of the circulation system between the sites, a system that allowed people to enter anywhere and then be carried from site to site by "a fleet of launches and land vehicles." Third, it was "a distributed fair," which made its gigantic scale possible and "permitted the exploitation of new ideas not feasible on one site." As a distributed fair, it would spread "financial benefits . . . over a larger part of the city" while easing traffic, because "instead of converging on one center, traffic would aim not only for the three elements but also for the fair circulation system."[158] Unfortunately, however, Chicago's world's fair submission in the national competition, no matter how ingenious its design, could not overcome the sentimental favorite—Philadelphia, the City of Brotherly Love.

Even though Chicago politicians and planning executives supported the special projects department where Caldwell and his cohorts produced one plan after another during his four-year stint there, all of these plans, like that for the world's fair, went down the drain. So did Caldwell. Mayor Daley and his planners could not swallow all his utopian recommendations or accept his criticism of the city. Caldwell and his team, by creating plans that would enhance the public good, gave the city ideas about how to manage Chicago's growth, but the private developers always resisted them. They were interested in short-term profit, not the public good. The proposals from the city's special projects department were too visionary, and as long-term undertakings they would take decades to create the financial return developers expected. For example, Caldwell's "Lakeshore Proposals in Two Parts"[159] analyzed the relation between the metropolis and the lake and proposed to bring Lake Michigan back to an earlier shoreline along Michigan Avenue. His idea involved creating "a city in a park" that included a lakeshore park, a new harbor between Randolph and Monroe Streets, an outer expressway under the harbor, and a series of tall apartment buildings on a strip of land "a mile or two in width" running parallel to the shoreline. Caldwell suggested that this city in a park could be expanded to forty square miles if the unnecessary streets of the grid system were removed. In part 2, titled "Urban Renewal as a Possibility," Caldwell provided a philosophical and poetic proposal to establish a new city order, the decentralized city in a living landscape. "To bring the true city back, and reassert the needs of life, and the spiritual nature of man, should be the purpose of planning. All else is heresy." No doubt the politicians and the developers scoffed at the details and scope of this living city, especially when Caldwell brought his professorial exegesis to an end with lines from "Milton," a poem by William Blake:

> Bring me my Bow of burning gold;
> Bring me my Arrows of desire;
> Bring me my Spear: O clouds unfold!
> Bring me my Chariot of fire!
>
> I will not cease from Mental Fight,
> Nor shall my Sword sleep in my hand
> Till we have built Jerusalem
> In England's green & pleasant Land.

Perhaps to give the politicians and developers less poetic but just as imaginative proposals, David Swan and Gerald Estes often wrote the reports in the special projects department. For example, the planning ideas in the April 1962 studies and proposals for the Illinois Central Air Rights sixty-acre area north of Randolph Street all emanated from Caldwell's fertile mind, but David Swan wrote the report in a straightforward, "professional" style. Mayor Daley wanted to avoid a skyscraper jungle on this important property, and Caldwell's group gave him a $1 billion proposal for a high-density development that would be carried out over fifteen years. This plan to build a complex where 30,000 people could live and work called for relocating Lake Shore Drive in tunnels to the east under Lake Michigan, included a huge elevated pedestrian plaza with shops, schools, churches, theaters, and recreational facilities, proposed a line of tall commercial and residential buildings carefully spaced facing the lake, placed all transportation links and parking on several levels under the plaza, and replanted Grant Park in the prairie landscape tradition. The mayor touted the plan, and even the developers said it "represented good thinking," but nothing like it came to fruition.[160] Nor did anything come of Caldwell's magnificent proposal for a Monroe Street–Grant Park underground parking garage with its circular garden terraces, prairie botanical garden, an indoor-outdoor swimming pool with a retractable roof, and a domed aviary. His pedestrian-oriented Chicago Riverfront plan, written by David Swan after Caldwell had left the planning department, envisioned crystal residential towers in a landscape of parks and lagoons. Although this plan never materialized, George D. Schipporeit and John Heinrich, students and colleagues of Caldwell at IIT, carried out the tower idea in perhaps the most striking skyscraper on Chicago's skyline, Lake Point Tower (1965–68). Caldwell provided this architectural jewel with an exquisite prairie landscape.

By the time that landscape took shape, however, Ira J. Bach, commissioner of city planning, had long since terminated Caldwell.[161] Caldwell made the mistake of opening up a private planning office in the spring of 1964 and employing Swan and Estes to work with him in the evenings on projects for developers. Caldwell had always had his own projects, and it seemed the natural thing to do, but Bach quickly fired him, ostensibly because his moonlighting created a conflict of interest in the department. In fact, remembered David Swan, "the city had been trying to dump him because his writing was very critical."[162] Right or wrong, Caldwell had banged away one too many times at developments in the city, especially Chicago's urban renewal projects. With the intervention of Larry Reich, Caldwell got two weeks notice instead of two days, but his departure eventually brought down the special projects department too. Estes and Swan wrote major planning documents in April and May 1964 after Caldwell cleared out, but the group of young idealists lost heart without him.[163] In his final project, the "Chicago Riverfront Study," Swan concluded sarcastically that "the lack of

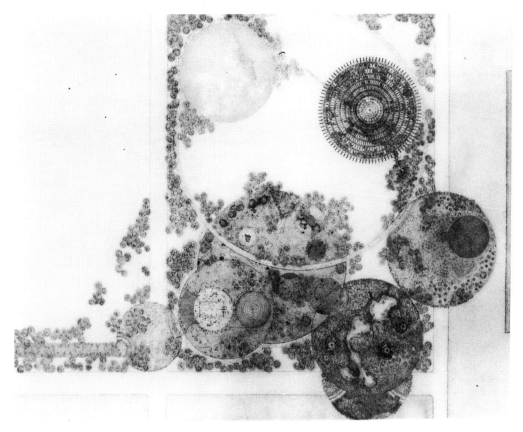

Upper-level plan, Monroe Street–Grant Park underground parking garage, Chicago, Illinois. (Chicago Department of City Planning; courtesy of Gerald Estes)

interest and desire for parks along the river is not something that is going to be changed by a group of governing aestheticians stumbling about in a half mesmerized manner, intoxicated with thoughts on civil beauty."[164] The urban realities of Chicago were too harsh for these young men to consider in the absence of their indefatigable leader. Disappointed with the politics of development and their prospects in the planning department, they became cynical and scattered.

When Caldwell walked out for the last time on April 22, 1964, a field of teaching possibilities lay before him. He had corresponded with more than a dozen schools while at the planning department, and early in his tenure there, in December 1960, he had turned down a job that Joe Passaneau offered him at the University of Washington.[165] But by the fall of 1964 no teaching jobs had turned up, money was running out, there had been no private projects and would be none until spring, and Caldwell was filled with self-doubt. In despair, without enough money to pay the rent, he remembers looking down from his balcony into the street, wondering what they would do if they were evicted, weighing how

Lake Point Tower, Chicago, Illinois, 1965–68. George Schipporeit and John Heinrich, architects. (Photo by Ralph Stark, Hedrich-Blessing; courtesy of Chicago Historical Society)

Geda would be affected if he took his life, and finally deciding to give it four or five more days. Then Charles Worley of Virginia Polytechnic Institute offered him a teaching job for two quarters, starting in December 1964. He and Geda moved temporarily to Blacksburg, where he taught so happily and successfully that Worley offered him a contract at a salary higher than Caldwell had ever made before.[166]

He and Geda often thought about what it might have been like had they stayed in Virginia; but they could not resist an offer that seemed to come from paradise, where the "sun set pink and gold over the ocean."[167] Crombie Taylor,

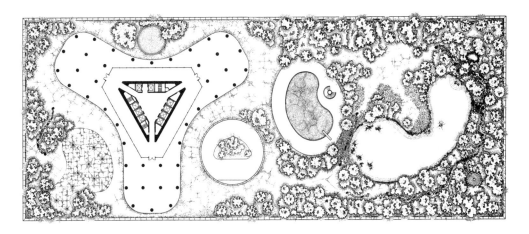

Plaza-level plan, Lake Point Tower, Chicago, Illinois, 1965–68. Alfred Caldwell, landscape architect.
(Photo by Hedrich-Blessing; courtesy of Chicago Historical Society)

associate dean of architecture at the University of Southern California, had known Caldwell from his IIT days when Taylor was acting director of the Institute of Design at IIT after Laszlo Moholy-Nagy died, and in 1962 he left his Chicago practice for the University of Southern California. By April 1965 Taylor desperately needed a proven teacher to instruct fifth-year architecture students in September. Taylor was desperate because in his view the architecture program at USC was moving in the wrong direction under the leadership of Sam Hurst, dean of the School of Architecture and Fine Arts.[168] With its new emphasis on research and experimentation rather than on design, Taylor believed the program would turn out students who could not become architects. This danger—that design would become mere talk—was real at USC and was exacerbated by the unraveling social situation in southern California in the 1960s, which included widespread protests against the Vietnam War and racial discrimination, the sexual revolution, drugs, and a general defiance of the establishment among the hippies and other dissidents who populated universities like USC. Crombie Taylor "went after Alfred because he was a sensible man, and he knew how to build."[169] Taylor's offer included arranging an apartment for the Caldwells in Palos Verdes Estates, a beautiful setting near the ocean where the "waves fall in scallops and the froth rolls over the rocks."[170] Geda could collect seashells and pebbles, and the two of them could "walk along the sand with these in our pockets."[171] Brooding at night over some word in a sonnet, Caldwell could walk "along the beach and in the pitch darkness hear the waves roll in from the shores of China." But the School of Architecture at USC was no paradise. With Konrad Wachsmann's appointment,[172] then Taylor's, and finally Caldwell's, the faculty and the profession thought the Bauhaus group from Chicago was taking over.

Garden, Lake Point Tower, Chicago, Illinois, 1965–68. Alfred Caldwell, landscape architect. (Photo by Dennis Domer)

Taylor recalled that "Mies was a curse word" among the faculty, who fought Caldwell and Crombie Taylor to an unhappy end.

As part of the recruiting process, Caldwell had flown to California to give a lecture. Taylor knew what Caldwell would do, for he had heard him speak in Chicago, but the cynical USC students could not have anticipated this remarkable stranger who brewed architecture, history, and the failures of contemporary society into a stirring tirade. "Be Your Own Man" was a "screecher and screamer" that the audience remembers thirty years later.[173] Caldwell set them back when he introduced himself as "a hippie too," and though he didn't look like one, he had more hippie credentials than the students did. He had worn bell-bottom pants thirty years earlier at the Chicago Park District. He had been a member of the Dill Pickle Club. Although never a card-carrying communist, he was certainly a leftist, as Mies recognized in Caldwell's master's thesis. He had always been antiestablishment and had been punished over and over again for sticking to his guns. With fire in his eye, his finger jabbing, and his voice piercing their ears, he didn't mind telling the truth to the USC students:

> I want a man to write with his blood. I accept him then as a force of Nature. Every word has cost him dearly. I demand that the professor profess himself, and prove that he is durable by putting his hand in the fire. The yawns and the spitball game under way are the wisdom of children who know that the lecture is really nothing, a mere pretense to fill up time.
>
> I like buildings with the mark of labor and wit and daring. I do not like the stones proper, sweatless, iced. The architect should have a strong arm to lift beams, and my spirit is lifted in the thought. I like buildings expensive in life. I count up the casualties and know that the building was in earnest.
>
> Most men are so cheap that they will not even spend themselves. They cannot love others because they cannot stand the expense of loving themselves. They want themselves for nothing. Love is knowledge. The need to love is the need to know, and the need to become a part of. If I know William Blake I become a part of William Blake; I love William Blake. Yet the basis of all knowledge is self-knowledge. Know thyself. The basis of all love then is self-love. Love thyself.

Alfred Caldwell with students at the University of Southern California, 1966. (Courtesy of Carol Caldwell Dooley)

The USC students had never heard anything like this, but they went wild when he attacked contemporary buildings in southern California: "Let us hoist the black flags and slit throats!" he roared. This brought the house down, and Caldwell went to California.

Thirty years later, his California students remember him as a savior. Caldwell certainly intended to work miracles. He taught the fifth year of architectural design, which was particularly difficult since students in the new scientific program usually had not designed a single building by the time they entered their fifth year.[174] The new curriculum was supposed "to create the super-architect of the future, the technologically savvy administrator who guided projects by delegation, and not by a deep understanding of construction."[175] They studied building processes, optimization, computers, and multimedia, created abstract forms "through an arbitrary series of decisions," made films, analyzed "water formations," and did research for Ralph Knowles's "amazing sun machine." "No instruction" was an experimental research teaching method many USC faculty members employed at the time. "We ran our own class" in the fourth year, and "under Wachsmann's graduate students we graded ourselves too."[176] The extent of the disengagement of the USC architecture faculty, in the opinion of many students, was dramatized in a teacher-student conference that occurred in May 1969. "We got a skeleton from a Fine Arts studio and set it up at the conference table and had conferences with it," remembered Dan Lawrence, now a teacher of architecture at the Arts Center College of Design in Pasadena. "We threw hamburger meat at each other. That was our history class."[177] "There was a great sense of frustration," in Dennis DePietro's view. "After all, we were the free thinkers of the 60's, and we simply were not finding the right answers as we continued our studies."[178] By the time students got to the fifth year many were bewildered about architecture, and Caldwell's task, as he saw it, was to teach five years of architectural design, materials, construction, model building, city planning, and architectural history in one year.

In the spring fourth-year students traditionally had the opportunity to hear what the fifth-year architectural design professors had in mind for the fall. In his presentation to the fourth-year class in May 1969, Caldwell spoke from the perspective of "nearly a quarter of a century" of teaching.[179] Passionate as the poet he was, he emphasized the importance of clarity, the significance of construction ("without that, nothing can happen"), the art of love, love of work, the teacher as a reporter of facts, the need to understand basic things "so that you can go on with your lives to lead a creative, satisfying, and I hope, beautiful life," and the centrality of the student in the educational process. Caldwell attacked the team approach to learning. To him the search for architectural knowledge or any other knowledge was an individual experience. "When the hippies say, 'Do your own thing,' . . . that's a perfectly truthful and profound expression. I understand exactly why they come to it." "You cannot fall in love in a group. You can only fall in love personally." Caldwell attacked Wachsmann's apotheosis of structural systems. "There is no virtue in a structural system. The virtue is in the human being." He also attacked research. "As defined by the dictionary, research comes from two words: Latin 're' meaning 'again,' and 'circare' meaning 'to go round.' To go round again. Now if you don't know anything about these things, how can you do research in it? You haven't gone round it once." Finally, he called for simplicity instead of complexity. "The most profound things in the world are simple; only poorly educated, trivial, and decorative men and women think complicated things are profound." In the spring of 1970 Dennis DePietro and his fourth-year class listened to Frank Gehry promote his "disposable architecture and cardboard furniture," and Ralph Knowles talked about doing environmental research. Alfred Caldwell, however, stuck to the basics of construction that he had practiced successfully since 1945. "One phrase he repeated often," DePietro remarked, "seemed to reach out and grab me by the scruff of the neck: 'In our class we will attempt to find reasonable solutions to reasonable problems.'" His presentation was irresistible, and he got by far the most students. By the second semester he had all but five or six. As DePietro remembered, "Suddenly, into this world of academic chaos, Mr. Caldwell came in and swept away almost the entire class. We too joined in to hole away in his Trojan horse, away from the whorehouse around us."[180]

Except for the daily coffee talks he had added while working with younger colleagues in the Chicago Department of City Planning, Caldwell employed the same teaching methods at USC that he had practiced at IIT and Virginia Polytechnic Institute. First of all he inspired his students by making them feel they were the most important people in the world. This was a shock because students got little personal attention during their first four years at USC. Whether a student liked him or not, Caldwell zeroed in on every one of them intensely and like Moses from the mountain convinced them they could be artists and architects. There were demonstrations and sit-ins outside, all manner of revolt against everything connected with the establishment, and a school full of furious and confused students. To each student who entered his class he offered a rational respite from this irrational storm, and he did it in the most personal way. Like him or not, David R. Kendall could not forget him:

> Much of what Mr. Caldwell teaches I must admit I find disagreeable, but I consider my time with him to have been a beneficial and extremely stimulating experience, and looking at it from the perspective of my previous four years of "education" in this school I firmly believe that his is an important contribution and one which I feel every undergraduate should be exposed to.
> I report, there is no love lost between him and me; I am not one of his zealous followers, of which admittedly there are a few. But I do believe that

Master's project of Dennis DePietro, University of Southern California, 1974. (Courtesy of Dennis DePietro)

he has a great deal to offer and that he displays several qualities which seem to be rapidly disappearing from the teaching profession: *genuine and total dedication to his vocation and a passionate concern for the development and success of his students.*[181]

Every weekday afternoon for thirty weeks, Caldwell met his students promptly at 1:15—usually on the run. "I can remember him racing around the corner," Dan Lawrence remembered, "and he said 'come up here, come up here, right now.' We all ran up to the table, and he started lecturing immediately, within ten seconds."[182] Caldwell gave an architectural history lecture every day, the first being the history of structural systems. This lecture cleared up a lot of confusion, because Lawrence and his friends "had studied structural engineering, but it was this standard structural engineering in which nobody ever once said there was a system."[183] After the formal lecture was over Caldwell went from desk to desk lecturing and talking until coffee time. Dennis DePietro recalled, "His talks were personal, always walking among us while speaking. He was never from afar."[184] While students drew he might talk to them about Spengler, or Ortega y Gasset, or Viollet-le-Duc, Sullivan, Wright, Mies, or Jesus Christ. He wanted his students to struggle, to try again, but he also helped them incessantly with structural calculations, showed them how to set up jigs for their models, explained construction details, and demonstrated how to lay them out on a Strathmore board.

Caldwell used projects he had worked out carefully at IIT: the 1,000-square-foot house, the brick project, a structural system, details of the structural system on Strathmore boards, a long-span structure, full-size roof details of the long span on Strathmore boards, and a plan for decentralizing the large city—in this case Los Angeles. He bathed his discussion in poetry, history, literature, philosophy, and parables. By midafternoon it was coffee time, and Caldwell raced individual students or students in twos and threes over to the student union for a personal interchange. Topics could be almost anything including the Vietnam War, the history of Greece, a design problem, or any questions students wanted to pursue. Lawrence and his peers used to talk about "soaking it up like sponges."[185] Perhaps the most important method of all was that Caldwell never missed a class, and he gave up his Christmas and Easter vacations to work with his students. Robert E. Stewart, president of the Adronicus chapter of Alpha Rho Chi at USC in 1971, wrote to Dean Hurst and described Caldwell as a professor "who would give his right arm if only one student would be the better for it."[186] On Thanksgiving he told them to bring him a turkey sandwich. Even during the "Four Days of Concern" on the USC campus when classes were canceled in response to the killings at Kent State University in May 1970, Caldwell refused to cancel his studio. Instead he lectured and led discussions on war while the university took its vacation. Through many dramatic acts of sacrifice like these, Caldwell proved over and over his devotion to students, and they, according to Michael Gould in a letter to John R. Hubbard, president of USC, recognized "midst all the confusion, one clear individual."[187]

Just as at IIT, no one at USC could compete with Alfred Caldwell as a teacher. USC students made this clear in letters they wrote protesting Caldwell's removal. Marc Glasser called Caldwell "the only person in the school I can honestly refer to as a Teacher."[188] Stephen Woolley testified in a letter to Dean Hurst that "Professor Caldwell was without doubt the best instructor I had at USC."[189] Roger Schultz wrote, "I have found that his vast experience, knowledge, and ability to communicate clearly are unequaled by any professor or teacher I have had in five years at this school."[190] Rollin Foss declared, "Our fifth year section voted unanimously that he was the best teacher we had while at USC."[191] "I have never met anyone so full of life and inspiring as Professor Caldwell," was Jeff Lundahl's opinion.[192] Dan Lawrence summed up his experience with Caldwell: "Nobody has changed my life like this, nobody under any circumstances."[193] The semester-end exhibit that he always required in place of juries convinced students that they were capable of art, and thirty years later many still keep their models from Caldwell's fifth year on their coffee tables.

Student work from the University of Southern California. (Courtesy of Dan Lawrence)

One of his biggest supporters was Craig Ellwood, already widely known by the time Caldwell arrived in southern California in 1965 for his steel-and-glass buildings in the modernist tradition of Richard Neutra, Raphael Soriano, and Charles Eames. Ellwood also admired Mies, and because of Caldwell's long association with this master, he considered himself lucky to land a teaching job "for a few semesters in the same large room at USC" with Caldwell. Ellwood was taken by Caldwell, describing him as an "architect, engineer, landscape architect, philosopher, teacher" who was "diligent, dedicated, giving, exacting, inspiring." Ellwood also recognized that Caldwell's students "were different. Serious young men with a real understanding of building and structure, and the capability of drawing and detailing—qualities rare among graduates in the late 60s and early 70s." In Ellwood's opinion they were so good that "the single prerequisite for being employed by my office was to have studied under Professor Alfred Caldwell."[194] By 1969 Ellwood recognized Caldwell as a "poet" and considered him a "friend."[195]

James Tyler, who had been Ellwood's design architect and had been in charge of Ellwood's office since 1967, taught the course at USC for Ellwood on a number of occasions.[196] Caldwell normally avoided contact with the faculty at USC, but when Tyler explained to him that he worked for Ellwood, Caldwell made an exception.[197] Tyler was otherwise primed to learn from him because he

Student work from the University of Southern California. (Courtesy of Dan Lawrence)

had worked in Utah for one of his former students, John Sugden.[198] Further, because of Ellwood's opinion of Caldwell and Tyler's lack of experience in designing the complex buildings Ellwood's clients needed, Tyler turned to him for advice. "Whenever I designed an Ellwood building," Tyler recalled, "I always reviewed the project with Alfred."[199] Caldwell critiqued Tyler's buildings, Tyler took his drawings back to the office, made corrections, and then checked his corrected drawings with Caldwell. In the background and without remuneration, Caldwell gave his experienced opinions to advance what he considered to be genuine architecture, and this system worked well in Ellwood's office from the late 1960s into the late 1970s. Ellwood got the jobs, and Tyler delivered the buildings while he went looking for the next job. During the time Caldwell worked as Tyler's éminence gris, the American and European architectural press published books and articles about Ellwood's buildings at a rapid pace.[200] To critics like Peter Blake, Ellwood's architecture captured the essence of Mies. In his view, Ellwood's buildings surpassed those of "Neutra and Soriano and even Eames" in their "precision and economy. Steel, plastics, prefabricated wall panels, large-scale components—all these seemed, in his hands, to come to-gether in the most logical, the most natural and effortless way possible."[201] With Caldwell as an adviser to James Tyler, and with the help of Caldwell's students who worked for Tyler on Ellwood's projects, Craig Ellwood's star rose higher over southern California.

In 1967 Ellwood stepped into the national limelight as the program chairman of the prestigious International Design Conference in Aspen, Colorado, and with him was his friend Alfred Caldwell, whom Ellwood had asked to deliver the opening salvo. The topic, "Order and Disorder," was organized as a response to Ben Shahn's praise of chaos in his speech "Bread and Butter to the Aspen Conference on Design" at the previous year's conference.[202] This plea for chaos touched a nerve among the conference organizers at a time when United States society seemed to be unraveling from nasty confrontations over a disastrous war abroad and to be splitting into camps of older versus younger Americans who disagreed radically about what was important at home. "Don't trust anyone over thirty," Abby Hoffman proclaimed. In his March 1967 statement on the theme, Ellwood argued, "Perhaps the designer's cry has become too loud. Perhaps it has been joined by some who blindly deny all order, some who mistakenly interpret freedom as a right to self-indulgence rather than as a privilege to produce within validly ordered boundaries of communal and intrinsic values." When Caldwell accepted Ellwood's invitation to give the opening speech of the 1967 conference, Ellwood wrote, "I am damned pleased about your acceptance, and I am counting on you to make some noise and to shake awake those who need it."[203] Ellwood surrounded Caldwell with good company in a conference program that included Jerzy Soltan, Jeffrey Lindsay, William Thomas, Charles Correa, Art Seidenbaum, Stan Vanderbeek, John Witney, William Arrowsmith, Christopher Alexander, Max Bill, Moshe Safdie, Theo Crosby, Robert Propst, Piet Hein, Paul Weiss, Paul Heyer, Peter Ustinov, and Jacob Bronowski. In "a few last words" to Caldwell six days before the conference began, Ellwood encouraged him to "hit hard when you agree or disagree."[204] Like the boxers he admired in his youth, Caldwell came out slugging, and he jabbed away at themes he had spent countless hours discussing with Jensen, Hilberseimer, and his students—suburban sprawl, the environment, and ecology. These were still new ideas to Ellwood, the reporters, most of the audience, and most of America, which was not yet "green." Caldwell pulled no punches:

- Nobody willfully intended the disorder; nevertheless there it is. It is the sprawling lunacy of the city. It is the far reaches of the wilderness of Manhattan and Brooklyn. It is the no-man's-land of Chicago, the thousands of acres of slums and ghettos west of the Loop, the gaudy acropolis of a frontier town, lined with catchpenny skyscrapers. Finally, it is Los Angeles, the American Baghdad, the city of beautiful women weeping in smog.
- The disorder that exists in the city also exists outside the city. Decentralization of industries, unplanned and chaotic, is now covering the entire region with smoke and fumes.
- Yearly, the nation uses 700 million tons of pesticides and agricultural chemicals of 45,000 varieties. This volume is expected to increase tenfold in the next twenty years.

- Modern man is poisoning the planet, making it unfit for life, including his own. The hydrogen bomb and its fallout become an anticlimax.
- Nature is the structure of reality. Fate is that thing which must be, that is, reality. Therefore nature is fate. When life itself becomes unreal, it is disorder. The one thing that nature will not tolerate is disorder.
- Disorder is the condition for death. Cancer is the disorder of cells. Of that cancer, civilizations, peoples, and cities perish.
- This is the destructive age, the permissive age: anything goes. The gods look down, and they are not smiling.
- Yet indomitable and perpendicular, man can go on in harmony and splendor out of his creative spirit, which is order.

The press spread Caldwell's punches in large headlines across the nation's newspapers. "Sprawling Lunacy of City Cited"—"Man Poisoning Planet"—"Declares Man Making Unfit for Life"—"Smog, Not Bomb, Seen Man's Way to Extinction"—"L.A.—City of Beautiful Women, Weeping, Smog"—"Cities Called Too Big and Too Dense."[205] Caldwell put no one to sleep in the Aspen tent that day, and thirty years later no one could call him a false prophet. The speech was another "screecher and screamer," and Ellwood described it as "pure poetry."[206]

Back at USC, the faculty's reaction to Caldwell, who never missed a chance to attack scientific architecture and its proponents, was mixed at best. In a lecture titled "Balderdash in the Universities," which he gave in 1967 with USC in mind, he complained that "the new schools are based upon what the professors call 'science,' which of course is not science, but rather a vast and ecstatic vulgarization. . . . It is Palladio and Vitruvius since *Sputnik*." He accused the faculty of "jabbering incomprehensible and barbarous polysyllables of educanese, a baroque and ornamental dialect derived from the misunderstanding of the exact and literal language of science." He lashed out at the new schools for being "antiarchitectural . . . anything to get away from architecture, to evade the facts of building, and to dissemble with hollow hocus-pocus." He ridiculed USC, where "the history of architecture was eliminated and the history of moviemaking and multimedia substituted in its place." He called research "an unscrupulous sophistry which fetches the unwary and impresses country cousins." He disdained computers, not because of computers themselves, but because the faculty believed computers would eliminate the struggle to produce architecture. Rather than struggle, "at this point Celeste, the lovely secretary, slithers in with refreshing drinks. Students can easily believe in Superman; they once spent thousands of hours viewing his exploits. 'Lois, it's time for outer space.'" Caldwell called the worship of science in schools of architecture idolatry. "It is voodoo. It has lost the right to reject the preposterous." Instead of voodoo, Caldwell demanded that the school teach what is useful. . . . Life is not long enough to spend time on the useless. Alfred North Whitehead pointed out that "pedants sneer at an education which is useful. But if education is not useful, what is it?" Let the school be frankly utilitarian. Born poets will make poetry out of it. When the useful in building becomes poetry it is architecture.[207]

Caldwell refused to go to faculty meetings, and with a few exceptions he refused even to talk to the faculty. Crombie Taylor "had to constantly fight [Sam Hurst] over Caldwell," and in the end he was fired as associate dean because he insisted on retaining him. The new associate dean, Panos Koulermos, after reviewing finished work of Caldwell's graduate students, denounced it as "working drawings."[208] In 1971 the dean agreed to keep Caldwell on another year[209]— USC required faculty members to retire at sixty-five, but with the dean's endorsement they could continue teaching until seventy—and the students unanimously chose Caldwell as their commencement speaker that year. He criticized the administration in a rousing speech, and the students "loved it."[210] But Dean Hurst did not love it, and the next year he retired Caldwell "after due deliberation in two successive years by appropriate faculty committees and in consideration of the best interests of the School, its students and Professor Caldwell."[211] Caldwell came back as an unpaid professor in 1973–74 to fulfill his obligations to a number of master of architecture students who refused to accept anyone else, and a few even continued to visit him at his Palos Verdes apartment for several years after their graduation because they wanted to learn more from him.[212] Jeff Lundahl, who had just completed his master's degree under Caldwell, proudly invited President Hubbard to come to Harris Hall on May 24 to see "the best teacher I have met in my life . . . you may never see the likes of him again."[213] President Hubbard did not show up, and most of the faculty breathed a sigh of relief when Caldwell was finally through at USC. Not everyone on the faculty dismissed him as a raving apostate, however.

During his California period from 1965 to 1981, Caldwell made few buildings or landscapes. In 1971 he drew the design and did the structural calculations for five steel-framed pavilion bathrooms and a nature center in Central Park at Huntington Beach, California, built in 1975. Eric Katzmaier redesigned the park according to prairie school principles under Caldwell's tutelage. Caldwell and Katzmaier also designed the prairie landscape for the Arts Center College of Design in Pasadena, a long bridge building of black steel and dark glass that came out of the Ellwood office in 1974. Caldwell's proposal in 1975 for a boat pavilion on a lake at Huntington Beach, though beautiful in its presentation, was never built. The same is true of the sun house of 1978 that he planned to build for his daughter, Carol, at the farm in Wisconsin. Its semicircular form was designed to let in as much sun as possible during the long Wisconsin winters. Not counting his indirect contributions to the Ellwood office, this was the extent of the projects

Bathroom pavilion, Huntington Beach, California, 1975. (Photo by Dennis Domer)

Caldwell completed or worked on in California. He was never an idle man, though, and throughout his life he always had his own projects, real or imagined. He had always lived for the creative moment. When he walked near the ocean, "along the top of the bluff," he wrote Gerald Estes, "I plan houses as I go. . . . I make the house and the court to the road and sheer glass on the sea side. . . . I could put the tee column house right at the very edge . . . stiffen the tees below the floor for 1 over r by welding a tee to the back making a star column."[214] At the bottom of his letter he added a delicate sketch for Estes to enjoy, but such drawings were also infrequent. Instead of making drawings, in Palos Verdes Caldwell turned to the pen.

By 1965 Caldwell had already been writing essays for thirty-five years, but his ability to understand the power of language and to use it poetically was nurtured in his mother's arms and perfected through his relationship with Geda. After they married he frequently read aloud to her: Masters, Poe, Frost, Donne,

Wilde, Eliot. He poured over Homer, Spengler, Gibbon, Ruskin, Shaw, Ortega y Gasset, Huxley, Mencken, Dostoyevsky, Kafka, Nietzsche, and Orwell.[215] He discussed what he was reading not only with Geda, herself a voracious reader, but at every opportunity with his students and friends. He was a self-educated man and a raconteur who loved to tell a story or a parable, bursting into a poem at the turning point of the conversation. Like a Greek chorus singing to Dionysus, he always had dithyrambs in mind.

Jens Jensen published Caldwell's first philosophical essay, "In Defense of Animals," in *Our Native Landscape* in December 1931. It was a harbinger of forty essays to come. With its attack on the assumption of man's superiority over animals, it set the philosophical tone for many a jeremiad over the next sixty-five years. "There is absolutely no evidence to support the belief that animals are without souls, yet the assumption that they are soulless is the reason generally presented as proof of their inferiority." Although Caldwell showed he could be scholarly in his encyclopedia articles, most of his published essays stem from his lectures in architectural history, in which he also considered the human condition, laid bare some timeless stupidity or failure, and enjoined his listeners or readers to reform, to believe, or to reason in order to gain redemption. The essays that Eli Bornstein faithfully published from 1967 to 1995 in the *Structurist* are at their core speeches crying to be heard rather than dry arguments to be pondered. They thunder with emotion and wit and flow with Delphic wisdom. Their common themes concern ancient, medieval, modern, vernacular, and landscape architecture; his masters Sullivan, Jensen, Wright, Hilberseimer; life as art and the disconnection of modern life and art; technology versus nature; man and nature; environmental degradation and ecology; harmony, structure, and the nature of ideas; cities and the twentieth-century escape from cities; Nietzsche, Spengler, and the failure of ancient civilizations such as Egypt, Greece, and Rome; the fate of modern man, the ingredients of his failure, and the hope of rebuilding. In spite of their wide-ranging content, Caldwell's essays are deeply personal. They reflect his struggle to win in the face of overwhelming odds and to convince others that they too must struggle to lead a significant life. As Gerald McSheffrey wrote, "For him it is not the search for utopias that leads to a better life, but the creative struggle of the artist and builder that comes from within."[216]

Caldwell's poetry is part of his struggle, his dream of life in sonnets and verse that tell the whole story symbolically. Although the language of these poems is clear, their meaning is difficult to grasp on a first or second reading. They are too autobiographical, and behind the words and rhyme the poet has packed layers of facts. Dreams like Caldwell's require study. Even without study, however, their poetic form offers a cadence and song that most readers can appreciate, and when Caldwell recites them from memory and piles one dream on another in a cascade of emotion, no one can avoid the conclusion this is an artist living his poem, as Frank Lloyd Wright commanded.

More than twice Caldwell's age in the early 1930s when Caldwell was only beginning to learn the craft of poetry, Wright considered his attempts amusing, yet he recognized his potential as an artist. That day at Taliesin, he told Caldwell they were both artists; but he advised his young friend to put a few years behind him, perhaps live a poem first, and then write about it. Wright could have heard at least eight of the early poems: "The Forthgoing" (1928), "Promise" (1929), "Frond" (1931), "Squares for Myself" (1932), "Lichens" (1932), "The Thaw" (1932), and "Prayer" (1932).[217] "Prayer," renamed "Sport at Gaza" but not otherwise altered in California in the late 1960s, is a rough diamond that shows a gift not only for poetry but also for prophecy. In this poem Caldwell forecasts his own struggle in the story of Samson, who killed a thousand enemies with the jawbone of an ass, was betrayed by Delilah and blinded by the Philistines, and was called from his grindstone to be made sport of before he pulled down the temple.[218] It was 1932, and he prayed for struggle to create his life:

> Their star's stallion still is tortured,
> And even crickets shout
> That figs have failed in every orchard;
> But turn and send me out,
>
> Oh Lord, a worthless slave forsaken
> In fields with thistles grown,
> To find the bitter mistaken
> Sustenance of stone:
>
> Deliver me from easy living:
> Swine's swill the butcher's bait:
> The fool's feast—and the snide's thanksgiving:
> Dog's dung on a gold plate; . . .
>
> With visions of eagles rearisen
> On World Wide Wings—send me,
> Oh Lord, where walls of hills imprison
> A deep valley and make me be.

Although Caldwell may have written poems intermittently after his fateful day with Wright—for example, "Poem on Peace" in 1945—he did not have time to return to poetry in a serious way for over thirty years.

He wrote the first of the twenty-five sonnets of "Atlantis and Return" in 1965 in Virginia, and the rest in California and Wisconsin. It was a worrisome time in Blacksburg, between his dismissal from the Chicago Department of City Planning and his appointment at the University of Southern California. Geda was away in Chicago, and Caldwell was always lost without her. With thirty years of struggle behind him, an uncertain future ahead, and the loneliness of the moment, Caldwell learned that he could squeeze a powerful message into fourteen lines of iambic pentameter. He took up his pen in praise: "Dear life be good and let me worship you." Although he admits that he is not a king and his life has come to an inevitable ruin, he believes it worthy of praise because it has been courageous:

> But lost in exile, I on midnight tours
> Thru all the fond and sleeping world behold
> Myself as such a one that he endures
> The dust of cellars—fugitive and bold—
> And will not cringe, though he be done and bled,
> And never more shall take his love to bed.

Then in Palos Verdes, where he could mull over a phrase while taking a midnight stroll on the beach, he wrote the next twenty-two. He wrote the last two in Wisconsin after Geda's death.

In addition to the sonnets from "Atlantis and Return" he wrote for the most part in California, Caldwell worked on other verse, including "No Love," "Day's End," "House," "Of a Life," "Innocence," and "Isle." They are not sonnets, Caldwell's forte, or woven into an epic. Instead they are reflective comments in a variety of poetic forms, and they explore various themes of mortality and the transitory such as in "Isle":

> Isle in the sea would I,
> Under the pine
> Warm in the sun; brine
> On the wind,
> And the long low line
> Of the sea bird's flight—
> Lest ever I die,
> In a slum, in a bed
> Under a quilt
> And ever so dead.

These poems emanate from a calmer period in Caldwell's life, after he left USC in 1974, but during that time he wrote more essays than poems. He would not write poetry again with the same passion and power of his early sonnets until after Geda's death on September 2, 1988.

From 1974 to 1981 he and Geda lived their poem peacefully, and these days were the happiest of their lives. They wintered in Palos Verdes, California, and summered in Bristol, Wisconsin, and they looked forward to the long trips by car between the two. Never had Caldwell's life been so quiet or so financially secure. For once he had no opposition, no faculty out to get him, no one to stir him up, and he was in no rush. In California he and Geda spent their days walking along the ocean, talking, reading, and seeing friends. Some of his former students at USC visited him regularly for tutoring, but otherwise he had no relationship with the university. On the other hand, when they arrived in Wisconsin in May each year, Caldwell always had some building project going on and work to do in the orchard or woods. His projects often took a long time. "When your farm is finished, your life is finished." In 1970, for example, he designed and began to build the workshop that floats like a Japanese pavilion in the clearing behind the house. He was still working on it in 1996, having converted it to a guesthouse. The broad hearth of glaciated granite boulders, similar to the one in the main house, contrasts with the long horizontal lines of narrow windows, the wide eaves, and the flat roof, creating an overall hybrid expression of the prairie architecture tradition gracefully married to the international style of Mies van der Rohe. Besides building and planting at the farm, Caldwell often gave visiting lectures at IIT, received many former students from Chicago and California who made frequent pilgrimages to Bristol to see him, and in 1980 was given the Distinguished Educator Award by the Chicago chapter of the American Institute of Architects. In recognition and appreciation of his many contributions there, IIT exhibited his work at Crown Hall in the fall of 1980. For a more usual man, this time when people paid homage and showed their gratitude might have lasted until his final hours.

On the recommendation of IIT dean Gerald McSheffrey in 1980, however, Caldwell interrupted his normal practice of packing the car and driving to California by accepting a position as a visiting distinguished professor of architecture for a month in the School of Architecture and Urban Design at the University of Kansas. He and Geda went to Lawrence, and he taught a fifth-year design studio with Professor Theodore Seligson. The time there was short, but Mount Oread represented the beginning of an unexpected new dream of life and his eventual return to academia in his late seventies. He renewed his old love of teaching and made lasting connections in Kansas that took him back there for lectures and discussions with architecture students. More important, the Kansas appointment made him more susceptible to the efforts administrators at IIT had been making to recruit him again after a twenty-year absence.[219]

The provost from IIT had visited Caldwell at Bristol without any luck. After the appointment at Kansas, however, Dean McSheffrey persuaded him to leave what he called "the warm Siberia of Los Angeles." Geda was against it initially, because it would reopen old wounds and recreate the nightmares they had avoided since the USC days. Both of them loved their home in California; however, when McSheffrey offered a tempting salary and agreed to give Caldwell his old teaching schedule of sophomore and junior construction as well as the history of architecture, Geda acquiesced. In May 1981 they made their last trek across the western United States to Wisconsin, and in September 1981 Caldwell

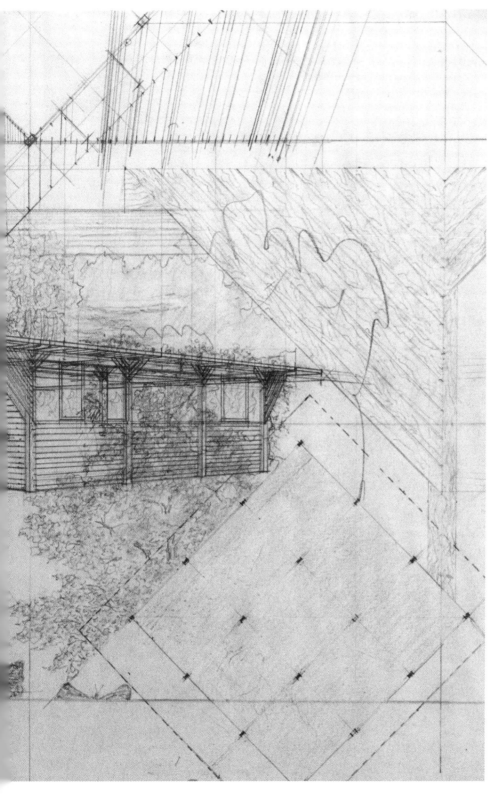

Caldwell garage, Bristol, Wisconsin, 1985. Alfred Caldwell, architect. (Courtesy of Alfred Caldwell)

Alfred Caldwell and friends at the council ring, Bristol, Wisconsin, 1994. (Photo by Dennis Domer)

became the Mies van der Rohe Visiting Professor of Architecture at IIT, where he taught until 1996.[220]

Coda

As landscape architect, architect, civil engineer, city planner, teacher, philosopher, and poet, Alfred Caldwell worked in the shadow of some of the most celebrated masters of design in the twentieth century. Wright, Jensen, Mies, Hilberseimer, and Ellwood all had greater public stature than Caldwell, but all of them recognized his deep understanding of nature, his superb drawing ability, knowledge of construction, experience in building, and capacity to envision vast urban spaces. At one time or another they all sought to bring him into their employ or under their influence, and they fought to keep him. Some unabashedly used his work as their own. In the shadow of these modern masters, improper attribution was a way of life that was abetted by historians who subscribed to the great man theory of design. Caldwell played his role behind the scenes for many years, but his story is just one of many sagas in which designers worked closely with gifted employees to produce the work that brought the master fame and fortune. Many accepted the "underling" role to learn from a master. Behind the drawings of the Taliesin Fellowship, for example, lies a nexus of underling tales that are only now being told in a few last confessionals. Caldwell was the hidden glue that sustained modern design, and he and many others like him have never gotten their due.

Caldwell's work is itself a masterpiece of modernity, and many aspects of that work have yet to be fully explored. Further, Caldwell has just finished converting his studio in Bristol, Wisconsin, into a small house. He is still working as a prairie school landscape architect, cutting new paths through the woods and making new clearings on his farm. He has just built a new bridge and added a hand railing to the council ring. He is still dreaming, living for the creative moment, and waiting for his next chance.

ATLANTIS AND RETURN

Caldwell wrote "Atlantis and Return" in California after he left the University of Southern California in 1974. He had time on his hands, and between morning and afternoon walks on the beach with his beloved wife Geda, he set down his early life in this short autobiography. The Pacific Ocean inspired Caldwell; "The waves rolled in all the way from China." Their roar at Palos Verdes conjured up a poetic nature that he had reluctantly relinquished in the early 1930s, when Frank Lloyd Wright told him it was better to live a poem than to write one. "Atlantis and Return" is an autobiography of both prose and poetry, never before published. Caldwell finished the last two sonnets after Geda's death in 1988.

These pages are an incognito journal of adventure and ideas, an autobiography of what happened and why it happened in my first thirty-five years. It records with abbreviations the fluid circumstances and thought of an ever changing life. A traveler who returns from a distant land finds it natural to relate what he has seen, what he has enjoyed, what he has endured, and his conclusions. If any part of it would contribute to useful knowledge, it is certainly admissible to relate it. Perhaps it may even be considered obligatory.

"Atlantis" is the dream of life. As a boy of nine or ten, I already had the aspiration. It is the world that does not exist, but which we feel ought to exist and could exist. In the case of "Atlantis," the world that we imagine actually did once exist. When Frank Lloyd Wright told me it is better to live a poem than to write one, I already knew exactly what he was saying.

So I became a scholar of life in order to implement the form—not for three or four years, but over all my life to this present moment. Books, thoughts, aspirations every day of my life. That is what I live for. I suppose that is why I am a good teacher.

Now I put a whole man in. In point that is what Walt Whitman said about *Leaves of Grass.* I think you cannot be a prude and live a poem. By the way, I quit IIT some twenty-two years ago because it was part of the poem—a canto by itself. You have to be true to the poem, or you cannot live.

Alfred Caldwell

1

He had always lived in cities. At the age of six he changed his city. He remembers an all-night railroad ride, the click of the tracks, the hurl and sway of journey, the Pullman porters, the green upholstery, and the muffled mystery of the sleeping car. He remembers at last the jerk and stop and the shouted name of the city, the steep steps down and the walk along the cars past the self-conscious black iron grandeur of the locomotive. He was to recall forever the hiss of steam, the hurrying crowds and enormous room of the station. He was to see the city forever as the city of the first morning in the chill and hostile air. He saw the brown and mighty buildings darkened with the ambiguous grime of cities, the lumpy cobblestone streets, the traffic jam of heavy laboring horses, and the teamsters on their drays red faced and legendary, wrapped in ragged coats.

He never grew up because he never left anything behind. He could recall the very words, the tone of voice and temperature of the day. He moved backward and forward, and nothing was more the past than the future. It depended only on where he began. At some moment any incident had still to occur. Once he asked, "If I had never been born, where would I be?"

That was a great moment. He was still in the first city and probably five. He was under a porch with another child playing a mythic game of connecting doorbells, a tense imagined procedure, as remote and unfathomable as connecting the stars. When he asked the question he experienced a kind of hollow sensation, not painful but certainly not pleasant. It was something he was to experience all his life. When he became a man and worked beyond his strength, suddenly the old sensation would flow through him again, poignant and a little startling.

The child of course never recognized any significance in his timeless memories. They were simply part of day-to-day living. He could never have understood even the meaning of significance. He lived like all children from moment to moment. He was by turns touched, joyous, or troubled, experiencing experience. A distant relative and her eighteen-year-old daughter Olga visited at his house in the first city. One morning in play he rushed into their bedroom, and what he saw on the bed astounded him. Olga, ordinarily a usual enough person, was here transformed. There must be two Olgas. The girl was sleeping naked. The large curved ivory hips, the sudden amazing wealth, in that instant smote the child. Then the mother covered Olga with the sheet. He had seen a goddess and had lost his innocence.

He remembers another woman who visited at his house in the first city. As a parting gift she gave him a medallion to take on the railroad journey. He lost the medallion in the berth and was forever bereaved. It was the greatest single loss of his life. It was the first enduring sadness. It could never be confided to another, and no attempt was ever made. It was an inexplicable misfortune.

However, in all other ways he lived a dream of life. "Let's play ancient," and Louie Haller and he, each with a garbage can lid for a shield and a lath for a sword, hacked and shouted at each other. In winter there were snowball fights. In the street after school, he joined one of the gangs of big kids and ran where they ran, through alleys and yards, and then perhaps to a last stand on the third floor of a tenement porch, and finally, with the snowballs flying, the hairbreadth escape, and the return home with stocking cap lost and shoes soaking wet from the slush. At the age of eight he read a child's version of the siege of Troy, of the exploits of Achilles, Ajax, Hector, Agamemnon, and Ulysses. The snowball fight was a dream of a fight. He lived to serve a fight. He read about Ivanhoe, Robin Hood, and King Arthur and the round table. A storekeeper on the street, noticing the small boy always fighting, called him Jim Corbett.[1] "You know who 'Gentleman Jim' was, boy—the great prize-fighter?"

He remembers that poverty was everywhere. Poverty marked the streets, the schools, and the calendar with indelible pencil. Once in the snow he saw a wagon being unloaded by a man wearing gunny sacks instead of shoes. In the winter the boy pushed a two-wheeled cart along the railroad siding, picking up tiny scraps of coal no bigger than marbles. When the cart was filled he pushed it home and then carried up the coal in baskets for the stove in the kitchen. He had a newspaper stand from the time he was ten years old. Coming home at night in winter's poverty, past a long and lurking street, he pounded up the long and narrow entry stair and shut the door behind him just in time. On zero nights he pulled the blanket up over his head, hearing footsteps creaking on the trampled snow outside.

---

1. James J. Corbett, 1866–1933. American pugilist who won the world's championship by knocking out John L. Sullivan in the twenty-first round on September 7, 1892. He was often called "Gentleman Jim" from his natty appearance and gentlemanly bearing.

He discovered that poverty is comparative and can even be official. The teacher in the third-grade class took up a collection for a poor family in the slums. The day before Christmas the entire class, carrying parcels and escorted by the teacher, took the elevated to visit the poor family. Hushed or giggling, the class walked up a rickety, snow-covered back porch stairway and came into the kitchen. It was clean and overheated, and a middle-aged woman kept thanking the teacher.

Summers he lived by fugitive preference the life of a street urchin among other street urchins, this small freckle-faced boy with red hair. He was to carry forever the indescribable essence of the street. He walked at high noon under the sidewalk awnings and jumped to touch the canvas scallops, breathing in the air of every store. There was the candy store, long, narrow, and dark, presided over by a Mr. Hovey selling kites, jacks, marbles, fire engines, chewing gum, licorice, lemon drops, chocolates, and last and best, caramels packed with picture cards of baseball players, two for a cent. There was the hardware store with dusty shelves and cabinets and bins for nails; there were hammers, hatchets, saws, and wrenches on the wall. He remembers the shoe store with the leather smell of new shoes and the delicatessen with the smell of dill pickles. There was the butcher shop with its sawdust floor, the slow electric fan on the ceiling, the hover of flies and the blood and musk of meat. There was the grocery store and boxes of cantaloupe fragrant and Arabic. There was the sweet, stale smell of the Greek ice cream parlor, with the marble-top tables chill on the hottest day.

He sauntered down the alley, stopping at the factory windows, watching the thin and sallow man ankle deep in oily sheet iron wisps, pulling levers for the bite and heavy champ. There were dozens of the self-same sallow man, and the ground trembled with the bites and heavy champs. In the grind and clang of metal, the flying wheels, the flapping belts, he sensed a sinister and driven haste of work. Then the shout from inside: "Watcha want, kid? Beat it."

Four blocks up was a corner saloon with a beer garden in the back behind a high board fence. Sidling past the sidewalk's wall of heat, he saw through the open door a cool and secret darkness, a deserted cloister of iniquity at once bewitching and malevolent and somehow forbidden and unmitigated. There was a sour and beery smell of terror in the sunlight.

Then the long walk to the baseball park down Clark Street and under the trees along Graceland Cemetery. At last over the tops of the buildings he saw the big signboard, and he began running. He ran among the crowds swarming toward the turnstiles, skipping past the hawkers selling hot dogs, soda pop, ice cream, peanuts, scorecards. At the edge of the crowd he stood a full minute panting. He ran along the fence and jumped to grab the steel bars. He climbed hand over hand, and there in a thousand feet of fence was the one spot big enough for a small boy's ribcage. Someone in the crowd yelled as he pulled his legs through, and he was in.[2] Then he ran again among the crowds inside. He found a seat beside an elderly man who was smoking a long, slim cigar. There green and gold was the playing field, and the practice warmup under way; the crack of the bat and the ball slapped across the infield toward incredible double plays. On the sidelines there was the tobacco-chewing pitcher warming up, snapping the curves with easy arrogance. Not the gods on Mount Olympus were more favored than these. Then the game and the seesaw back and forth and the futile ninth inning. The small boy walked home along Clark Street: Ulysses home to supper.

One day he called for Louie Haller. Louie came out on the porch: "I can't come out. My mother's sick. Go away." Then Louis didn't come to school anymore. He saw Louie on the street dressed in a delivery boy's green uniform. Louie said, "My mother died. I've gone to work on the wagons. I've given up school. I don't like school." Louie lit a cigarette. He even looked different: "So long. I have to go now."

He thought about Louie, but he never saw him again. Where have you gone, Louie? And asking, he became acquainted with his days and years. Louie slid away. He vanished into the enigma of alleys. It was a lost thing, authentic and final. He acquired the knowledge of lost things, to go with the lost medallion.

It may be that in this way he came to the lost Atlantis. Someone had told him that a civilization had fallen into the sea, the streets and the palaces. He thought he could raise the lost Atlantis. Once he confided it to another boy, who merely stood impassive and unimpressed. Nonetheless he saw it all, the vast derricks and the enormous undertaking. That was what he would do. He would grow up, and one day he would do it.

2

It was September,[3] five o'clock in the morning, and he was waiting for a Clark Street car to take him south on State Street as far as 67th. Then he would hitchhike 150 miles on the Dixie Highway. He had a suitcase, and he lugged it over to the newsstand. "Fatty Arbuckle Kills Virginia Rape." Just then the street-car came, and he was on his way to the university;[4] cash in hand, twenty-three dollars. He was on his own and eighteen. Everything had happened. Nothing much more could happen. They said, "Without money—are you crazy?"

It was late afternoon by the time he reached Danville. There was still a distance of twenty miles to go. He walked along the sidewalk of the main street hungry. He put a penny in a slot machine and got a handful of peanuts. Two more

2. Wrigley Field, home of the Chicago Cubs.
3. The year was 1921.
4. The University of Illinois at Champaign-Urbana.

blocks and the storefronts ended. He walked out in the street with his suitcase. A red roadster came to a stop: "Going to school? Thought so. Hop in. Put your suitcase on the floor. My name's Bill Kaiser. This is Jim Lange. Jim's on the varsity. We're both seniors, Delta Tau Delta. Where are you from, Chicago? That's where we were last night—long, long party."

They rode fast, cut out open. They talked to each other. Bill Kaiser said: "Boy oh boy, that was some babe you had. She sure could dance and what a sax that was. When he walked out on the floor he practically made it talk. Jim, we ought to get him for the Delta dance. I feel real good, Jim, not tired at all. Only one thing, I keep wondering about that goddamn math course. Everything else I take this year is a pipe. Fellows in the house say the two courses in social thought you can sleep through."

Another stretch of road and they were in town: "Suppose I let you off here on Green Street? You'll find rooms on the bulletin board right over there. See ya around."

So he found his way and found a room and lived in the town and went to the university. In the first few weeks he was asked to be a pledge in a fraternity.[5] He accepted and went to live in the house. This was a new experience for him to live with other young men. When guests came to dinner there was the ritual of introductions, the scattered talk, the bell and then the filing into the dining room. The waiters carried in the plates of food, setting them down carefully. There was the stiff and formal conversation in the effort to be very proper for the sake of the guests. Afterward he stood with others around the piano singing songs. He supposed that this was college life and was pleased with himself.

Sometimes on Saturday nights after dinner the entire house went to Orpheus, the vaudeville in the town. Once Sam Langford,[6] the battered and aged prize-fighter, was an act on the bill. There he stood in the fighter's ring on the stage, a heavy Negro perhaps fifty, a deadpan flat face, and matched to a tall, gangling boy. How many fights had Sam Langford fought, and how many fortunes had he squandered to be brought finally to such a tatterdemalion end in a cheap vaudeville? He stood in the middle of the ring, for all his bulk with something like ballet grace, but barely moving. Suddenly, so quick that it was impossible to follow, the left hand would jab out, and the gangling boy would dance away. It was only one round and not in earnest, but in those three minutes Sam Langford was a master. Seen thirty years too late, after the thousand all-night sprees, after the women, after the Harlem bars and the gang around him, here was still the real article, the accomplished pro.

5. Caldwell pledged Zens, a local fraternity.
6. Sam Langford was a heavyweight boxer. Caldwell remembers that Langford never made it to the top.

So from that time on he began to think about superiority, about what it means to be really good at something. He began to notice that nearly everything around him was emphatically not the genuine article. He noticed, for instance, a way of shaking hands that was a fraud. The hand came down and then up again to clench the hand of the other person and hold it with great determination. It was meant to seem like something it was not. Plainly it was meant to create an impression; it was a facade. He went about looking at the little world around him, seeing frightened people pretending assurance. Or he saw the shamelessly dishonest imposing upon credulity. A very few had the gift of humility, accepting themselves for what they were, and to these he was drawn. But of pros the equivalent of Sam Langford, he knew none.

Whatever he was—at least he asked the most of himself. When he worked, he worked to exhaustion. What he believed, he believed totally. He recognized no middle ground, only the extremities. It was a process of development which only had its inception at this time. It was to continue all his life. He saw his life symbolically.

Once after a fraternity dance he walked his girl home through the streets of the town. It was April and he could smell the new leaves. He remembers that the girl's gown was a pale lavender. He put his arm around her and they stood on the sidewalk at two o'clock in the morning in the country town. They walked up to her porch and sat on the swing, and he trembled with fervor. This was not a mere girl, for he had come suddenly to a mythological moment in his life. And the girl wondered at the trembling fervor; her eyes were dilated, and she whispered against his cheek.

It was the mythos of love, recurring in his consciousness for days on end. He trembled again and again with the intensity. A year before at the age of seventeen he had taken a nurse twice his age. She was the great earth mother. Garment by garment she had stripped the half-grown man for her wholesome and magnificent embrace.

So he existed in the town, living the life of the fantasies of youth. Shy, withdrawn, ignorant, he could stand at high noon on the awkward village street and call to mind the dream of life. On and on forever he lived the life that never dies. It mattered not the crowd and place. He crossed the threshold of reality that stretched before him like a fairyland. He became the life he dreamed. He entered into distant vistas and was never seen again.

How he lived so long in the town on twenty-three dollars capital is uncertain. It was part of the insignificance that he forgot. To be sure there was scrabbling for money, waiting on customers in stores, selling trees and shrubs house to house in the town, selling chrysanthemums at football games, washing dishes in restaurants. It was endured. It was a process without dignity, without intelligence, without meaning. Whenever in his life thereafter he would hear someone extolling poverty, the life of the lowly, the frugal, the sensible, he could hardly restrain himself. It was, he knew, imbecilic platitude. He knew that in such a life there is rarely anything worth extolling. Save for the weakest and dullest of men, the necessitous existence is degenerating. All aspiration and all respect for self are involved in the effort to get out of poverty and stay out of it. Poverty is a sticky river, a fog of smells. He had known poverty all his life. Poverty was not a young girl with a shawl over her head. Poverty was a whore eager for wages. Poverty was not a young man whistling down the street. Poverty was foul mouthed and always waiting in alleys.

This period of his life in the university was not important enough even to be disappointing. Judged as life, it was simply nothing. There was no clear idea in the university, no clear idea in the students, and no clear idea within himself. The experience left him merely with a mild distaste for formal education. There was in the classwork nothing to believe in; consequently there was nothing to disbelieve. The teachers impressed him as commonplace and dutiful. They were exponents of courses but not of knowledge. The lectures were dull and uninspired. No lifted word, no beautiful infallible phrase ever disturbed the pedagogical cemetery. In exquisite boredom he grimly foresaw a Chinese-like perpetuation of the same for hundreds of generations and thousands of years.[7]

So he returned to the city. He was eager to pledge himself, to offer his life. But to what? He imagined the crossing of perilous bridges bastioned in space. In mountain rain, in the clouds, he traversed the dizzy footpaths of the Andes. He demanded the unequivocal. He asked no odds. For one so young he could contemplate the most appalling defeats. For the sake of something or other—he was not sure what—he saw himself hiding away in a room neat and plain. He warmed his hands at the candle flame. He ate three crackers, looked at the falling snow, pulled the shade, and went to bed. He saw himself in a small brown house in linden woods. The rain dripped from the heart-shaped leaves. He bent over the drawing board; the triangle clicked against the T square. After a while he stopped and sharpened the pencil. Raindrops hissed against the smoldering logs. It was getting dark. A puff of smoke blew into the room.

He would endure hardship, defeat, enemies, but never the insignificance of nothingness. In a world safe and mean he saw himself beset, betrayed. In imagination he leaped on the rooftops of the city, twirled on the tar and gravel, and was gone. His legs were like the wings of a moth. He was too tremulously alive to be frightened. He flattened against a wall and became the wall, feeling the gaunt embrace of the wall against his back, and the sharp mortar crumble against his wrist. He ran in the darkness with back hunched. He was a soundless machine

---

7. Caldwell entered college twice and withdrew twice. After the second withdrawal he went to Cleveland to be with Geda.

invisible in the shadows. The soles of his feet conformed to the cobbles of the street, to their round and rut. He moved in an aura of power. It is something to be one against the many, to hear the aroused crowd in the street and to careen swiftly under the drunken stars and to crouch and leap beyond the wingless. Could he enmesh them in the skein of streets, turn and turn and leave them twisted and livid in the lamplight somewhere? He slipped through the velvet canyons of the city and touched a darkness that was like the veined black petal of some enormous flower, soft, cool, and so smooth that his fingertips rasped the skin of the darkness.

3

Then he married. His wife was seventeen. They were two small children, almost absurd. Her adolescent shoulder blades would sprout wings, and lo they did. He lived penniless in paradise. To live one must have money, and paradise is not enough. Yet he wanted no part of what he saw around him. In his chosen work he could see nothing but what was degraded. The last thing in the world he wanted was to be an employee. He chose a simple expedient. He borrowed money and opened an office of his own. It was impossible and ridiculous, but he did it.

He remembers that his office was on the second floor in the old Reaper Block, a dull and dingy building in the very center of downtown. The traffic all around it was wild, and at the change of the traffic light like stampeding horses. The first morning, a cold and wintry day, he went out and bought a drawing board and two cheap paper letter files, a T square and triangles, tracing paper, an engineer's ruler, pencils and colored crayons. He set the drawing board on top of an old mahogany desk left in the room by some former tenant. He was in business. Now to hit the street and get some jobs.

He succeeded after a fashion, for he had a kind of Gaelic eloquence. The businessmen he solicited—mainly speculative builders—were hard bargainers, and they knew what they were doing. They risked their money.[8] That was genuine and something one could respect. He had an old flivver which he drove at all times at its maximum speed of twenty-five miles an hour. Sometimes he was up at five o'clock in the morning, returning home at ten that night. In the mornings he parked the car in some discovered cranny in an alley west of downtown, blocks away. He saw himself as a businessman, a magnate, walking into his office. The phone would ring, and then he would be off back to the car again, and into the wilderness of the city, the West Side or the South Side. He was one well acquainted with the city, remembering the bits and pieces of his childhood and adding to it what he saw from day to day.

8. This was George T. Donoghue, who was later superintendent of the Chicago Parks District.

The city was a place of sweat, of filth and squalor, of winters ten below zero, of stove-heated tenements, of windows thick with frost, of gaslights, of lurking tenement stairs, and of deserted midnight streets. It was a city always with the distant clang of streetcars. It was a city of summers ninety something in the shade, when the sun cooked the asphalt of the streets so it wrinkled underfoot, and the brick walls of buildings were ovens radiating heat far into the night. It was a city where the el trains looked into the kitchens and bedrooms of the poor and down on the sinister, can-littered yard with its privy. It was a city of rats big as terrier dogs; it was a city of garbage, of slum geography and flies; it was a city of alleys and the snatch of waiting and omnipotent evil. It was a city of switchyards, where boys of the poor stole coal in the winter and ice in the summer and were chased and cornered and beaten with pleasure by the railroad bulls.

There were the winter slums and the summer slums. There were the breathless Sunday afternoons in August. There were the crowds of children playing in the street. There were the men and women in doorways or leaning out of windows and the idle, sheepish workmen on chairs or stools in front of doors, seeming to be waiting in the heat for something that would never happen. There was the distant smell of the stockyards, mixed of burnt hide and hair, of dung and blood and entrails. There was the cheap, sweet doughy smell of the bakery across the tracks. There were the women wasted and formless, bloated or emaciated. There was the drab clicking by, pitiably decked, yet with a certain drawn and poignant comeliness, frizzed and antiquated. And in the winter there were the gray, trampled snows, crusted at the edges beyond the foot tracks and dusted with soot. There were the early morning faces on the street, pale and blotched. They seemed to be abroad who had no right to be abroad, walking into the sick sun in that polluted whiteness.

It was a city of wealth beyond the avarice of emperors or the gold of the Incas. Borne in on the galleons of the stock market were the new bars of bullion. A corner on wheat, and fortunes would be made by inflating quotations. Even the far-off places of the earth would feel the pinch of price. Profits overnight from combines and mergers could pay for the pyramid of Cheops. Steel, farm equipment, tools, and foodstuffs made dollars like paper confetti.

It was also a city of fraud, of the rake-off and the payoff, and the thick cigar clamped in the mouth: "We gotcha down for ten bucks, sister. Every Monday morning ten bucks, see." It was a city of violence and bought killers, where the police fished the dead men out of the river or found them out in the lake bumping against the piers.

It was the city of the Maxwell Street open market, with poor peddlers selling watermelon slices a penny each, dotted equally with flies and seeds, and other peddlers selling thread, aprons, dust mops, brooms, hats, shoes, and suits of clothes. It was the city of Kinzie Street near the river, with the smell of roasting coffee. It was the city where warehouse wagons, still drawn by dappled teams of heavy Norman Percheron horses with feathery fetlocks, were loaded up with iced boxes of smelt, perch, and whitefish. It was the city of the Randolph Street market, where the truck farmers drove in their wagons loaded with gunny sacks of sweet corn and cabbages and piled tiers of carrots, beets, onions, cucumbers, and lettuce and where commission houses along the sidewalks of the market were stacked with fragrant boxes of lissome white celery, phallic cucumbers from the earth god Priapus, embryo-shaped green peppers, and baskets of shiny Nubian eggplants.

Once at two o'clock in the morning, driving through a pouring spring rain, he shouted in exultation: "O my city in the night, scatter silver arrows bright on the pavements of the night. Did you think that I could live without you, beloved thief and darling slut?" It was a city in the pleasure of thought, like the thought of sunfish caught at dawn, boned and gutted in the still forest and roasted over a fire of green hickory boughs, or the thought of a handful of chilled honeycomb; or of ripe figs bought from a Greek girl at Corinth and eaten at Mycenae, tasting like Wisconsin clover smells cut on a hot and windy day by Olympian horses with flying manes, or the thought of Early Richmond cherries stolen from the tree and stuffed in the shirt of one long ago, who ran pell-mell down the alley and across the lots.

It was a city of buying, selling, and making. It was the thriving city of the factory districts and the imported Polacks, Hunkies, Liths. It was the city of the stockyards, where they packed the doped and contaminated meat and worked the immigrants to desperation. It was the city of all these things. It was also the city of dreams. It was the one unique city with electric air and a cosmic tremolo.

It was a city on the great prairie far to the horizon. Here was the power of the prairie, the power of the great simplicity, the stretched, straight line of the earth. This was the long line, the long vision of the autumnal prairie, far as the eye could see over the fields and the distant farmsteads, and onto the rim of the world. It was the prairie at the beck and call of joy and melancholia. It was the prairie of the old farm villages: Niles, Wheeling, Halfday, Dundee. It was a city on the shores of an incomparable lake, with the waters changing country and color from Aegean blue to gray to green by hours, days, or seasons.

It was a city of mighty railroad stations from which the salesmen left for the distant towns, returning on weekends or month's ends to the city's Englewood, Hyde Park, Ravenswood, and far-off Wilmette. The vast and frightening stations were ports of entry for families from farms and distant countries. It was a city that had burned down in 1871 and had been built up again. It was temporary before the fire, and the air of the temporary and tentative still clung to it. From the el platforms the view westward over the thousands of acres of slumland, with factory water tanks and chimneys thrust up through the tenement aggregations, always looked like a catastrophe that had yet to be cleared.

It was the one expectant city. It had yet to be made. It was a vast stage, and the players had yet to appear. The possibilities were limitless. It was the one city with an Aladdin's lamp to raise the lost Atlantis or to reach the stars. The city was one enormous industrial cinder heap lacerated by railroads and sidings, attempting to make the entire city a switchyard, and not of the nation merely, but of the universe—as if cars were being loaded there among the tenements, bound for Saturn, Jupiter, and Mars.

4

So he worked in the city, and the months became a year, and then it was two years. Slowly he began to see the futility of what he was doing. It was a great effort, and it came to nothing. He had fondly imagined the labors of Hercules. An ant could move a grain of sand, but he had moved nothing. The world went on in its own way. It was not hostile; it was not even curious, not even aware of his existence. And he was shamed in his vanity. He thought his arrows had shot straight to the mark, the shaft of each splitting the shaft of the other. His fallacy was indisputable. He had believed that he was headed straight for the goal, whereas in reality he was running in the opposite direction.

Neither mover of mountains nor archer nor runner, he had to begin again. He had merely been trading dollars and—what was worse—borrowed dollars. The work itself, looked at harshly enough, was close to meaningless. He had to learn something first. He went to the one man and asked for a job. It took all his courage because the man was great and famous, a legend within his own life-time.[9] The man asked, "Are you any good?" and laughed low to himself. Then the secretary came in and asked, "Will you stay and have lunch with us in the studio?"

He stayed and was silent and merely listened, for he had come to learn. The man talked about what interested him; about nature; about the parts of the state that he wanted preserved against exploitation; about protecting the redwood forests of California, the Appalachian forests of Virginia, the Everglades of Florida, and the remnant wilderness tracts of Minnesota. The man talked about river valleys, bog lands, and canyons, disposing of these vast sections of the earth's surface with unique and beneficent grandeur.

The man talked about ecology, the relationship of living things to each other and to the soil, explaining that the landscape enables mankind to survive on this planet. So if we destroy the natural landscape we will inevitably destroy ourselves. Therein lies the great danger of modern technological industry, with its built-in leverage for destruction. For the first time in the long course of human

9. Jens Jensen, 1860–1951.

Jens Jensen and Alfred Caldwell, about 1945. (Courtesy of Alfred Caldwell)

history mankind actually possesses the power and the might to alter and throw out of harmony the natural order of the earth. We cut down the forests and erode the hills into gullies; we poison the lakes and the rivers with industrial chemicals, incidentally killing the fish, and then drinking the water ourselves; and we poison the very air we breathe and call it progress. What is happening to the once beautiful landscape of America is a catastrophe of the first magnitude. The future will curse us. The man at that time was about sixty years of age, and he had been saying this to deaf ears for approximately three decades. Besieging state governors and legislatures, he had set himself up as a one-man lobby representing nature and ecology, and the interests of the citizens of the United States. His professional practice as an artist—he was one of the outstanding artists of the nation—he had relegated to an avocation.

This was a September noontime in 1925. Fifty years later, the truth of what was said that day would become a world ideal in an already tragically collapsed environment. The word "ecology" would be, as a state official would then scurrilously put it, "the political equivalent of the word motherhood." But in that far-off time of 1925, it is probable that only this one man really understood the importance of the word, and the fatal consequences of ignoring its meaning by destroying the balanced equilibrium of nature. In a few brief sentences the man explained it, as a naturalist, a philosopher, and a poet. The entire explanation could not have taken more than fifteen minutes. Presently the boy walked out to his flivver. He sat in the seat awhile, dazed. It was the most astounding experience of his life. Then he started the car. He kept saying to himself over and over again: "At last I have found a man. I have found a man." He drove along laughing.

It was in this way that he came to work for the one man. Years later people would say, "Oh, you worked with so-and-so." And he could only reply that no one worked *with*, but only *for*, so-and-so. He was always quietly amused by the flattering pretense of even that much implied equality—as though the word "with" at once courteously and pleasantly lifts a person up, while the word "for" would tactlessly demote him to the reality of himself.

He remembers that he began his work by hiring teams of horses and drivers to dig a lake on a country place forty miles from the city.[10] The first morning, hurriedly rushing up, he found the teams and the men in the woods waiting. Then they began, the scrapers pulled by the horses cutting into the heavy clay that had lain undisturbed since the passing of the last glacier. The teams moved in a circle, one following the other, first loading the scraper, and then, beyond the precinct of the lake excavation, dumping it. He stood in the center of the circle, breathing in the smell of the autumn woods, the smell of the horses and of the cut earth. He rejoiced in his thought that this was genuine, that this was real work and he was a part of it. At noon a whistle blew somewhere, far off in the countryside. The teamsters unhitched the horses from the scrapers and led them to a place under the trees, putting on the horses' heads nosebags filled with oats. The teamsters sat about the ground nearby eating bread and pieces of meat. The men seemed like giants in the woods.

Then the work began again, the teams moving one after the other in the circle. The sun itself moving in the great circle of its journey beat down from above upon this minute activity, this clock of work ticking out the earth. The sun slanted down the sky until it was a great orange ball on the horizon. The men stopped work, hitched the horses to the farm wagons, and drove off. He stood alone in the hole that had been dug, slapping the wet clay with his hand and feeling the grit of gravel here and there. He climbed up the bank of the hole and paced out the length of lake again. He calculated how many weeks of work would be required. It was dusk when he started his flivver and went home.

10. Caldwell remembers this project as a private estate of about twenty acres belonging to a lawyer, just west of Highland Park.

He continued with the teamsters digging the lake day after day, leaving the city in the dark and returning in the dark. His life was swept along in the curve of days—the mysterious life that can change so completely and so quickly, leaving of all the former haunts and lairs of place and thought only the essential identity of self. It was like an exile. He came back at night to the once-familiar streets like a traveler returning unexpected from a distant land. The happenings of two months past seemed years removed. He was untouched. What he had lived through was a thing finished. The office he had set up for himself and the struggle had happened, but he would never go back. He was alien to this unregretted past. It was a sweeping conclusion. To be irrevocably finished with something is a luxury that maturity cannot afford. Only the spendthrift rich can throw away things. To start adding up assets and calculating costs is to be already old.

Certainly employment with the one man was never very much as a job. The wages were minimal, and the work was hard. However, it was the most valuable experience of his life. When winter came he was out all day with the men, sometimes at ten below zero. He would grab a grub hoe and work along with the men to keep from freezing. An extension of the lake had to be excavated through frozen clay. He bought a hundred sticks of dynamite, putting in a dozen charges a day. Holes were augered for the dynamite, the fuses were placed, the teamsters held the horses against fright, and men ran behind tree trunks. Then the explosion shattered the ledge of clay. In thirty minutes the teams of scrapers removed the chunks of clay. Then the operation was repeated.

For the first time in his life he began to understand how to work, how to go about doing something. Often the men knew more about it than he did. Then later he would laugh at himself for his ignorance. He was supposed to be the boss. But now he had the experience at least in this. Now he knew how to do it, and he felt enriched. But there were hundreds of things, and each had to be solved. He discovered that there was a knack or rationale, and once you had learned how to think in that hard, practical way, in that way of doing, then you could solve the problems. He froze in the winter, was drenched in the rains of the spring, and cooked in the heat of the summer sun. But at length he began to understand. Nobody could call it an easy life.

Twice during the autumn, in fine weather, the one man came out to the job, apparently to see how things were going. And apparently he was satisfied. The man had a few suggestions to offer, but no orders as such. It was possible to believe that the work was satisfactory. This man was a showman of a very subtle and superior kind, elegant in dress and demeanor, friendly and knowledgeable and obviously in manner an artist. In fact, with his mane of silver hair and mustaches he looked more than a little like Mark Twain. Instead of saying that the lake should be drawn in at one particular place, it should be "foreshortened," as if the lake and landscape were being painted on an easel. "I say too much water surface will produce a glare when viewed from the terrace. Be careful—that would be bad." The advice was excellent, and of course the manner was impressive beyond words. It was so much so that this neophyte, at that time twenty-three years of age, would have defended it right up to the gates of heaven or to the hinges of hell. Not for many a year would he be able to reflect that at least part of the excellence was in the eager belief of the believer and that by trades like this it is possible to learn and profit. People ordinarily would call it hero worship.

Once on the way home, driving in the pitch dark along the highway entering the city, suddenly a wagon without lights appeared in front of his flivver. He had the split-second choice of smashing into the wagon or going into the ditch. Into the ditch he went, landing upside down. He crawled out unhurt. He looked at the car, its wheels in the air, and set off at once to find help. He walked perhaps a thousand feet to a farmhouse. When he returned twenty minutes later with the farmer and a team to right the car, the tires had been stripped from all four wheels. He drove all the way into the city on the rims. He pulled into the alley by his street, and onto the pavement of an automobile accessory shop still open. He had no money, but he talked and pleaded for four new tires, payment deferred until Saturday.

It seemed a major catastrophe. He was shocked and appalled. The memory lingered for years. It reminded him ever and again of the predatory nature of man. He really did have the weakness of innocence and ignorance, and in his naïveté the incident called to mind the dangerous imperfections of at least some of the inhabitants of this planet. Years later he would only grin. Somebody had stolen four tires; it was nothing. Later they would steal everything in sight. They would steal ideas, steal credit, steal a job, steal an earned reputation, steal anything. Nature protects the young and breaks the news gently, little by little.

5

He worked and so continued for some years, going from one part of the country to another. He built roads and planted forests, living in distant towns a life remote as a dream. He saw the world around and withdrew into himself as if he were a visitor, a superfluous person who had merely wandered in. He had come from another planet. He had landed in the dead of night in the middle of a plowed field and had started out thus, hobbling over the furrows toward a distant light. He had passed under a bridge, and through weed-choked lots into the gregarious town.

It was their town, the town of the world around, but certainly not his. He would say: "No, I intend to leave in a day or so. No, not at all; I always walk at night." In such ways he went about disengaging himself. He was an alien mindful of his separateness. He scarcely noticed what the inhabitants of the world around did with their hours or their ten minutes. He was looking for a purpose in his life, "This is the earth, and this is the world around, and now what do I do?" The world around was an aimless welter of trivialities. He could find no relationship between himself and the world. He made no small talk. If he spoke his heart he alarmed the inhabitants. They went scurrying away, some angry, some embarrassed, some simply astounded. He was a wolf among sheep. He was a dynamo wired to a toy train.

He made enemies, certainly. If he said not a word he still made enemies. His very strangeness ensured it. He discovered that the one outstanding characteristic of the inhabitants was their fear, and hence their hatred, of strangeness. Whoever was not like everybody else aroused distrust and fear. It was a wild, unreasoning fear of strange persons, strange thoughts, strange manners. Silence could arouse the bitterest resentment, while a sentence could bring down an avalanche. The inhabitants were ridden by secret anxieties. They lived in nightmare rooms filled with psychological bric-a-brac lying around waiting to be broken. Platitudes of all kinds reassured and consoled them.

The suspicion and hostility were easy enough to observe. Passing by a group of men lounging at a street corner, he was measured with sidelong glances. As he walked into a room, suddenly an animated conversation would lapse. When he was talking to two persons, each of those addressing him would look at the other as if there was a secret understanding between them, from which he was of course excluded. Yet such hostility was the hostility of perfect strangers. He began to see that the world is truly unfriendly, and that country towns are tribal. Anybody who is not a member of the tribe is a stranger and, by supposition, an enemy. The big cities, in contrast, were anonymous. Nobody belonged and nobody cared. The big city was not friendly; it was simply not tribal. In the city it was possible to live for years as an inhabitant of an apartment building housing fifty or a hundred tenants and, as the most natural thing in the world, never speak to one of them. It was possible in this way to be absolutely alone, and with no sense of being alone.

In the small town of the university he had observed that nearly every person was friendly. The townspeople, when students passed by on the sidewalk in going to classes, would invariably say, "Good morning, boys." It was apparent that they must have been happy to say it. Because he had lived all his life in a big city with its noncommittal detachment, that attitude had really surprised him. Someone, however, explained to him that students are special; in that sense they live a charmed life. Definitely the townspeople thought there was something special about the town because the university was there.

Now, however, he was living in small towns that were not university towns. So he began to see the normal and usual face of small-town America—resentful, turned inward, grudging, disagreeable. All outsiders please keep out. He who had only a few months to stay wondered grotesquely how many generations one

Alfred Caldwell, about 1935. (Courtesy of
Carol Caldwell Dooley)

would have to stay in order not to be an outsider, in order not to be a dangerous character. In one small town there was a report that he was really Dillinger—an escaped convict of the day, at that moment famous as a murderer and desperado on the loose.[11] The alarmed townsman would say: "Here comes Dillinger. Look at the blue car. It's the same. I read about it in the newspaper."

Once, walking into a construction shed on a project in a southern town, he received the full message in a hurry: "I thought we'd killed all you damn Yankees.[12] Well, we still got the niggers, and now we got you too. The niggers, we know how to put in their place. Around here we gotta have lynchin' fun, jus' about one nigger a year—jus' to keep 'em nice and quiet for a spell. Las' year a bunch of the boys buckshot a nigger offen a tin roof. Funniest thing you ever seen—roof real slippery, steep as kin be. One of them boys give 'im a shot in the legs, and he be lettin' out a yell and slippin' back some. All them boys a-shoutin' at 'im he scairt some more, and climbin' up the roof. Three times he done it. Las' so scairt he got uppen to the top and plum fell offen t'other side. Boys string him up

11. John Herbert Dillinger, 1903–34. With "Pretty Boy" Floyd and "Baby Face" Nelson, he was responsible for sixteen murders. He was gunned down by law officers in Chicago.

12. During World War II Caldwell built military camps. This particular experience happened while he was working on Camp Forrest in Tennessee.

anyhow, but he wuz sure one dead nigger. Lit a fire under 'im—always do that 'round here—didn't do no good, there warn't kick in 'im—one dead nigger."

A few days later he casually mentioned this testimony about fun lynching to the president of the little bank in the town. The banker smiled in a deprecating way: "Yes it's true. Only sometimes they get the wrong nigger. A little town tart, just to stir up excitement, can make up the whole thing. This last one—the nigger you were told about—was certainly innocent. His name was George, and he was a good boy. He had two mules, ten acres, five kids, and a wife. A pretty spot of farm—house all fixed up nice. In fact our bank held the mortgage. We lent the money, the money for him to buy the place. We'll do that when we know that the borrower is a hard worker. That kind of loan to niggers is extremely profitable. The interest comes to about thirty percent a year, in the way that we do it. Those farm and town boys should have cleared their lynching through me. I'm the pillar of this community. That lynching cost this bank a damn lucrative little mortgage. The trouble is that they get so enthusiastic about what they call 'protecting white womanhoo'd.' Wherever they got that fancy way of putting it, I don't know—the Klan I guess. But it sure heats them up."

Then he added, gazing off into space and adjusting his glasses: "I wouldn't talk about it around here if I were you—being a stranger and all that. It's just a local affair. These town and farm boys, after all, are the real Americans. Why, their people go back two hundred years and more in this country."

It happened that very next day he stopped at a farm in the hills to confirm a delivery of soil for the project. When he drove in the farmstead the farmer was standing and talking to a neighbor. The farmer's wife, a slip of a girl, was some twenty feet away, shelling peas on the porch. The farmer was a gigantic man with tousled yellow hair, about thirty years of age. He was saying to the neighbor: "You kin be havin' that hay. Add them twenty-five dollars an' be takin' that thar sorrel colt you been a-likin'."

With that the wife on the porch came rushing down: "Yore not a-sellin' that thar colt. Ahm likin' that colt—a-feedin' it out uv a bucket."

The farmer turned, his faced flushed: "Ahm a-doin' the famin' round heah. Whea you thinkin' you is? Ah gotten you to fry mah meat, an' a-straddle tight. You a-wantin' to keep that thar colt—til ah get round to you, wal you be keepin' this." With that the giant arm swung and struck the girl across the hips. It toppled her into the dust of the yard. The farmer advanced and stood over her: "You be gittin' up and gittin' in the house. Or ah be a-markin' you up in fron uv these heah gent'men. Don' you be a-playin' possum. Gwan. Gwan in the house."

The girl got up on her knees, then stood up, turned, and walked into the house limping, head bowed, and crying. The farmer concluded the transaction with the neighbor: "Be a-sendin' yore boy fo' that theah colt. An you be a-cuttin' that hay bout nex' week I s'pose." Apparently embarrassed or intimidated, the neighbor turned away, walked over to his dilapidated pickup, and drove out.

The farmer turned: "An' you be a-wantin' those loads? Iffen you say ah kin gib em. An ah 'pologizes fo' this heah woman. It ain't fittin'. Mah pappy tol' me. Her pappy done tol' me: 'Huey, yore a big boy. You gotten yorself a lil' ol' mountain vixen ain't growed up yet. You be feedin 'er good an iffen she not be a-mindin', an a-sassin' you, why you strap 'er good an be a-keepin' it up.' So ahm a-fixin'. Ah can feel it in mah ahm. She be sittin' down on 'er sittin' place, real edgy like, lemme tell you. An you be a-drivin' out an' a-lockin' the gate."

6

It was evident that some of the inhabitants not only were hostile, they were dangerously insane. He was looking down into a pit. His intentions for his life were suddenly ludicrous; he was shaken for days. Nothing in his life had prepared him for such realities. He had supposed conflict between adversaries. But here was no conflict; here were no adversaries. He had gone forth, and he had just returned with an appalling message. He had been a fool, been fooled by illusions of his own contriving. He had been warped and twisted into believing fairy tales. These fairy tales were merely a mirror reflecting his intentions. And he had imagined that was life. Valor and truth, like a copybook saying, had been written in swirling script at the bottom of the mirror. Now he had been given, by casual and extreme experience, some part at least of unacceptable reality.

So it was at this time in his life that he became uninterested in the world around. That lack of interest was to be permanent. Ambition to be successful, that is, to participate, left him. Quite possibly ambition to be successful had never been very great. Now it did not exist at all. Why should he extend himself? The world would not change one iota. It was pleased with itself. Let it be. He had no desire to interfere. Let the earth take care of its own. Let it turn its own back into the earth. It did not require his urging or permission. He would keep the swirling words written on the bottom of the mirror—even though the words were illusions. For they were better than the reality. The illusions were his secret sanity.

But his indifference extended only to the world around. In contrast there was another world, the world of work. The inhabitants were the workmen. There were the companions of his days. They were rough, unsentimental, practical. They were something solid—a rock or a clod, not a shadow or a sham—something all of a piece that went clear through. He sat around the fire and ate his lunch with workmen, listening to their talk. Sometimes, in a project near a big city, they were Italians. They ate the hard sausage with chunks of bread and garlic, drinking red wine out of small clay jugs and then lighting their pipes or the licorice-like black stogies. A kind of peace descended on him, almost as if he were hypnotized, will-less and enchanted.

It was at this time that he began to work with stone. He built a small bridge, gathering the stones in a creek bottom.[13] The pieces were mainly sandstone, brown and gold, with the colors rippling from the waves on some ancient geological beach. He would wade into the creek with the men, and working together they would pry the stones up and onto the bank. Using a heavy, wide plank as runway, they would lift the stones over and over, and so onto the wagon. After two weeks' work there was a large pile scattered out adjacent to the foundation of the bridge. What a pleasure it was to lay the stones in the work, each slab in turn squeezing down into the mortar. What a sense of accomplishment to tap the just-laid stone with the hammer and thus bring the high side down so the top would be level. And then to point the edges of the still-soft mortar, making the joint neat and workmanlike. Could anything be more beautiful than the golden glint of the wall in the sunlight and the natural and rhythmic pattern of the bonding? How fortunate he was, how enriched, to have such work to do.

At the end of the summer there stood the work complete. He walked around and around it like one bewitched, put his head down to see the world upside down and the wall against the blue sky. Standing alone by the wall he put his arms around the corner to embrace it and laid his face against a stone.

It remained to plant a forest, to cover the banks with native trees and thus prevent future flood erosion. A man named Jim Collins owned the adjacent farm, a vastly neglected sixty-acre holding grown up with young trees, volunteering like weeds where once there had been tilled fields. It was said that Jim Collins lived alone in the old house. A man then of about thirty-five, he had been the hired hand of two spinster sisters, who had died and left him the farm. Now on Saturday and Sunday nights gamblers came from miles around to wager on cockfights held in the barn. So he called on Jim Collins, knocked on the door, and waited. And then he knocked again and again. Suddenly the door flew open, and the man stood there holding a shotgun, shouting, "What d' you want?"

"I want permission to dig young saplings out of your fields. We expect to pay you of course for what we take. I'm planting the creek land on the other side."

"You are, eh? Well, let me be tellin' you somethin'. I don't want any part uv the million bucks of that dandy little widow yore a-workin' fer. Tell her there's one thing I first gotta get from her. Tell her that's what I want from her—what's up her skirt, see. Then she can be a-havin' every goddamned tree on the place." With that, Jim Collins slammed the door.

He stood on the rotting farmhouse porch, sick, insulted, seared by the

---

13. This was a project for a Mrs. Barber, who lived near Cleveland. Her husband, a banker, had bought land to have a country life, but he died before this dream was realized.

sudden violence. Then he began to laugh. He sat in his car and laughed. Then he started the car and went down the rutted road. He crossed the highway and turned to the right. It began to rain. The road went up the mountain and down the other side along a meadow. There everywhere were clumps of sugar maples, white birch, dogwood, and Juneberries, the leaves flaming in the October rain, red and orange and purple. He stopped the car and walked out among the young trees. It was the very place for the men to dig. The owner of the land would certainly be glad to get a few dollars. He began to laugh again—at the shotgun, the man's dirty, ragged shirt, the musty smell of the dark inside of the house when the door was opened. He laughed at the snarling malevolence, comic, awkward, imbecilic.

Of such was his experience in rural America. It was a million miles away from the usual picture of the rural or small-town scene conjured forth by writers and homespun philosophers. However, it was a vital part of his education, for the sake of which he had left the university. Now he was dealing with life itself—not abstract theories such as classroom sociology and psychology—but rather with life as he encountered it from day to day in his obscure and remote existence. Certainly the most brutal portions of it shocked and stunned him. But equally certain, none of it ever hurt him. It drove him away from easy sentimentality about his countrymen and into the useful direction of trying to look at things firsthand, and if possible to discover some kind of reason or truth behind them. It made him intolerant of facile generalizations. He had an eye trained now to look for the actual details. The details, like an X ray, showed everything. Never mind grandiose assumptions. So most of all his experience made him his own man. He was launched now, come what may—and possibly on a perilous sea.

In brief, his experience made him even more what he had really been all along—a radical. He wanted to approach things at the root level, which is in fact the Greek derivation of the word "radical." Not for nothing was he a gardener and a planter of trees. No doubt—and especially at that age of twenty-four—he was perplexed and unsure much of the time. But one thing at least he was positive and clear about; that there is always somewhere a root level of meaning. To his credit, he had already rejected success as something not worth the trouble and the time. Success meant being a lackey. It actually demanded it. It meant doing what everybody else does, saying what everybody else says. He was sure the emphasis and effort were wrong.

The two years ridiculously in business for himself had purged him of success illusions. And really that was why he was now indifferent to what he called the world around.

Because he was serious in his work, and competent, inevitably some measure of material success would from time to time normally occur in his life. Yet over and over again some fundamental issue would arise, and normally then he would act according to the root level of things, and the success—such as it was— would vanish like a mirage. He would be out of a job, perhaps with angry enemies. At the most some few persons might say, usually long afterward, that he had been courageous. But nobody is in that implied sense "courageous," for nobody really wants to lose. It was always simply that the success, as such, was not worth a dime, and the fundamental issue was worth everything. The difference in worth was so plain that there was never even the smallest question of choice. So beginning at this age of twenty-four, he was to acquire the dubious reputation of being a reckless fellow, generally by quitting his job or having the job quit him, whereas in reality he was merely being a serious student of the small affairs that happened to touch his life and being ready to act on them. He never claimed more, nor had he any right to claim more. For he had no vanity, that great goad for success. He had no money, but that fact never nagged him into devoting his life to making money. The small sums he earned of course necessitated extremely restrictive expenditure. His net property worth, including clothes and broken-down automobile, could hardly have exceeded three hundred dollars. But he considered that he owned himself. If that belief was vanity, then he was in that case vain. To cap it all, he was ignorant. However, he did not intend to remain so.

With such thoughts he worked from day to day and year to year. Slowly he began to see some general drift of meaning in what he experienced. Yet it was a process of learning so gradual that he was never able afterward to say just when it began. Nor did the meaning ever appear as any kind of grand enlightenment. It was rather a vexation. For every question it answered, or seemed to answer, it asked a hundred. He would need to read whole libraries. Familiar giants of books he carried about for years.[14] They filled his leisure by night or by day. He ruined all the pockets of his coats by carrying them. He read on trains and buses and at every lunch counter. Single sentences impressed a lifetime.

He read history and discovered that, as men are, so have they always been. With a shock he discovered himself in the pages that he was reading. Evil was his evil. With a kind of despairing bravado of honesty he recognized that—given the situation—the hatred and cruelty, the murder and plunder of history were not some other person's but his own. He lost province after province of imagined virtues. What had once seemed like a kingdom dwindled away into empty pretensions. The ignorance of some historical folly was simply his own ignorance, blown up by chance and by enormous encounters, by treachery and sacked cities. So at length—as a kind of disreputable by-product—a fugitive and unwilling

14. Books that influenced Caldwell most, besides Pepoon's *An Annotated Flora of the Chicago Area*, include Oswald Spengler's *Decline of the West*, *The History of the World* by H. G. Wells, *The Decline and Fall of the Roman Empire* by Edward Gibbon, José Ortega y Gasset's *The Revolt of the Masses*, and the Bible. Caldwell loved the Greeks and Shakespeare. He memorized the English poets, especially Swinburne, Keats, and Shelley, as well as Frost, Whitman, and Emerson.

knowledge of himself enlightened the pages. He stood in the midst of some ancient carnage and could not pull a spearhead from his side.

He saw life as a chaotic striving at cross-purposes, without intelligence, without pity. The forlorn and helpless individual, fettered by frailties and old mistakes and victimized by illusions and by the relentless pressure of events and circumstances, impossible to control, was driven on to destruction. It was a game of chance that no one wins. The inhabitants of the planet seemed like mere pieces set in motion by some incredibly powerful and sardonic being, himself perhaps driven on by some inscrutable bent or beguiled by some futile gesture. And perhaps he too was a prisoner of an even higher tyranny.

He read works on the history of man. The creature with shambling gait came out of the cave something more than an animal, and something less. He was a timorous hunter of small game and, with good luck, a jackal skulking behind the lion or the tiger, consuming what was left of the kill. This creature would attack sick or dying animals. In times of dearth he would turn cannibal and eat his fellows, smash the heavy skull and scoop out the brains. Reading far into the night, he was overwhelmed with nausea and shaken by the appalling revelation that man has only a thin skin, and that under the skin is still the craven hunter in the rocks, the jackal, the cannibal.

This, or something like this, apparently was the beginning of man, a creature hostile and disagreeable. At length this man developed a property sense. It was likely that the first property, aside from food, consisted of cherished natural flint slivers, at some time picked up loose on the ground. With these slivers men could scrape the flesh from the hide of game and so produce fur blankets against the cold. Later on men learned to flake flint by hammering and thus to make knives, spears, and arrowheads. With these as an arsenal of weapons, man at once became a more successful hunter. He was now able to kill large game. Men could also attack other families and tribes of men, killing them and taking away their weapons and any other possessions. Thus man became a bandit—or speaking plainly, a thief. Plunder became an economic means. Sometimes the vanquished would be taken alive and retained as slaves, that is, as property. Thus men were divided into the two fundamental estates, the slaves and the slaveholders—or precisely those who obey and those who command.

He remembers that at last grasping this simple and elementary fact of human history was like a great light coming down. Slavery was not something relatively recent; it was the second oldest profession. All kinds of things that he had observed and been repelled by in the world around were at once as clear as crystal. For instance, envy was no longer puzzling. It was the instinctual atavistic reaction of a slave. Self-pity was the same, the normal mental attitude of a slave. Self-advertising, a thing in one form or another everywhere on every street corner—a veritable leitmotif of civilization—was but the obsequious and ingratiating effort of a slave to impress a master in order to gain preferential advantages. Power of all kinds, and in all degrees, was simply the vantage point of a slave-holder. The bully was the man handling slaves. And then suddenly he saw money as the Stone Age weapons heap. He saw it as the modern means of impressing others into slavery. He saw it as the means of seizing the bodies of men and making them property in order to own and use their labor. With a start he realized that envy, self-pity, self-advertising, power, money, and its built-in compulsion are not faults to speak of overcoming. They are the intrinsic bred-in qualities of mankind, going all the way back to the tribal encampment. It is what walks down Main Street.

In his imagination he would climb to a desolate peak, to some final pinna-cle of ice. Or he would withdraw to an island in the sea, to swim in the sea and sleep in the night, and wake in the morning and walk on the sand naked and immaculate. The longing to be beyond himself, a sublimation walking in the morning, became at last the secret meaning of his life, his utmost hope, forever fading like a rainbow for a child.

7

He was a man in love with his wife. When it was necessary for him to go away to start another job, his wife would visit her family. He would be alone in a distant town for some weeks. He was lost. Every morning he woke up with desire, and every day was empty. He had no peace. He walked the town at night for hours. Then he went up to his hotel room and couldn't sleep. Nor could he eat. The three daily meals in the restaurant were like a penance. He thought it was just his body—that he was too healthy. Then he saw a pretty girl in the hotel lobby, and it meant nothing. So it wasn't that simple.

He wrote long letters to his wife, filled with voluptuous dithyrambs and the Anglo-Saxon words of love. If his words had ever been discovered, given that benighted age, they would have shocked people to righteous consternation. He saw people all around him playing sly little games of infidelity. If his love words had been discovered he would have been ruined, at least in the general estimate, and these people would have remained pure. For this was an age when the sexual encounter was considered only a little less dreadful than a murder. A girl who had been emotionally beguiled into even one transgression was by the usual appraisal morally damned forevermore. She had lost her honor; she was soiled. Quite often her family disowned her. Even after marriage the sexual encounter was consid-ered at best a mortal weakness. A proper and refined woman agreed only under duress. For the wife to have amorously participated would in many instances have lowered her in the eyes of her husband. Only prostitutes gave evidence of desire. He recalls that an acquaintance had once parenthetically and rather proudly

Virginia Caldwell, about 1940. (Courtesy of Carol Caldwell Dooley)

alluded to the attitude of his wife as "dignified acquiescence," thus explaining the existence of his six children.

In these circumstances of national prudery, both cynicism and hypocrisy were usual. This was the period after World War I which legislated the prohibition of alcoholic drink in the United States; if it had somehow been possible to legislate nationally the prohibition of sexual intercourse, that prohibition too would have had many advocates. As it is, sex outside marriage is a criminal offense on the statute books of many states even today. The prohibition of alcohol produced gangsters and drunkards, while the prevalent sexual prudery produced sleazy infidelity and dishonest and thwarted lives. Yet nearly everybody, it seemed, had it in the back of his cranium that he ought to help in improving everybody else. Being a nation of prudes, it was a nation of world savers.

But the amorous words written to his wife were really not necessary. Just having her love was quite enough, because he never had enough of her. So all of his life he was to live in a love affair. And like all persons in love, he supposed that he had invented it. He had not the slightest idea—it had never occurred to him—that his misery of separation was only part of the magnetism that held the universe together. It was in reality invented five billion years before the Anglo-Saxons had invented the word "I," the exact 50 percent of the magnetism. The infidelity had no "I," since in the general proceedings the rumpled bed, the sleep, and the awakening could be for anyone—and by anyone—and not for and by the "I."

Finally, on the appointed day his wife would return and would be met at the railroad depot like visiting royalty, despite only the one suitcase (they were always poor). Stepping down from the coach was an image so beautiful. The poise and the delicacy of her manner made him suddenly shy, whether he had been married five years or fifty. Now he had to be accustomed again. He was one, in his special thoughts, for whom nights were bridal nights, and mornings bridal mornings. So why wouldn't he be shy? He wasn't one to make a joke of it, to make it coarse with rough words and a laugh, carrying the suitcase to the car—just another adulterous couple going away someplace for a weekend. No, instead they sat in the car and looked at each other. Then they held hands for a moment, and her fingers went under his cuff caressing his arm as if trying to get close to him. Then at once he was even more shy, aware of the flames licking above his knees and the inexorable tightness and the surging and the familiar heat.

All of the inner loneliness of his life melted away in the incorrigible consciousness of the good, sweet heat and in the power and the glory of male desire. In the sense of losing his persistent, tense, and lonely self, he felt now free like a god let loose. He had been entombed and shut away in a world which is too much to be endured and too bitter to be borne. Now bearer of the bright phallus, he had arisen and then walked right through the massive and canted stone walls of the tomb, through the ramparts of guarded loneliness and separation, now as insubstantial as translucent mist breaking into the sunlight. So over the heather he could walk like a god, bearing the pride of gift. In this momentary unspoken soliloquy in an automobile, holding the hand of his wife, he saw that this very instant with its intimation revealed that the world had once been the pride of gift, that the world had once been as glad as the eagles. The world had died of fear and shame and hatred, and the inhabitants had been shoved in the tomb of loneliness and separation, each man and woman in his or her own private cubbyhole of hell. The gods left the earth. The bright phallus as the pride of gift was no more. The glad titans were conquered. The world had died.

"What are you thinking about?"

"I'm thinking how much I love you. You see, my wife is so beautiful. That's truthful flattery. Did you get my letters?"

"Yes of course. Do you know what? All the way on the train I kept thinking how much I want to see my husband, how much I want to look at him. And that's my truthful flattery."

So memorable were the many rejoinings with his wife that fifty years later he could still recall them in detail. The little furnished apartment in the town, the door through which they entered, the chairs and the couch, the big double bed in the bedroom, and the low table on which he set the suitcase—even these were remembered. These were the visual periphery when he turned and at last embraced the whole person, kissing her mouth and cheek, her neck and arms. With the masculine impatience not to be brooked, the dress would quickly be unbuttoned and slipped to the floor and then the underwear exquisitely, exposing at once, new and virginal, the nakedness, the newfound land. As explorers kneel and kiss the earth, he knelt and kissed his girl. Pulling the stockings down and taking them off with the slippers, he kissed her feet, her knees, her thighs, his hands around, in front, in back in stroking adoration of loveliness too good. She stood and endured the worship, like a slave or a goddess. Her head was bowed, eyes closed, around her head the halo of crisp black curls. Her forehead was very high, giving the face an expression of nobility and intellectuality. Aside from the few freckles on forehead and arms, all of her was creamy white, that sudden gleaming color that only nakedness possesses.

She stood like a captive queen, a prize beyond all of the prizes of the earth, accepting the impetuous homage. So standing there being adored, in a tidy and impoverished apartment, was not a mere girl who had traveled three hundred miles on a train to be kissed. He couldn't accept that. All of his life his imagination just simply leaped over the mere factual reality—whether it was his love, his work or anything else. The realism was nothing; it wasn't worth the living it. Yet he kept his phantasmagoria to himself, knowing full well that no one would either accept it or understand it. His secret and unspoken poems were his life. He could be seemingly irrelevant to the prosaic point and plainly bewildering to others. Without the Rosetta stone of the poems the meaning of his life could be totally indecipherable.

Here in his wife was the intimidating and terrible beauty. Here, and for thousands of years, was the implacable dream of life. If a man could possess it for but an hour he would venture any price, and forever afterward be like the sere autumn leaves blown by the wind. For this kingdoms were once paid, armies launched, and cities sacked. He pressed her to the bed, and now, not to be longer deprived of his booty, he hurriedly pulled off his clothes, feeling the joyous air on his skin. He opened his girl like a fan and they were joined, writhing together like two serpents entwined. Under him the girl moaned.

This was his love affair with his wife. It would be the easiest thing in the world to ridicule. Worse yet, to make it ordinary, obvious, perhaps shameless. These were two small persons living together from day to day and year to year. In being happy they hurt no one. They even kept their happiness a secret. Now and again, however, someone with shrewd observation and deduction would possibly penetrate it a little. Once a neighboring woman, with more than a bare hint of malevolence, commented to his wife, "I guess it's what you call love."

He always considered it something far better than he deserved. It was the bounty of nature. It gave verve, delight, and pride to his life. He awoke in the morning for the pleasure of living, and he went to bed at night for the pleasure of loving, and the long sleep, passionless, deep.

8

It was a sunny autumn day. He had been surveying a park site in Pennsylvania, and at four o'clock they loaded up the transits and the rods.[15] An hour's ride and they were halfway back to home base, passing right through downtown Pittsburgh. The car could barely move through the heavy traffic. The rodman was sitting on the outside, and he kept leaning out: "Say there's something going on. Look at the black headlines on the newspapers. Pull in. I'll get one." It was Thursday, October 1929.

It arrived so casually, that afternoon—almost, it seemed to him afterward, like someone who had just dropped in, put his hat down carefully on the opposite chair, saying: "I'll wait. Just mention that I'm here." It was the stock market crash and the beginning of the Great Depression.

News was newspaper news. In 1929 radio was just beginning and television hadn't appeared. Years before, on a hot Sunday afternoon when he was nine years old, he had been sent to buy an extra paper. That too had a black headline: "Germany Invades Belgium." It was August 1914. Five years later at war's end he had sold extra papers himself, shouting through the alleys and looking up at the tenement porches: "Wukstra. Wukstra, five cents, Kaiser jumps in the Rhine River."

So they called it "the depression." He who had hated poverty now saw the poverty of an entire nation, and with the poverty, terror. Millionaires jumped from ten-story windows; chorus girls were no longer bathed in champagne; real estate first mortgage gold bonds could be used for wallpaper; savings of a lifetime were wiped out in bank runs; canvassers went around buying up gold teeth, crumpled little rings, all sold for a pittance. And workmen walked the streets for months looking for work. Their shoes wore out looking. Finally they began staying home most of the day. And then the wife went out looking—for anything—for a scrubwoman's job—anything—but generally there was nothing. Then the last dollar, the last dime. The next day the children went to school hungry. In the richest nation on the face of the earth, with the warehouses bulging with food and goods, a fourth part of the population had virtually nothing to eat. It grew like a disease. Soon there were twelve million unemployed. Like

15. This was a park near Pittsburgh. Caldwell was still working for Jensen at the time, but for political reasons Jensen had not gotten the commission. Geda's father, Al Pullen, had a business in Pittsburgh selling mining equipment and knew the superintendent at the park. He helped his son-in-law get the job, but before Caldwell accepted he consulted Jensen, who told him to take it.

bubonic plague, it was no respecter of persons. It hit the bottom income, it hit the middle income, it hit the top. It hit the top hard, and the top collapsed almost at once. This top income was loaded with fake: fake confidence, fake fortunes. Even the collapse was fake, because there had never been anything to collapse.

It was, after the winter's sunset in the darkened office, lighting for a moment the notes of avarice on the desk; after the exhilaration of so much so easy; after the chauffeurs and the lacquer smell of new cars; after the smell of leather and its cool, accomplished touch; after the doormen in plum-colored uniforms; after the laughter and the bare arms of women; after the marble thought that all of wealth was there simply for the taking, and that this was the one great fortunate life—it was, after the dream of backing a Mack truck up to the mint, suddenly and irrefutably to have arrived at exactly nowhere. It was to have lost, but in reality to have lost nothing. It was to have squandered the futility of fortunes and bought nothing. As the entire national opulence went slithering down into the desperate reality of the depression, it was to have awakened like a drunk in a gilded gutter. It was to have endured tragedy without tragedy. It was to have been not Hamlet destroyed by the just frenzy of his nature, nor Oedipus by the decree of gods—it was to have been discovered a fool playing with buttons.

What was the reason behind all that astounding procedure? Quite plainly he was now not merely reading history; he was actually living in history, living in one of the great historical moments of folly. For instance, he simply couldn't get it through his head why—through what compulsion—men, women, and children must go hungry in the midst of plenty. What possible purpose is served? He couldn't understand Napoleon's march on Russia, or the Crusades. Quite plainly man was mad, was triggered for madness, and the weight of a speck of dust, given the special situation, could send him off on some wild course of action. An obscure Austrian duke that no one had ever heard of had been killed—and the result was the vast and bloody war of 1914. Now at this very moment in Germany there was a man named Adolph Hitler screaming at the top of his lungs to multitudes screaming in answer.

From earliest childhood one is brought up to accept the proposition that mankind is rational. Every schoolbook presumes or asserts it and changes or glosses over hard facts to prove it. Every infamy of history is presented as a dialectical argument. Yet underlying it all, in reality, is a substratum of irrational origin. Upon that substratum rest the beliefs of a person, of a group, of a nation, of an epoch. These beliefs are not the beliefs of people in insane asylums, nor are they the beliefs of criminals. On the contrary, these are the commonly accepted beliefs of nearly everyone—their sincere judgments. Yet about all of this there is a conspiracy of silence that fatuously supposes a network of closely reasoned propositions, whereas in truth the beliefs rest upon the promptings of deep-buried fears and phobias, old hatreds and rages, forgotten but not to be erased old hungers and longings. Upon this kitchen midden of irrational debris is erected what people fondly imagine to be the very citadel of reason. This structure, not on rock but on old rubbish, inevitably topples. Apparently there is nothing that can be done about it. Invariably the new structure that replaces the old is put back on the same queasy foundation. It is the one certainty of nations.

"Don't Sell America Short" was the logos of the twenties. America was speculation, speculation piled on speculation, subsidiaries of corporations piled one on top of the other to the moon. A pound of real wealth was buried under tons of speculative rip-rap. It was gold mining in reverse. The holding companies of the public utilities corporations were so deviously contrived and interlocked that, in the investigations afterward, financial experts were bewildered by the intricacy and mystique. One operator turned five thousand dollars into fifty million during a period of some six years. In order to create just such miracles, the poor and the middling poor of the nation had invested many billions of hard-earned dollars in merely fictitious securities. All was lost.

Blue-jowled men, the heavy, the commonplace—presidents and vice presidents of corporations and chairmen of the board—sat in their offices conjuring forth leprechauns of finance. Or like alchemists in cobwebby garrets of the medieval town, they transmuted paper into gold.

It was a nation speculating on unearned wages, that is, buying on time, and paying in the process an enormous surcharge of interest. The good fairy waved her wand, and here was a new automobile, a new refrigerator, a new house, a new anything. Even money itself could be bought on time. Sign the paper and the good fairy, disguised as the man at the loan company, would hand across the desk two hundred dollars or five hundred. Name it. How much do you need?

The American people had reached the high plateau, the Utopia of capitalism. The nineteenth-century premonition of beneficence had at last come true. In the movies everyone was rich and good-looking. No one worked very hard or had money troubles, but only love troubles. The hero leaned against the marble mantelpiece in the unexplained sumptuousness or walked across the lawn during working hours swinging a tennis racket. There was no problem so abstruse that it couldn't be solved by the hero punching the villain in the jaw. The feminine sex was inevitably represented by a pretty face and a voluptuous figure. Every virtue without dispute automatically accompanied these obvious physical stigmata. So in the feathery darkness of the movies, like cult palaces now curiously perfumed not with incense of aphrodisiac, but with crackerjack and popcorn, millions of Americans—perhaps very nearly the entire population—were vicariously living out the daydreams of adolescence.

It seemed as if nearly everyone above mere subsistence was, in one way or another, out to make his pile, little or big. Looking back from this distance at the depression, that historic catastrophe of America, there were no good guys and no bad guys. The virtuous fleeced by swindlers was a nice thought, but it really wasn't so. Nearly everyone would have jumped at the chance of being a swindler—of course never calling it such—and would have, like the real practicing swindlers, represented it as simply business, as progress and a service to the country. It was merely that the American people as a whole were absolutely convinced that something could be made out of nothing. Avarice and enthusiasm reduced to a shambles the hard realities of basic economics. In the popular understanding, money gave up whatever meaning it might once have had as a token to represent the expenditure of labor in the production of goods and services. Money took off on its own, disembodied in a never-never land. The office boy on his lunch hour played the stock market. The secretary put three dollars on Yeah Boy to win in the third race. The shoe shiner invested in a weekly lottery. Questioned closely enough, the least likely person would turn out nonetheless to have invested in twenty cemetery lots—"bound to go up."

The dentist, the doctor, the grocery man, the tailor would invest the proceeds of forty years' work in a thirty-six-apartment building. Apartment buildings were built by speculators who, in many cases, borrowed quite fraudulently in first mortgage gold bonds more money than the total cost of the building plus the land value. The speculator then could take two profits: one, the surplus from the mortgage, which could be immediately pocketed, sale or no sale; and two, the eventual profit from the sale of the building. In order to fill the building with tenants and so present to the prospective buyer the pleasing semblance of a profitable investment, tenants were given a "concession" of two or three months' free rent as inducement to move in. When the crash came the people who had lost their jobs moved out. Buildings were commonly only half filled. Consequently the "investor" couldn't make the mortgage payments, and the mortgage house foreclosed. The many buyers of the mortgage bonds eventually lost ninety or ninety-five cents on the dollar, for they were holding mortgages on half-empty and bankrupt property, a good portion of whose real value had already been pirated out by the profit of the original building speculator. Nearly all the rest of the value just disappeared somewhere out in the ether due to diminished demand. Of course the dentist, doctor, grocery man, or tailor, far from making his pile, lost everything.

He remembers that the depression gave him his first real understanding of the economy, and what a curious mixture it was of the grotesque and the ridiculous. It wasn't at all the classical economy of books, but rather the economy that is in real life. For instance, he remembers how people defended the various procedures for money getting. "Why, he's only earning his living—what's so wrong about that?" So far as he could judge, that reason seemed to justify just about everything. Was the world this and no more? Was there no other possibility? After all his thought on the subject, he was still asking the question incredulously if society was only a process of plunder—mean and sniveling for the little and gigantic for the big. Was his own country only that? All of his former pessimism about the nature of man now seemed silly and puerile in the face of the actual, concrete fact.

He was innocent in the extreme. For of course everyone and everything works nearly exclusively in its own self-interest. To be appalled at that is to be naive, approaching basic stupidity. At this time, in 1930, he had been out in the world some seven years. Beyond question he had learned a great deal. But his surprise now was an expression either of how vast an amount there was to learn or of his own incapacity to learn. He hated cynicism because its negativity destroyed the exuberance of life. He was sexually exuberant, emotionally intense, and by consequence happy. Thus his hatred of cynicism. But he hated ignorance as much. This was his dilemma. So he observed the passing world of the depression with watchful eye and a painful uncertainty.

He saw a breadline two blocks long. He had never seen so many miserables in his life. Some were plainly depressed, head slightly down, staying in line but lounging against the brick wall. Others, quite apparently pleased, were chatting. Perhaps a third of the line gave the general impression of being not only pleased, but definitely relaxed as well. There was one rather short man who stood out a little distance from the line; this one was belligerent, his legs spread defiantly as if looking for a fight. There was one man studiously reading the newspaper, very possibly the want ads, as though some job had been overlooked, or as if his eye could sweep into existence on the page the one ad that no one else could see— and that once he answered it he would be cheerfully assured, "Step right up." Then his coat would be thrown down and the big wheelbarrow would be light as a feather in the thought of a day's wages.

Passing under a railroad bridge in the slums of the city on a January night during zero weather, he saw men standing around an iron barrel with burning newspaper inside. He had seen that sort of thing before, but for some reason he had never thought very much about it. Now he wondered where such men slept at night, for apparently they had no place to go. Did they sleep in some protected niche of the bridge's concrete abutment, perhaps under blankets of newspapers? The police were always finding men dead from the bad weather.

9

So he entered into the depression. He had never had over three hundred dollars at one time in his entire life. Now suddenly he had no work at all. The few dollars melted away. Presently there was nothing to eat. His wife prepared boiled cornmeal served with sliced raw cabbage flavored with vinegar and a strip of chopped and fried bacon. In substitute for packages of cigarettes he bought Bull

Durham tobacco, four cents a sack, and rolled his own. Miraculously a few days' or a few weeks' work would appear, and so the rent could be paid.

Then the rent would be due again, and again there would be no money. The landlord served a five-day notice to move. The gas company shut off the gas. The electric service was shut off. On a hot summer's night he strung wire to the apartment building light fixture in the hall and plugged in a fan and a light to read by. Perishables like butter or milk were kept cool by running a trickle of cold water over them in the sink. At eight o'clock in the morning he would start out looking for work. He had no money for carfare, so he walked. He walked to the North Shore towns, the suburbs where he had once laid out gardens for wealthy private estates. Going and coming back he often walked thirty or forty miles in a day. Invariably the rich weren't home—and what did they care about him in any case?

Once, as he was walking around the grounds of a place he had laid out a year before, pausing and inspecting every tree, a cop in a squad car suddenly stopped by the curb, challenging his presence. Thinking even better of his authority, the cop pulled out his gun, walked over, and knocked him down. Before he could get to his feet he was handcuffed. Later, after a long explanation at the police station, he was released. He walked twenty miles home, his one good shirt torn in half and hanging from his shoulders.

But he was undefeatable. No chance was too forlorn. He was told about a woman who had acquired eighty acres of land, intending to subdivide it into lots. It was 250 miles away in the next state. He wrote a letter offering his professional services, and he received a reply. Yes, they were interested. An appointment Thursday forenoon would be satisfactory. So Wednesday at six o'clock in the morning he started out a poverillo, in his best clothes, but determined to get there somehow or other. After an hour of walking a truck picked him up and took him fifty miles. Then there were three different cars, all adding up the miles. By 6:30 that night he stepped out of the last car only twenty miles from the town.

It was getting dark and getting cold, and he was way out in an enormous emptiness of farmland. Right along the barbed wire was the edge of a tomato field already harvested. He stepped through the barbed wire, smelling the acid pungency of tomatoes rotting on the vines. Here and there were good tomatoes, and he filled his pockets, setting them in gently. Now he could eat and with some left over for breakfast. But where could he sleep? He had always heard about sleeping in barns. How do you go about it? Walking along the road, thinking it over, he rounded the top of the next hill, lonely, a little frightened, and certainly cold. In ten minutes it would be dark. Then suddenly a miracle. There, not fifty feet from the road ditch, was a barn. He had inherited the earth. The farmhouse had long since burned down, the chimney still standing among sumac crowding the old farmstead lilacs now grown up like trees. There was a well with a pump handle, and a dipper on a wire hung over the crotch of a tree. And no yelping dogs and no shotguns for bums.

He opened the door and discovered that the barn was filled with last month's cutting of summer hay, more fragrant than dreams of Arabia. Outside he worked the creaking pump handle and drank from the well the water ice chilled. Then he went inside, laid on a shelf his tomato breakfast, hung up his coat and hat on a nail, lay down on the hay, pulled some over, and went to sleep.

He arrived in the town by a farm truck the next morning at 10:00. By 10:30 he had walked to the address of his prospect. He rang the bell, and directly a pleasant and handsome woman appeared at the door and invited him in. He was seated in the living room, and a maid presently brought coffee. His prospect entered the room, sitting at a small desk opposite. She set a notebook in front and began to ask questions. He explained his work, how he went about it, the various necessary procedures. His prospective client was an excellent audience, knowledgeable and intelligent. He was scarcely aware of the passage of time. Suddenly his audience said: "I am interested in what you are saying. Now you take me to lunch and continue your talk, and then tell me something about yourself. After lunch I can drive you to the site."

Here was a catastrophe. How could he have been so stupid not to have foreseen that particular possibility? He didn't have a penny. Before he had left home he had doled out his last dime for a bottle of milk. Take a guest to lunch indeed. So what he said—lying outrageously—was this: "I am sorry. I didn't realize it was so late. You have been such a kind listener that I completely forgot my previous obligation. I have to meet my associate who drove me up here, for he and I have an appointment for 2:30 at Baraboo. I'm to meet him at Main and Center at noon. May I come again to see you—at your convenience? Anytime you say. You could write me the time. You have my letter address."

With that we both stood up: "Then you are late already. My car is at the curb. Let me drop you off at Main." A pleasant good-bye, and that was the end of it. Never a word thereafter. It was four days' traveling for nothing.

When he arrived home he took a bath and went to bed. In the morning, with the sun streaming in the window, things looked a little better. He stretched tracing paper on his drawing board and started to work. He had no clients. Very well, he would be his own client. He wouldn't waste his life chasing around for work that didn't exist. He imagined a job—a house this time—and started to draw it. He drew the floor plan; he drew the garden, dreaming about raspberries and vegetables, hollyhocks and roses, maples and oaks. He could smell soup cooking in the kitchen. It was six o'clock already and time for dinner. Tomorrow he would draw the house elevations. And tonight he would read poetry to his wife. At nine or ten they would go out for a long walk, then come home and go to bed together. Yes, he was happy.

And every day he went to work at his drawing board just as if it really was for real. Sometimes a paid job would appear, and he would be off to wherever it was for a few days or a few weeks. In that terrible depression the pay was miserable, but putting the little money together like misers, somehow they survived. At the end of the paid job he had months at his drawing board. He began to make geometric structures, rhythms of structures with secret hieroglyphs of meaning; he colored them with crayon laid on with fastidious care. He filed them away or mounted them on cardboard and hung them like paintings. He made a geometric nature pattern on the window in the kitchen where the winter sun came through. He pasted on elements of colored onionskin paper, defined with taut black lines of heavy thread stretched and glued. He had his own stained glass window. Once he made patterns for napkins, and his wife stitched them in. He tried to block print with linoleum dipped in paint and then pressed on cloth.

There would be days when he was too discouraged by poverty to do anything. Then he wrote poetry to try to say what he couldn't say. Thus he learned that poetry is always saying what cannot be said. He did all these things, day in day out, as a way of life. Yet it was only later that he realized how much he had educated himself. His drawings of houses and gardens and geometrical rhythms taught him to think and to work structurally. The poetry taught him something at least about the terrible plasticity of words in a prism of structure.

And he read. He read all the poets. He was steeped in Whitman. He read the books that people talk about but never try to read. He read the Bible and the Bhagavad Gita, the Upanishads, and the *Iliad* and the *Odyssey* of Homer. He read Gibbon's *Decline and Fall of the Roman Empire*. He read Mommsen. He read Marx, a very great man but a very bad writer—not in the least to be confused with the political myth of tyranny that uses his name. He read Spengler's *Decline of the West*, a sledgehammer blow on the ox skull of mankind. And he read the great soul, his guide and genius, an architect still living. He was a frequenter of libraries, looking up references to this man in any available papers, magazines, or books. He found "In the Cause of Architecture"[16] and read it like one hypnotized. He walked home from the library through the snowdrifts, his mind whirling.

Working alone—totally alone—he began to realize a direction in his life. Even if his poverty and isolation were to continue all his life, he would still go on. Even if no one would ever see his drawings and no one would ever listen to his thoughts, he would go on. He explained nothing to anyone. He just worked. Why should he stop? What would he be waiting for? Thinking that thought, he was standing pencil in hand, eyes closed, and swirled over by that loneliness which is always at the root level of creative work. It is true that at the time he imagined that

---

16. Frank Lloyd Wright, "In the Cause of Architecture," in *Architectural Record* (New York), 1908, 155–65, and *Architectural Record* (New York), 1928, 49–57.

the sense of loneliness was something special to himself, perhaps an emptiness of some kind. Years later he realized that it is universal, and that it can be the indication of glad tidings. For loneliness is the basic material. There can be no work of art without it. He was sure of it when he read Blake: "Great things are done when Men & Mountains meet; / This is not done by Jostling in the Street."[17]

So he could work alone with his thoughts and fantasy. He could look into his drawing and see a whole world revealed. He could turn over the drawings one after the other. This one was imperial. He entered the drawing as if entering a palace with its broad corridors and its rich and sumptuous rooms. Somewhere just beyond, a flute was being played. He held his hands out loosely and moved them as if to the music. In contrast, this other drawing was an entirely different world. With its gay pastel colors it was like a spring garden, and it was forever leading on. He who had left the earth, walking on and on, enchanted, bemused, wondered which was his real life, the everyday mundane existence or this other existence of his fantasy where he could disappear into thin air and perhaps never be seen again. How strange that just these rhythms and colors could release him into this other existence, mysterious and magnetic.

He discovered then that there is an inner world, entirely within oneself, and that it is possible to live in it. Making that discovery had at least one distinct advantage. Forever thereafter he was saved from the fear most people have of being excluded from something. He knew that no technique of shunning could hurt him. He could be his own man with impunity. In this depression he had gone through three years of hardship and poverty, living totally on inner resources. He had come out unscathed. He had shown that it could be done. He had gone hungry, he had worn tatters for clothes; worse yet, he had endured periods of despair and melancholia. But he had worked from morning to night every day of the three years, exiled in the world of his imagination. Without clients, and hence without a job, he had created them by imagining them. At the end of three years he was an established architect in the kingdom of his imagination.

A few acquaintances who came around from time to time—and there were a few—could only shake their heads. They looked at the drawings on the walls and shook their heads some more. "It's all ridiculous. Why don't you get a job. Get any kind of job—a salesman's job—anything. Stop wasting your time. Nobody has money for buildings and gardens today. Give it up. Get into something else. Get into something serious. A hobby, yes—but first get a job. A salesman's

17. *Blake: Complete Writings*, ed. Geoffrey Keynes (Oxford: Oxford University Press, 1966), 550. This epigram is a part of Blake's *Epigrams, Verses, and Fragments from the Note-book (1808–1811)*, no. 43. Another authoritative source is *The Poetry and Prose of William Blake*, ed. David V. Erdman (New York: Doubleday, 1965), 502.

job would be a million times better than this waste of your life. Who do you think would pay for all this stuff? It's laughable. And you with not even a dollar to buy groceries."

One person, uninvited, picked up his notebook of poems and read through it. He announced that it was frightening. "It is insane and nothing but gibberish."

10

An old town on the banks of the Mississippi needed a park superintendent. His name was proposed, and he received a letter inviting him to visit the town. On a Saturday morning in March 1934 he stepped down from the train and was met by the park board members. After a tour of the various parks in the town, the specifics of the job were discussed over lunch in the hotel. The federal government's WPA unemployment relief program would furnish labor and materials to develop the parks. The federal government's stipulations required an experienced man to take charge as the town's park superintendent. Would he accept the job? They would give him all the help he needed. A local architect could draw the plans for the park buildings and so relieve him of that part of the work, since the time was short. In fact it was immediate. In order to qualify for the project, the work had to begin Monday morning. There would be fifty men to begin work at eight o'clock in the morning. His salary would be extremely modest, but he would have a free hand.

He replied that he would accept. But he would accept only if he made the building plans. No need for the local architect. He would make the plans for the first building that afternoon and that night. He would drive himself and turn it out. He would have the plans finished by morning. The men could start on the foundations Monday. He would return home for his family, and he would be back in town again by the middle of the week.

With that agreement, they terminated the meeting. They would meet again at ten o'clock the next morning to approve the plans. After they had gone he went to a nearby store and bought a small drawing board, T square, triangles, pencils, and paper. He took a room in the hotel and started at once to work.[18] This was his chance. He had prepared himself over the past three years. Now it had actually happened.

This building was to be a shelter house at Eagle Point Park. It was to be used by groups of picnickers in the summer, by strollers in the spring and fall, and with its big fireplace it was to be a haven in winter to warm the adventurous, out for a walk in the snow. Now how to build it. Why not make it out of the native stone,

18. Caldwell stayed at the Julien Dubuque Hotel, where he stayed once again in 1991. Caldwell made only one other trip to Dubuque, at Ludwig Hilberseimer's request in the late 1940s.

Gateway Pavilion, Eagle Point Park, Dubuque, Iowa, 1936. Alfred Caldwell, architect. (Photo by Dennis Domer)

out of the limestone underfoot everywhere in the town? These slabs were golden, delicately pitted in texture, almost like Italian travertine. Aside from the labor for quarrying, the stone would be a material costing practically nothing. The slabs could be laid up in the walls without cutting, very nearly like the face of the rock cliff. The stones could be placed weathered face out. He began to draw.

After an interval of time that could only have been a brief while, he straightened up and walked over to the dresser to look at his watch. He could hardly believe it. It was midnight. He had only ten hours left—no time to get anything to eat. Just keep working. The steam radiator went off, and soon the room was cold. He blew on his hands to keep them warm enough to draw. There was the familiar and pleasant click of the triangle against the T square. Once again he sharpened the pencils. Then he looked at his watch. It was six in the morning. One more tracing paper sheet tacked down, and he was on the cross sections. Only four hours to go. This sheet was what they would build. It had to be right. He calculated the foundations, and that took an hour. Then he drew the detailed sections, showing the materials—the concrete, the steel, the stone. He proceeded to the roof, calculating and spacing the rafters and drawing them on the sections, again showing the materials—the timber, the sheathing, the shingles, and the plaster ceiling. He dimensioned all parts throughout and lettered in the construction notes. The phone rang. The park board was waiting in the lobby: "I'll be down. Give me ten minutes."

Now back to the plan sheet. He sketched in a garden and grouped big trees around the building. It was the fastest landscape that he ever made. Five minutes. He threw on his overcoat, grabbed the tracings and was out the door.

So he drove the park board car back to Chicago. Wednesday morning he drove the car around to the front of the apartment building. He rushed upstairs and down several times, loading in suitcases and bundles. And then the last trip up to look around the now empty flat, the scene of so much poverty, despair, dreaming, and covert hard work. He carried down his son, two months old, while his wife walked ahead with their two-year-old daughter by the hand. They started out through a late March snowstorm to drive into an unknown world. He had a job, and a wonderful one.

It was a town of hills, and below the hills was the mighty Mississippi. From a vantage point on high ground, and looking northward, there was that mystical channel of America, dividing the nation into east and west. At this interval in its course, and in the distance far as the eye could see, it was disappearing into islands. So it was a river town, once sighted by the eighteenth-century French explorers. It was also a railroad town; it was a shipping town. It was right in the middle of the agricultural hinterland of America. Certainly it was a hick town, but it was also an industrial town, with the great factories a block long each. A short way down the factory streets were the impoverished cottages of the poor, hardly distinguishable from the factory cottages in towns along the Atlantic seaboard.

Thus there was an air in the town as of something old in manner and usage, and in that sense it was an urban town. It is a feeling that no new towns can have. The factories were three generations from the founding. All the big buildings in the town were old and substantial, with heavy walls sometimes brutal in proportions. It was evident that behind the facade was the power of money and ruling prestige. The wealth was old wealth, and the poverty was long-established poverty. Yet like all of America, the town of course was essentially middle class, up and coming, and very Main Street.

The town was hard hit by the depression. Factories had laid off up to 80 percent of their workers. The wages of the workers had never been very much above bare subsistence. So naturally with no jobs at all workers' families were without food in a matter of weeks or months. With a continuing lowering of agricultural prices due to diminishing food consumption throughout the nation, the farms in the vicinity were being foreclosed for nonpayment of mortgage loans. The once somewhat prosperous middle class in the town, largely dependent upon industry and agriculture, was soon almost as bad off as the factory workers and the farmers. The special economic alignment of the town seemed to make a situation particularly disastrous, even when compared with some of the worst areas in the country. The owners of the factories dug in just to survive. The largest industry in the town had not paid city taxes for two years, being in arrears nearly $100,000. Small businessmen, with proprietorships such as small industrial shops, simply folded overnight. A lifetime accumulation of industrial tools would be locked up in sheds. The owner would go home to wait it out, on rainy nights contemplating the rust on the tools. Retail stores by the dozens failed, the owners possessing at the last scarcely more than a drawerful of bills. When Franklin Roosevelt became president of the United States and proposed welfare work relief programs, the wealthy in the town indignantly opposed him. A leading man of affairs in the town, a person of considerable wealth, proclaimed that the only solution—the true solution—was for the neighbors to feed the poor and the hungry. He pointed out that federal help programs could be paid for only by increased taxation, which would inevitably be confiscatory. It would destroy the owning class in America and hence destroy free enterprise.

Thus there was, perhaps for the first time in the entire history of the town, a great and abiding bitterness. The factory workers were bitter because—through no fault of their own—they were now objects of charity; the up-and-coming middle class were bitter because they had not made it; and the wealthy were bitter because they were frightened. Added to this was the fear of communism. Anybody could be a communist. You had to be on your guard night and day. They were about ready to take over the country. The Roosevelt administration was filled with them. There ought to be some kind of concentration camp to throw them in as soon as they were apprehended. It was the only way to save America. On this point, at least, the factory workers agreed, the middle class agreed, and the wealthy agreed. The town was particularly vulnerable to an invasion. If the one bridge across the Mississippi was taken, the entire town would be cut off.

The work began under dark gray skies.

11

He arrived in the town early enough to superintend the pouring of the concrete. At eight o'clock in the morning on Thursday, there were the men at the building site. The sand, the gravel, and the cement were precisely piled for the work. The concrete mixer was started and loaded, and the pour began. The wheelbarrows of concrete were trundled up to the foundation edge and dumped. All day the pour went on. As soon as one portion of the foundation was filled, the top was leveled and then roughly scored with a trowel to form an adhering bond for the mortar of the stone wall. All the men were happy and laughing, and he was in his heaven, for there is nothing more exhilarating than laying a foundation for a building. It is the beginning and the hope of things. Into the hard clay was established the heavy monolithic rim of concrete that would support the stone walls for centuries. After the workmen had gone home, he stayed on. It was too wonderful to leave. He walked around and here and there touched the still-wet concrete with his fingers. It was dark before he went home to supper.

That night after the dishes were cleared away, he laid paper on the dining room table and started to draw. He drew the bond pattern of the stone wall. In four days there would be masons on the job. He wanted to work it out in detail, in order to have the bond clearly in mind by the time they began. The wall must be strong and enduring and simple to lay up. It would be beautiful; he was sure of that. He would no more have doubted it than he would have doubted the geology of the earth — as if the rocks of the planet had still to be rectified.

The limestone of the town, like all limestone, was laid down vast eons ago as sediment under water. Cementitious material in the water and in the sediment solidified the deposit, making stone. Layer after layer of sediment would be built up in this way, making stone strata, one layer on top of the other like the leaves of a book. These strata might be hundreds or thousands of feet deep, depending on the geological situation, and their formation might require millions of years. Other millions of years of erosion would wear away part of the topmost strata and generally cover the strata with a blanket of soil and geological debris. Exposed cliffs and mountains dramatically reveal a small part of the sedimentary foundation crust of the earth, which nearly everywhere has its top layers only a few feet, or a few score feet, underground. All of the strata were once laid down as exact horizontal layers, because they were formed under water. Thus the horizontal stratification, so apparent in the limestone cliff or in the stone quarry, not only is the history of the stone, it is the principle of the stone, its irreducible fact — its truth.

For this reason, then, he planned the walls of the park building as in-and-out cadences of horizontal bands. The sun would strike the projected courses of stones, and they would cast their shadows on the walls. The wall would have over its surface these fluctuating bands of sunlight and shadow, moving in expressive rhythms, musical in character. At the same moment this would be a method of building stone masonry so simple, so natural, and so easy of execution that on extensive work such as this it would save many thousands of hours of labor. In its naturalness, like nature's cliff, it would have that rarest of all qualities, the quality of innocence.

Some years earlier he had tried this stone-laying method, and he had been amazed and delighted. His guide and genius, the man he had followed from afar, had built such walls, and with compelling force and beauty.[19] Now he himself

19. Frank Lloyd Wright, 1867–1959.

had the chance to try his hand. Could he really do it? Could he enter that Valhalla? He believed he could earn the right with honor and hard work.

He truly used the words "honor and hard work" in this soliloquy at a dining room table. He was no longer a boy, one to use such words lightly, just because they were high sounding. He was a man who actually thought and talked that way. It had been ten years since he left the university. Over half of this period he had spent with the one man—the inspiration of his youth—that great and famous landscape architect.[20] His debt was enormous. He was to hold this man in his mind with love and veneration for all the days of his life. But he was not a disciple. He was his own man, one to go his own way, one to try for himself and if necessary to err. This was his character. He even looked the part, perhaps even a little defiantly.

He wore his hair long, and he wore an ascot tie. He wasn't a dandy; he was just old-fashioned and dead serious, using the old-fashioned words. In appearance he was a man of about medium height, slender, blue-eyed, and with fair complexion. His Scots ancestry was apparent. His straight, rather prominent nose he had from his small, olive-skinned mother, inherited perhaps from her French forebears. But from what source he had derived his definitely archaic attitude toward life—his personal *Weltanschauung*—he never knew for certain. It might have been from reading or experience or from inheritance. People ordinarily called him "romantic," meaning by that term, in the usual circumstances, a mild rebuke or evidence of unreliability. Nonetheless, when he used the words "hard work" it was certainly genuine. He had worked hard all his life, and that was, to say the least, old-fashioned enough even in that day. In addition he had the curious ability to get others to work hard too. He wasn't a driver. With his obvious enthusiasm, hard work simply became contagious. The men in his charge caught it as you catch the measles. Workmen liked him, and he liked them. He enlisted their interest in the work, continually pointing out the reason and importance of what they were doing. He remembered bits and pieces of their personal lives and referred to these from time to time. If a workman was mad about something that had happened—a construction job is not a tea party—he did everything in his power to correct the situation. He enjoyed the work, and he wanted everybody to enjoy it.

Such in brief were strong points of a sort in his favor. However, he had onerous faults, and he knew them thoroughly. Under duress he could be indignant and harsh in judgment. He had a bad temper, and so he commonly worsened difficult problems that required tact. It was just as if he believed that being right was sufficient; worse, as if he believed that there was such a thing as right, nicely separate from self-interest. Because he required much of himself, he was

20. Jens Jensen.

often intolerant. So he was an idealist and probably doomed. He was a doughty hater of unscrupulous behavior and low cunning. Contempt became him well, and Jonathan Swift delighted him. At such uncongenial moments, his despair of the fallible world he reduced to ludicrous hyperbole. Too objective to believe in *Homo sapiens*, he considered that even the most rational hopes were at the very best problematic. Without being a cynic, he was convinced that the universe was a tragedy. He was an optimist of the immediate present but a pessimist of the future. These were the impedimenta he carried around, clanging and clattering behind him. Still, he was happy by disposition, sometimes hilarious, certainly amiable. Among strangers or slight acquaintances he was accommodating in manner, but withdrawn rather than forward. He loved to laugh, and he was appreciative of wit and goodwill.

Neither his high-handed acknowledgment of his own faults nor his reticent acceptance of his own talents and intelligence had ever contrived to make him vain. No doubt he could be abrasive to others, but he was much more abrasive to himself. He was too modest to be humble.

12

It was spring, and every day was a pleasure. It was a pleasure discovering a quarry site, a mile or so away, and setting men to work stripping the soil from the ledges, revealing the ancient, weathered stone under the loam. The men drove in steel wedges between the seams, lifting the layers and then prying them up. In order to have a quarry face to work the stone out, holes were drilled a foot apart in a line fifteen or twenty feet long and four or five feet back from the face. Then blasting powder would be packed in the holes and fuses connected. After the charge, the entire stone face for some three feet down would be shoved out an inch, freeing that much stone from the solid formation behind. Then the prying up would be very easy. At the end of a day several truckloads of the golden slabs would be stacked ready for hauling to the park.

Every layer had its individual character. Some were hard as flint, fine grained and cream colored. Some strata were mottled gray and gold together. Some contained minute sand pockets, giving the stone a pitted pattern, rich and delightful in texture. He planned to select the stone in such a way that each type variation was used for the best place in the walls according to its nature. The strata hard as flint were reserved for lintels and for copings especially vulnerable to weather. The building walls rested on a stone platform two feet wide, which, besides being a powerful architectural base for the building, provided continuous seating under the roof eaves all along the walls. The textured slabs would be reserved for this platform's top course. These textured stones were far too beautiful to be buried in the wall. It would not be excessive to say that he dreamed stones.

Hearth, Eagle Point Park, Dubuque, Iowa, 1936. (Photo by Dennis Domer)

So he began his great job, working from morning to night. He was possessed. There were never enough hours in the day. He set up a drawing board in the bedroom. Many a time far into the night he drew. At three or four o'clock in the morning, too exhausted to continue, he would fall into bed. With laughing self-commiseration, at breakfast his wife would recite to him complaining lines from a poem about the empress Josephine, "The drums beat in my boudoir."[21]

The work was just something that had happened to him. It was something

21. The source of this quotation is unknown.

too splendid to believe. Every single part of it was a blessing. He would stand by the walls and run his hands over the rough stones. There were especially beautiful parts of the walls, and these parts he never grew tired of studying. By preference he would arrive at the job ten or fifteen minutes early so that he could walk around alone and muse about the work. Then the masons would arrive, the mortar would be mixed, and the day would begin.

Adjacent to the buildings, he was constructing a large public garden with an extensive pool and a waterfall. The garden was in several levels or terraces, retained by great stone ledges — some single stones were twelve or fourteen feet long. These ledges he was building were veritable cliffs, faithful to the geological formation of the region. The original site had been a steep slope, and by building the ledges he obtained a series of flat and usable areas which stepped down, one after the other, all the way to the tops of the ancient bluffs high above the Mississippi. Stone-flagged walks and stone stairs joined the levels together.

The terraces created by the stone ledges were planned as sequestered flower meadows, interrupted by groups of white birches with their long slim trunks, and by stronger groups of sugar maples at the edges. Stepping stones would lead across the flower meadows, terminating at council rings. Each ring was a low, circular stone seat about twenty feet in diameter that would hold as many as thirty persons. The garden was planned as a good-time place for both individuals and groups, and as a picnic facility which could, with all of the council rings, accommodate hundreds of park visitors at one time.

He planned it to be a miracle of nature, as if in some unaccountable way just this space of the beautiful earth had been left unspoiled. He saw it as it would be in all seasons. In the spring, with the catkins on the birches limp in the sun, and the first flowers — hepatica, bloodroot, spring beauty, and perhaps trailing arbutus — under the birches. There would need to be a few Juneberries, with their twisted gray trunks and their white flowers against the white birch. Sometimes there would be a late spring snow, and the white feathery flakes would fall against the white flowers, white against white.

In the late spring and summer, all the terrace meadows would blossom with their native flowers. There would be shooting stars and violets, lupines and the little blue-eyed grass, anemones, meadow rue, meadow phlox, and the splendid native Turk's cap lily. Every month would have its flowers. The finest of all would be late summer and autumn, with its purple coneflowers, black-eyed Susans, gentians, asters, goldenrod, and sunflowers. In all, he estimated at least sixty varieties. The park greenhouses could propagate these now-rare native varieties from seed gathered along remnant strips of virgin prairie, found here and there in the surrounding countryside. The meadow gardens would bring back the prairie flora which had been destroyed over nearly all of the vast stretches of middle America. In the winter, perhaps the season most beautiful of all, there would be,

Ledge garden, Eagle Point Park, Dubuque, Iowa, 1936. (Photo by Dennis Domer)

adjacent to brown-gray trunks of sugar maples, the clumps of white birch ascending through the drifting snow. Groups of wild roses would loop in pink and thorny brambles.

Given time, moss would cover the rocks. Ferns and many a flowering native plant would root in the crevices. This garden would be the identity of the town's own native landscape. Since it was not artificial and forced but, on the contrary, natural, it would be by consequence very nearly maintenance free.

So he worked on the public garden just as he worked on the buildings, the construction of the two proceeding together. The original building, the stone shelter house, had now grown to a project of four buildings. The park needed a large water reservoir. The existing automobile road through the park had created a pedestrian hazard. To solve this he planned a crossover timber bridge. The stone abutments for the bridge were water reservoirs. Thus the practical needs both for water storage and for pedestrian safety were provided in the same facility. Since a small restaurant for the park was also needed, he planned that as a wing adjacent to one end of the crossover bridge. There was no workshop for maintenance in the park, in fact not even a place for tool storage. So in addition he planned a shop building, placed in appropriate relation to the other buildings and to the park as a whole.

By grouping these necessary buildings together he created—instead of several disparate and unrelated buildings—the sense of one harmonious and extensive building, with courts, little gardens, and terraces. A powerful architectural expression resulted. As the stones were built and the plan and the spaces became evident, he, who had dreamed it and made it in his head, could only stand amazed. The actuality so far exceeded his hopes and imagination that he could scarcely believe he had made it.

In this way he discovered that a work of inspiration is never familiar. It is always a stranger from afar. No wonder the Greeks attributed inspiration to the Muse. It is unfamiliar because it is the gift the god has imprudently given. So

Terrace, Eagle Point Park, Dubuque, Iowa, 1936. (Photo by Dennis Domer)

Gateway Pavilion, Eagle Point Park, Dubuque, Iowa, 1936. (Photo by Dennis Domer)

inspiration is that part of a work of art which costs the artist nothing. In mortal naïveté he may explain, "It just came to me."

Of course the remaining part of work—that is, the actual making of it—is toil and sweat and sleepless nights; it is anxiety and the hammered brain; it is danger poised and teetering over an abyss of fear. So at the end the inspiration is paid for, every bit and piece of it. It engenders enemies with well-organized opposition. Doing the work is a kind of warfare. It is a battle against sometimes overwhelming forces that charge the ramparts of reason and creative work. Any day they may be victorious and the work destroyed. There is only the inspiration, that nothingness of air and thought, that fond figment of an idea. If that goes down, everything goes down, ignominiously vanquished, hacked and meaning-less. Years pass and the ruined scene is like an old battlefield, where wondering persons stop and ask, "What happened here?" A spade would turn up skulls.

These of course were merely fugitive reflections. He was far too busy to dwell on them. Later he would recall that these reflections were really like a chorus in Aeschylus, foretelling the shape of things to come. However, at the moment he was not only too busy but far too happy to think very much about it. A visit to the garden construction in the morning, a visit to the quarry, a stopover at Glenview Park to oversee the work under way there, and then back again to the buildings before ten o'clock was the usual beginning of the day.

At once he would be up on the scaffold with the masons, talking the work over, explaining the idea—not his idea but the stone's idea. He asked questions and solicited advice, to let them do some of the explaining. Almost from the beginning they understood the idea. A mason would pick up a stone, set in on the wall, step back a little and squint at it. If it looked good he slapped down mortar and laid it, adjusting it to the line, laying the level on it to make it true, tapping it down, and finally pointing the joint. It all went like a charm. From the very first week of the work, there were established differences of interpretation, veritable schools of thought. Later he could pass along the wall and see at a glance who had built that part. But all of it was good.

They were artists, and not one of them had ever supposed it. He wouldn't have spoiled it by mentioning it. They were just laying the stone. Whenever he would see three or four stones together in a particular expressive relationship he always made a point of praising it. It was just a few words—never excessive—and always about the stone and its meaning. It assumed that the mason had simply discovered the combination and therefore had opened the door of the safe. That much was evident.

He began to see that common working men are capable of getting the point of a proposition, that is, of education. When he considered how little actual instruction was required, he realized the tremendous force of learning. No doubt laying stones was a small affair. But why could not the same principle be extended to big affairs? Why could not the world be a learning world? When not enough professional union masons could be supplied by the WPA, he trained young men to lay the stones, teaching them to be masons. This process of work and learning was so natural that it seemed to him, in imagination, as if the work were work of a medieval guild. Up there on the scaffold the union masons and the young apprentices worked together in perfect harmony.

But in reality not only the building masonry but the entire park project proceeded on substantially the same learning basis. All of the work was original; it had never been done before, and the workmen had to be trained to do it. All over the parks there were men doing things totally different from anything they had ever done in their lives. As a kind of consequence their work had élan, freshness, and care, and practical understanding as well. The great ledge stones for the public garden were moved from where the trucks had dumped them by inserting pipe rollers between the stone and the plank runways. The stone would be

WPA worker, Eagle Point Park, Dubuque, Iowa, about 1935. (Courtesy of Dubuque Park Board)

hitched to an improvised portable windlass. When the stone reached its destination on the ledge, the rollers and the planks would be easily removed by simply prying up with pinch bars, letting the stone down on its bed. The work proceeded with surprising efficiency and rapidity, saving many thousands of dollars compared with the cost of equivalent retaining walls built by the usual conventional construction.

To give another example, the caretaker of Grandview Park, a small tract at the other end of the city, was only partially employed, although of course he had to be paid for full time. Security reasons demanded that the man be on the premises, even though so little actual work was required. So he talked it over with the caretaker. Why not make something for the park instead of being idle? Why not make a stone council ring? Then the park visitors could have a beautiful place to sit under the trees. There would be picnics and eventually group meetings of all kinds. Certainly it would be a very popular place, whereas now it was just nothing. At once the caretaker agreed.

A few hundred feet distant, but still on park property, there were outcropping ledges where stone had formerly been quarried. With brief instruction and direction the caretaker pried up fine limestone slabs and carried them over to the site of the ring on a wheelbarrow. In a week's time enough stone had been stacked to build the council ring. Given a load of sand and gravel, a few bags of portland cement, and a mixing board, in eight or ten days' time the caretaker had excavated a circular trench and poured the foundation.

The caretaker, supplied with chisels, stone hammer, trowel, and mason's level, laid out the first course of stone, setting the pieces in place tentatively and without mortar. The next morning he worked a few hours with the caretaker, mixing the mortar and setting some of the stones. With just that initial instruction with these first prototype stones the actual stone laying could begin. Thereafter, stopping by every morning for additional coaching and discussion was all that was necessary. By the end of the summer a splendid council ring had been completed. The caretaker was a changed man. Every morning his smile was broader. He had discovered a talent he never knew he possessed.

This same man for years past had fired and tended the greenhouse furnace boiler during the winter months at Eagle Point Park. This was a night-shift job which he filled when Grandview Park was closed at the end of the summer season. This job too required mandatory time but very little actual work. Since the man had enjoyed the stone laying of the council ring, why not continue stone working during the winter to utilize the long periods of unoccupied time? Isn't all that empty idleness after the brief firing of the boiler unendurably boring? His agreement was almost immediate.

So slabs of quarry stone were brought over by truck and stacked adjacent to the boiler room. These slabs were planned to be precision cut for use on the buildings, as special copings and other stone elements. These pieces were to be bush hammered on the top surfaces, resulting in a delightful texture as fine as Italian travertine. This innovation to get the job done worked out perfectly. With instruction to the caretaker on many an overseeing night visit to the boiler room after supper, the net result was an increasing accumulation of excellent dimensioned stone. The stone was trucked up to the building site as it was needed. None of this had cost the park board a penny. The man himself was pleased, proud, and happy. As a consequence of the dimension stone, the building work had here and there at special and appropriate places, in contrast to the heroic roughness of the walls, an eloquent note of refined and piquant quality. Like a kind of counterpoint, it enriched and subtly emphasized the wall's heroic roughness.

It would be a pretension of modesty to deny that the greatest pleasure and pride was his own. Certainly the pleasure and pride of creation was his motivation. However, quite in addition, through the process of initiating the various methods necessary to build the buildings and the parks, and then by finding the way to use what was there—the men and the materials—as a sort of by-product he discovered something he had not known before. He discovered that everything is special. Nothing is more special than men, and nothing is more special than the hard reality of materials. So he lost whatever respect he might once have had for mere abstractions and rules, that is, for the stereotype which generalizes everything and understands nothing. For instance, he could see that this particular historical moment of the depression, this particular place and these particular persons, made everything possible. For every creation is the expression of a particular situation. Thus it cannot be formulated. It is always unique and original, and it would never happen again.

13

With the deepening of the depression, by late summer of the second year there were two hundred WPA men at work in the parks.[22] This was in addition to the twelve regular staff employees of the parks. What had started as a small project thus became a large one. As the project increased in size and importance, conflicting interests began to appear. When the project was small, hardly anyone had paid much attention to it. Now, however, the people in the town became definitely aware of what was going on in the parks.

Nearly everyone was in favor of the work and emphatically impressed. But inevitably a few were not in favor. So these few people began to say in effect, talking it over far and wide in the town: "With so many of our own men in the town unemployed, why did the park board bring in a stranger from outside, to plan and direct the work? Surely there must be able men in the town for that sort of thing. And what in the name of common sense is so great and special about that fellow? You elect the park board members to office, and the first thing you know they do something irresponsible and silly like bringing in a total stranger."

Sometimes such persons came out to the park to look at the stone walls and engage him in conversation. Perhaps they would say something like this: "Yes, to be sure, that method of laying up stone would save labor. But today it is unfair to save labor. Because we did save it is why we have a depression. Besides the whole thing is a kind of foolishness. Today thousands of people in this town are hungry and without even bread, and here you are talking about architecture, which is nothing but a luxury. They want bread and you give them stone."

In reply he might explain: "But don't you see, the WPA pays them wages to lay the stones, and then they can buy their own bread? And I am not doing it. It is

22. The year was 1935.

Stair buttress, Eagle Point Park, Dubuque, Iowa, 1936. (Photo by Dennis Domer)

the federal work relief program. It is all over the United States, and it involves millions of the unemployed in just such projects as this."

But of course such explanations, however mild and persuasive, would usually gain nothing. The complainer would leave angry and indignant, perhaps flinging out at the end: "Yes, that's just wonderful. The federal government pays the wages and we pay the taxes. Some system. In the end we are all going to be bankrupt, I guess."

Now, the three park board members were in retail trade. If the work in the parks caused serious controversy and criticism, they could as a result lose customers in their own businesses. Naturally they were sensitive to such complaints. They understood in a general sort of way the quality and excellence of the work and the hollowness of the complaints as well. But they also were aware that it would not take very many complainers to organize a secret boycott of their businesses. And this they feared.

At approximately this same time, several persons in the town—notably a jack-of-all-trades prominent in the American Legion and a local building contractor temporarily out of work—each began to see himself as just the person to be the man in charge and to take over the work as superintendent of parks. Even in a midge dance, opportunity knocks and ambition has no limits. So these men began to talk privately to the park board members. They could do everything better, and of course they could do it faster, and besides they were natives of the town. As a result, first one of them and then the other one contrived to get a job working on the project. Now on the inside, they could twist and turn to their advantage—at least in the telling—any situation of any part of the construction and then report back to the park board. The very walls had ears.

Yet another part of the town became aware of the park project at this time. In general they were the very wealthy daughters of the old, three-generation industries. Thus Mary Hazeltine appeared one day in a chauffeur-driven Packard. Imperious, and about fifty years of age, she addressed him as royalty condescending to a new vassal in the town which was her fief: "So this is what they are talking about. Show me around and explain it. I want to know everything."[23]

So he did. At the end of thirty minutes, as the chauffeur opened the door of the car: "Imagine it. And in this town. And where in the world did you come from? Don't tell me. You can tell me later. I want you to lay out a garden at my house."

"I'm sorry. But I don't have time to do outside work."

Then, like Blanche of Castille: "Nonsense. I insist. Come at ten tomorrow morning."

A few days later the Millay sisters appeared. They were small, delicate, lighthearted in manner, and apparently about thirty-five years of age. One of them put it: "This is amazing. We had no idea. We read about it in the town paper of course. And all of stone. Like the stone houses of Tuscany. You see, we went to Italy every summer for years on end. Alice studied in Florence and

23. Mary Hazeltine was a fictitious name. Her actual name, according to Caldwell, was McDonald.

Ladies at the council ring, Eagle Point Park, Dubuque, Iowa. (Courtesy of Dubuque Park Board)

I just romped around. Could we go inside that one building? Could you show us around?"[24]

Similarly, there were other wealthy and influential people who came out to the park from time to time, and they too were impressed. Just by this fact the park board was impressed. Everyone loves millionaires and respects the opinion of millionaires, as if that opinion represented some rare and special kind of wisdom. Nothing is any nicer than being on their side. But at the same time, the approval of the rich was a little alarming. If the work was so fine, maybe it was costing a great deal more money than it should. Rolls-Royce work was certainly finer than the town could afford. Besides, had they any right to spend money just to please the rich? Chevrolet work was their limit.

One park board member stated it very clearly: "You go around trying your

---

24. Caldwell recalls making a drawing of a building for stray dogs for the Millay sisters. It was never built, but they sent Caldwell thirty-five dollars for the drawing. The Millay sisters eventually took Caldwell and his family to the train as they departed for Chicago.

best to make everything so good. We know how hard you work. I drive past your house sometimes at eleven o'clock at night and see you through the window slaving at your drawing board. But in reality you're just wasting your time with all that effort. Nobody in this town except those few people would ever know the difference between good and bad. Slop it through and get done with it. Those farmers coming out for picnics—what do they know?"[25]

He did his best to reassure them. He pointed out that nothing in the park work was expensive. On the contrary, the entire method of the construction had been initiated to save money and time. If there were no other points of excellence in the work, just the saving of expense would recommend it. So the architectural excellence had not cost anything. The very method was economy. The comparison between a Rolls-Royce and a Chevrolet is deceptive and sophistic. However, the comparison of the buildings to the stone farmhouses of Tuscany is apt and just. Those fine old Italian houses, standing there for centuries, had been built by shrewd and practical farmers—in truth, poor folk—who would not have spent the stroke of a chisel for extraneous expense. Such is the real meaning of this park work, and such is the expressive character of the architecture. In that sense the park buildings are like the American log cabin, or like the stone barns of the eighteenth-century Pennsylvania Dutch. The expression is use and economy. In a way of speaking, it is architecture without architecture.

In that way he tried to explain it, answering their doubts. But in a few weeks they were back on the same subject again. Someone in the town had talked to them again. Their old worries and doubts were in operation once again. It was evident that the situation was untenable. The park board were not bad men. They were just limited men. They were not strong enough; they were not intelligent enough. Simply said, they didn't want anything. They were right on top of something great, and they were frightened to death. They were *Spiessbürghers*, that is, mere townsmen given spears to help defend the town. When the actual enemy scaled the medieval walls, they were terrified and threw away their spears.

Apparently for some months past they had been talking it over. They had been surprised at the bitterness leveled against them, and for no other reason than that they had brought in an outsider to be superintendent of parks. They had been surprised and alarmed at how effective a few objecting persons could be in building up a boycott against their retail businesses. Naturally they concluded that the superintendent must go. However, they assured each other that a man so able and so eager in his work could easily find another job somewhere. A dirty trick, some people would call it. But it couldn't be helped. Presently even he would forget it. And probably laugh, if he happened to remember some part of it.

Meanwhile, as the governing park board, they themselves had done very

25. Caldwell says this was Charles T. Landon.

well for the town. The project had been estimated as worth half a million dollars. They had been told that an architect's fee would have come to 10 percent. That would be $50,000. As an employee of the parks, he had prepared all of the drawings, besides initiating and directing all of the construction. So he in reality had performed all the services of an architect. They had paid him $175 per month. In the two years' time the salary equaled only $4,200. So they had in that way procured for the town some $50,000 worth of architectural services for about one-twelfth their normal market value. In addition, they had the services of a park superintendent thrown in for nothing at all. The actual cost of the construction had been paid for by the federal government as a work relief project. So the whole project had cost the park board nothing at all. Whoever in the entire history of the town had ever contrived such a bargain for the public? Boycott their businesses indeed! And for such a fine and useful piece of work—why, even the vociferous detractors agreed on that point. So they rationalized.

Thus after two years it ended. They would continue the work as best they could. They would follow his plans, using the men he had trained. They would appoint a native of the town to be superintendent of parks. If that was what the town wanted, that was what they would give. So on a winter's day he visited the job for the last time. He looked at the buildings now nearly complete. He walked into the garden and out onto the stone ledges. He patted the stones with his hands. Part of his life was here. Suddenly and terribly he was alone. The next morning, with his wife and two children, he boarded the train to go back to the city he had left just two years before.

SONNETS FROM
ATLANTIS AND RETURN

Alfred Caldwell's mother, Kitty, gave him books of poetry on his birthdays, and he memorized works of many romantic and Victorian poets—Shelley, Keats, Wordsworth, Swinburne, and others. He used these poems to illustrate the problems of life, to teach, and to tell his own story. Frank Lloyd Wright told him that it is better to live a poem than to write one. Caldwell did both. His twenty-five sonnets from "Atlantis and Return" are autobiographical. They portray a tragic life, exclaim over the joys of love, criticize the devilish politics of academia, express the gloom of the nuclear night, and grieve for a wife. Caldwell wrote many poems besides these, but the sonnets are the heart of his story.

1

Dear life be good and let me worship you;
Black as the night, I say, and strewn with jewels
Is this forlorn desire that is your due.
I cannot claim how, like a king who rules
In sunlight, I do fling largesse down
In that America. I cannot claim
To give to anything by any crown,
By any marble preference, praise or name.
But lost in exile, I on midnight tours
Through all the fond and sleeping world behold

Myself as such a one that he endures
The dust of cellars—fugitive and bold—
And will not cringe, though he be done and bled,
And never more shall take his love to bed.

2

The sun that reaches to the sill of hope,
The spring that ventures to the world of men
Outlaws the legacy of chain and rope
For one, who beaten to his knees, still then
Arises on limp legs to charge the door,
To scream and foam against the hollow air.
Till like a child, exhausted on the floor,
He dreams of orchards and the summer fair.
He lives illusion out and so do I.
Intransigent, it comes to simply that.
A moment wings myself into the sky
To ride above the planetary flat.
Beleaguered on that circumambient day
I see the world and you from far away.

3

Close to the hand were you, close to the heart.
Somewhere a girl is walking on the sand,
No counterfeit of you to tell apart.
There was an idle legend in the land
That on your adolescent shoulder blades
Would sprout the wings to fly without.
Just so, forever as a rainbow fades
Is color that the sun is all about.
Not with my words were you encumbered then,
Not with my deed to do—no need of these.
Received alone beyond a mortal ken
This gift from great Apollo if you please:
Your freckled forehead and their enmity,
Your upper lip and your gentility.

4

There is no single inch I do not love;
I say there is no fairer field than you.

A wealth of wheat encircled just above
Is what you are, as suddenly and new
As if I had not seen you so before.
A valley in your pale self endlessly
You are, a pilgrimage, a distant shore
Of rain and sunlight and a golden tree.
But for your loveliness I would not care;
I would not mind to let them do their worst.
Since that is what they want, to let them fare
As best they can and I alone accurst
Live on, and in some hovel stitched with pain,
Or caked with blood and in some alley slain.

5

Grim armies meet outside your window pane;
A plunging horseman rides the night athwart,
And these marauders from afar are slain.
Your sleeping then is triumph of a sort.
Dark are the curls upon the pillow white;
Gone in a sleep are all the treacheries
A gentleness endures, come day, come night —
The want and all the little poverties.
The crazy clock that will not keep the time
Ingeniously is turned upon its side.
The broken pan, the pan that twirls, is crime
Enough endured thru all the years beside.
I ask of the high gods and a world lost:
To buy it new just how much would it cost?

6

A Frederick Barbarossa learned to bless
Both popes and antipopes in purple gowns,
That they beguilingly would acquiesce
For good of him — but Oh those Lombard towns.
Because the world is not mechanical,
Nor will it make the state and engines hum
So men obey, all men are not in thrall
To those who think they are, but only some.
Yet if it were the truth, supposing so,
Still order then is not authority
In dim Atlantis or in Sicily.

And one who cannot tell a friend from foe —
Sad commentary on a man of parts —
Can only see the horses drawn by carts.

7

Go ride a comet to the end of time,
Out on the shattered tremolo of space.
Oblivion and the planets in their prime
Address themselves to some demoniac place
Beyond the furthest reach of this aghast,
This nothingness, this galleon that implies
The stars are burning cinders of the vast,
A gesture flung across the cancelled skies.
In that omnipotent blood of man survives
The sulphurous smoke and fury of his fate.
Not for the altar that a god contrives,
Not for an anger, I, who soon or late
Expect an Armageddon or their thug,
Should knowing go to bed without a shrug.

8

Precisely back a lost precarious cause
For sake of loyalty betrayed and true,
And from that vantage all my mortal flaws
And fallacies with valor would imbue;
Alone and by a midnight vow invite
Their leprosy of envy and of fears,
A harvest of the vintage in the blight,
A paltriness of unregenerate years;
In country love embrace a slut of slums;
Have worthlessness as better than the good;
And take as penalty whatever comes
For reason simply that he said he should.
And I, who knew so well their timorous habits,
In consternation watched them run like rabbits.

9

And some have been the gayest and the best,
Whose ramparts were the citadel to die,
Whose towers were a blasphemy and jest

Hurled down on men a millimeter high.
Not less are envious they, however small;
Not less are vicious they, who are afraid.
The man was honest, diffident and tall,
Brought down to them, torn coat and bloody braid.
This one was shunted in and shunted out,
For weeks in dungeons and in steamy places;
And as the huddle and the lamplight shout
Their shame, he, dying, grinned into their faces.
Yet mediocrity is not a price,
Take all in all, to cover cowardice.

10

There is no worser thing than this: to be
As decently despised as if they were
The vermin in the wall—as if the key
To turn the tumbler meaning that they are
Could open then the door of what is not,
Close littered with dry bones and closeted
With dusty rags; and in that crumpled slot
Announce at last the living that are dead.
For cobwebbed then, and in the room of filth,
A monkey of the sick against the well
Could giggle torture's shriek and scream its illth
Across a hairy diadem of time—I tell
You this, across a shackled skeleton,
Clean wormed by flies, now whitening in the sun.

11

These vassals kneel in no medieval times.
Their flattering word of loyalty is bland
As a grail engraved with thirty dimes.
Baghdad, Damascus, and the holy land
Is this crusade against your livelihood
By tourists of a nether world. They shun
The single hazard not in crowds, nor would
They stand and fight though they be ten to one;
Nor pry with iron against a castle door
Until the stout oak shivers into splints,
To match with men at arms upon the floor.
They deal with innuendos and with hints,

Who lisp and turn and walk with waspish waist —
In easy laughter then outdone, outfaced.

12

Now are the circling eagles sore beset
Who fly alone that limbo of the brave —
I daresay out of date. Wherefore a knave
And ragamuffins guile with trap and net
Fair game in open season. I am fain
That they and only they shall then betray
To ominous death in some dissolving day
The lean and bony frame of my disdain.
I would not be the bird safe in the cage,
Nor townsman in the town, nor farm the land,
Nor shine in trifles — thus to countermand
A scorn and laughter and specific rage
That trembles on the air though I go dying,
Fluttering to the last and no more flying.

13

No village, town, or city shall unravel
This desolate unwillingly retrieved,
For I would lose the tincture of my travel
To ask when have I not in Chaos lived?
When have I not upon the street called What?
Nay I had longed to find a quiet town,
And far beyond the raucous and the rut
Live out my life in peace and lay me down.
There is no puny help against the state;
There is no door nor any sense in fleeing;
There is no guard nor any use to wait;
There is no wall nor any height in seeing;
There is no nark punctiliously to quiz —
When all the world around a prison is.

14

The mighty state is that obliquity
In man which conjures forth the anthropoid,
And sets him up in bold conspiracy
Against a hapless weak by force and fraud.

The tarnished means assure a troubled end;
Go wage a war that none may quite escape;
And guarantee that no man is a friend,
Where none are wise and good, but all are ape.
Impugned upon the fact that none are clear,
A hope as such cannot survive past this,
A history's brief kaleidoscopic year
Of shattered foes in some atomic bliss.
It is the state. It matters not the name.
Three men on dead and cratered earth the same.

15

To put away the tense and brittle spear,
For sake of blithe invasion from the mind,
And pick up failure then and all its gear
Is what I would. I know the traced and lined,
Involved and crimson courage of the brain,
A sacrament construed within the heart
To pump the dark vermilion of the vein
And take their gilded alchemy apart,
Is bound to keep a man in hurt and harm.
Yet if perchance I go, or if I stay,
Or sojourn in a hamlet far away,
Pass off myself as one not worth alarm —
Well might they fear a Trojan fear that drifts
From incommunicable bastion bearing gifts.

16

Whence came the spawn of tyranny in man?
This animal which preys upon its kind
Still knows and balances the distant span
And hurl of unseen stars across the mind.
The lion's swift and hot terrestrial lust
For antelope, now down the wind, is animal
For animal—no scarlet more—but just.
Here is the fitful thing: a cannibal
To crush the heavy skull, scoop out the brain.
A slave makes slaves in irons his bidding do,
Till they the treadmill of his fear attain.
The jailor is avidity in lieu,

Who in a craven day or two unlocks
A jackal and a hunter in the rocks.

17

This the swart of that corrupting self
The dust of man will carry to the end.
For all the saints alive or pitying elf,
The best and worst are idle to defend.
The dust will blow in great Sahara's van,
Solidify in seas to vex the earth
As rock in brief geology of man,
In hard ironic shapes of meager mirth.
Ruined, strayed, grotesque, and beaten at the start,
Naked and fit to no environment,
Forsworn he stands to live by hostile art,
Who has no home but for the thatch or tent,
A foeman farmer or a nomad slender —
A bravest coward crying "no surrender."

18

A warrior came with all his golden crew
To fall with ripping knives and savage swirls
On tumbled men with some of death to do;
On naked flesh as if it were a girl's
To plunge the eager blade up to the hilt,
For quivering awe of that ascending breath —
In one convulsive leap without a guilt
To give or take the ecstasy of death.
A captive lass would follow, cuffed and bound,
To tend the fire and lie beneath her lord;
Though once, with supple ivory to astound —
Gone and returned a moon from bed and board,
And trounced in lust—delivered up thru wiles
A fondness more than death in Stone Age smiles.

19

Dreamed I that on the winter solstice day
I lit a candle in a darkened room,
And they had taken everything away.
But dreamed it not in my enraptured gloom

How every trifling treasure would be stripped:
Ideas new minted once and bright to see,
And trays of malachite in anguish dipped,
And worthless then to anyone but me.
I walked abroad and held the taper high
Against a sun as black as midnight glows.
Then ventured forth across the stricken sky
The pulse and beat of that enormous rose.
Therefore these faded garlands that I fling
Against their malice, their poor helpless thing.

20

Is there no torch to hold against the sky
To give new life; no fable and no trance,
No magic circle that could turn and try
The fiery disk from dead? Is there no chance
That man could equal quite a savage grace,
Enough to warm a mouse in thistledown,
Or legend of the faltering sun to face,
On earth's primeval calendar of stone?
The clock of sun and time is running out.
The members of this mythos will not shine,
Nor tender throat of spring be kissed about —
Alas remembering bees in the columbine —
So dark a Stone Age that is now, and sheer
The circumstance. The shortest day is here.

21

Now falls and glistens in the heat of stars,
Now longs the winter in the flake of snow.
No evening flue is loud; no fire chars
Wet hickory logs, by morning to endow —
Black and obdurate — ashes soft as down.
No slush of spring nor hard of heart to care;
No arctic melts the glacier of the town.
Withal there is no harvest anywhere.
So white in hate the meadows and the tarns,
The moment that the sun and moon went out,
No fish could swim the ice; no hay in barns
Fragrant and Arabic; and no orange shout

And tumult of the pumpkins in the field;
No lissome celery in the loam was heeled.

22

And no lascivious summers, no rash young;
No cool caress of wheat in granaries,
No haft of pendant sweet, no rubric hung
Astronomy of apples on the trees,
No melons ripe and languorous in the sun;
No blunted pears are heavy in the hand,
No genitals of grapes—forever none
The juice and stain of that forsaken land.
So every road will rut in poverty,
And every huddled house will lurch and fall—
Dismay in avalanche of gravity
Brief candle ends upon the spinning ball.
For every life will whimper in the fate
Of this, and in the polar night of hate.

23

You are my very life my only one;
I shall not venture down this road again.
Once is enough; I want no more be done.
I do not need a mountain or a plain,
And continents in thousands passed me by.
I do not need a sea nor need a cloud,
Nor yet a promontory or a sky,
Or anything allowed or disallowed.
From all of pretext then be you undressed
For me, and smooth be you in nature's skin,
For I am glad to labour ere I rest,
And lie with you who now are closest kin.
The time at best is short. You are the life
Of me, and I have taken you to wife.

24

So I should wander thoughtless on the street,
Who once was sure and beloved by you,
Forget the stride when once I was complete,
Since what I had—forlorn—is not my due

For you have gone away I know not where,
Some place I guess where constellations end,
Where try my best I could not venture there.
Within that furthest space there is no friend
The void is what the gods forgot to own
Is where you stand serene—not hurt nor hurled.
I laugh at fire and all the molten stone,
At distant stars and all the meager world
And desperation's planetary loam.
The void where nothing is—is now my home.

25

I ran around a lonely mountainside
That led forever downward to the sea
I staggered past Saharas thirst untried.
At once the crowd of vultures turn and flee
The sudden onward haste of my traverse.
The very stars have vanished from the sky
Rain that fell is here a curse
On my forsworn and wild antipathy.
It will not vanish like the sanguine rose,
For all its scarlet, ended and undone
Enough to scatter petals on the sun
But my omnipotent love I cannot give,
As hopeless as eternity, I live.

Jens Jensen published Caldwell's first essay, "In Defense of Animals," in *Our Native Landscape*. It attacked a false assumption, in this case the relationship between animals and humankind, and set a tone for many essays to come. In "Columbus Park," published by the now defunct journal *Parks and Recreation*, Caldwell lays out the prairie school landscape philosophy he learned from Jens Jensen. He interprets this philosophy in his own work at Chicago's Lincoln Park in "The Lily Pool, Lincoln Park."

In Defense of Animals (1931)

Instead of the cross, the Albatross / About my neck was hung.
Coleridge, *The Rime of the Ancient Mariner*

The idea that man is the one exalted creature over the whole earth, and that the beasts of the fields, the fish of the sea, and the fowl of the air exist solely for his benefit is a pretty little conceit, older than the Book of Genesis, and even older than the hieroglyph. The notion is a deep and apparently permanent crease in the human brain.

In all of its ramifications, it is so illogical that good philosophers and theologians have worn themselves out trying to make it sound plausible. It is insulting to the cosmos, and yet it lacks the vitality of an insult because it is too preposterous.

I believe this assumption of superiority is unique in its stupidity—that is, none of the other animals could be that stupid. In fact, none of them are stupid at all, except domesticated ones like pigs or sheep. Not any of them play bridge, go to the movies, or chew gum, for not any are so insincere as to substitute semblances or pictures of reality for the reality itself. And not any are so lazy as to be constipated, or so filthy; and not any have halitosis, or disgusting advertisements about it. All are endowed with a fine sense of good taste and decency: they have no brothels, dance halls, pay toilets, or beauty parlors.

And there are no animals so ignorant as to play tricks on their own bodies, and so none require crutches or appendages of any sort comparable to toothbrushes or false teeth, hospitals or hair tonic. But every one is endowed with the tremendous astuteness of seeing straight and smelling straight, of tasting and touching and hearing straight. And not any, once these things are gone, make much to do of dying; for every wild beast that ever lived possessed a native and unlearned courage that would put the heroics of the Spartans to shame.

Now, while it is true that man has a cunning and highly sensitized brain, I believe its importance, as a token of superiority, is overestimated. And especially is this so since the brain prostitutes his other powers and steals away the astuteness of his five senses. The South American anteater has a cunning and highly sensitized tongue, which serves him far better than man's brain serves man; for there is no virtue in merely owning a tool whose use is neither known nor mastered.

It seems to me also that if there is such a thing as immortality of the soul, it is large enough to pertain to animals as well as to man. There is absolutely no evidence to support the belief that animals are without souls, yet the assumption that they are soulless is the reason generally presented as proof of their inferiority. It is interesting to note in this connection that there are still people who believe that savages are largely without souls, or at least so until some missionary talks one into them. This business of harping on who has a soul and who doesn't proves nothing except that he who harps the longest and the hardest is himself possessed, as in the case of the missionary, of a soul probably smaller than the ameba's. Things worth having at all are inclusive, not exclusive.

The cosmic pattern is not so simple that mankind can catalog the other creatures as to their importance to God. I believe the threads of the universe are infinitely long and the weaving infinitely fine, with colors, forms, and lives overlaid, one upon the other, in kaleidoscopic rhythms of equality.

Columbus Park (1942)

Columbus Park is located on the west boundary of Chicago. It is not only the finest of made parks, but also one of the most penetrating expressions of our age. It is the work of Jens Jensen.

The baroque parks of Versailles were an expression of a despotic culture. The clipped hedges, the strict avenues, the extravaganza of fountains, expressed the courtly despotism of Louis XIV. The distortion of living plants by clipping their growth, and the tyrannical insistence on reducing nature to the mode of a geometric artificiality, imply a will to power founded on a philosophy of cruelty blind to human dignity and rights. Such parks could be proper only to a society where the few were lords and masters and the rest mere slaves. Yet the influence of the now meaningless forms of that era lingers on even today. Culture expressions follow slowly the great social and economic changes. Columbus Park is perhaps the first completely clear park expression of the new age.

In the grand manner of Walt Whitman, this park celebrates the common citizen. It celebrates the largeness of "these states," the vast sweep of the open landscape, the thrill of space. Profound expressions are possible only by simple means. This is a simple park. Its essence is the intimate charm of the flower by the roadside. The park is an exposition on the eloquence of simples. The plan of the park is of the utmost simplicity. A large meadow is bordered by forests. This meadow symbolizes the prairies of Illinois. No trees are planted on the meadow. It is a tremendous clear floor of grass and space. Just so were the primitive prairies of the West with their fertile grass-growing black soil, too rich for trees, but a pasture for the roaming herds of buffalo.

This park interprets the spirit of the native landscape. Like the landscape, it too is an organism, and the sense of the whole is evident in all the parts. A prairie river flows through the park. The river is fed by a waterfall slipping over moss-covered limestone ledges deep in the forest. The trees and shrubs of this park are all native to Illinois. The forests are maple and oak, elm and ash. Masses of wild crabapple, hawthorn, plum, cherries, sumach, dogwood seek out into the meadow from the forest edge. Wild roses and the prairie flowers are everywhere.

The plants are used with consummate understanding of the processes of nature. The species possess the innate horticultural fitness to climate and topography. Associated together in the groups with knowing skill, they become at once the finest esthetic formation. So deftly harmonious are the foliage textures that it seems as if all the park might have been planted with just one plant. Yet within that unity there is still the rich, colorful individuality of the many species. Thus by the simplest scientific means, by the planting of those plants that will best grow, the work teaches this very highest aesthetic level.

Columbus Park is a creation, a conscious imaginative work of art, and not a duplication of nature. It is a structure created by the working of organic principles. Indeed, this deliberate creative character of the park is singularly evident throughout. The planning of Columbus Park is based on a conception of integrity—the oneness of things—and a sense of life and space. That sense of space rejects the tyranny of closure. It repudiates the sterile masonry terrain of cities today that are as prisons, spaceless and visionless. It asserts the rights of man to the wide green earth. In this park an island of forest stands free on the edge of the prairie, and the prairie flows around the back of this forest. The prairie space between the freestanding forest and the forest background is like a broad pathway to a world unseen. It possesses a mystical quality of infinite space, like the premonition of some irrational dimension. This quality of otherworldliness is a spirit and beyond definition. Columbus Park is a landscape located in the universe.

The Lily Pool, Lincoln Park (1942)

Water has cut deep into prairie soil. The clays and gravels of the Middle West are merely a tread on stone floors. In this loam, oak trees, grass, and corn take root. But in places forgotten rivers have swept away the debris of soil and cut a path through the solid stone. Outcropping ledges in the landscape, and the fern-grown canyons in the forest, now mark this ancient path of water. Today little brooks and rivers seek their way through the old valleys to drain the land of rain.

The landscape of all Chicago was once a lake formed by the melting ice of the Late Wisconsin Glacier. These dammed-up waters finally broke through the moraine ridge at the southwest extremity of the area. This surging torrent carved out the underlying strata of Niagara limestone. The present Des Plaines River, in part, follows that channel; and the stone bluffs are a veritable statement of the natural forces that created the terrain of Chicago.

Thus do the stratified ledges of the prairie embody the structural essence of the landscape. But this essence is more than scientific. The outcropping stone is architecture; strangely, deeply harmonious. Low mesas, rising from the rolling fields and pastures of the Middle West, are like cities in the landscape—incredibly beautiful horizontal formations that march with strong rhythm. The stones of the prairie are sweeter than the mountains, comprehensible and human. Of their delicate selves, a garden can be made.

The garden at Lincoln Park was planned as a sanctuary of the native landscape, a place sequestered from Megalopolis, the jungle of profound ugliness; a cool, refreshing, clear place of trees and stones and running water—an exposition, in little, of the structure of the land. It was planned as a hidden garden of the people of Megalopolis. And the very poor, naturally without hope of escape in Buicks—the disfranchised citizens of the slums—could come here.

A small elongate lagoon, made riverlike in character, flows through the garden. This river, in a sense, has cut a channel through limestone, and the ledges are intermittently revealed. A waterfall at one end is the river's source. The entire garden is planted as a forest. A stone walk winds through the forest near the water's edge. Wildflowers cover the ground each side.

The planting is designed as an integral part of the native terrain and the stones. Sumach, aspen, and crabapple cling to the ledges, anchor in the crevices.

The white blossoms of hawthorn and plum overhang the river. The waterfall springs from a bluff of white birch. In April the Juneberry blossoms are white in the white birch.

When Caldwell returned to Chicago in the middle of World War II from building military bases in Tennessee, Wisconsin, and Nebraska, he took a job in the Merchandise Mart designing training aids for the War Department. He always had a creative energy that spilled beyond his eight-to-five job, and since there were no materials or clients for nonmilitary landscapes and buildings on the home front, he continued to work on a long manuscript, "The Living Landscape," that he began during the depression but never finished. It would never be published. The selections here from "The Living Landscape," along with "The City in the Landscape," published in *Parks and Recreation*, and "Atomic Bombs and City Planning," published in the *Journal of the American Institute of Architects*, describe the failures of the centralized industrial city. Based on his belief in the value of a Jeffersonian rural landscape and the importance of a sustaining ecology, Caldwell proposes the decentralized alternative that Frank Lloyd Wright advocated in his *Broadacre City* (1934) and Ludwig Hilberseimer outlined in *The New City* (1944) and later books.

The Living Landscape (Excerpts) (1943–54)

Preface

This book is about the city and its slum and about the landscape and its use. The city is the native landscape of well over half the population of the United States. The bravest fantasy could not imagine more hideous environs. Dante's Inferno had grandeur and beauty; the dead piled at Verdun would possess a certain tragic and fragile beauty. But the city, in its truest and most intense expression, the slum, has nothing but hideousness.

There were the winter slums and the summer slums. There were the breathless Sunday afternoons in August. There were the crowds of children playing in the street, the men and women in doorways or leaning out of windows, and the idle, sheepish workmen sitting on chairs or stools in front of doors, seeming to wait in the heat for something that would never happen. There were the distant smells of the stockyards in the air, mixed of burnt hide and hair, of blood and entrails. There were the cheap, sweet doughy smells of the bakery across the tracks. There were the women wasted and formless, bloated or emaciated. And there was the drab clicking by, pitiably decked, yet with a certain drawn and wasted comliness, frizzed and antiquated.

Perennial plan, Lincoln Park Lily Pool, Chicago, Illinois, 1937. (Courtesy of Chicago Park District Special Collections)

The Lily Pool Pavilion, Lincoln Park, Chicago, Illinois, 1937. (Photo by Dennis Domer)

And in the winter there were the gray trampled snows, crusted at the edges beyond the foot tracks and dusted with soot. There were the early morning faces on the street, pale and blotched. They seemed to be abroad who had no right to be abroad, walking into the sick sun in that polluted whiteness.

Also, this book is about the land. Compared with the land, everything else is illusion. The cities are the startled thoughts of sleep.

The land of this book is like all of the land, floating on molten magma, supported on girders of granite. There is only a tread of clay, and over the clay no more than a film of soil darkened with life. There is only a space of breath, for life is the blush of time; it is an innocence dividing eternity in two.

This is the land begetting the silvery breasts of women, breeding the grass and breeding the corn. Out of the land is begotten the yolk of the song sparrows' eggs and the cool caress of the deep-piled wheat in granaries. Out of the belly of life, out of the land, is ever and ever born the curious sense and sinew of the quick—the wit of crows, the malignant and fanatic stare of goats, and the oracular snake like a tower under the fingers.

It is out of the land that the stuff of the engines comes—the iron, nickel, copper, tungsten, tin, and the bland sheen of aluminum. Out of memorial jungles that were out of the life, out of the land, are begotten the coal and the oil, the engine's unctuous hunger.

The use of the land is the use of life. Venereal and done to death is the land. Fertile and good is the land.

The brook runs fresh in the winter's thaw, out of the caves of snow, boating the oak leaves over the granite. Wet with the rain are the meadow boulders; wet and green are the lichens there, sucking the basalt, sucking the flint.

This is the land, like all of the land, of spring and sowing. It is the land of the cold gray day and the first birds—not two or three—but twenty brown winged, suddenly and out of nowhere taking over and putting an end to the mystery of the spring's exact moment. It is the land of the smell of the wet thawed earth.

It is the land of the plowing under of weeds, the refuse of things, the distillation of the winter's snow, the fragments of the stars and the dung of beasts. It is the land of the lineal furrows, rippling up to the sun the glistening underdark of the sightless soil. It is the land of the disk and the drag, and the final fields pieced and stitched with crops.

It is the land of the harvest, of the heavy cluster, and of the abundance never understood; of the secret weight of grapes touched in the dark; of the succulent sweetness of the hillside clover cut on a hot and windy day by Olympian horses with flying manes.

It is the land of the water that springeth from the rock, of the pool in the forest, and the naked swimmers exhausted and fallen to the fragrance of the rock, to the brimstone smell of ancient fire.

It is all these things. It is equally the land of abuse. It is the land that is too much land, yearning for the Chinese, for the patient tillage. It is the latifundia of Carthage and Rome. It is the sandy wastes of Babylon. It is all the sick and leprous land, the worn-out money crop land, the dust bowl land, the gully land, the strip mine land. It is the land of the cities.

When the roots of the trees have broken the asphalt, and the walls have crumbled into low heaps, into green and mossy banks of rubble, when the great turbines have returned to red and sterile knolls, in that wandering silence no man would remember. No vagrant tribe would recall dams that were fallen mountains of decayed concrete, or broken spans of suspension bridges protected from rust in the waters of rivers they once cleared in one leap.

It is life that gives meaning to what otherwise would be nothingness, like the stars without meaning as the last man dies, or the last insect falls in the moonlight, or the last blade of grass withers on a dead and cratered earth. So this book, being

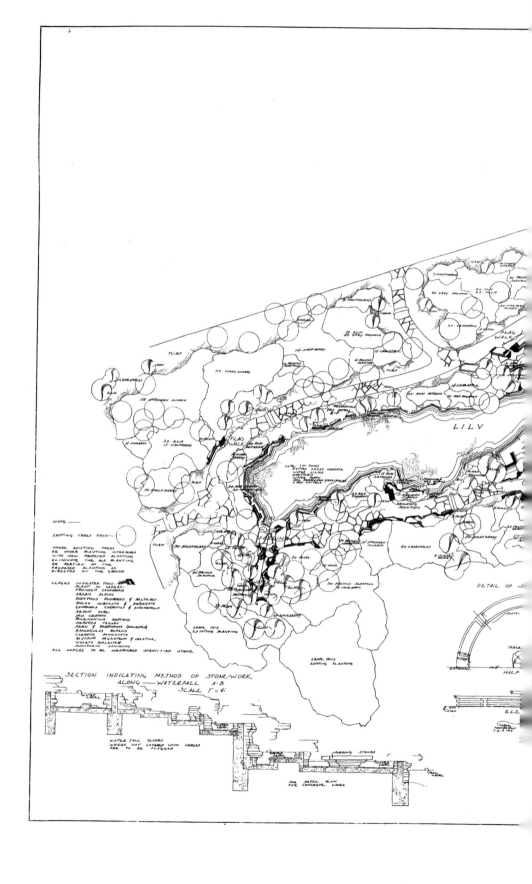

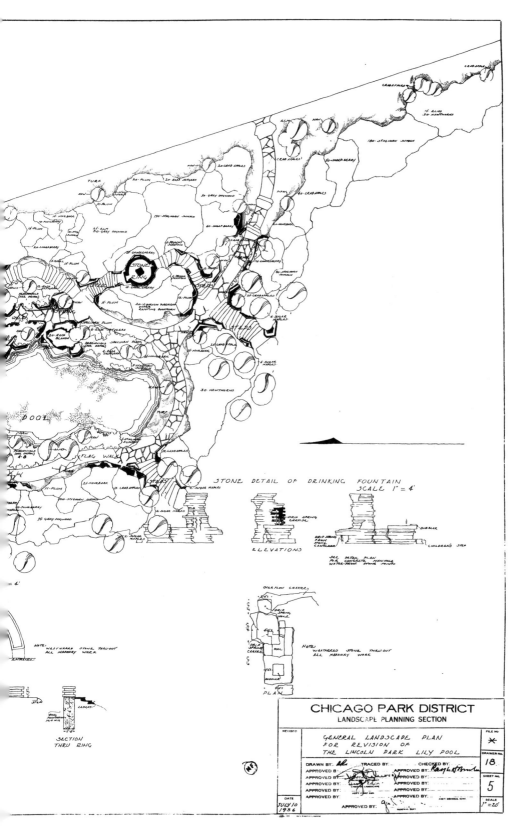

General landscape plan, Lincoln Park Lily Pool, Chicago, Illinois, 1936. (Courtesy of Chicago Park District Special Collections)

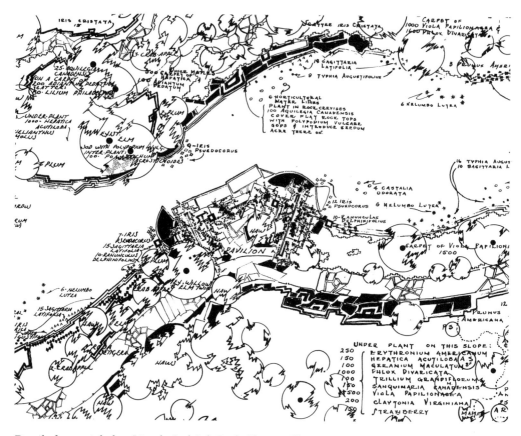

Detail of perennial plan, Lincoln Park Lily Pool, Chicago, Illinois, 1937. (Courtesy of Chicago Park District Special Collections)

about life (whatever else it may profess), is an impossible statement no apology could pardon or explain. Life is like the spring that cannot happen but happens nonetheless, like the immaculate plum blossom out of the dead black branch, or the quick, sweet fragrance of Arabia, strangely heavy as death, yet a white multitude under the sash of the cold frame, and all from a few shriveled roots set in October.

No one knows how it happens. The known things are dead things. They are become like x in an equation. Nothing can ever happen to x. It is frozen in death. Life is the other sense, the sense of the becoming to which everything happens. But x has a cause. Life has a fate. It is a proceeding like rivers dividing the night, or like ice on the point of melting. Life is a spontaneous particle independently crossing the threshold of inertia.

It has neither purpose nor moral, because it neither accomplishes nor establishes. It is a vain prodigious protest against the tyranny of the forever enduring void. It ends in the defeat which is characteristic of fated things. Hence it is the one tragedy of the universe and the Dionysian song of songs. When gigantic stars collide in space, nothing truly has happened. Result has simply followed a mathematical cause. However, the last flutter or the last breath of the last still live creature signifies a profane and willful struggle even the inscrutable gods must envy.

These pages are a discussion of the environment and the means of human life.

The Genesis of Life

Once the earth was a spinning, molten ball. Once it was part of the sun, just as the sun was once part of something else, all in some unimaginable tremolo wheeling through the black void. Once the void itself was perhaps no more than a punctuation mark in a sentence, indicating something after following something before—and the sentence no more than an indecipherable jest flung across the canceled skies.

A split second ago, say at some tick of noon, the molten ball of the earth cooled and crusted. In cooling, the rock crust wrinkled into mountain ranges. Torrential dews fell upon the parched rocks and, heated, rose as steam and fell again as torrents on the hot and misty earth. The rocks cooled and accepted seas blue as the Aegean. Tiny rivers, silver as the spittle of the spider, twisted into skeins and tumbled into cataracts, clutching at the flanks of rocks, bearing minutest fragments in the foam. Thus were formed the first sediments on the floors of the clear Aegean seas. Thus the first sandstone and limestone. These, pressed and enfolded as in a groin of basalt, formed metamorphic rocks and the marble thighs of earth.

The sun cooled, and earth vapor sparkled into snow. Films of water, insinuated through rock crevices, froze. The giant shoulders lifted and rock fragments broke and slithered down and broke again. Mountains were undone piece by piece. Crustal folding thrust up new mountains; these too were leveled. The sheer blocks of Himalayas, Alps, Andes were reduced to the size of sand grains and the microscopic grains of clay. These were carried by the rivers and laid out as beaches, bars, and floodplains.

Over this landscape nothing stirred. No seabirds, no sand peep, no salamander vexed the pure world. No hankering bees trod flowers with soft, lascivious feet. Nothing clung in terrestrial lust. Nothing was desired, nothing sated. There was no fragrance on the dead planet. Nothing moved save the wind drifting the sand of the antediluvian beach.

There was only the bulging sea licking the black roots of the mountains. Nothing lived in the sea, neither sea anemone nor moon fish. There was only the gray mud of the dim sea bottom, and no gardens, azure and lavender, waved on the bottom of the deep sea.

No marsh was bright with the green scum of algae. No moss covered the rocks of the land. There was nothing that crawled on its belly, because nothing lived. There were no insects. No beetles brightened like jewels of amethyst and malachite the gray mud or the gray rock.

No seed quickened in the mud, in the sand. Nothing brought forth, since nothing attracted nothing. There was no beast of the field to find its kind. There was no wanting of anything. There was no life.

At what time there was first life on this planet—and just how it came about—we do not know. The complex relation of substance and energy, which possesses the awful and inherent gift of self-perpetuation, of separate existence, of will, of conflict and defeat—this relation we call life—baffles explanation. In attempting explanation, the magical misrule of science is exposed as fraud. As well explain love by chemistry or death by statistics. To the physicist the plum blossom is a few milligrams of cellulose, and the eggs of the song sparrow are protoplasm. It is not cellulose or protoplasm which numbs us.

In reality we know as much concerning the genesis of life as did the Stone Age: which is precisely nothing. We only know that the earth is teeming with life. There is life under the sea; there is life on the ground and under the ground; there is life in the air.

We are bewildered by the kaleidoscopic variety of life—its forms, colors, patterns, structures: the sea fish polka dotted blue, with the last two polka dots the two eyes; the sea shells' logarithmic curves past all telling; the snake diamond-headed svelte, the pink tongue lisping air; the spider black and furry, and golden spiders, and the brown-legged matter-of-fact spiders.

We who are a part of all life formed billions of times, out of the belly, out of the ovule—the ovule that in the microscopic darkness was set upon at hard odds, breached, and entered like a lost citadel, arrogated thus to life's dominion—we who are a part of all this, part of the wild rage of life, are bewildered. We are bewildered because man is so small and trivial a part of this—one species of all the species of creation, of the roses and lizards, and the brilliant bits of life on the sea floor.

The Definition of Soil

Since the soil is so important—since if it is destroyed peoples and empires vanish—let us analyze briefly what soil is.

All life is growth: dead things do not grow: they disintegrate. Disintegration is a process of nature by which the structure of the whole is broken down into parts. The rocks of the earth's surface are continually disintegrating. The hardest granite is soluble in rain and time.

The tree falls in the forest, and bacteria and fungus feed on the dead trunk.

In a few years the wood of the tree is transformed into millions of soil particles. What was once a living structure of trunk and branches, bearing leaves and fruit, has disintegrated into the soil from which it sprang.

Yet soil is not dead. It is a world of activity, the habitat of countless bacteria in manifold species; some feed on the cellulose of dead leaves and stalks, some on animal remains; some feed on the dung of animals; some are attached symbiotically to the roots of plants, transforming nitrogen out of the air into protein available for plant use. Earthworms burrow through the soil consuming enormous quantities of organic material; their castings, containing in immediately available manurial form all necessary nutrients, are perhaps the very richest of all plant foods. Charles Darwin estimated that earthworms often deposit as much as two-tenths of an inch of new topsoil annually. Earthworms, by working down into subsoil six feet beneath the surface, continually import to the top of the soil, in their castings, minute rock particles of clay and sand. Thus, quite in addition to the manure supplied, the mineral content of the soil is continually replenished from beneath. The burrows of the earthworms aerate the soil, aiding the growth of plants and beneficial microorganisms; the burrows allow rain to enter and percolate through the soil and, by reducing runoff, prevent excessive erosion of the soil surface. Fungus is another form of life inhabiting the soil, interacting with other forms in the endless rhythm of growth and disintegration. Tiny mycelium roots thread through the soil, feeding on plant remains, breaking down the dead structure into humus content, which can then be used as food for higher plants. Fungus, in the form of a mycorrhizal association, transfers, by symbiosis, the nutrients contained in humus to the living roots of higher plants.

Life—willing itself outward from entombment in the crystalline inertness of primal rock, apparently flowering free—is yet bound within an order embracing all living things, from fungus to sunflower, from bacteria to men. Life is dependent on life; life feeds life. Generation is the fate of life; therefore life is not possible without death; growth is not possible without disintegration. The plant transforms from the disintegrated fiber of once living structure, and from the subtle juice of stones, new living fiber, miracled into life by sunlight and chlorophyll, that green stuff of the leaf.

The soil of the earth varies in thickness from a few inches or less to sometimes a foot or two. All life, both plant and animal, is entirely dependent on this thin film of soil. It is only soil which contains the life process of growth and disintegration. Subsoil does not contain the bacteria or the other agents of disintegration, simply because it does not contain the organic matter upon which they must feed. Disintegration does not take place, and plant life cannot subsist. Just as plants must derive their sustenance from the soil, so all animals, including man, must directly or indirectly derive their sustenance from plants. The life within the soil, which by disintegration produces the food for plants, is therefore the most precious of all life.

The Hilberseimer Plan

The city planner Ludwig Hilberseimer, in solutions for specific cities, has demonstrated how unnecessary the urban maladjustments really are.[1] It will clarify the issue to briefly discuss these solutions.

When we began by considering the city just by itself, a multitude of other interrelated maladjustments nonetheless soon revealed themselves. It became apparent that any valid solution of the city must be a whole solution. We must find not only a specific answer to the chaos of the city, but a general answer to the chaos of the time—of which the city is but a part. Fragmentation will not do.[2] The great value of the planning of Hilberseimer consists in that it solves, or implies the solution of, all these interrelated things.[3]

The city and the landscape are considered in fundamental relation to human needs. The planning is founded on basic principles, and its structure is built on these principles just as a building is built on its foundations. These principles are simply the needs of life,[4] and that they seem so novel today—and must now be fought for—is a measure of the chaos of our time.

In this planning there is a firm discrimination between realities arising from human needs and the pseudorealities arising only out of the chaos of our time. A certain naive quality of objectivity is necessary in order to see the problem clearly, as if for the first time, and stripped of all the too insistent irrelevancies that are merely the immaterial facts of the moment. Beneath is the real significance for the future. Hilberseimer demonstrates how, by planned decentralization, cities can be made an integral part of the broad land. The new city illustrates veritable criteria for the future and a skillful and always tolerant know-how. These proposals for the replanning of our cities lead to a new and stimulating conception of the landscape and an affirmation of man in possession of his earth. In the words of the planner: "Plan we must, not only economically, but always and primarily for the benefit of man. We should always bear in mind that at the center of all things is man—man who creates everything and for whom everything is created. Our real problem is life itself. Agriculture, industry, and transportation are important only as they contribute to the richness and fullness of life. We should plan to make this earth a better place to live. Life has cultural as well as material aims. Planning can be one of the means for their realization."[5]

1. Ludwig Hilberseimer, "The Elements of City Planning," *Armour Engineer and Alumnus*, December 1940, 4–13.

2. Ludwig Hilberseimer, review of *New Architecture and City Planning*, *College Art Journal* 6, 2 (1946): 165.

3. Albert Howard, *Agricultural Testament* (London, 1940), 180–99, is an excellent criticism of fragmentation.

4. Ludwig Hilberseimer, *The New City* (Chicago, 1944), 55–128.

5. Ibid., 166.

Hilberseimer's conception is a city in the landscape composed of units, which we may think of as the size of small towns, each surrounded by parks and by the fields and forests of the region, and all interconnected by highways and railroads. The size of the typical unit is determined by convenient walking distance, say three-quarters of a mile in length by half a mile in width. Each unit has its own industries, shops, and other working places closely adjacent. The citizen could walk to work and so be released from the tiresome and expensive back-and-forth haul morning and evening. Naturally then all street traffic would be greatly reduced. But within each unit a changed street system would still further obviate the present-day hazards and nuisances resulting from traffic.

In our existing gridiron system every house is on a thoroughfare—a highway, really—and so every block is an island surrounded foursquare by traffic. To reach schools, parks, stores, and even transportation, one must cross many death-dealing streets.[6] These solutions, however, propose a street system so planned that all the houses are on byways and none on highways. The byways are like garden lanes, tree shaded and intimate; the pavement would carry only the automobiles going to or leaving the houses on that block. These byway pavements are tributary to a large main street which would carry the traffic of all that unit. Underpasses and ramps connect the main street to the highway. The traffic could flow on unimpeded through the open landscape like a river. No thoroughfare directly crosses another thoroughfare, and so traffic lights and stop signs would of course be unnecessary. Travel would be swift, safe, and pleasant.

Large parks, within a short distance everywhere, would be reached without pedestrians' crossing a single traffic street. The schools are in parks, and the parks are all continuous and therefore form one park extending into the countryside.[7]

The typical houses planned for these communities, now released from the gridiron embrace, are quite simply oriented to the south. Every room in every house receives the winter sunlight. The building lots are now of good proportion—no longer the thin, useless slices of today, but broad and fitted to purpose. The houses now, no longer tall and squeezed, sequester sunny courts and little private gardens.[8]

A large city is composed of many of these units repeated at planned intervals over the landscape. The future city grows by adding more units. Thus growth would always be free and lateral, not tortured and centrifugal like the urban

6. *Statistical Abstract of the United States, 1941* (Washington, D.C.: Government Printing Office, 1942), 455. The number of deaths in the United States caused by automobile accidents for the decade 1930–40 totals 315,859 persons. It gives some idea of the consequence of the present-day unsafe street and highway system to compare these numbers killed with United States war dead. If we assume major wars would occur every twenty-five years, then those killed in each war would need to total over three-quarters of a million to equal automobile deaths from war to war.

7. Hilberseimer, *New City*, 104–13.

8. Ibid., 74–98.

growth of today. The idea of lateral city growth was first proposed in 1882 by the Spanish writer Soria y Mata for a ribbon settlement connecting two densely populated cities.[9] In the planning of Hilberseimer, however, the conception is broadened in application and becomes finally a flexible organic method applicable to all the diverse types of settlements. This method creates the structure of the new city, as if by a miracle. Within that structure, all the difficulties of the old city are simultaneously solved.[10]

The old industrial concentrations, surrounded by smoke-blown slums, need not persist. In these solutions factories, as they continue to decentralize in the next few decades, would be located according to a basic plan of the region. Such a plan would zone manufacturing by prevailing wind direction, so that residential areas would occupy only the geometrical sectors of land receiving the least (or no) wind from the points of manufacturing. The typical units, each with their supporting industries, would occur at intervals so computed as to avoid the windward side of the manufacturing points of neighboring communities as well as their own. The landscape space between these decentralized communities would become farms, forests, orchards, and vegetable gardens in parks. The city then would be a living thing, related to the living landscape. Within this disorganized pattern all the communities, interconnected by highways and high-speed transportation, would become one organic whole. The region would become a symphony of many parts.[11]

By the planned use of the same technical developments, which are now only degenerating the suburban region,[12] we could change negative destruction into positive creation. By planned decentralization, city and landscape could be joined. Industry and agriculture would exist side by side, each complementing and therefore enriching the yield of the other. Both worker and workshop would go back to the land. The countryside would be industrial, and the city would be agrarian.[13] Life would be simpler and freer, more secure and more satisfying.

Just as the steam age required the concentration of manufacturing in cities, so today the automobile and electricity now plainly imply its dispersal. Planning could supplant the present-day urban maelstrom with new cities in the landscape. All could possess, besides manufacturing and commerce, a sun-spun economic fabric of vegetable gardens and small farms. Such a simple alchemy could transmute leaden poverty into golden wealth, for truly we already possess the technical means. It remains but to use them rationally.

The commercial zone of today—our own vexatious and archaic downtown—

9. Arturio Soria y Mata, *La ciudad Lincal* (Madrid, 1931).

10. Hilberseimer, *New City,* 71, 72.

11. Ibid., figs. 103, 104, 105.

12. Ibid., 165.

13. Ludwig Hilberseimer, *The Regional Pattern* (Chicago, 1948).

need not continue. It would all be supplanted by a few tall office buildings placed far apart in the landscape, with department stores, markets, and larger theaters in the parks between. Both worker and shopper would be freed from filth, noise, and the hazards of insane street traffic. Transportation would be by highway and electric railroad, connected to all the communities in the landscape. The residential areas for the commercial workers would be in the midst of parks and gardens, within a short walking distance of the shops and offices.[14] Only shoppers, and the few workers who might choose to live at a distance, would require transportation. Parking, then greatly reduced, would no longer defy solution, for it could easily be provided in buildings. Utopia? No—but something rational and possible like a turbine, an airplane, an apple tree. To build such a city nothing of worth need be destroyed, nothing prematurely torn down. The useful of today could be used. The new city would simply be built; according to reasonable plan, by the gradual process that even now customarily replaces obsolescence.[15] Most of our existing buildings are short-lived at best, and few will be standing fifty years hence. So soon might the new arise complete from the obsolescent rubble heap of the old. No new billions of dollars are necessary. All that is necessary is the vision to see it and the heart to make it.

Just as machines have altered the methods of industrial production and created values impossible by past means, so too can the form of cities be altered, liberating the human, economic, and aesthetic values rightfully and properly belonging to the machine age, though still buried beneath habit and debris. The planning of Hilberseimer points the way to a new spatial freedom and the true values implicit in machine culture.

The City in the Landscape (1945)

The small area occupied by the cities of antiquity and the Middle Ages allowed little or no space for parks. The primitive means of transportation and communication always demanded extreme compactness of urban area and the ultimate density of population. Fortification walls, to resist sieges in times of war, likewise limited the size of cities and their outward growth.

Today, however, mechanical means of transportation, communication, and manufacture have made this old requirement of spatial limitation obsolete beyond question. Flight from the city—the feverish suburbanization of recent years—shows it precisely. And of course at this moment aerial warfare dramatically demonstrates the piteous military vulnerability of massive cities and their centralized industries. Plainly, the conditions for urban settlement have changed

---

14. Hilberseimer, *New City*, figs. 91, 92, 109.
15. Ibid., 158–64.

diametrically, and a new structure of city making must take the place of the old. That new structure will liberate clear space from the tyranny of closure. *The New City* by Ludwig Hilberseimer (Paul Theobald), demonstrates how cities, by planned decentralization, can be made an integral part of the broad land. This book sets forth the basic principles of city planning—veritable criteria for the future, and a skillful and always tolerant know-how. These proposals for the replanning of our cities lead us to a new and stimulating conception of parks and an affirmation of man in possession of his earth.

The typical parks of existing cities consist of relatively small isolated areas, imprisoned within the masonry mass of the city. This inadequacy is a direct result of economic and social maladjustments following the Industrial Revolution. At a time when the medieval need of urban compactness was no longer valid, due to the technical and political changes in the world, land speculation created a false scarcity of urban area and so artificially limited the extent and the availability of parkland. The great industrialization of the nineteenth century was accomplished in a period of lowering social conscience. The attitude largely repudiated civic responsibility. The need of adequate parks hardly troubled the leaders of that era. As the city grew, the little parks bound within naturally remained the same. As a result, now these parks represent a trivial proportion of total urban area. To correct this insufficiency, circumferential park sites have generally been provided on the outskirts of the city.

Still, neither the parks within the city nor those outside are adequately related to the city itself. The green open area of the interior park abuts only the brief surrounding zone. The great extent of the city remains as solid urban formation, spatially unqualified and unrelieved by the landscape. But the recent exterior park is even less a proper solution. The circumferential park type, by the very fact of its removed situation, has therefore no architectonic relationship whatever to the dense interior of the city. If the site adjoins the city at all, it is an area of minimum population density, where comparatively there is the least need of a park. Subsequent city growth might increase the surrounding density and even make such exterior parks interior, but it could not alter a wrong structural principle.

Automobile traffic has, in addition, reduced the effective usefulness of the existing parks. The hazards of crossing city streets have made all parks increasingly inaccessible. The automobile, a means to extend human powers, today actually reduces them instead. In a system of dangerous and improperly planned city streets—and therefore improper in every regard, including parks—the citizen on foot and the citizen mobilized are equally thwarted, equally imperiled.

In the new city proposed by Hilberseimer, all the residential areas are adjacent to parks, and the parks penetrate the entire city. The city is in the landscape, and the landscape is in the city. Parks within a short walking distance everywhere are reached without the pedestrian crossing a single traffic street, for the dangerous and archaic gridiron street system, so unfitted for fast-moving modern vehicles, is replaced by a rational street pattern planned for the actual needs of today. Schools are in parks. Industries too are in parks, and these industries producing smoke and fumes are located according to prevailing winds, as a protection to the health of the people—a true and simple solution to this most serious problem of industrial cities today. The old industrial concentrations, surrounded by smoke-blown slums, need not persist. Factories, as they decentralize in the next few decades, would be placed according to a basic plan of the region. This plan would zone manufacturing so that the residential areas, located always in a certain direction from the industries, would be free from windborne smoke and fumes. Still, the industries are within walking distance of the residential areas. Thus the citizen could walk to work through a park and so be released from the present-day tiresome and expensive back-and-forth haul, morning and evening in streetcars and trains, over the vast slumlands of Megalopolis.

The commercial zone of today—our own vexatious and archaic downtown—need not continue. It would all be supplanted by a few tall office buildings placed far apart in the landscape, with department stores, markets, and large theaters in the parks between. Both worker and shopper would be freed from filth, noise, and the hazards of insane street traffic. Transportation would be by highway and electric railroad, connected to all the communities in the landscape. The residential areas for the commercial worker would be in the midst of parks and gardens, within a short walking distance of the shops and offices. Only shoppers, and the few workers who might choose to live at a distance, would require transportation. Parking, then greatly reduced, would no longer defy solution, for it could easily be provided in buildings. Utopia? No, but something rational and possible, like a turbine, an airplane, an apple tree.

Parks were not so essential to the cities of ancient times because the cities were small, and the open countryside at the periphery was but a short distance from the center. But the big city of today is tremendously enlarged in scale. It is precisely the gigantic monotonous extension of pavements and buildings that makes our cities unbearable. A few scattered oases of green landscape in a vast desert are inconsequential. Within this boring, inhuman formation, the citizen is held by economic force, awaiting the first opportunity to escape. The growth of our fugitive and cottage suburbs (with their own ominous future) records the escape.

Because flight from the present large city is caused by profound human needs, nothing can permanently stay its course. The city cannot continue even as it is, for the disintegration cannot be stayed. By planning, however, it is possible to direct this destructive dispersal into creative channels and thereby provide the means for the ultimate achievement of permanent settlement, in place of the expedient and wholly fallacious suburbanization of today.

The city and the landscape must be considered in fundamental relation to human needs. It is necessary to discriminate between basic realities arising from human needs and the pseudorealities arising only out of the present urban disorganization. Indeed, a naive quality of objectivity is necessary in order to see the problem clearly, as if for the first time, and stripped of all the too insistent irrelevancies that are merely the immaterial facts of the moment. Beneath is the real significance for the future.

This book by Hilberseimer shows how parks might be. It presents a conception based upon real possibilities and the needs of today. Parks combined with orchards and vegetable gardens would enter and surround the city. Close to his house, the city man could till land and harvest the fruits of the earth. This part-time garden work would help to offset the many disadvantages of industrial and office occupations. It would bring release from indoor drudgery, and the soil and the sun would bring good health. The return in produce from these vegetable gardens in parks would give the householder a new measure of economic security—we have only to remember the unemployed and helplessly hungry of yesterday.

Play meadows, with the school adjacent, would be an integral part of these garden parks. The meadows would provide the space so necessary for sports fields and community buildings. These would be parks for both use and play. Large tracts would be planted as forests along river courses and to encompass lakes and regional places of geological and ecological significance. Such forests would be recreational areas of primitive beauty. There camping, fishing, swimming, canoeing, and sailing would be easily available to all the city.

These new parks would be productive parks, active, living, self-supporting: planned for gainful purpose and for pleasure. Because the agricultural fields and the forests of all the region would be an inherent part of the park, the landscape would be very large indeed. The great size, and the agricultural and forest use, would give this park a character infinitely finer than the merely decorative and expensive park of today. These would be parks of the natural landscape, staple as a potato.

The differentiation between city and landscape would disappear: in its place would be a vital and rational interpretation of landscape and city. The city might comprise an entire region—the entire city a park—the park the entire landscape. The city would then be a living thing related to the living landscape. Within the pattern of this disurbanized city, all the decentralized communities—all interconnected by highways and high-speed transportation—would become one organic whole. The region would become a symphony of many parts.

The steam age required the concentration of manufacturing in cities. Electricity, together with the automobile, now requires its dispersal. So planning could supplant the present-day urban maelstrom with cities in the landscape—cities for living, slum-proof, poverty-proof, and unemployment-proof. All could possess, besides manufacturing and commerce, a sun-spun economic fabric of vegetable gardens and small farms. Such a simple alchemy could transmute leaden poverty into golden wealth, for truly we already possess the technical means. It remains but to use them rationally.

By the planned use of these same technical means that are now only degenerating the suburban region, we could change negative destruction into positive creation. By planned decentralization, city and landscape could be joined. Industry and agriculture would exist side by side, each complementing, and therefore enriching, the yield of the other. Both worker and workshop would go back to the land. The countryside would be industrial, the city would be agrarian. Life would be simpler and freer, more secure and more satisfying.

Just as machines have altered the methods of industrial production and created values impossible by past means, so too can the form of cities be altered, liberating the human, economic, and aesthetic values rightfully belonging to the machine age, though still buried beneath habit and debris. The machine is now the tyrant of life only because we have failed to use its immense power to serve and enrich life. The planning of Hilberseimer points the way to a new spatial freedom and the true values implicit in machine culture.

Atomic Bombs and City Planning (1945)

Surely the single bomb dropped on Hiroshima has shaken the foundations of every city in the world. The secret of the atomic bomb will not long remain a secret, and inevitably, in the next war both sides will use it. But atomic bombs and concentrated cities cannot both exist in the same world. Something terrible and new has been added, and cities must be changed. From today on our city, and every large city, can be completely destroyed in a moment.

Perhaps we may like our city just as it is. We may even like the slums. We may talk bravely about rebuilding the blighted area—and of course there are some very interesting arguments to show that all this could be done on a "sound basis." Unfortunately, however, you cannot argue with an atomic bomb. One day it just drops out of the sky. Maybe it leaves a big hole in the earth where the city used to be. Or maybe it simply burns everything up and melts the streetcar tracks. Or maybe it only knocks down the buildings. But most important, it kills all the people for miles around. Indeed, there is nothing more incongruous than atomic bombs and babies. It would be a city without people, however much rubble and real estate.

Throughout history—even as now—cities have always been the chief military objectives in war, for cities have always been the seats of government and the centers of manufacture, trade, and storage. In olden times cities were surrounded by fortification walls for defense. Cannons, developed in the fourteenth century, could easily batter down the walls, and so finally—by necessity—these closed and independent cities became open cities, mere parts of a large nation dependent for defense on a standing army.

Just so aerial warfare (like the cannon) makes the city no longer feasible. A few brief months ago Berlin was demolished by means we must soon consider needlessly laborious and primitive. Plainly the city, once a place of refuge in time of war, has now become the very place of greatest danger. Naturally, we must do something. To be sure, we can do our best to keep the peace. Still, if war comes there is one defense and probably only one. During the years of peace we could disperse our cities and decentralize our industries. Then the city would be agrarian and the countryside would be industrial. The city would be everywhere and yet nowhere. The enemy would have practically nothing to attack. In our time weapons of offense have developed far beyond those of defense. Consequently an aggressor is always encouraged by the prospect of quick and easy success.

Wholly aside from the military need, to disperse and ruralize our city would be truly no loss, but in reality a positive gain. Through the years, our city has become unlivable. The smoke- and fume-poisoned air, the dangerous streets, the helplessly congested traffic morning and evening, the crowded and sunless tenements, and the infinite and monotonous extension of pavements and buildings—these things are surely no boon. In a sense we have really repudiated the city. One-third of our population has already moved to suburbs. Obviously we would want to change our city even if airplanes and bombs had never been heard of. People move to the suburbs—if they can afford it—in order to live in a country community, away from the city. So unlivable has the city become that they are willing to travel an hour or two a day just to get away from it. However, in the new rural city, thoughtfully and properly planned, of course, everyone could live in the country. Slum clearance, then, would mean not perpetuating the slums by building new buildings on top of the old, in the dirtiest and smokiest section of the city; rather, it would mean that every family would have the chance to live in an adequate house, with gardens and parks adjoining. This would be a city of incredible fresh air and sunlight.

We may object that there are many problems, and it wouldn't be easy. But of course there are problems. Still, it would be very strange if a civilization cunning enough to split the atom and realize the primal energy of the universe must somehow confess itself unable to provide the simplest need of mankind; a simple house in a safe place. If we lack the wisdom to provide for our own safety in the immediate tomorrow by performing the relatively easy task of replanning our cities, how little likely it is that we can cope with the much more difficult planning problems of world security. Then perhaps, after all, we are men on a doomed planet, and destruction is our domicile at last.

By the mid-1950s Alfred Caldwell had been a professor for a decade in the
architecture school at Illinois Institute of Technology under the direction of
Ludwig Mies van der Rohe. He taught construction—an architectural design studio with an emphasis on structure—to sophomores and juniors, and
also architectural history. Caldwell made a strong impression on students,
who remember him as a riveting lecturer. The essays that follow all come out
of lectures in the classroom. Alfred Caldwell still gives the lecture "Louis
Sullivan," published in 1956 by *Dimension* at the University of Michigan, as
well as "Jens Jensen: The Prairie Spirit," published in 1961 in *Landscape
Architecture*. The *Structurist*, edited by Eli Bornstein at the University of
Saskatchewan, has published all of Caldwell's remaining essays, including
the six included here. Although Alfred Caldwell has been a landscape architect, an architect, and a civil engineer, he is above all else a teacher.

Louis Sullivan (1956)

Louis Sullivan was defeated in his life and work, and he knew it, yet he
never gave an inch. He made a war, in which he was slain.

The acceptance of Sullivan today raises the question whether the war is
forgotten and all is forgiven, or whether the war was won posthumously, or
whether his fame now is simply part of the idiocy of time, touching—as in a
trance—one man by the sleeve, out of a multitude.

Sullivan's architecture was based upon a philosophy, which he expressed in
eloquent dithyrambs. Nearly all of his voluminous writings are treatises on this
philosophy. Its center of gravity lies somewhere between Jean Jacques Rousseau,
Walt Whitman, and Friedrich Nietzsche. The rolling and expansive prose demonstrates the following propositions:

Man is by nature good. Man is creator. Democracy is the natural life of man as
creator. The beneficent idea of democracy is opposed by the archaic and oppres-
sive idea of feudalism. Feudalism is in control of the law, of government, of
education, of the marketplace. Yet feudalism, in one form or another, has always
controlled the world: the world has never known a decent social fabric. The
consequence of feudalism is slavery. The consequence of democracy would be
freedom. By means of this freedom, man at last would have the chance to develop,
to expand, to differentiate, and thus actually to become the individual. The
individual, free of fear, and able to govern himself, would be an individual
sovereign, an individual god. Architecture would be the expression of this democracy of the individual, the expression of the creative power of man, aware of the
"infinite creative spirit" of the universe. In this architecture things would be as they
seemed to be: they would be sane, reasonable, honest. Deceit is diametrically
opposed to the idea of democracy. If architecture is honest (and things are as they
seem to be), form follows function. Indeed this is a principle of all living things.

Yet Sullivan's hopes came to nothing. America was turning in the opposite direction. Sullivan wrote, concerning the Roman classic style foisted on the World's Columbian Exposition in Chicago in 1893:

> These crowds were astonished. They beheld what was for them an amazing revelation of the architectural art, of which previously they in comparison had known nothing. . . .Thus they departed joyously, carriers of contagion, unaware that what they beheld and believed to be the truth was to prove, in historic fact, an appalling calamity. For what they saw was not at all what they believed they saw, but an imposition of the spurious upon their eyesight, a naked exhibitionism of charlatanry in the higher feudal and domineering, culture, enjoined with expert salesmanship of the materials of decay. . . .Thus did the virus of a culture, snobbish and alien to the land, perform its work of disintegration; and thus even works the pallid academic mind, denying the real, exalting the fictitious and the false, incapable of adjusting itself to the flow of living things . . . that turns its back upon man because that is its tradition; a culture lost in ghostly misalliance with abstractions, when what the world needs is courage, common sense and human sympathy, and a moral standard that is plain, valid and livable.

Since Sullivan's death in 1924, the world has experienced feudal despotisms more grinding than any Sullivan, in his worst moments, could have imagined. The concentration camps of the Nazis and the Soviets, the annihilation bombings of World War II, culminating in Hiroshima and Nagasaki, have made any former estimate of world morality and sanity very high indeed. In nearly every nation former individual freedoms have been restricted or entirely abolished. The restriction of traditional freedom of thought in America is now a commonplace, and classified as a national necessity. Plainly, the acceptance of Sullivan today cannot be because his philosophy, even in the least part, has been adopted or is about to be adopted. The mere mention is drollery.

Neither is the Sullivan architecture adopted. That is as much a lost cause as the philosophy. Over a clear and rational building frame Sullivan cast a poignant and fragile shell of symbolic ornament. The exuberant traceries, delicate as the Moors', symbolized the unfolding process of life, from the embryonic seed, through rhythmic differentiation, to fulfillment. In low relief, scarcely a fraction of an inch beyond the surface plane, the repeated imagery asserted, like the alliterative cantos of some ancient scripture, the song of life.

The steel skeleton has been developed to eliminate the use of bearing wall construction, an impractical means for tall buildings due to the excessive thickness of the walls. Henceforth the building could be sheathed in glass from column to column, as in the Carson, Pirie, Scott store. Beginning with the Wainwright Building in St. Louis (1890–91), Sullivan had first made the skyscraper one thing from the bottom to the top, and the architecture soared. The building at last became itself, integral and entire. The height, the new thing about the skyscraper, was to Sullivan the opportunity of architecture. To the other architects of the time it was an embarrassment, which could be resolved only by piling up a series of classical replicas, one upon the other, in layers like a masonry cake.

The mercantile establishments for whom the buildings were built were considered by Sullivan as a necessary part of society. Hence the buildings were works of interpretation and sublimation, and hence the expression in ornament.

In contrast, the classical architects, with their imported and bogus architecture, in reality were grossly insulting and patronizing the institutions they represented themselves as serving. The steel skeleton's marvelous flexibility only lent itself to the most astounding abuse. This treasure-house of light and space was weighted down with the stone quarries of the earth. Under the big buildings, under the caissons, ninety feet down, bedrock groaned. For the sake of "architecture," so called, massive mimicries of bearing wall and antique colonnade were hoisted up upon this superb and patient frame, twenty and thirty stores overhead. Thus resulted not a positive architecture, but a ludicrously negative one. This is the formless form, the faceless face, the mask of Main Street — or almost any street anywhere.

This is the wilderness in which the few Sullivan buildings are to be seen today. There were exceptions, such as the technological work of Jenney and the Chicago school. There is the Monadnock Block, John Root's great work of the nineties — its steep flank with the sharply pierced windows making a looming diagram, as symbolic of today as the guildhall of Hildesheim was of the Middle Ages.

But with all, the Sullivan buildings stand out as distinct as if they belonged to another civilization, which in reality they do. They seem to show what life could be. Architecture was religion to Sullivan. It was not a business, and not even an art, except in the ancient and primitive sense of artist as priest — an avocation which was already old in the Stone Age. Dilettantes would have rough going with Sullivan. Children, or normal and healthy common people, would understand the Sullivan architecture much better than the sophisticated, whose misfortune generally is not to be sophisticated enough.

Many still living remember distinctly the fascination of the golden door of Sullivan's Transportation Building at the World's Columbian Exposition. The crowds knew they were supposed to admire the Roman classic grandeur of the Court of Honor as architecture and culture. Secretly a multitude preferred the one dissenting building, which spoke to everyone in the sign language of architecture, becoming to the sensitive an emotional experience. In just that sense art is always primitive until it is talked to death. The small-town banks, in the making of which Sullivan eked out his last years, stand on the awkward village streets like sumptuous strongboxes, perfect in function as banks, looking like banks, admired as banks—and by people who had never thought about architecture before in their lives. The three tombs Sullivan built seem like small personal temples blessing life.

Louis Sullivan is as unknown now as ever. His fate was the stigma of his time. What he said and did still has little meaning. The fact may not flatter, yet the triumph of understanding is the augury of action. His meaning can only be the meaning of a future. Like Whitman, he was poet of a democracy not yet born. Like Nietzsche, he conceived of man as an infinite possibility, of man the creator surpassing the creature man. He was fire bringer and a going beyond. The tall graven buildings show that once there were giants on the earth.

Jens Jensen: The Prairie Spirit (1961)

Jens Jensen, Danish-born landscape architect, became a legend within his own lifetime. The personality of the artist and the force of his beliefs are known to a multitude who have scarcely any knowledge of his actual work. The earliest work, in the West Parks of Chicago, dates back before the turn of the century. The healthy beauty of these parks, powerful in form, still lifts itself above the sordid mediocrity of the surrounding city.

These once splendid parks have suffered greatly at the hands of politicians and all manner and conditions of men. Yet the very moment one enters the area one draws deeper breath. It is not simply the air of nature, the cool, green oasis in the desert city. These parks are works of art; the landscape is the carrier of an idea. Symbol, gesture are primal language to express what Jensen knew as the prairie spirit.

The analysis of the forms—the extended meadow, the water in the landscape, the billowing forest masses—will never lead to an understanding of the work. Form is nothing by itself. Form is merely the vessel of existence. Only that which has no existence is formless. It was the existence which was the concern of the artist: the form resulted. The final reality is not the thing itself—the form— but the idea, the existence from which it emanates. Jensen called this idea in his work the prairie spirit.

As an immigrant to America, trained in Danish and German gardens, Jensen first planted foreign plants in the parks. He discovered that they were, in this different landscape, expressionless, decorative; they were nothing: formless. Little by little he began planting, instead, the hawthorn, wild plum, sumach, crabapple, chokecherry, which were native to the prairies of Illinois. Then something opened on the mystery of existence.

The parks and gardens of the baroque were expressions of political power. Clipped hedges, strict avenues, the extravaganza of fountains, expressed the courtly despotism of Louis XIV. The power of all France was centered in one king. His palace was centered on the perspective of the avenues. The distortion of living plants by clipping their growth and the insistence on reducing nature to the mode of a geometric artificiality have their precise parallel in the facade of baroque architecture, where truth is distorted behind a mask of entablatures and pilasters and architecture is reduced from structural significance to decorative surface.

The park of the eighteenth and nineteenth centuries was the expression of romanticism. The simulated ruin of castle or temple in the landscape was a direct emotional appeal to the past. Rousseau had discovered the noble savage (as Tacitus had once discovered the noble Germans); the nineteenth century discovered the noble Greek, the noble knight. Archaeological findings in Greece and Pompeii, the writings of Ruskin on Gothic building, stimulated the thought of the time. The romantic park, in its appeal to the past and its vague idealizations, was parallel to the architecture of both classicism and medievalism.

The Power of Nature, Not of Man

The parks of Jensen are diametrically opposed to the baroque; nature determines and not style — nature is style. The plant and the landscape have their own expressions. The expressions are not foisted on — they are out of. The power of Jensen's park is the power of nature — not man's despotic power.

In principle, Jensen's parks are also opposed to the romantic park of the eighteenth and nineteenth centuries. The romantic park, like the baroque, was a style too. It was concerned with the simulation of nature and the provoking of mood, melancholy, or ideal. The raptures of Prince Puckler on seeing the ruins of Tintern Abbey — Wordsworth's Tintern Abbey — would scarcely be felt by Jensen, who in another age was concerned with living nature, not with the patina of the dead past.

Such differences become very clear in Columbus Park in Chicago, which is the finest and most complete of all the Jensen parks. The plan of this park is of the utmost simplicity, for profoundest expressions are possible only by simple means. The park is an exposition on the eloquence of simplicity. A large meadow is bordered by forests. This meadow symbolizes the prairies of Illinois. No trees are planted on the meadow. It is a tremendous clear floor of grass and space. Just so were the primitive prairies of the West, with their fertile grass growing in black soil, too rich for trees, but a pasture for the roaming herds of buffalo.

Limestone Ledges, Deep in the Forest

This park interprets the spirit of the native landscape. Like the landscape, it too is an organism, and the sense of the whole is evident in all the parts. A prairie river flows through the park. The river is fed by a waterfall slipping over moss-covered limestone ledges deep in the forest. The trees and shrubs of this park are all native to Illinois. The forests are maple and oak, elm and ash. Masses of wild crabapple, hawthorn, plum, cherry, sumach, dogwood push out into the meadow from the forest edge. Wild roses and the prairie flowers are everywhere.

The plants are used with consummate understanding of the processes of nature. The species possess the innate horticultural fitness to climate and topography. When associated into the proper groups, they become at once the finest expressive formation. So harmonious are the foliage textures that it seems as if all the park might have been planted with just one plant. Yet within that unity, there is still the rich, colorful individuality of the many species. Thus by the simplest scientific means, by the planting of those plants that will best grow, the work reaches this very highest level.

Columbus Park is a creation, a conscious imaginative work of art, and not a duplication of nature. It is a structure created by the working of organic principles. Indeed, this deliberate creative character is evident throughout. Columbus Park is based on an idea of life and space. That sense of space rejects the tyranny of closure. It repudiates the sterile masonry terrain of cities today that are as prisons, spaceless and visionless. It asserts the rights of man to the wide green earth. In this park an island of forest stands free on the edge of the prairie, and the prairie flows around and back of this forest. The prairie space between the freestanding forest and the forest background is like a broad pathway to a world unseen. It possesses a mystical quality of infinite space, like the premonition of some irrational dimension. This quality of otherworldliness is a spirit and beyond definition. Columbus Park is a landscape located in the universe.

From Public Parks to Private Estates

Jensen, due to continual and disheartening political pressure, left the West Parks at the completion of Columbus Park. Henceforth his work was to be almost exclusively the country places of the wealthy. These private places planned by Jensen gave a dignity to wealth that all the show and pretense of Philistia—the formal gardens and the copied clutter from abroad—could only make abortive and ridiculous.

There was no straining for effect, no tricks, nothing supercolossal—everything modest, normal, simple—hence the greatest possible dignity. One feels, on seeing one of these old places, that the owner should be some generous and noble democrat, the American ideal, some Jeffersonian person. A road curves from the highway, entering into a forest, emerging into the sunlight of a meadow, with the great house in the distance under groups of large trees. Aside from a garden for flowers, there is nothing more; there is only the beauty of the native landscape.

To Jensen, as to the ancient Greeks, there was an essence or being proper to a spring, a hill, a meadow, a ledge of rocks. The art is not to impress but to make this being clear, to make the landscape speak.

The Edsel Ford place on Lake St. Clair expresses the essence of a lowland landscape. The Julius Rosenwald place was land cut through with forest-covered ravines. Each place was planned to reveal the inner meaning of the landscape. When the landscape became itself, it became more than the landscape because it then revealed what had once been obscure.

At the Alexander place, Spring Station, near Lexington, Kentucky, there existed some springs. With this water, Jensen made a waterfall to supply the swimming pools in the garden, using the native limestone ledges. It is no more copying nature than is a landscape painting of the Sung dynasty. The Sung painters did not paint a mountain, but the symbolic essence of a mountain. These giants of imagination were creating not mountains, but peaks of enlightenment. The figures which occur in the paintings are not men; they are man in nature.

This waterfall, which is the idea of a waterfall—not the mere simulation of waterfall—exists in a region which is touched by no railroad line. To deny the existence of this region is to deny the existence of art. This region we may identify as the world of ideas, explained by Plato in the parable of the cave. What men consider to be the real world is in reality an illusion, where things are but the shadows of ideas thrown upon the screen of experience. The artist is one who is able to pass through thin air into the world of ideas. In the words of William Blake, he sees "not with, but through the eyes."

A Meadow Path to the Setting Sun

The Becker place at Highland Park, Illinois, is dominated by a long meadow, slanting westward, tapering indistinctly into the forest: a path to the setting sun. Works of art cannot be photographed. What is always missed is the very thing which is important—significance, emanation of idea. It is like explaining a poem. What is there to explain? Poetry is sign language. It is the expression of the inexpressible; it says by not saying. If it could be explained it would not be inexpressible; therefore it would not be poetry. Imagery, symbol, allusion, cadence are not themselves poetry; and no poem is all poetry, since only a part of anything is inexpressible. It is just this part, however, which is poetry. We understand very well the geometry of a plum blossom, or that the eggs of the song sparrow are protoplasm; it is not geometry or protoplasm which numbs us.

Just as these places by Jensen expressed the spirit of the landscape, so too they expressed human qualities. The Harley Clarke place, in Evanston, Illinois: friendliness. There is never anything arrogant in Jensen's work. The Clarke house which, due to its size, might so easily have seemed alien and overbearing in the landscape, becomes, under the large trees planted, a part of the landscape. The meadow, on the pretentious and showy racetrack of Sheridan Road, becomes pastoral, secluded. The public is not asked to be impressed by the wealth of the owner. Because there is no straining for effect, there is the greatest repose. One waits at ease and expects only perfect beings.

A Job for Durga and Shiva (1967)

1

Almost any observer must come to the conclusion that the old world is disintegrating or has already disintegrated. Of course what lies about us everywhere is a ruin that we do not truly see, because we have always seen it. It is a ruin of defaced and broken stones, with graven images of bankrupt gods overturned upon a marble stair. There is a door ajar in an ancient alley, and someone passes fugitive and anonymous. Nay, it is a Paleolithic kitchen midden, a junkyard of used parts like the automobile dumps, both fact and symbol.

However, almost any street scene in the commercial section of a modern city shows us the extent of disintegration. What meets the eye is filth, ugliness, a jangling disharmony, the brutality of the architecture and, despite the hurrying crowds of people, a general and pervading air of utter desolation. Not all the shine of new buildings can dispel it. The old, covered with the ambiguous grime of cities, and the new, gaudy and self-assertive, somehow turn out the same. Through all the raucous cacophony of street noise there is something deserted, ominous, and silent in the glass canyons.

In the old buildings of fifty years ago, the steel construction's marvelous flexibility only lent itself to the most astounding abuse. This treasure-house of light and space was weighted down with the stone quarries of the earth. Under the big buildings, under the caissons ninety feet down, bedrock groaned. For the sake of "architecture," so called, massive mimicries of bearing wall and antique colonnade were hoisted up upon this superb and patient frame, twenty and thirty stories overhead. Thus resulted not a positive architecture but a ludicrously negative one. This is the formless form, the faceless face, the mask of Main Street, or almost any street everywhere.

In the new buildings, the very same steel construction now results in an equal, although dissimilar, abuse. The glass curtain wall costs less to build than the classical colonnade. That is the real difference. The building itself is a pathological straining for effect. And interesting shapes are the doctor's order for the day. Every building is meant to set a new fashion and outdo the others. What results, an assault upon the optic nerve, is a crass and repellent vulgarity, as it were, a love of ugliness for its own sake, a thing unique within the history of the human race on this planet. It is a parade of fashions, if such they are to be called. But far and beyond that, it is a dampening meningitis of the brain, a palsy of the heart. Architecture is the document of society—But what of the society?

It is now largely a society of mechanical men. These are the days that have happened. The old rough abundance of the earth is gone. Fields of ripening grain, orchard, vineyard, meadow, forest are apocalypse and scenery in a world impoverished and contrived. Depleted modern man, like Fabre's insects, now treads with machinelike and mindless ritual the cogs and trackways of instinctual behavior. The advertising writer knows what gears are meshed, what wheels are turned, and by what. He plays man into the computer on the chart waves of response. The proverbial greed, fear, and sex are fed into the machine, and predetermined man comes out like a punched card: a prodigious consumer of food and goods, a monstrous plutonian appetite from the lower depths. It is, as everyone knows, a mass-produced identical man, plugged in at identical super-markets, triggered for identical alarms and aversions, and snapped on at a mo-ment's notice by identical prurience. Literature becomes pornography and, it is said, cannot be sold without it.

Quite apparently the former values of Western civilization are being beaten to death. The metaphor is an exact one. Crime and street gangs—considered uncontrollable—are on the increase, as they were in Rome of the imperium. The streets of the cities are no longer safe after dark, and many not even in daylight. Central Park in New York is a no-man's-land of rape, murder, and robbery. The unhappy of Watts, although given a dole and a winning baseball team, proceeded to take Los Angeles apart, as Rome at the last was taken apart, stone by stone.

Add to this the fact that the American cities are otherwise unlivable. Amer-ica less than two centuries ago was a new continent, a new hope for mankind. Now the cities are a lost world of ghettos and slums, a million miles from Mr. Jefferson. The very air, burdened with its industrial sewage, is unfit to breathe. On particularly bad smog days inhabitants of New York are advised to stay in their houses. Chicago and Los Angeles, and many another city, are scarcely better. The automobile on the city's hysterical streets, and equally hysterical highways, adds to the smog and runs over the inhabitants, killing more people than are killed for the nation in wars. No one seems to care very much—an aimless lethargy under chaos—or the vitality of the civilization is not strong enough to deal with the problem. A civilization, planning to land a man on the moon, cannot land a man on a safe and livable city. Such evidence, here merely listed at random, could be extended almost indefinitely to indicate that something is happening, or has happened, to the society.

Nevertheless there are those who still are optimistic and point out that this something is simply a change or natural mutation of society and not ruinous at all.

Others, however, see a grand finality, a twilight of the gods. The greatest of these was Oswald Spengler. His *Der Untergang des Abendlandes—The Decline of the West*—leaves little doubt that the thousand-year cycle of Western civilization (Spengler uses the word culture), like equivalent historical sequences before, is nearing the end of its journey work and will be extinguished in darkness. Still others accept the ruin as a fact but repudiate the finality. Frank Lloyd Wright said in conversation in 1932: "Spengler?—The old Europe is only a compost to enrich the new world; America will go on." The ill-starred Hart Crane, following the same Whitman tradition, but with tragic frailty, saw America as a bridge to the future and the beginning of a new world: "Dance us back to the tribal morn." In addition, there are those who say that since nothing apparently can change the fact—whatever that fact may be—it really doesn't matter: only we ourselves matter, and whatever we are we are.

All of the foregoing raises at once the question of human existence and all human aspiration, and any answer is at best a hard chance. The old gift of assurance is gone. For instance, science is a vast lore, but it has created more new areas of doubt than areas of solution. The bomb is a case in point; and there is many another, such as reported United States Defense Department explorations to destroy the climate of an enemy country, or to scorch a hemisphere, or to spray human disease from the air, like an enormous Flit gun for vermin, or perhaps to crack the planet like an egg—and all in the name of science.

As specialization, science—or its counterfeit—knows more and more about less and less until, as Patrick Geddes put it, eventually it will know everything about nothing. Albert Einstein asserted that this period is characterized by perfection of tools and confusion of aims.

Certainly no man knows the future, and few know the present. The god of knowing is not locked in the temple with someone having the key. In our uncertainty, there may not be the god: there may not be the temple, let alone the lock and key. It was once thought that everything was known. Aristotle was right and known, and then Newton was right and known. Now—and speaking in unforgivable generality—science knows that virtually nothing is known—we may say irretrievably known—and that is the knowledge. But from such a brave and arrogant encounter with the god of knowing, for the godlike skepsis of existence that only gods have known, man has not gone unscathed. Not sleeping when he sleeps, but waking when he wakes, is the plundered gift of unregenerate doubt that lies upon the troubled world. William Blake said:

> The Bat that flits at close of Eve
> Has left the Brain that won't believe.
> He who replies to words of Doubt
> Doth put the Light of Knowledge out.

If the Sun & Moon should doubt
They'd immediately Go out.

If nothing is known nothing is believed, and nothing is wrong since nothing is right. This is the permissive age, and anything goes. Thus Hitler's technique of the big lie suddenly demonstrated the wide open space for lying. Therefore it is now easy to lie, and the world is much improved, freed of yet another impediment. So fraud and deception, from governments to individuals, once at least relatively rare in occurrence and always a stigma, are now a commonplace, accepted and expected. The last question anyone would ask about nearly any issue under debate nowadays would be its honesty. The important question is the pressure group behind the issue, or the public relations method of presentation—that is, the method of public persuasion through illusion, guile, and deception. As we see on every hand, bazazz—putting it over—is a holy grail. Honor is a foolish word. Everyone laughs. The person who uses the word is assumed to be—and generally with justification—a hollow fellow, a fool, or a charlatan. At length, and carried to conclusion through some such procedures as these, all that will be left will be bare life itself. In that harsh and primitive moment man will have come to the final rampart.

2

Once the earth was a tiny star fragment clocking out its million timeless years around the hurtling sun, and the sun itself a gesture flung across the canceled skies. The spinning ball in space cooled and thrust up Himalayas and at last accepted seas blue as the Aegean. On that antediluvian beach no life stirred. The roots of the mountains grappled the basalt crust of the earth, the rocks aged, the black flanks crumbled, a thousand stars collided, but nothing happened because time was not born. It was neither yesterday, tomorrow, nor a billion years ago.

Time is the endurance of life. Only that lens finds time. Time is the duration of a midge dance. Time is the distance of life. Past time is time become what we call history. Present time is time becoming—time as act: the process of living, or as we say, activity.

The community of mankind experiences time both as activity and as history and hence possesses a life both as fate and as death. This time and life of the community of mankind is civilization. It is what surrounds human life on this planet. It is the structure of society. It is what man cannot escape from, though he fain would have it otherwise.

We may say that civilization is the stage upon which the human drama is played. Just because the individual life is important, it is important to understand the civilization. That understanding is both the wisdom and the valor of personal life. Yet civilization offers no Utopias right around the corner, and nothing is going to happen to make a coward's paradise secure. Civilization cannot be designed. It operates on its own laws, and nothing will finally turn them aside. Long ago Euripides said:

> And the things men look for cometh not,
> And a path there was where no man thought;
> So hath it fallen here.

All life is turned toward the light. "More light," said the dying Goethe. Light dominates being. We say we see when we mean we understand. In this light world man alone stands upright. It is a tactic for seeing afar. What the eye sees in the lonely landscape is the world. The extent of the world is space. The how far is the journey of the soul. Thus the sense of space is a synopsis of the mystery of existence. It is the distinguishing quality of a people, of a civilization. The sense of space of ancient Egypt was diametrically different from that of ancient Greece, as both were different from Byzantium, and all were different from that medieval space of the Gothic cathedral, with its great window, a painting hung in space—jewels dissolved in light—or the later Gothic-like Rembrandt paintings, with their dark and brooding backgrounds, out of which miraculously the figures stand forth, lit up out of the infinite depth. As another world, the eyes of Egyptian portrait sculpture, with strange and noble fixity of expression, stare straight ahead—straight toward the tomb, straight toward the Osiris-resurrected life hereafter—in the one-directional aisle of space between life and death.

Space is expressed in an inner and terribly specific awareness. This awareness is that which gives meaning to existence, which colors the merely physical phenomena, such as birth, life, death, in its own hues so specific that all others in final analysis must be alien, barbarian. This awareness is not transferable from one age to another. We cannot feel the compelling force that raised the circle of Stonehenge; neither can we feel the faith that built the cathedrals of the twelfth century. Their true awareness is some distant and un-traversable shore. The world—whatever that may be—that is ours is now. Only in daydreams, or in the nostalgia of defeat, can one ever go back. The attempt is futility of both individuals and civilizations, for life is bound by inexorable time, and time only goes on.

The Greco-Roman world is of course an excellent illustration. Nothing could bring that civilization back again or allow it to continue. By the third century A.D. the Roman Empire had exhausted itself. There was less and less to believe in, less and less to live for. What was left was a spiritual vacuum, without impulse, without force. We can see this very clearly in the rise of Mithraism, the Isis and Horus cult, and at last Christianity with its surging intensity, all of which came in from the East to fill the void produced by the drying up of the fountain of the classic.

Rome fell from sheer boredom. To the rich, the empire was a gorgeous, pretentious, and yawning emptiness. To the middling sort of people, and especially to the farmers ridden by debt and victimized by jumpy markets, it was a system frustrating and restrictive, so rigged by the power clique that it was impossible to feel either loyalty or interest. When the barbarians arrived it hardly mattered.

We know that a vast proportion of the population of the Roman Empire consisted of slaves. We know that the greater part of those who were not slaves were little better than slaves. They were penniless proletarians, like the ghetto Negroes, the Mexican braceros, or the Puerto Ricans, all on the fringes of the American commonwealth; or like the kulaks under Stalin, or the Slavs under the Nazis, to say nothing of the Jews—it is a long list. All manner of evil could befall a man without desert. He could for the veriest trifle, real or trumped up, be fined to the point of ruin if he possessed property; he could be exiled; he could be tortured or killed; he or his family could be suddenly kidnapped and sent away into slavery. The Nazis and the Soviets did not invent such procedures. That condition, much like the condition over a great part of the world today—and barely yesterday—is just what always announces any great revolutionary movement.

That revolution was one of the great reversals of the world's history, turning everything inside out, including man's sense of himself, that is, definitively man's sense of space. The Doric temple of the early Greeks, the type form of the Greco-Roman space, was corporal. It seems to stand alone in the landscape. Even a group of temples, as on the Acropolis at Athens, spatially do not merge, but each building stands detached and distinct. The temple is all exterior and stands sufficiently to itself as sculpture stands. Its spatial sense is a crystal sublimation of the idea of body. In the Erechtheion the roof of the porch is actually supported by bodies, that is, the caryatids. The Greek city state was the polis, the point-formed body isolated in the landscape. The Greek vase, the great plastic achievement of antiquity, was the quintessence of elegance in the detached object. We have only to compare this with Gothic sculpture, equally plastic but growing out of the cathedral structure, and unthinkable without it. To the Middle Ages God was everywhere, flowing through everything—through stones, through philosophers and their stone figures, and through the body of Mary transfigured at the portal of Chartres. To the Greeks the gods were at Olympus, a detached point in space. So the Doric temple is a certain godlike nonchalance of standing. From the exterior we have no feeling of an inside world within.

We feel at once, however, that the exterior of an early Christian domed church is but a shell, enclosing a fabulous world within. Just as the space of the Gothic cathedral, nearly a thousand years later, was to move outward with irresistible fluxions through the mighty nave, just so, the diametrically different space of the Byzantine Christianity created a quiescence, symbolizing the Savior's announcement that the kingdom of heaven was within. The dome itself, as structure, is a gesture of enclosing. Beyond the curved periphery is the netherworld. The dreamlike, hovering, wavering, inner contained interior of Saint Vitalie at Ravenna is a space based upon a proposition antiphysical and mesmerizing. This was the proposition which came out of the East to fill the emptiness of the Roman Empire.

Perhaps once again the world endures the hard undedicated moment of a dead idea. Perhaps something had meaning for Western man that no longer has meaning, and the esprit, the clear sight, the tense hand, the elastic touch are gone. This then is the moment of Durga, the ancient Hindu god of destruction. It was Durga when the vast empires collapsed and crumbled from internal weakness. It was the god at Nineveh and Tyre; and the god piled the bodies high at Verdun, at Hiroshima and Nagasaki, and at Auschwitz and Buchenwald. Not only empires, cities, armies, populations, but everything that lives is partly Durga's. Durga is everything that fails, that comes to nothing. Durga is desert land and seamless sky that brings no roots rain.

Durga is part of life and Shiva is the other part. Shiva is spring green and the Dionysian song of songs. Where men are working and making, there stands Shiva, for Shiva is the god of creation, the god of structure. Shiva is the god of what is being put together, and Durga is the god of what is being taken apart.

3

If the world today is being taken apart, then it is Durga's until there is a basis for putting the world together again. That basis would be structure. We may define structure as a relation of parts. It is idea of parts, using the word idea as Plato meant idea in the parable of the cave, demonstrating that things are but the shadows of ideas thrown upon the screen of experience. Yet what is the idea of the future? Alas, here again we do not know. It is idle to say that the idea of either the present or the future is science and technology, as some say. These are simply artifacts and not causes. To hold such a belief is attachment to a thing: thingism. Only the creative spirit of man is cause.

The future is clothed with impenetrable darkness, and the past is known only as from a great distance. We are like travelers looking down from a jetliner upon some improbable country, girt about by green seas. From the great height, so great that we have lost all sense of distance and the far seems something near that is strangely diminutive, the little indentations of the coast are the legendary harbors. The impregnable castles and fortresses, which once defended them, do not even register on the retina. Minute texture clusters, faintly geometric, are the three-thousand-year-old cities. The broad and important river of our childhood books, now less than the silver spittle of the spider, waters the brown plain.

So only the present is possible inquiry, and since the present is always the ruin of the past and the edge of the future, the present is always equivocal—equivocal as the oracle at Delphi. It all depends, as we commonly say.

We do know this, however: Durga and Shiva coexist in the same world. Nature is a compound of both destruction and creation. The tree falls in the forest, the length of a ruined thing. In a very few years its tree structure is changed into soil structure. The once living fiber rots and becomes humus, to be transformed at last into new tree structure; and so again and again in the endless continuity of nature. Structure is the dynamic impulse of life. It is time's cadenced heartbeat of death and rebirth. Civilizations throughout history have died over and over again (and always will, for nothing—excepting to the sentimentalist—is ever permanent), and new civilizations have always arisen out of the old. Society exists today in just such a period of structural disintegration, out of which must come finally a new civilization. In the springtime of an epoch architecture comes forth out of clear structure, like a flower out of the subtle and nourishing earth.

The evidence is in these industrial tanks of metal in the landscape. This perfect silver sphere, seen once across spring fields pieced and stitched with crops—the strange ball deft in the distance—would make even the better buildings of our time seem dull, pretentious, ill at ease, at best tentative. This metal ball is an entity, a completeness magically flowering. The unpremeditated loveliness of its form is as spontaneous as a spray of sparks flying from a spinning wheel, and as much a result and not a purpose.

We can see in the steel tower, the trussed arch bridge, or the trussed vault, as we do in the great architecture of the past, a grand symbol. The space destined mind of man, reaching always ever outward—in the cathedrals of the twelfth century reaching up, scarcely less high than heaven—here pierces through finally, through space into the core of the universe, comprehending realities within realities, worlds within worlds, atoms within molecules, electrons within atoms, swinging on propositions as terrible and comprehensive as pendulums within yet other pendulums. It is significant that the commonplace analysis of stresses in beams and trusses involves an insight unknown to antiquity. In the past, shear, compression, and tension were recognized only as effects. Whereas antiquity saw the beam only from the outside, the modern understanding has entered the inside of the beam. The forces of shear, compression, and tension have finally become in reality only attenuations: taut black threads within a sunlit phantom. The very materials of building are lightened to mere space inhabiting filaments and lines. The space beyond, even as in the cathedrals, is like the premonition of some irrational dimension. The halting mind stands amazed upon the threshold of the immaterial.

The vast spans of suspension systems project into the future. A suspension hall with a clear span of 2,000 feet, may not be bold enough. The Golden Gate Bridge, spanning 4,200 feet, may be only a beginning. Perhaps man has crossed in blue morning to a new world, perilous in sheer space, shrill wind upswung. It is as if, centuries hence, a figment race would unravel from the earth, like a spider's filament, some longer span anchoring in the bastions of unpeopled space.

The dams impounding the waters of a continent, the beautiful intricacy of derricks swung against the sky, the high power transmission lines, the factory with its mile-long shell of glass, all are the creative spirit of man, like a giant out of the ruins. Once again, as in the ancient past, is a powerful statement on the soul of man. Architecture is not in the bogus and self-conscious playing with shapes and fashions for a crumbling civilization. Architecture is the world of making and doing. That is structure: that is Shiva.

Here it is not necessary to enumerate great men. They always exist, some famous and some unknown and obscure. But they are always there, and we can have absolute assurance about that. They constitute the overwhelmingly valuable and indispensable part of the human race. Without them nothing could ever be achieved in the first place; and if achieved, without their continuing and tremendous efforts, everything would promptly go to ruin. So it has been, time out of mind. The dull, the weak, the complacent by themselves can do nothing. Yet the point is that man is the measure, and so it will be until the last man dies on a dead and cratered earth. Man being the measure—there is a time when men lead on to destruction, and there is a time when men lead on to creation.

We may be certain, however, that all the while destruction is at work there are compensating forces of creation at work. Nature—of which man is part—is a balance. Under the dead weight of mediocrity a society, a morale are destroyed. Under degenerating and corrupting success the highest revelations of mankind are perishable. Nothing fails like success, and nothing is as dangerous as a sure thing. Societies can survive famine, pestilence, lost wars, and humiliation like the last increment of pain. But a long and protracted success is invariably fatal.

Yet something there is in man that, when everything has broken down completely, comes back and builds another world. What is built is never the same as before. It has changed from a former position in time. It is neither better nor permanent, but different. That is civilization. What exists today is the interval between. It is the moment for Durga and Shiva.

Lost Cities of America (1970)

1

The first art was magic, a practical proposition meant to produce a practical result. Drawings on cave walls were not playing with shapes; they were not artistic or doing your thing. They were ceremonial statements intended to control a situation. Geometric lines on artifacts were not decoration but symbolism, communication, incantation. Intellectually arcane, the work of art was addressed to men in this world and to whatever is under the world and above it. All life was circumscribed by art, and men existed in the verve. The first words were poems. Poets really were Shelley's "legislators of the world."

For thousands of years, throughout all the course of human history, art retained its original practical necessity. It wasn't something nice; it was a necessity. And when we speak of the magic of a work of art we are unconsciously saying more than we suppose. The worst thing—the most damning thing—we can say about modern art is that it is unnecessary. Remove it from modern life and nothing is changed. It is at best a kind of diverting bric-a-brac, an embellishment—in a word, an irrelevance.

The art is an irrelevance because the expectations of modern life are an irrelevance; and the expectations are all part and parcel of the materialistic delusion. That is why this counterfeit art is always a kind of play. Art can be fun. On the contrary, the genuine work of art, since it is addressed to the eternal sense of things, is always the contemplation of significance. That is where the magic lies; that is what catches at the sleeve. It is as serious as the mad voice of Cassandra. Nothing can ensure it, and no hovel is safe from it.

Man is more than a consuming and producing animal. He cannot be an animal because he has lost his innocence. He can never achieve the Nirvana of animal existence. For what came out of the cave was something less than an animal and something more. The more is the subject matter of art. It is the relevance of man, the spell of harmony.

Without that harmony man is merely an outlaw of nature, a degenerate animal. Man, for some curious reason ill fitted to his environment, managed somehow to survive by creating an arsenal of weapons against nature. This creature with shambling gait was originally a timorous hunter of small game and with good luck a jackal of sorts skulking behind the lion or the tiger, consuming what was left of the kill. He would attack sick and dying animals and in times of dearth would turn cannibal and eat his fellows—smash the heavy skull and scoop out the brains. At length this early man developed a property sense. It is likely that the first property consisted of natural flint slivers picked up on the ground. With these slivers men could scrape the flesh from the hide of game and so could provide coats and blankets against the cold. Later on men learned to flake flint by hammering and thus to make knives, spears, and arrowheads. With these as weapons, man at once became a more successful hunter. Emboldened, man now made war on man, attacking alien tribes and families and taking away their possessions. Man became a bandit or, saying it plainly, a thief. Plunder became an economic means. Sometimes the vanquished would be taken alive and retained as slaves, that is, as property. Thus men were early divided into the two fundamental estates, the slaves and the slaveholders, or precisely, those who obey and those who command. Attitudes developed which persist to this present moment hardly abated. Envy was the atavistic and instinctual reaction of a slave. Self-pity was the same, the normal mental attitude of a slave. Self advertising—braggadocio—a veritable touchstone of our present civilization, was but the obsequious and ingratiating effort of a slave to impress a master in order to gain preferential advantages. Power in all degrees was simply the vantage point for commanding the labor of slaves. The bully was the man handling slaves.

Here, we may hazard, was a disagreeable creature, filthy in habit, shunned and feared, an outlaw of nature. Every individual's hand was turned against his neighbor. Yet the more sagacious members of this leper colony that was mankind must have inevitably and sadly compared the miserable life of their fellows to the majestic grandeur and harmony of external nature.

We may imagine a fable wherein they saw the sun rising at dawn out of the garlands of the east to warm the chill marrow of the darkened earth, complete the awful circle of its journey work, and homeward hasten. They saw the selfsame stars we see. They saw the seasons in their prime, the haggard spring worn out by love, the blunted heft of fruit upon the bough, and then the gold and scarlet of the autumn flaming in the ancient woods. And in all of this they must have imagined some mighty power, far beyond man's puny weapons against nature: a power that had given the eagles of the air their prey, and the beasts of the field their meat; that had given the horse its quiver and the fierce speed of its feet; that had laid the foundations of the earth and had given the soil its fertility and the seas their fish and sparkle and brine; that had divided the earth with the rivers, running with sweet waters and teeming with life; that had enveloped the earth with a mantle of fresh air for the gasping of breath of brides and bridegrooms and the first breath of newborn infants and the last breath of the dying. Before that mighty power—we may imagine—they saw themselves even as the witless locusts.

Finally they put this new way of seeing into whatever they were making. At that moment the method of making became art. The things were still the same things made for use, but now the use was sublime, for it was part of the mighty power and possessed that power. The cart was no longer a cart but a chariot of fire, and the hearth of the primitive house was the navel of the earth. Suddenly they saw everything differently, they from whose eyes the old scales had been lifted. It was no longer a leper colony of outcasts from nature but was a community of men in league with the mighty power of the universe and using that power for the purposes of everyday life. Man escaped thus from his exile, from being hermetically sealed within himself, within his hostility that knew nothing but hostility.

2

Zoologists call this great change in the species culture. It was the greatest revolution—really the only revolution—that *Homo sapiens* ever had. Down the ages it stormed the Bastille behind the standards of the great revolutionary leaders—of all the legendary Christs, of the legendary authors of the Upanishads and Bhagavad Gita, of Buddha, of Lao-tsu, Socrates, Gandhi—a list beyond space to enumerate. In point of fact the entire species goes along on credit based on this list. Yet the revolution at its best never carried the day, not two thousand years ago or a hundred thousand—and not even in a ramshackle fashion. For men on the whole always kept to their old zoological ways, making of the revolution only hypocrisy and cant, or simply another expression of tyranny. Ignorance rode victorious, but perhaps its ranks were thinned. Men were drilled by their betters into at least an outward conformance with the revolution's principles and propositions. That was a triumph of a sort—and with hardly pausing to mention that the revolution, in one way or another, gave all the art ever made.

Now we stand on the threshold of what appears to be a great counterrevolution in the world. If we will allow the metaphor, it is as if man is belligerently returning to the old zoology of the tribal squatting place. However, it may only seem to be so. In final reality this present time may be only one of those extremely negative historical periods that almost invariably follow upon any considerable material success—say the period at the decline of ancient Greece, or at the collapse of the Roman esprit from the emperor Augustus onward—or say the world of the Judean masses following the long prosperous reign of King Uzziah, and as presented by the orations of Isaiah—or say the period of the sixteenth-century peasant wars in Europe on the eve of the Reformation, as presented by the shriek of a Gruenwald Crucifixion—or say finally the world of fascism, as presented by Picasso's *Guernica.*

Yet certainly the technology of the past two centuries has launched man once again upon the course of his old onslaught against nature and his fellows. Man could not resist his toys. The toys were too powerful, and the humane revolution had too weak a hold. Man began with spears, and he is apparently ending with the earth-destroying missiles. A rare and fugitive species in the gloom of the antediluvian forests, he began with aggression: on the deserts of the then desolate earth, a population multiplied to compaction may crawl like the vermin and die. In that sense man is success incarnate. He began with cunning, and he is ending with the fatal flaw of his engines. He began with hunger and now promises glut. He calls it his dream: his American dream, his Russian dream, his Chinese dream—his screaming, nationalistic, earth-sundering and destroying dream. The books of the humane revolution are not being burned; they are part of the garbage piles. God is spelled GNP. Back to zoology—man has set a sick monkey up in office. Of course the environment is polluted. Man is polluted. Based on the facts, no other explanation is admissible. The machine by itself is a poor, helpless thing. As the situation now stands, man is the world as plunder, the world as spoils: the old slave ethic of plunder or be plundered. Man then is every man for himself, and the devil take the community. "What is art?" asked Tolstoy—and the sick monkey laughed.

Contact with the technology of Western civilization, and with its exploitative force, has shriveled the native art of every culture on the face of the earth. No peoples have survived the electric light bulb and the tin can. By beautiful ceremonial art, American Indians once sang up the corn and danced down the rain. Once art gave every meaning of life, and to every culture. As ritual practice it explained birth and death—for Western civilization, with its present high rate of suicide, the great futility. Thus art lifted life above the intrinsic absurdity of mere zoology. Every human activity from the commonest to the highest was once expressed by art. Every man was an artist. Ditches were dug by art, and bread was baked by art. According to a medieval guild stipulation, "Bread must be baked in justice." The art was a moral statement on cosmology, for the practical use of an everyday life, cast in the role of sublimest allusions. It was what we now call superstition—we for whom everything that cannot be transmuted into dollar bills is folly and ignorance. We would not like that art if suddenly we were set down in the austere midst of what made it. We would suppose that even Michelangelo believed rot and nonsense and worked like a fanatic in sweat and filth to prove it.

So we have killed the life that produced not only our own Western art, but the art of everyone else as well. However, we want to be prettily confessed. We are filled with sentimental longings for art but are empty of the life impulse to produce it. We are the sleeper dreaming he must run, and he cannot pick up his feet. The last man who imagined the life we have destroyed was Gandhi. He imagined peasants in their cottages, living in harmony, singing to Brahma, spinning cotton and making sandals. He called that *swaraj*: freedom for India. Aldous Huxley suggests that Gandhi's idea was an intolerable affront to progress and war and to what we grandly call science and art; and therefore we killed him.

In the nineteenth century William Morris witnessed the destruction of town and countryside by factories and slums, the demoralization of common folk everywhere by the brutality of workshop enslavement to machines, and the debasement of everyone's life by the degenerated products of machines. He proposed armed rebellion against the merchant industrial state, in order to reestablish in England a humane society based on morality and art—all as related in his beautiful and nostalgic *News from Nowhere*.

Today it is plain to nearly everyone that, even at the mildest estimate, we are living through a period of unprecedented historical crisis. Indeed, now the very perpetuation of the human species seems problematic. Yet the man in the street would be outraged to be told that the crisis was the failure of art. But is it really outrageous? Perhaps William Morris after all was right. We must bear in mind that just as art is an expression of life, so any criticism of art that is not at once a criticism of life itself is no criticism at all.

It is possible to illustrate this point, taking as an example the collapse of the art of city making. No art—save perhaps architecture—touches so closely the daily life of so many. Historically considered, to name the peoples is to name their cities, for the civilization is the cities, whether we are speaking of the autonomous walled towns of the Middle Ages or the polis of the ancient Greeks, or the mysterious cities of the Maya deserted and overgrown with jungle. The form and structure of the old cities was the life that produced it, crystallized in streets and stones. The development of the nineteenth and twentieth centuries, wherever it reached, destroyed the old cities and left chaos in their stead. To the few remnant old cities of Europe, in out-of-the-way places still untouched by progress, tourists now flock by the millions to see the beautiful things still left. But to see the cities of what we call progress, in Europe or anywhere else, they might just as well go to Chicago.

3

From the el platforms in Chicago you look westward over the tens of thousands of acres of slumland, with the factory water tanks, chimneys, and church steeples thrust up through the tenement aggregations in a kind of grim self-assertion. It has always looked like a catastrophe yet to be cleared. However, business and industry are still going on there, and so is the god of things as they are. After World War II, with its terrific concomitant imagery, that view westward suddenly looked like a bombed-out city—say, like Hamburg after the English and American airmen got through with it, the just-missed buildings sticking up through the desolation like ragged teeth. After the assassination of Dr. Martin Luther King Jr. it was briefly, in part at least, a burning city, a city that the infuriated inhabitants had put to the torch.

Chicago is the type form industrial city of the nineteenth century. That city was a place of work and sweat, of filth and squalor, of winters ten below zero, of stove-heated tenements, of the windows thick with frost, of gaslights, of lurking tenement stairs, of deserted midnight streets. It was a city always with the distant clang of streetcars. It was a city of summers ninety and something in the shade, when the sun cooked the asphalt of the streets so it wrinkled underfoot, and brick walls were ovens radiating heat far into the night. It was a city where the el trains looked into the kitchens and bedrooms of the poor, and down on the sinister tin-can-littered yard with its privy. It was a city of rats big as terrier dogs; it was a city of garbage, of slum geography, and flies; it was a city of alleys and the snatch of waiting and omnipotent evil. It was a city of switchyards where boys of the poor stole coal in the winter and ice in the summer and were chased and cornered and beaten with pleasure by the railroad bulls.

There were the winter slums and the summer slums. There were the breathless Sunday afternoons in August. There were the crowds of children playing in the streets, the men and women in doorways or leaning out of windows, and the idle, sheepish workmen on chairs or stools in front of doors, seeming to wait in the heat for something that would never happen. There was the distant smell of the stockyards, mixed with burnt hide and hair and blood and entrails. There was the cheap, sweet doughy smell of the bakery across the tracks. There were the women wasted and formless, bloated or emaciated. There was the drab clicking by, decked pitiably, yet with a certain drawn and poignant comeliness, frizzed and antiquated.

And in the winter there were the gray trampled snows, crusted at the edges beyond the foot tracks and dusted with soot. There were the early morning faces in the street, pale and blotched. They seemed to be abroad who had no right to be abroad, walking into the sick sun in that polluted whiteness.

It was a city of wealth beyond the avarice of emperors, or the gold of the Incas. Borne in on the galleons of the stock market were the new bars of bullion. A corner on wheat and fortunes would be made by inflating quotations. Even the far-off places of the earth would feel the pinch of price. Profits overnight from combines and mergers could pay for the pyramid of Cheops. Steel, farm equipment, tools, and foodstuffs made dollars like paper confetti.

It was a city of fraud, of the rake-off and the payoff, and the thick cigar clamped in the mouth: "We gotcha down for ten bucks sister, every Monday morning ten bucks, see." It was a city of violence and bought killers, where the police fished the dead men out of the river or found them out in the lake bumping against the piers.

It was the city of the Maxwell Street open market, with the poor peddlers selling watermelon slices a penny each, dotted equally with flies and seeds, and with other peddlers selling thread, aprons, dust mops, hats, shoes, and suits of clothes. It was the city of Kinzie Street near the river, with always the smell of roasting coffee; and where the warehouse wagons, drawn by dappled teams of heavy Norman Percheron horses bearing curly fetlocks, were loaded up with iced boxes of smelt, perch, and whitefish. It was the city of the Randolph Street market where the truck farmers drove in their wagons loaded with gunny sacks of sweet corn and cabbages and piled tiers of carrots, beets, onions, lettuce, and tomatoes, and where commission houses along the sidewalks of the market were stacked with fragrant boxes of lissome white celery, phallic cucumbers from the earth god Priapus, embryo-shaped green peppers, and baskets of shiny Nubian eggplants.

It was a city of buying, selling, and making. It was the thriving city of the factory districts, with their imported Polacks, Hunkies, Liths. It was the city of the stockyards, where they packed the doped and contaminated meat and worked the immigrants to desperation. It was also the city of dreams. It was the one unique city with electric air and cosmic tremolo.

It was a city of mighty railroad stations from which the salesmen left for the prairie towns, returning on weekends or month's ends to the pleasant elm-shaded streets of Englewood, Hyde Park, Ravenswood, and far-off Wilmette. The vast and frightening stations were ports of entry for families from farms and distant countries. It was a city where anything could happen. It had burned down in 1871 and had been built up again. It was temporary before the fire and temporary after the fire, and the air of the temporary and tentative still clings to it.

It was the one expectant city. It had yet to be made. It was a stage, and the players had yet to appear. It was the one city with an Aladdin's lamp to raise the lost Atlantis or to reach the stars. The city was an enormous industrial cinder heap, lacerated by prodigious railroad sidings, attempting to make the entire city a switchyard—and not of the nation merely, but of the universe—as if cars were being loaded there among the tenements, bound for Saturn, Jupiter, and Mars.

4

That the cities of America are unfit for human habitation is a well-recognized fact today, attested by the federal government's frantic efforts to do something about it through urban renewal. However, all these planning efforts, if such they are to be called, are simply directed toward establishing a little more permanently the same essential disorder that already exists so terribly.

For one thing, all the cities are too big and far too dense. They are out of all human relation. They began in the nineteenth century as land speculation. For the up-and-coming part of the population the city was a Horatio Alger place to get rich in—"Work and Win." Frank Lloyd Wright called the city "a rent meter." And that of course is what the cities are today: places where the populations are, more or less indirectly, exploited through land speculation expressed as rent. Given that purpose, the more numerous and concentrated the population, the greater the competitive pressure for land use—and therefore the greater the rent and the greater the profit. The city as a wholesome environment for living was never the question. That is why the cities are so ugly. The notion of the "city beautiful," that incredible platitude, comes to little more than a beauty parlor mask for plunder.

It only illustrates the benign fraud to point out real ills of the city which are persistently and shamelessly ignored, such as the dangerous streets and the hysterical traffic. More people are killed in automobile accidents on the city's dangerous streets, and the equally dangerous highways, than are killed in the wars. The comparison is a commonplace endlessly repeated. But more important even than the killed and injured is the callous fact that no one thinks very much about it; ergo, that it is commonplace. The smog of the cities, perhaps in the long run even more lethal, is just as much a commonplace. On particularly bad smog days, inhabitants of New York are officially advised, with perfect equanimity, to stay in their houses, as if the fact of poisoned air were part of the natural order of things. A city planning official in Chicago once commented: "Everyone has to die sometime."

Crime and street gangs—considered uncontrollable—are on the increase as they were in imperial Rome of the third century. At least half of New York, Brooklyn, and Chicago is a two-cop jungle, where one cop will not walk alone. A Brooklyn housewife called the police because there was a prowler in the vestibule. The desk sergeant cut off the complaint: "Look, lady, we ain't got the time—keep your door locked or else move—murder and rape are our problems." According to the *New York Post*, the leading causes of death for all persons under thirty-five in New York City are drugs, suicide, and murder.

Following World War II automation opened Pandora's box. The tractor and improved machinery dislodged from their precarious livelihood millions of the poor in the American rural hinterland. Out of the starving hill towns of Appalachia and the Cumberland range, and out of the one-mule sharecrop patches of Alabama and Mississippi, they came. They arrived in the cities at the very moment that automation had canceled in the urban industries the unskilled shovel jobs they might have filled in the nineteenth century. These are the new masses of the cities. A great percentage, and through no fault of their own, are charges of the state. They are unemployed, excluded, frustrated, disillusioned, and therefore dangerous. They are motivated by brooding and musical aspirations, incomprehensible and alien to the old bourgeois ruling class of the cities—that is, to the financial pirates of yesteryear: to the merchant princes and dominant business interests, with mayors in tow, and to the heirs, managers, lackeys, do-gooders, forward lookers, and suchlike frayed bits and pieces of the old wealth and power clique. These, of course, fail to see that a dole cannot buy men out of frustration. Man is the most deadly of the carnivores. *Panem et circenses*—bread and circuses—is the triumph of chaos, the sentimentality of the social worker, and the last resort of the political scoundrel with new votes to count.

Consequently all the current talk about new housing in the ghettos is arrant nonsense. The last place in the world where the poor want to live is in the ghettos, refurbished or unrefurbished. All God's chillun got slums. They want to get out of the dirty, crowded, unhealthy, and unlivable city, just like everyone else. However, to the prosperous whites, the ghetto is a way to keep the poor invisible—and incidentally a way to keep the land rent coming in, and hopefully the tax rolls up.

This exactly is Chicago, *Urbs in Horto*, the city in a garden. It is the city not of refuge, but of escape. Suburban dormitories now cover the flat Illinois landscape, practically from the Wisconsin state line to Indiana. The tract-house inhabitants, as if chained to the tortures of Tantalus—always reaching for a life in the country always daily denied—fiendishly commute back and forth, either to tottering factories of the old Chicago or to the central business district, that is, the Loop, that is, the gaudy acropolis of a frontier town, lined with catchpenny skyscrapers.

Yet this is the tragic dilemma of every metropolis in America. People are talking about it today as though it is something new that just happened. In reality it is a very old affair, and so is our reaction now. Bad as the city is, we think, nothing after all is fundamentally wrong that machines, computers, and mass production can't make right. One day spending a hundred billion dollars, or two hundred or three hundred, everything automatically will turn out rosy. Isn't that what machines are for?

America is the machine state, the corporation state, the state on ball bearings. America grew up under the tutelage of that great machine the railroad locomotive. Under the impetus of the railroad, small towns suddenly grew into giant cities. The city was a labor market, a handy bin full of men. The iron horse hauled coal and materials and the mill wheels spun, and a new time began. We call it the Industrial Revolution. We speak of it as progress, and with that certain patronizing inflection as if we believed that all the life on this planet, and the cities of that life for the ten thousand years, were hopelessly and incorrigibly not progress.

5

Just as America leads the world in that progress, out on the west coast of land's end, California leads America. It is a drive of one day on Route 66 from the red rocks of Arizona, through the bitter brimstone heat of the Mojave Desert, over the San Bernardino mountain pass, down onto the plain and over the interminable freeway corridors of Los Angeles—the latest of the big cities, the American Baghdad, the city of beautiful women weeping in smog.

The pioneers took perhaps a month or two to make the trip. But month or day, it is still another world because it is the future, or at least evidently so. It is as if, beginning in the mysterious silence of New Mexico, all that harsh and beautiful wasteland of mesas, and the stupendous geological ruins of fallen ramparts littered across the sky for a thousand miles, was really meant to be some unnegotiable and hostile gateway of time, separating the ambiguity of today from the fatality of tomorrow.

For what is on exhibit in Los Angeles, more than anything else, is the perilous emptiness and triviality of a mighty nation, carried to its logical conclusion. For instance, with hardly let or pause there are thousands of lineal miles of Love Bungalows, every one a movie set. The full impact of it is like some

Gargantuan practical joke. It is the projection forty years later of all the nation's movie houses in the twenties. These in the feathery darkness were like cult palaces, perfumed not with incense of frankincense and myrrh, but with aphrodisiac of Cracker Jacks and popcorn. The dwellings of the Los Angeles region are in a very substantial sense this American dream created by the movies. They are no longer a mere wish, a mere abstraction—that nameless longing for a home in the West, in order to scuttle the humdrum and escape from the snow and the slush—but the final reality of it, Utopia actually arrived. Thus there is something about even the meanest dwelling that has the undeniable air of the movie plot.

Everyone was rich and good-looking, and no one had money troubles but only love troubles. The movie hero bounded across the lawn during working hours, swinging a tennis racket; or indoors he leaned against the marble mantelpiece in the unexplained sumptuousness. The feminine sex was represented inevitably by a pretty face, lovely hair, perfect breasts, winsome buttocks. Every virtue—kindness, honesty, courage, loyalty, intelligence—automatically accompanied these obvious physical stigmata. One hundred and twenty pounds of love object, simple to understand and to the prurient point, sabotaged Mr. Jefferson and became the national ideal.

So Los Angeles, a somehow approximation. To be sure suburbia everywhere is much the same, but nowhere else is it on such a scale as in southern California. There it is the world become a suburb, and there it is architecture expressed almost totally as the daydreams of adolescence.

The bastions of big business—that is, the skyscraper office buildings, the plush shopping centers, the Civic Concert Hall, the County Art Museum, and even the university campuses—are all conceived as a kind of Shangri-la monumentality, grandiose and fortissimo. In all that posturing of steel and concrete, a sensible building wherever it occurs is so out of place it is shocking. You wonder how it happened.

So it is abundantly apparent that the inhabitants live their dream, at least insofar as it is possible to live it: they or their parents who nearly half a century ago came out from the Great Plains, from the Dakotas, Kansas, Iowa, Illinois, from all those farms, hamlets, and small towns. Of course some came from the Atlantic seaboard, from the early settled states of the Union; and some came from the old Confederacy. Landing in Hollywood, Los Angeles, Pasadena, Riverside, how like a miracle it must have seemed to be actually in the real locale of the movie stars—a long list in say 1925.

World War I was over, and the nation under Harding had entered upon its great era of banality and prosperity. America itself became a movie plot, a vast spectacle, broad as the continent, ten years in the running: became it paradoxically out of the bitter violence of its actual past, out of the ironic spit and fury high in oath of all its history past. And in this movie it won the war, it rounded up the reds and deported them, legislated prohibition, preached its virtues to the world, had all the pure and noble thoughts and made them hum.

Thus southern California, born out of the twenties, is by tradition curiously puritanical, precisely as were the movies. Advertisements address both husband and wife, and the copy often shows both. The wife is lovely, and the husband has a jaw like Francis X. Bushman. Perhaps both are swimming in the swimming pool. It is the movie's happy ending. People go to bed early and get up early and go to work. It is almost pure Calvinism. For a city the size of the Los Angeles complex, there is very little nightlife. In cities like New York and Chicago, always a derelict part of the population turn night into day, frequenting till all hours restaurants, bars, and theaters. Walking along such an all-night street one feels the richness and variety, the exuberance and the profligacy, of the human experience—the diametrical opposite of puritanism, however lush may be its expression. In the dark a woman's heels staccato on the sidewalk are part of the poetry of a city. In that sense Los Angeles is a small town. It is worse than a small town, because it is a suburb and purity is its boredom—just as Glencoe, Winnetka, Lake Forest, outside Chicago, are so bad because they are so good.

Yet half of all marriages in Los Angeles end in divorce, the highest figure for the nation; and no place else are the young as alienated. Beatniks and hippies were a California innovation. The campus militants began at Berkeley; the race riots began at Watts, the now famous bungalow ghetto of Los Angeles. Thoreau's observation about men leading lives of quiet desperation finds expression today in a fiercer kind of desperation, never far from the surface in Los Angeles. It is possible to see men of fifty and more wearing long hair, mustaches, and beards in imitation of the hippies—apparently agreeing with the unshriven young that there is no problem so abstruse that hair can't solve it. Some wear Nehru jackets and beads and go to hair stylists. People at a cocktail party, got up in their fantastic clothes, look like nothing so much as a troupe of down-and-out movie extras hired for the occasion. Around the shopping centers you see old men getting out of expensive cars in bare feet, as if they thought they had recaptured the rural charm of a young lad on the farm. Members of the feminine sex from seven to seventy walk through the store in bikinis. Psychologically the child may be already without childhood; but the mature woman, in all that expanse of no longer lovely flesh, has completely destroyed sexuality. By comparison, one reflects, a pale Victorian lady with a bare wrist showing could have the sexual appeal of Helen of Troy, Astarte, and Swinburne's Dolores all rolled into one.

6

Along the sand beaches fronting the Pacific the boys and girls lie on blankets or walk in pairs. They seldom laugh, and perhaps they seldom talk, and that seems strange. For they really are the beautiful people, these seventeen-year-olds. The young men in their trunks—slim, strong legs, flat bellies, supple backs—are not parading in masculine fashion. Toward the girl, the boy seems almost indifferent. The girl in her brief costume snugging her bottom—a sun-tanned Nordic, nay, a Valkyrie leading the slain to Valhalla—takes the initiative, and by casual and almost unnoticeable gestures conveys infatuation for a blasé and world-weary consort.

Touching in its absurdity, it is like the players of a tragic role who do not even know they are playing it. There is a vast frustration of some kind, a futile realization that nothing really works. Suddenly life is not very valuable. One thinks of people walking around in a plague-ridden city. The hippies are not harbingers of spring, for all their flower symbols. Like mute backwoodsmen with their long hair, they both act old and look old. Their eyes seem infinitely sad. At twenty they look used up—but by what? They have experienced no attrition of defeat, nature's great aging device.

There is an ominous silence, as if something is about to happen. The old optimistic illusions are breaking down, perhaps to be replaced by other illusions comparable to the old one—come and get it, here is paradise, sex, palm trees, sunshine, and beauty. And money. A banker put it imperishably: "Someone has to pay for all that sunshine."

Southern California, in point of fact, is not an urban region at all. It turns out that the thousands of lineal miles of Love Bungalows are simply speculative real estate developments. Perhaps nearly every house owner looks forward to selling out at a profit and moving on. The costs of raw land are staggering. Often the smallest building lot is ten to twenty thousand dollars, representing perchance a dozen profits by a forty-year dynasty of speculators.

That is why there was never any consistent effort to make a true city, a city for living, with the parts of the city properly related to each other—with parks, playgrounds, and pleasant squares within walking distance; with a community of residences sensibly and agreeably located within a short walking distance of places of work, in order to avoid the onerous and expensive daily back-and-forth automobile travel; with safe streets throughout the community; with high-speed public transportation to connect all the communities. In a word, there was no genuine intention to practice the art of city making; there was only the intention to make money.

Due to all this fond delusion of land speculation, with its resultant disorder, the traffic volume generated by the disorder is unbelievable. The smog from the traffic is the worst in the nation, perhaps in the world. Thus Los Angeles the uncity. Meanwhile the mails are clogged with real estate brochures offering inside buying privileges for an exurbia escape from it all, from the ugliness, the dirt, the pollution, and all so easily at the newest speculative development, a hundred or two hundred miles away, at "Fun City," "Joy Ranches," "Sleepy Hollow Mountains."

The wealthy part of the population is certainly bewildered by the kaleidoscopic changes in California and appalled by the hydra-headed problems. Theirs is no longer that hacienda on the Mediterranean. They see the pollution of the air by industry and automobiles; the poisoning of the land by DDT and other chemicals; the wholesale ruin of the landscape by the bulldozer; the killing of the old California, the Golden State. They see the drug addiction of the young; the rise of the militant Black and Mexican groups; and whole stacks of other problems from the enormous welfare rolls to mindless pornography and smut. Perhaps they lump them altogether as part of that thing out there. They are beginning to be afraid. The American dream promises to turn into a nightmare.

The militant young are interested not in reform but in revolution — nonnegotiable. They want the whole mighty shebang of the state brought down. Said Jerry Rubin, speaking at Los Angeles: "Destroy America — spell it with a K." Intellectuals, all their lives impotently hating the pious and self-righteous power of the merchant industrial state, can only applaud to see the enemy now hilariously bedeviled by striplings. As for the poor, they have nothing to lose, in this case not even chains. No one really wants them, chained or unchained. They are simply the superfluous men, as things now stand unemployed and unemployable. They are something like 30 million men, women, and children, depending a bit on who makes the estimates. It is a remarkable number, and in the instance of California especially remarkable: all that tremendous wealth of the region to leave so many in the lurch. And to keep the untenable peace there are only the cops, "the pigs" to the militant young, for whom the American eagle has grown a snout.

The catalyst of it all is the war in Vietnam. As in Macbeth, the raven himself was hoarse that croaked the fatal entrance, and not within the battlements of some mere liege lord, but within the collective consciousness of the most powerful nation on the face of the earth. However, to the Blacks, the war was just another example of the White man's insincerity and tyranny. To the poor generally it meant billions for butchery and pennies for bread. To the young, who were expected to die or be maimed in the bogus cause, it was indisputable evidence that the American system was rotten at the core. The rage and contempt launched by the militant young against the state would have brought credit to Isaiah had he spoken in the invective of Anglo-Saxon obscenity.

To be sure, the scale of all this is the scale of the world, and far beyond one particular place, a Los Angeles, a city of Euphoria by the sea. In addition, the collapse of the American esprit really began in the depression of the thirties, was halted briefly during World War II, and was resumed in the hollowness of the Cold War years. It was resumed in the terrifying momentum of the arms race, in the gathering frustrations of suburbia and the tract-house culture, in the glowering enmities of the big city ghettos, and in the pitiable and helpless rural poor of the South, starving with the starvation of the Ganges.

Yet all the while multitudes of Americans were becoming very rich, and far vaster multitudes were becoming moderately rich. Newspaper editorials gloated. Poverty had been conquered; it was the American millennium. The official class and their intelligentsia, blind as bats, unable to see their own country right under their noses, projected messianic and imperial plans for the distant parts of the earth. The great corporations throve and panted for foreign markets. Technology, aided by corporate research, permeated every aspect of life.

Under the straitened discipline of machine technology life itself became, for a great percentage of the population, exquisitely boring. The technology, while releasing men from hard physical labor, could still leave them curiously enervated. The machine in sparing the muscles sweated the nerves. This tedium of mechanical work is not something simplistically applicable only to factory and clerical workers but is rather a fixed condition all the way up the ladder to managers and company executives, gulping down two martinis at lunchtime and calling their life and their job that infinitely expressive inanity, "the rat race."

Paradoxically, the very success of the American technology, while making material existence gaudily secure and comfortable by any standards of the past, in the process somehow robbed life of a considerable portion of its original challenge, adventure, and zest. The sons and daughters of this prosperous middle class, relatively pampered and spoiled—the usual prerogative of prosperity— witnessing daily the harping dissatisfaction of their parents, quite naturally rebelled against duplicating more of the same in their own lives.

Thus were the young alienated from their parents, and hence from the nation—that is, from what they with superior glee and naive disdain quickly called the "establishment"—to wit, the imperfect organization of affairs that had been feeding and clothing them from the day they were born. These intransigent young, whose responsibilities were nil and whose indulgences in day-to-day Thunderbird and Volkswagen living would have drawn envy from Croesus, in their adolescent discontent outlandishly penetrated the various buncombes of the American hypocrisy.

Then the war in Vietnam against a resolute enemy who simply refused to be defeated. Then the enormous power of the draft, as if the American generals imagined themselves in the role of the ancient Persians—as related by Herodotus—driving their troops into battle with whips. Never did the leadership of the nation exhibit itself as such a spectacle, one significant of dementia, failure of reflex action, the blanketing of the brain. Then all the gorgeous GI coffins for the young snuffed out. And for what, they might have asked? For the lies of politicians flying around like flies? For the profits of Pentagon corporations, always instantly denied? For the star-spangled hope of one day selling Pontiacs and washing machines in East Asia? For a world in reality falling apart at the seams? "For an old bitch gone in the teeth," in a 1920 phrase of Ezra Pound's? So it was that the nation became discreditable. The revulsion was a long time coming.

So it came to Los Angeles too, and broke the dream that had really been broken for a long time, there in the smog like a mist always hiding the mountains. It had been broken a long time before the young men burned the Bank of America at Santa Barbara and went off screaming and shouting into the night.

Perhaps Furies are today working underneath, in the subterranean depths of southern California, to emerge as some enormity of retaliation. These Furies may emerge through some crevice of the broken dream and spread it out over the entire nation. A broken dream is a dangerous thing. The Hegelian dream of the Germans, broken by the defeat of World War I, twenty years later, with the advent of the Nazis, released monsters out of the chthonian regions of the underdark.

7

Notwithstanding all of this as presented in these notes, if America has the vitality, it is still possible to turn about. Perhaps it is not likely, but it is possible. It is possible to plan and build livable and beautiful cities, just as men have always built cities, according to reason and the needs of life. These cities would be limited in size — as cities have always been — and closely surrounded by the fields and forests of the region, and by parks with vegetable gardens and small farms in them. These would be cities of the living landscape. Life, at least estimate, could be simpler and freer, more secure and more satisfying; in a word, more humane.

Both poverty and welfare would disappear. They are only the expressions of land monopoly, expropriation from the land, and consequent economic exploitation. In these cities any man could earn his living by applying his labor to the land. It is possible to bring our common life into harmony. That was the problem in the leper colony of early man, no less or more than today. What is needed is not new machines but new morals. That is the only hope worth having. All else is simply a new Babbitry. To hope for the best and go on doing the worst is no hope at all. Emerson answered that by pointing out that the laws governing cause and effect are "the chancellors of God." Society gets the cities it deserves. No new machine provides an escape hatch.

Putting a man on the moon was irony. This event was achieved in the very midst of a ruinous war, in the midst of the ecological desolating of the earth, the withering and hostile touch of person to person, the brutality of cities. It was like a kind of spermatozoon out of bygone earth: that missile's hurl to leave it all behind—polluted corpses of American Baghdads, speculative lechers of suburban hill and dale, virulent rivers and cesspool seas, industrial fumes like rotten eggs of the air. In flicker of box those billions of dollars for bravo. A girl's white breast, moonglow on the lost earth, suckles the strontium young, curdles the milk from the vats. A million years' adventure—once to run before the tusk of boar, to whimper in the dark, to search for lizards in the rocks—at last betrayed the earth to strip it bare.

After all the technological virtuosity of the moon landing, no one will ever again be able to doubt the awesome feasibility of nuclear annihilation. Looking at the glittering and luxurious kitsch of cities, and then looking at their favorite ghettos, who would doubt the moral zero that would do it? All of mankind can go in one moment of atomic bliss. On some beach of that oblivion, the lonely tides can nudge the toothy skull of the last man.

Alas poor man—in many ways so admirable and dear—brought down before your time. What gods would have imagined that out of the vast and wheeling cosmos, trillion starred, the little speck of knowledge you had found would prove too much?

Yet just as well man could go on. He could go on and on, positive, optimistic, defiant: a new race of man born out of man, to give the slip to the anthropoid. Once such purpose came to the squat, hunched dwarf, chewing flesh and cracking bones in the dark man stench of the cave. It came in the night and the dwarf screamed. There was a light, and then it was gone. It came again and again. By the red rock it came. It gave him no peace by night or by day. It came as an apocalypse and led him forth he knew not where.

It was a purpose exactly as old as art; as old as the fantasy of man in the pageantry of nature. It is older than the sculpted horses of the Parthenon; it is even older than the rocking horses of our childhood.

Since it is man who decides now whether man goes on or goes under, the Greeks and their *paideia* were right: Man is the measure of everything. Art is the measure of man.

Light and the Conquest of Kitsch (1973)

1

In the darkness there is the light of the stars. In the cold countries there is the light of the snow, refracted from the stars by the trillions of hexagonal crystals. There is the light of the now tarnished moon on the snow. It still lights up all the valleys and the snowy wastes when far from home, even though the scientific kitsch of the moon landing has violated the splendor of its once unapproachable femininity.

In the summer there are stars too and the moon, and the song of insects in their palace haunt of strident lust. The gigantic moth clings to the screen, a poised and lascivious wingspread opened like a fan, powdery and silky. It cannot resist the light. There is something light centered in the hankering and hesitant tremolo of its wings.

Yet how could it be otherwise on this planet, since all life is the child of the sun, turned toward the sun? All over the turning half of the planet are the great sheets of light coming down. So everything depends on light. Whoever has made something—he may be vain as a peacock and just as ridiculous—yet if he is a genuine maker, a genuine article himself, he stands back and looks at it won-deringly and asks himself equivalently, in rare and unconscious homage to the sun, if it was really he himself who made it and lifted it into the light.

For light is understanding. In our common speech we say that we see when we actually mean that we understand. Socrates in the dialogue of Theaetetis could not prove knowledge. So light cannot be proved. Its effects are known. Its speed is known, but what is it? We exist in a relative world. One thing is related to another in kaleidoscopic complexity; and that is really all there is. Final answers therefore are impossible. A thought is a portrait that is never finished. If it ever should be finished—that is, perfected—it would be dead. It would no longer relate to the actuality of the relative world. Only in the split second that we die are we perfected. Rossetti wisely and secretively claimed as his secret that he mixed his colors with brains—which told practically nothing. Descartes said *cogito, ergo sum* (I think, therefore I am), meaning that there are no assurances about particu-lars. The realities of existence may be only a dream. This piece of paper may be only an illusion. However, the intimation of that possibility, or of any other possibility, proves the one firm fact: existence—life. The final nature is unknown. Alice, in her adventures through the looking-glass, is about to wake up the Red King. It develops that Alice may be only his dream—and then what will happen to her? Thomas Aquinas, in a way of speaking, logically proved God. However, in making God a matter of proof rather than a matter of faith, he unwittingly opened the door for making God a matter of disproof. Seven centuries later, God is dead.

If the world is relative, then it is a balance. To every action there is an equal and opposite reaction. Thus there is a cause for every effect. Now if the world is a balance—weighted on both sides of the scales—it then follows that it is a dualism. This pairing of opposites is the phenomenon of life and death. We may express it as creation and destruction or as light and darkness. We are back once again to Shiva and Durga, the Hindu gods of creation and destruction.

The world which is the world of death is the destructiveness of the ape animal. It mashes down into nothingness whatever lives, whatever reaches to the light. It is the dark nature of mankind. It is that part of the universal dualism which applies to man. It is the frustration that cannot create and therefore destroys. It is the pure pleasure of killing, the power of torturing, the sadism exquisitely thrilled. It is murder, war, and the deep need to make an end of whatever lives. It looks down on the dead and mutilated and is reborn to new darkness. It cries out in the ape throat the triumph of transmuting the crux and the quiver of life to a suddenly still and vanquished nothingness. To repeat: it is the power of darkness in man that is there because of the power of darkness in the universe. It is the mathematically balanced equation of ticktock, from midnight's promontory whirling forever onward with the stars, to a forever oblivion matched to a forever creation.

Diametrically, the power of light reclaims out of the dead and the dark. It forms—not mutilates—out of a nothing a something. It is in the something that it is reborn. In the significance it is reborn, in the signal, the hand uplifted, the vertical finger, the perpendicular gesture. It is the upward, the through—not the trampled underneath.

The light comes down on the poor helpless thing, which is really everything. And because it is the light it is no longer a helpless thing. It is no longer poor. It is the wealth of whatever is, and the power and the glory of aliveness: for the gift of the sun is life. It is the masculine moment of exultation and the femininity of creation. It is the frailty of white on white, frailer than flowers, whiter than white, than white bird in the white snow.

Down in the dark there is either the womb stuff, seed stuff, root stuff—or else there are only the vast unregenerate regions of death. In the regions of death there is no good, because these regions are beyond the need of light. But the roots of the trees grapple in the dark, suckle the stones, anchor the trunk rising upward into the light. So down by the roots of things there is light out of the great incandescence of the sky, invisibly lighting all the workshops down under the earth. No eye can see it, no meter measure it. We know it is there, because there are preparations down under the earth. It is the sleep of light which will awaken into the air.

2

The present age is an age characterized by anxiety, insecurity, and boredom. Yet materially no age has accomplished so much as this present age. Every day science and technology achieve new wonders. Yet this is also the blowhard age. Therefore these wonders are announced far and wide, and so loudly and persistently that even the most obtuse could scarcely be unaware of them. If telling the good news, to say nothing of the wonders themselves, could make happiness, the people of the United States should be the happiest people on the face of the earth.

Luxuries and nonessentials by the thousands of kinds have become the commonplaces of only average opulence. As a matter of course these put to scorn the trifling aspirations of all former avidity. Perhaps two-thirds of products on the market today were literally unknown seventy-five years ago. Of the remaining products, the majority have been so warped and distorted that original use and context have for all practical purposes disappeared. Clothes have become erotic costume. Houses have become the means for impressing others. Food, once daily bread and now largely denatured, is now daily glut, gorging the beleaguered and plutonian intestines. Life itself, the end product, has become "lifestyle," a painful platitude.

The kitsch of cant has become the official language of the nation, supplanting the plain intelligible order of things and bringing the dictionary to rack and ruin. For nothing is what it was. Thus "free enterprise" means corporation monopoly. "Prosperity" means higher prices, and therefore greater poverty for the already poor, in a nation where the top 1 percent of the population possesses eight times as much money and assets as the entire bottom 50 percent. "Peace with honor" turns out to be the honor of My Lai, and no peace in sight. Pious euphemism replaces truth, lies flying around like flies.

We are surrounded by kitsch. Kitsch to the right of us, kitsch to the left of us—kitsch in front of us—volleys and thunders. Politicians run on kitsch, and kitsch is the patron god of industry. The sweatshops and factories of the American Sahara turn out the stuff at the billion rate. Nothing is more forlorn than trying to buy an article that is not kitsch. Everything is "beauty." An article may fall apart after a few hours or a few weeks of use, but it was made for beauty—no question about that. Beauty is a sales line; it is attractiveness; it is customer appeal. There is no advertisement so mean that it does not want beauty. It is the great Gallup poll that always wins 99 percent of the vote.

Some 200 million people are apparently yearning for beauty. For all that sweet and stupid nonsense, it is what you see out of the windows everywhere, from Los Angeles to Las Vegas, to Chicago to New York. All of this obvious tawdriness was for beauty and business; and the business was beauty. This "beauty" of course is what kitsch really is. It is cheap, mass produced, egalitarian and 99 percent of the vote. Kitsch is the opiate of the people.

Doubtless the world has always had its vulgarity; and if kitsch were only vulgarity one should be ashamed to spend thought upon it. If the peasants of the Middle Ages were vulgar, there was a childlike innocence about it. People were having a good time in Pieter Brueghel's paintings—an exuberant and robustious good time—and of course the church took a dim view of what the peasants did for fun. However, kitsch exhibits quite different characteristics. It is the vulgarity of universal boredom. It celebrates not a good time, but a bad time. And practically no one takes a dim view of it. In point of fact, it passes for art. So steadfast is the public affection for it, and so overwhelming is its occurrence, that it is possible to wonder today if there really is any other kind of art.

Once everything that was made (to say this again) was made by art. This seems strange to us because we are so accustomed to thinking of artists only as painters, sculptors, musicians, architects—a very few occupations—and everyone else excluded. But once art, as in the traditional society, was simply the proper method of making, so eloquently presented by Coomaraswamy. The artist was every man, and daily art was both daily life and daily bread. For instance, a pair of shoes was not made as an erotic gesture, advertised as sex, and hence as kitsch; shoes were for walking and Eros was for love. If the shoes were not properly made, that is, if they were not made by art, no one could walk in them. If love was not properly made it would be unclean. Dirt is simply irrelevance. The dirt in the farmer's field is clean because it is relevant. Kitsch is irrelevance.

The irrelevance of pornography, said to be a half-billion dollar business peddled by the Mafia, is no crime save for the merchandising. It is not even a sin. Mawkish and unimaginative, it misses Victorian Swinburne's "fierce midnights and famishing morrows." It does not produce in devastating actuality the daydreams of adolescence. It makes you want to laugh.

A revolution it is not. A reaction it is. It is a symptomatic reaction to the emptiness, the unaliveness, the meaninglessness of modern life, resulting from the materialist success ideal. Pornography, revealing its derivation in kitsch as irrelevance, assassinates individuality. These are not persons in the pornographic procedure. They are mechanistic robots perpetually—and unrealistically—in rut. Fool simple, there is no character and no complexity, and hence no plot. It is the furthest no-man's-land of banality like all kitsch—all verve and drama is gone. It is profitable fraud perpetrated against the lonely, the defeated, and the bored—in reality an antisexual paper and celluloid swindle of banality.

Hannah Arendt, in discussing Eichmann, asserted that evil was banal. What could one make of such a man? He was a bureaucrat shuffling papers on his desk. Lucifer was a gentleman. Here was a law-abiding bourgeois, a former traveling salesman frequently bored—and appalled when he actually saw the concentration camps, to which he had sent millions of Jews. Yet on trial for his life in Jerusalem, there was no need for him to be a liar. He was ensconced in the cocoon of party-line clichés—that is, kitsch. The orations of Hitler were nothing but kitsch heroics—and so dangerous because the kitsch was catnip for the German masses. A German writer (Reck-Malleczewen, *Diary of a Man in Despair*) later executed by the Nazis, watching Hitler through binoculars, noted in his diary that the man looked like a streetcar conductor. There exists a photograph showing Hitler sitting by his Christmas tree, receiving his criminal henchmen and grinning while he repeats the commonplaces of a benign uncle.

Kitsch is banal because it is pretentious. What it is, is never what it is. The ranch house is not the house on a ranch. It is the monument to a pretension on a fifty-foot lot. It has lost the sense of a house, not because of the lot size but because of the pretension. Similarly, our cities are not cities at all. They are in reality only commercial ventures. so the City Beautiful is the City Kitsch. But what is a house—the house in its deepest meaning?

3

From primeval times the woman has crouched by the dead fire. She has blown on the embers until the bright yellow flame flickered and the little sticks caught. It was necessary because the flame was a kind of life. It was a light, even a torch to hold against the darkness. So the woman knelt before it. Yesterday the American Indian woman knelt before the fire. But long before that the Asiatic woman had tended the fire for the bronze wayfaring men who first crossed the Bering Strait, fifteen or twenty thousand years ago, and started from Alaska the long thousands of years journey southward across the American continent.

At least two-thirds of that journey had already been completed when the Egyptian woman ground the grain in the courtyard, under the stair of the two-story mud-and-wattle peasant house. She too, in the valley of the Nile, served the fire and blew upon it. When the crackling momentum of the fire had subsided and on the hearth were the cherry live embers, she laid over them a clay dish containing a bread dough of grain. The life of the fire went into the bread, and thence into the man who had entered the body and the rapturous mystery of the woman; and also into the young who had come out of the loins of the woman. And this vestal woman felt the fire that was part of her woman's body; and she felt the fire's warmth between her legs.

Just so a woman of the early Stone Age, walking along the beach with a basket of clams, would come gladly to the fire by the cave's mouth, and stand a moment so, with cold legs and feet still wet from the sea. She too felt the life of the fire, as it flickered up through the curls of heavy smoke in the half rain and the mist.

But these of the early Stone Age were the little people of the wide world. Catastrophes of nature, and pestilence and famine, would turn them back into the earth, and their fires would die. Violence and wars would drench the fire with blood and scatter it. There would be raiding devastations so thorough that it would seem as if this species must destroy itself and so disappear from the planet. Yet inevitably a few individuals would escape. A girl and a boy might elude pursuers and wander together. It was the wide world, for man was rare, and certainly it was then possible to travel for months, over hundreds of miles, and never see another member of the human race. Still, if several others with scattered fires would eventually meet, another beginning could be made. A fire would be kindled at last, perhaps from lightning igniting the grass. And the life of the fire could then go on again.

However, the fire was the woman's. The house that was built was to protect the fire. That is why the house is, in its deepest meaning, essentially feminine, for it is the place of the fire. Men return to their houses at day's end when they are tired, and close to the primal femininity of sleep, the daily repeated womb of forgetfulness. They leave their houses in the alien masculinity of the morning, eager to be gone.

Thus the house is the archetypal sense of life, and as such it is the center of the earth. The hearth is the navel of the world. The chimney, or the path of the smoke, rises to the heavens. At its base is the femininity of the fire. That is as it should be, for it reaches to the source of life that only the gods bestow. It is sacred because it reaches upward to the stars, and its gift is the stuff of stars. The sons of the sacred act of cohabitus are therefore the sons of stars. The vestal girls are the daughters of the sun. Therefore they tend the fire which is the sun's image.

So the body of the man and the woman are archetypal too. The house both shelters and completes the man and the woman. Without the house—without this proper archetypal house—they are lost, like bees without a hive, mere waifs of the world, frayed and lusterless.

This archetypal harmony of house and human is the structure of human life; and it is life that requires it so that life can go on. Man is no beast of the field. Men and women die in the ecstasy of love and so are born again. For thousands of years, long before the Song of Songs of Solomon, and long before any recorded language, love and the house were poems of the poets. Just as in darkly distant times, love in all of its oceanic expressions is still the ultimate meaning of the house.

The house, although it may be only a primitive hut, is still the image of the world, the *imago mundi*, in which man through love becomes a part of the world. Man escapes from his tragic disconnectedness—which is aloneness. It is not possible to conceive of one's existence independent of the world; and it is not possible to conceive of man without the house. If technology could provide some capsule battery capable of warming the body to an ideal temperature, or of cooling the body perfectly in the heat of the day, and of deflecting rain or snow or wind, and could somehow provide a secret and perfect radar privacy—and if all of this could be made as simple and economical as a transistor watch—still men and women would need to live in houses. For human beings are the cosmology that the house asserts. The house is not a machine for living. It is man's sense of himself. The house is the epitome of all art. It results from the same psychic need and cause.

When there is no longer a possible sublimation of life, there is no longer a possible art. What has happened to art is what has happened to modern life. It may be difficult to imagine that a civilization as materially successful as this one can have anything fundamentally wrong with it. The mere suggestion seems to deserve a hoot of derision. Plumbing, prosperity, and the gross national product sufficiently guarantee the quality of the civilization in this approximate Utopia which is now. So it is commonly believed.

However, if in the process art becomes kitsch, then it can only be that something is wrong with life itself. For it is idle to suppose that the understanding of art is separate from the understanding of life. Intense art is related to intense life. Bored art is related to bored life. No new techniques, and no new art from the techniques, are going to change that. They will all end up (and they do) just as boring as what they replaced. The bourgeois-baiting shock of today is the yawn of tomorrow.

4

Down underground the crowds of initiates gathered, drank big beakers of wine, stood around, and then finally sat on the floor. Psychedelic paintings of a sort were all over the walls. A topless dancing girl came out, in the manner naked to the waist, but trailing a long crimson gown past the flickering light of the torches. The frankincense she wore was so strong you could smell it all the way across the room—she wriggling and twisting in some sort of sweating hypnotics. Presently there were eight or ten others—men with long hair and masks, wearing costumes of brightly colored fabric. These began twirling and chanting. Over the top of the music the noise was deafening. The initiates began to take the trip— weaving back and forth, eyes dilated—down to adore Isis under the ground, where the sun shines bright at midnight, and death is ever so lovely. It was in general essentials a mystery chapel in ancient Rome, third century A.D.

It was one of the ways that inhabitants of ancient Rome could get out of a bad, humdrum life.

> Just to be a ticket taker at the Colosseum, and Cassius riding you all day, is no joke. All that penny ante shakedown—"What's my cut of your cut?" Right. So you get a handful of coins payday, and give over half of them just for that hole in the wall eight floors up. I'll be barbecued some night. A rickety firetrap by the crookedest contractor from here to the Sabine hills, breaking every law on the books, passing the graft out right and left, even to the emperor's brother with his influence racket, and his thumb in every pot.
>
> Right again. Sure it was a better life when Octavia was around. There was a real girl. No question. So who can afford to keep a wife these days? You might just as well keep a chariot and a stable of stallions. And what kind of a banquet at hizoner's, your lousy patron? Banquet indeed from that skinflint. Table scraps. So all you have here at home is the same supper of lentils, and then lie on the bed alone and look at the ceiling. Nothing to do but just that. The emperor's official ceiling looker.

What had happened to the Roman world was success—a dazzling, unprecedented success. The Roman system was a machine that worked. There were forty-five provinces, and they stretched from Britain to the Tigris and Euphrates. Rome had started as a little city-state in Latium, founded according to the Virgil legend by a god-obeying Aeneas, a refugee from the fall of Troy. On the voyage from Troy he met and fell in love with the beautiful Dido, a queen. Although sojourning awhile in her kingdom and availing himself of the pleasures of her person, he nonetheless ended up by piously leaving the lady in the lurch in order to found the city of Rome, a city of manifest destiny. Thus the great hero of Rome comes down to us over the two thousand years since Virgil, exhibiting a character with curious inhibitions, and a strong drive of purpose matched to an excess of piety.

We may say that Rome began as a puritanical state. Significantly, it ended as a bordello. Just as the American colonists fought the Indians and took their land away from them, using muskets backed up by Bibles, so the Romans fought and conquered the aborigines of Italy, using their phalanx backed up by Roman virtue. After about four hundred years of nearly continuous warfare, Rome had conquered the world and had reached the pinnacle of success.

Centuries before, Alexander the Great, a mere Macedonian, could weep because there were no more worlds to conquer. He had conquered the world for honor, that is, to be the greatest of the Greeks. He wept because in the achievement the honor had seemingly ended. However, Rome had conquered the world for spoils, for what the politicians and the powerful quickly turned into money. The Roman Empire was a money-making machine, grinding out the taxes—the profits—from the oppressed provinces. Money, unlike honor, never seems to have an end. It always looks as if it could go on forever and ever. Therefore Rome did not weep the day the world was conquered.

Just so, American corporations do not weep because they have conquered a world market. Quite the contrary, they rejoice and declare dividends. The chairman of the board is bound to be asked to address university graduates at commencement. His words, unmistakably benign, with just the proper touch of gentlemanly truculence, will present all the Roman virtues (although he will certainly call them American), and he will end on a note of Roman optimism.

Now materialistic peoples are always optimistic. Yet optimists are really pessimists, because they are materialists. All notions of materialism are in rudiment finally cynical, and therefore they are pessimistic.

What Wordsworth called in the nineteenth century "getting and spending" always presents the exciting prospect of getting something for nothing. It can go all the way from getting a bargain at the store to backing a Mack truck up to the mint. It means, in last analysis, the dedication of life to the exciting possibility of striking it rich—that is, in one form or another, plunder. The Roman world operated on that basis. To a great extent so does the modern world. Speculation is plunder. It presumes the acquiring of wealth (money) without directly or indirectly applying productive labor to the resources of the earth, and therefore taking the wealth away from somebody else who has.

During the recent riots in the ghettos the frustrated poor folk looted the clothing, liquor, and television stores. They stormed no Bastilles—only the outlets for consumer goods. They stormed no bakeries; they weren't after bread; they weren't starving. The miserable relief saw to that. Neither did they have any genuine plans for a revolution, that is, for the liberation of man, the establishment of justice, and the defeat of tyranny. They had solid grievances, to be sure, but they were innocent of revolutionary abstractions. In a way of speaking, they were good Americans. They wanted to get something for nothing; just for the once to have the excitement of striking it rich. They felt they had been unjustly excluded, through poverty and racial discrimination, from this American privilege, more or less shared by the rest of the population. They seized the privilege openly and crudely, and therefore criminally. They ignored the fact that in the national mythology a small theft is bad while a large covert one properly disguised by abstractions is respectable no end. It is what made America great.

The notion of plunder is optimistic because it presumes that it can go on forever, that there is some kind of good fairy protecting the nation against the immutable laws otherwise governing cause and effect. Something like that was the general psychology of the Roman conscience.

How all of this worked out with the empire is well enough known. We could walk blindfolded through the corridors of ancient Rome—our very own. The virtuous materialism, the success ideal, resulted in the economy of plunder. The plunder resulted in the gradual impoverishment of the general population. Rome became at length an empire of millionaires and beggars. The impoverishment resulted in the welfare state, in bread and circuses, in the terrible cry through the streets: "Games forever and bread for nothing." Thus the citizen existed at the favor of the politician who got his votes. The politician and his wealthy backers took over nearly every affair of life, and managed the takeover with ever increasing inefficiency, corruption, and brutality. So the economy of plunder resulted in the gathering power and prestige of our enemy the state, then and now a conspiracy and a monopoly.

The state—as distinguished from normal and necessary government and law—is that system in America of elected or appointed officials and their fat cats. And in Russia it is the system of commissars, secret police, and Party bureaucrats. In that Roman process of the state everyone, excepting the rich and the powerful, became finally a part of the general rabble—bored, frustrated, and consequently unscrupulous, and entertained by the sadism of the gladiatorial games.

Slaves were the machines of the Roman Empire. The slaves were the by-product of wars of conquest. Into Rome, through the centuries, they came by the hundreds of millions, and in far more numbers than any labor use required. There was not enough gold in the world to represent, as legal tender, the new wealth of Rome. So the bodies of slaves became *pecunia*—coin. Just so in America and the modern world, the great development of machine technology came out of the wars—what is today called the "spin-off." The development of the tractor and the airplane, for instance, came out of World War I. Electronics, the jetliner, missiles, atomic fusion, and an enormous accumulation of gadgetry came out of World War II. These machines, like the slaves, are far beyond any real requirement of gainful use, and in themselves are always verging on the pointless, like the moon landing, a kind of nationalistic science fiction braggadocio. The machines become for us possessions for the sake of possession. In a word they become *pecunia*, the coin, a mark of wealth, what Veblen called "pecuniary responsibility," from three automobiles and three television sets all the way to anything that it is barely possible to machine-ize. It is a vast kitchen midden of pecuniary junk. It is what fills the stores—the kitsch, the useless.

Money floated the Roman people right off the ground. The rabble had once been the free farmers of Latium, farming with their sons the little eight- or ten-hectare farms. As such they were able to conceive and found the first free republic in the world, a genuine government by law. These farmers, ruined by the neglect of their farms during the wars of conquest, as soldiers of the legions, or else later unable to meet the competition of slave-grown corn, finally gave up and moved to the city. Modern statisticians would call it "urban migration." It is going on today all over the world, due largely to the competition of the tractor and other farm machinery.

In Rome everybody was after money, from the poorest to the richest. Most got it—when they did—by the easy expedient of going into debt; the wealthy got it by sly and crude schemes to corner it. Above all, people had the illusion of progress. There was all that money everywhere. There was much hope, but there was much disappointment. Disappointed and mendacious officials, and such like, were forever concocting rapacious plans to take over the government or some branch of it. If apprehended they could claim national security as a loophole—the borders were in hazard. Watergate was all the time. Nearly every election was rigged. The emperors bought themselves into power with donations (Gibbon) much like our campaign funds. After the assassination of the emperor Pertinax, the empire itself was auctioned off like a drove of cattle to the highest bidder.

Along with the illusion of progress was the equal illusion of the necessity of mere bigness and expense. Excepting for the pyramids of Egypt and the skyscrapers of Chicago and New York, there is in all history nothing comparable to the giantism of Roman architecture. Until the end there were bigger and bigger baths, amphitheaters, and forums. They were built not only in Rome but all over the provinces. Their purpose was to impress and intimidate the population. The projected buildings of Hitler were on the same scale. Who would dare to oppose such a mighty power?

The emperor Augustus boasted that he had found Rome a city of brick and had left it a city of marble. He neglected to mention that the marble was only a veneer. And a veneer was the entire pretense of Roman art in the centuries of decline. As Gibbon points out, the highest rewards sought out the faintest glimmerings of artistic merit. The foundation racket—so familiar today—found its expression in the favor of a wealthy patron surrounded by admiring sophists and pandering charlatans. Poetry become the avant-garde avocation of dilettantes and triflers. By the time of Constantine the art of sculpture had entirely disappeared in Rome. No one could be found to produce the pieces to cover the emperor's triumphal arch. It could be completed only by stripping marbles from the arch of Hadrian.

With the decay of art came the degeneracy of manners and morals. Finally there was no Roman virtue. It was a sham like everything else. Presently the barbarians of the North appear, eager for spoils in the effeminate and degenerate city. Rome had simply become filth. Reading Juvenal is like dredging a sewer. The sexual perversion, to say nothing of the repellent tawdriness, taxes the ingenuity of the translator. Yet Juvenal, for all his savage brilliance, was only talking about what was going on all around him. Not only had Rome become filth, nature herself had become filth, in the guise of the once beautiful Eros now tittering and possessed of warts, scabs, and pus. The sewer was so deep it took a thousand years to clean it. Nature was wholesome and sweet once again only in the troubadour's song of Francis Bernardone of Assisi.

5

The light came down on the new world which was the medieval age, built over the ruins of the Roman Empire, the very stones weathered clean by the rains and snows of the thousand years. The light was the *lux nova*, the new light discovered by the Scholastics at the school of Chartres. The light was the source and the essence of all visual beauty. "Lucid," "luminous," and "clear," the light was the creative principle of the universe, illuminating the world; the light was both order and the hierarchy of values. It created the Gothic cathedral.

Light was defined as the uncorrupted body of Christ. If we are not to be provincial, we must bear in mind that it was a religious epoch. The cathedral was the exact archetypal image of the house of heaven. It was believed with exact medieval literalness that, as the house of heaven, it was the temple of the immaculately conceived son of God. Therefore the stones are dematerialized by light. Nearly everywhere the walls are perforated, opened, and fretted so that the light passes through them. Since light is the luminous glow of heaven, the construction is dissolved in light. The heavy bearing walls of the old Roman basilica are thus transformed into a skeleton of piers and flying buttresses, diagramming on the naked air a metaphysic of engineering. The intervals between the buttresses became stained glass windows. Light is the child of space, so the glass paintings, with their translucent blues and greens, colors of distance, were as jewels dissolved in light. Space in the guise of light passes through them. The symbolism is perfect. Just as Christ was the child of God, so God appeared on earth in the guise of Christ.

Since God is infinite, God is everywhere. Therefore the space of the cathedral is infinite. The great long line of the nave was as long as the burghers could make it. At the transept crossing, the piers proceed upward, onward and diagonally in mysterious, never terminated, and irresistible fluxions. The space beyond is like the premonition of some irrational dimension. The gods of the old Greek and Roman pantheon were sublime bodies, but not an infinity. They dwelt not everywhere, but at a certain bodylike place—Mount Olympus. Therefore Greek and Roman temples are always bodies, sculpturelike, static in space as bodies stand. The Doric temple was the grand expression.

So saying that the space of the cathedral is infinite is not to imply a mere architectural manipulation or a poetic fancy. The space was infinite because of a genuine idea, one of the great historical ideas of life. For genuine idea, where and when it exists, is the only human beneficence, the one salvation from catastrophe. The entire race of man goes on its credit. Idea is the light coming down on the poor helpless thing. Suddenly the illegible is legible.

Abbot Suger, in building Saint-Denis, in one stroke invented the Gothic from the Scholastic idea of light. The stone walls were penetrated everywhere and were thus transparent, thus dematerialized, letting light into the body of the once illegibly dead stones. The recognition must have been like a thunderclap: that is the body of Christ, and of course that is his temple.

To be sure the *lux nova* was recognized because a new life, and a new hope for mankind, had come to release Western man from the cellar of the feudal castle, and from the dank serf's hut, into a new possibility of life in the new villages which quickly became the free autonomous towns, with their free life and their guilds. The feudal period—what we call the Dark Ages—had resulted from the breakup of the old Roman Empire. It was another expression of slavery. Now these new towns of the medieval age were simply populated by runaways from the feudal fiefs. The baron sent his emissary to these upstart fortified towns, and the burghers met him at the gates. They asked whose law the baron meant to invoke—the law of the town or the law of the baron. If he said the baron's law, they handed him in symbolic gesture a sword; if he said the town's law, they handed him a bouquet of flowers.

According to Peter Kropotkin, the same spirit of emancipation in the twelfth century ran through all of the towns, the richest as well as the poorest. Especially was this true in Italy. It was the Lombard towns which defeated

Frederick Barbarossa, the German king. In defeating the king and thus preventing his conquest of Italy, the medieval city was proved as the great counterforce against feudalism.

To guarantee liberty, self-administration, and peace was the chief aim of the medieval city. Labor was its foundation. Speculation on production was not allowed. All products had to be first offered at the common market. No one got a "corner" on anything by speculation. There were no deals under the table, no nimble arrangements of finance. There was simply the market open for anyone to buy until the ringing of the bell had closed the market at day's end. Only then could the retailer buy. Even then his profit had to be an honest one, not excessive.

We laugh at the proposition that work ought to be pleasant, because we are today dominated and bullied by the slave psychology that work is drudgery. However, a medieval city ordinance, as the most natural thing in the world, stipulated: "Everyone must be pleased with his work." Meister Eckhart, a medieval philosopher, pointed out that "the craftsman loves to talk of his craft." Of course he did, because his craft was a pleasure. The modern factory worker, standing at his machine, mechanically repeats brainless billions of times the same minutely small part of the whole, and he hates every moment of the day.

On the contrary, in the medieval town everything that was made, all the way from bread to plowshares to the cathedral, was made as a work of art. Everyone was an artist of a certain kind; and a man's art, by human reaction, was the great delight of his life. It was himself in the highest sense. Our notion of work as drudgery and art as kitsch would have been considered insane. If anyone had proposed or demanded it, the neediest man would have picked up his tools and gone home.

In the eighteenth century, long after the medieval town had collapsed, Adam Smith, the English economist, could boast that by the new division of labor, and the money as plunder economy, it took eighteen men to make a pin; and that by this method pins could be made ever so much cheaper. Of course today there are vast machines that make pins and spout them out by the ton; and no doubt the pin is again ever so much cheaper. But in the process the workman has been turned into a robot; work has been turned into drudgery and life into boredom. In distinction, the medieval workman made the pin all by himself as a work of art. The guild process used the whole man. Whether it was pin making, boat making or barn making, the making required a knowledgeable and particular man, a *Baumeister* of his craft.

Today the whole process of mass production and the division of labor is bitterly challenged everywhere, even by industrial management, but more importantly by the guy on the assembly line. Yet over fifty years ago the archly good and shrewd George Bernard Shaw could point out the fallacy, noted above, as had William Morris fifty years before Shaw in *News from Nowhere*.

The medieval city was eventually ruined by destructive forces both from within and from without. It was ruined by the rise of a privileged class of merchants and entrepreneurs who merely used the structure of the city for their own profit. From the outside, the city was thwarted by the development of a centralized state—the nation—with its imperial pretensions and its standing army. Within the city the old religious faith, which had originally formed the city, quickly died down to something very ordinary, finally to be replaced by *skepsis*. Emancipation from tyranny and the brotherhood of man were no longer the ideal. The light had gone out.

And there the cathedrals stand to this day, obviously unfinished. In many instances, there the great towers stand without steeples. Men just gave up. So the remnant town and the cathedral today are very still, like something bewitched, an enchanted world that had simply stopped one day, as a clock stops. But all medieval works of art have the same feeling of arrested beneficence. A drawing from the Book of Kells, with its unbelievable draftsmanship and detail—even to the two rats nibbling the eucharistic bread under the eyes of a benign pair of cats—fills the most callous person with nostalgia for a world now inexplicably vanished.

The medieval world has something to say to everyone, each according to his particular nature. In that sense it was vernacular and popular, and miles and miles from the avant-garde and the corduroy-coated cocktail boys. To repeat, it was that world revealed by *lux nova*, the mystical sense of light; and it was developed in the name of the religious aspiration of man. In a word, it was the very essence of what is most jeered at today. Intellectualists and ignoramuses, haughtily and easily soaking up our present derogatory materialistic attitude, extol the medieval works of art and deplore the religion as though they were two separate things—indeed, as though art were a thing, an objet d'art fabricated for the shelves of museums.

Medieval people never made that mistake. To the Scholastic, the Gothic cathedral was an intelligible proposition in logic and philosophy which conclusively demonstrated the structure of faith. To the *Baumeister* and the masons who had built it, it demonstrated that God was in his heaven and that stones were as they should be. The shawl-covered peasant woman come to the great cathedral to kneel before the Virgin. She had lost a son in the king's war. The Virgin had lost a son too, and so the Virgin knew all about the grief that wants and needs no words.

6

It is unknown whether Western man has the vitality to begin over again. However, it is evident as affairs stand—and presuming that they continue as they are with only normal acceleration—that the modern world, judging by history, will now proceed very rapidly to the familiar situation from which there is no salvation. It is familiar because history records the situation over and over again. Every civilization occurring on this planet, each in its fatal time, has been brought down groveling and dying in the same situation. "The lion and the lizard keep / The courts where Jamshyd gloried and drank deep."

So what alternatives remain while there is still time? There is only one: understanding. It is a rare article, and especially so if, modestly, we do not presume to enroll ourselves. Understanding is the art of knowledge. Understanding is knowledge sublimated. By knowledge alone it is possible to destroy a world; by understanding, to create one. Understanding is light, forever a new light, a *lux nova*. New light is new life. New life is the conquest of kitsch.

In the Renaissance Alberti could say: "Men can do all things if they will." Certainly men and women today could pick up and leave our favorite serfdom. They could resign. They could refuse to be anymore a part of it. They could give notice to the state to get out of our lives—the state with its official power rolls so generously dotted with unconvicted felons.

Just as eight hundred years ago men and women escaped from feudalism and founded the medieval city as the city of refuge, so today the same is possible, and for the same tremendous reason of survival. It was not then a fancy, nor is now. A society cannot be designed. It is organic. Great world changes are rooted in the bedrock of reality. If modern man is to go on, he must break the hold of the incipient industrial and commercial fascism and its grinding bureaucracy, the modern equivalent to feudalism. With all of its grim promise of slavery and a world soon to be exploded into nuclear rubbish, now is the Dark Ages. Man must escape to freedom.

Certainly men and women today could leave the terrible cities with their ghettos, both the poor ghettos and the rich ghettos. They could make new cities in the landscape, cities for living. As in medieval times, the city could be a work of art. Everything made could be a work of art. And most important, life itself could be a work of art. Said Frank Lloyd Wright: "Better than to write a poem is to live one."

True, we ourselves have forged our own chains by following the mechanistic success ideal. Yet technology is not at fault, but rather selling out on life for it. Technology is not a hobgoblin, it is a tool. The machine was made for man, not man for the machine. The machine is now the tyrant of our life only because we have failed to use its immense power to serve and enrich life. So of course we could carry our technology along with us, as the tool to build our new cities and the artist's tool to make whatever is made. The light would come down on technology too.

Nor need everyone do it. However, such a superior quality of life would be emulated. That is how every advance of mankind has occurred. It may be objected that the innate destructiveness of man would eventually bring down the new life and so reduce it to a shambles. Very well, perhaps it would. Then men and women would need to begin over again. There is no help for it.

There is no final solution to life. There is only life. Its inner content may be impoverished and empty, or it may be enriched and full to the brim. Only the solemn ass imagines that either case by itself results in happiness. The happy never think about happiness. Happiness as a purpose is an illusion, just as much so as any supposed final solution to life. Are butterflies happy? The very thought is a leaden knell and reveals at once the tragedy of man, who cannot himself be happy and so imagines the happiness of butterflies. Life can have valor, and that is better. The illumination of valor is art.

In the creative process there are ever and ever again new cathedrals. Nature, of which man is a part, is not frugal but abundant. Yet the world is imperfect and must remain so, because that is its nature. This basic imperfectibility of the world is the reason for every creative act. That is its catalyst. Mankind has never arrived at any ultimate anything. Utopias are delusions. The true creator looks at his work quite otherwise. It was brief and fragmentary, and it tuned his soul. It was one triumphant moment out of the infinite imperfection, close under chaos.

And that is why man must always go on, out of the creative spirit, which is man, and in the world of his making, which is art.

Nature and Architecture (1983)

1

Except for the national economic paranoia of making money, there are few things today more important to the megalopolitan consciousness than nature and architecture. This is a curious paradox because our civilization is in reality rapidly and ruthlessly destroying actual external nature. It is a commonplace that rivers and lakes, and even the mighty seas, are being poisoned—to say nothing of villages, towns, and cities and the very air we breathe. By strip mining, vast areas of the beautiful wilderness deserts of the western states are being turned into hideous man-made deserts. In point of fact it is a national policy.

By this and similar destruction, eventually hundreds of animal species will be exterminated and become as legendary as the unicorn. Religious folk used to call these species—these creatures—the handiwork of God. But today everything has changed. Even the rain has changed. It is acid rain that now falls on the land. And it doesn't fall on God's land, it falls on technology's land. Technology is God. Far better the childish gods of ancient Greece with their golden curls and vacant brows. For, like Faust, we have made a deal with the devil. Now pay up.

Perhaps that is the reason for our nuclear bombs. It is the bottom line, as we commonly say. One day, not so near and not so far, our technology's mindless computer, stuffed with its appropriate data bank, will interpret on the screen as enemy missiles merely a flock of fugitive geese or enraged condors. At once the computer will begin cranking out the retaliation instructions. An hour later not even the insects will be alive, not even the seeds of the field. The earth will be a sterile ball in space—scorched, dead. The account paid up, stamped, perforated.

Since all of this situation is plainly so—that we are actually in the process of destroying nature—why our affectionate interest in nature? But of course the same question might be asked about architecture. Today the public interest in architecture is truly enormous. However, stated with near exactitude, today there is no architecture. Why? What in the world is architecture?

The confusion on this subject is bedlam. For instance, people today think that architecture is simply a matter of fashion, forever changing. This week's architecture is not last week's. So always the big question is, What's next?

More specifically stated, the goal of architecture is assumed to be the quest of interesting shapes—or as the term is applied, "exciting shapes." Thus the purpose of architecture is to relieve boredom. This is obviously an impossible function. Boredom, as clinical records show, is a grave psychiatric problem, not an architectural problem at all. Boredom is boredom with life. It feeds on itself, and unless root causes are eliminated, it is insatiable.

However, with such a false motivation of relieving boredom, inevitably the very buildings themselves become perversely boring. Nothing is reasonable, nothing is true. The buildings run a long gamut from the merely comic to the malignantly grotesque. Plainly it is idle to speak of such buildings as being architecture, since they lack altogether that essential delight of the beautiful, which is the radiance of truth.

In their search for excitation, architects at last discovered structural engineering, and they proceeded to apply its structural forms—which for them were just a surprising novelty of shapes, such as arch, vault, parabola. Felix Candella, the eminent Mexican structural engineer, pointed out that architects were never interested in engineering, and in reality they know nothing about it. They have the naive notion that just about any shape can be built. They are only fascinated by the novelty. This false structuralism is an escape hatch from the boredom of their modern architecture.

But of all absurdities, nothing is quite as bad as the new tall buildings of the big downtowns of America, from New York to San Francisco. The excitement in these is not so much the shape as the gigantic size. They are just big advertising signs—the corporate image is the usual term.

But the back of the giant size is perhaps something much more sinister. The buildings are meant to impress, and hence to intimidate, the crowd in the street. Who would dare to oppose such a mighty power? The pedestrian is reduced to the scale of an insect in the glass canyons. Is America drifting toward an industrial and commercial fascism?

Of course no one knows, but long before the great spasmodic changes of society, symbolic harbingers have occurred. The building of the palace of Versailles, with its strict geometric avenues, its extravaganza of fountains, and its reduction of nature to a despotic mode of artificiality, in reality announced the final end of the medieval period and the beginning of the baroque with its will to power.

These new tall buildings only add to the already preposterous density of the commercial areas. Such peaks of traffic morning and night stall to a halt. With this welter of traffic as a given, the old department stores surrender in despair and move to the suburbs. The new skyscrapers must have a symbolic reason; they certainly do not have a practical one.

Now add to this the military hazards of such concentrations of population. How long would the downtown last if bombarded with merely conventional high explosive bombs of TNT, delivered by a small armada of thirty or forty terrorist or enemy airplanes? Perhaps twenty minutes—say 200,000 dead. Or how long would the downtown last in even the mildest nuclear war? Seconds—the strike of strikes—everybody dead. To any enemy, the concentrated population is an irresistible target for destruction—and asks for it.

Certainly we have a strange notion of architecture. But in contrast, what should architecture be today? What should be its nature?

2

Nature is not merely what we usually mean by external nature, such as the landscape, the flowers, and the seasons. Nature is the entire context of the universe. Hence nature is reality. The unreal is *contra naturam*—against nature. A single word could do: nihilism. That means the nothing, the meaningless, the empty. So architecture as the expression of nature is not some special kind of architecture. There has never been any other.

Thus the ancient Egyptian temples, with their close-set mighty columns, created groovelike aisles of space, representing the journey of the soul to life eternal. To the Egyptians, the explanations of religion supplied all explanation. Religion was not simply the care of the soul, as medicine would be the care of the body, agriculture the care of the crops, and government the care of the people. Religion, because it dealt with the whole apparent reality of the universe, was everything. It was the architecture.

The Nile River, in its inundation, bestowing annually its offering of rich mud which, under the desert heat of the sun, yielded several crops a year, was a dominant force in the development of Egyptian architecture. The Nile carved as permanent a groove in the thought of ancient Egypt as it did in the rocks of its riverbed. The flowering column capitals of the temples, as conventualized papyrus and lotus, expressed the yearly springtime miracle of the resurrection of life following the inundation of the Nile.

This brief explanation of Egyptian architecture is an explanation of an idea. It suggested to the Egyptians a synopsis of all life. But the history of the world is simply the history of ideas. The absence of idea is simply historyless nullity. These were the dead times, the empty times, the times without architecture.

To speak of ancient Greece is to speak of the idea of the Doric temple. It said everything that the Greeks meant. Entirely different from the groovelike space of ancient Egypt, Greek space was point formed. The Doric temple stands alone in space, as the body stands, as sculpture stands. The Greek city-state, the polis, was point formed, standing alone in the landscape, unmerging. What we mean by Greece was a multitude of these little independent city-states—usually only a few thousand citizens. The Peloponnese of Greece was by geographical nature broken up into small segments of land between mountains and inlets of the seacoast.

The original formation of the point-formed cities was of the utmost simplicity. A piece of land separate from the landscape, with a square at the center for public affairs, was the first condition and gesture of the city. It implied a contract of free citizens to live and work together. The simple dwellings were merely arranged around this center point, this polis.

The history of nearly all of the ancient world is a history of universal despotism, a history of kings and dynasties and of antlike multitudes of population. The history of Greece is a history of individuals, of fearless freedom of thought, and of the ideas of individuals. In this sense the individual is the point-formed connotation of life. The Greek tragedy is simply the drama of the individual standing alone against gods and fate. Of such is the sublime proportion and the statuelike space of the Doric temple, the idea of Greece, the idea of the architecture.

But when this idea of freedom and the individual—somehow through the savage vicissitudes of time—at last lost its original purpose, its responsibility, its relevance, its vitality, then the mass man took over. Greece died. Greece became a hinterland and a geography of ruins.

Yet so persistent is historical idea that its life span extends over many centuries like an ancient tree. It was a thousand years from the *megaron*, the type-form house of the godlike heroes of the *Iliad*, to the final development of the Doric temple. It was a thousand years from the first Christian basilicas in the late Roman Empire to the building of the Gothic cathedrals in the twelfth and thirteenth centuries.

Architecture gave the meaning to the great ideas of the world, because architecture was the idea. It was the sense of life; it was the sense of ultimate reality. It was in everything. It was in the common dwelling of the peasant or the farmer with surprising—even arresting—expressive similarities. The "soul houses" of ancient Egypt—little pottery replicas of the common farm dwelling, a few inches across, discovered in Egyptian excavations—spontaneously suggest the style of the prodigious Egyptian temples. As a parallel, the common house of ancient Greece was innately similar to the *megaron,* and hence to the Doric temple. The half-timbered houses in the medieval burgher town at once suggest the rib-vaulted structure of the Gothic cathedral.

Everything goes together because idea is a harmony. Thus a knowledgeable critic standing in front of an artifact from the historical past—say a cup, a painting, a sculpture—may say with perfect assurance, how Egyptian it is, how Greek, how medieval, or how Chinese. In each example the artifact is a kind of architecture. In that time, in that culture, life itself was a kind of architecture, a perceived harmony. Just because the human experience itself is so problematical, so tragic and so comic, so self-defeating, as well as sometimes so triumphant, the sense of harmony—the sense of the successful resolution of fate—is sheer necessity. We can call that harmony structure. Architecture is its sublime symbol. We are so affected by the profane eloquence of Beethoven because the structure of the music is architecture in sound.

All of this seems so strange to us today because we live in a screaming cacophony which we defend; we call it freedom, whereas it is only license for chaos. That is for us the normal. To the insane, insanity is always reason.

3

Such is the essential problem of nature and architecture. In our time, what would be the solution? We have no architecture today because architecture is a social art, and we do not have a genuine society. As Robert Hutchins said: "Every man for himself, and the devil take the community."

The old cities of Europe were beautiful, and they belonged to everyone. Even today, as any tourist sees at once, that is still the normal. What we have is the diametric opposite: the cheap theatrical, the sham, the straining after effect, the forever changing moment-to-moment inspiration, and the total lack of any logical sense of purpose. Consequently we have shape without form, material without substance, intention without idea. But even this is flattery. To properly estimate the pomp and show of the newest glitter, suppose a tribe of barbarians incredibly enriched.

Modern man has accomplished miracles with technology. But much of it is dangerous, and nearly all of it is pointless in use. Albert Einstein characterized our civilization as "perfection of tools and confusion of aims."

Yet the machine itself is a natural tool. The trouble is that we do not know how to use it, as Frank Lloyd Wright splendidly showed so many years ago in his Hull House lecture "The Art and Craft of the Machine." We do not know how to use it because we lack any genuine purpose of life, like a fool playing with buttons. We are at once technological giants and social pygmies.

Here are some 200 million persons—the American nation—heirs to an ample and generous past. They are materially enriched beyond any period of history. There is simply nothing comparable to the American wealth. It is beyond the furthest dreams of avarice. But what has been the net result?

The American cities are among the most squalid in the world. The public buildings are among the dullest and most pretentious in the world. The streets are among the ugliest and most dangerous in the world. Automobile-related deaths, resulting largely from the archaic gridiron pattern of the streets and the contiguous highways, exceed every year the numbers killed in disastrous wars. Apparently no one cares very much. The multistory slum clearance projects are like prisons, repellent and terrifying. But at least 75 percent of the average American metropolis could be classified as a slum by any reasonable standards. The city as a whole is dirty, shabby, disreputable—with automobiles parked bumper to bumper around the block, making the entire city a kind of used car lot. Quite a touch, that—a kind of fiendish unloveliness.

It only emphasizes the poverty in the midst of plenty to point out that there is an enormous housing shortage of millions of dwellings. As poor as the dwellings of the nation really are, there are not even enough. However, this very fact could be a great opportunity to build a true architecture—not in the old city which, in its present form, is doomed—but outside the city in the landscape. This exodus could eventually create a new city, a city for living.

So then, what architecture for America? Architecture should begin at home. Historically, it always has. The American republic was not founded to give a job to emperors, kings, or millionaires, but rather to be the homeland of free citizens. So, in principle, the dwelling was the original idea.

This prototype house could be of any material, and infinitely various. But every house would be in some form a work of art, for art is simply the proper way to make something. In that sense every house could be a poem.

Thus houses could be built of stone, the great nature material, laid up in a natural way suggesting cliff or outcrop. Or the walls could be built of boulders, like old stone walls dividing farmers' fields. As well, houses could be built of wood, the boards laid in beautiful wood-grain bands.

But all materials and methods of construction could thrive. Houses could be built of brick, that ancient prefabricated material older than the pyramids of Egypt. Brick can make walls so enduring, so precise and exact, so delightful in color, so logical in the lapping and bonding. What walls could be that rich—what ornaments that splendid? In a natural architecture the facts are the ornaments.

Or the house could be built of steel and glass, a crystal house, built like a pavilion in a garden. It could be as much a part of nature as if the trees and flowers were actually in the house—or from the insideness of such a prism looking out: delicate springtime, full leaf of summer, vibrancy of autumn, purity of new snow.

So of course houses could be built of any material practical and useful for the purpose. The quality of the house is not guaranteed by the material, but rather depends on how we use the material. Each material has its own intrinsic meaning, its own intrinsic nature. To find that and express it is the art of building.

Such a house could be so natural that it could actually be a growing house. Let us say that a boy and a girl get married. As usual, they have very little money, but they need a place to live. In this instance let us suppose they choose to have a prefabricated industrialized house—remember, any material that is useful is a good material. They could buy the prefabricated parts for a basic irreducible minimum of space—a minimum bath, a tiny kitchen, a little living room, and a place for a bed. They could carry the light steel or aluminum prefabricated parts in a trailer in back of an automobile. On their plot of ground in the nearby countryside, they could bolt together these parts, following a diagram and instructions. After two or three weekends they could move in and begin planting trees, flowers, and a vegetable garden.

After a year or two, with a little more money for the necessary parts, they could add another unit, and then another and another, until the house was as large as they wanted. They would own it. They had made it themselves. That truly would be free enterprise, not the fallacious and empty slogan that it is today. There would be no rent, no mortgage, no terrible and ruinous interest rate, where the so-called owner, after some twenty-five years, finally pays back perhaps triple the original cost of the house. In contrast, how sensible would be the procedure of building the house oneself. How natural it would be in America, a country of born mechanics. That procedure of course would not apply to everyone, but it certainly would apply to many. Plainly such part-time building work by the owner would be possible with any material, with any construction.

These various types of houses, here briefly listed, are in reality nothing new. They have all been built again and again. They are the best in America; they are the best in the world. The trouble is that the houses are not America. They are only what America ought to be, and could be. So the houses are an architectural debt that cannot be paid and was never meant to be paid; the houses were just meant to be built.

It should go without saying that this new architecture should not be crammed into the old city. The city as we know it is an anachronism. There cannot be a new architecture until there is a beginning to make a new city.

The present city, economically, is an absurdity. It is everyone's pick-pocket. The dollars-and-cents cost in taxation, in order to somehow prop up the collapsing assembly of dangerous and wasteful streets, alleys, and slums—to say nothing of crime and misery—all of it comes to bankruptcy. Witness the example of New York. The city's sister ugliness is a nightmare and a scream. As already stated, the military vulnerability of the city is the single greatest danger of society in our time. By any just analysis, the whole city is a slum: and a slum is simply a place where no one really wants to live. Thus the enormous growth of the fugitive suburbs. Meanwhile the population density of the old city remains unbelievable. Walking down the street in the worst areas, it is possible to see more miserables than can be seen in any place on this planet, save perhaps in India. However, it is often objected that a new city cannot replace the old city, because the old city represents such a tremendous capital investment. The point is nonsense: nothing is an investment that is itself valueless. The present city does not represent a value; it represents money that is already lost. Nay, more—it represents the decline of Western civilization. All of the old civilizations were at the last eaten out from the inside. So what we now witness was the same in old Thebes of ancient Egypt, in Babylon and in Rome. If Western man is to go on, he must create a wholesome, livable condition for life: a new city for life, a city in the landscape with parks and vegetable gardens and sun-filled houses; with safe and adequate streets and highways; with schools in parks, and with meadows where children can play and really belong in the scheme of things; a city with nearby shopping areas and working areas, reached without the pedestrian's crossing a single traffic street; a city as a part of the farms and forests of the region; a city for living. This proposition, here compressed in a paragraph, is a precondition for vital architecture.

It may not be likely, but at least it is a possibility. Since the possibility is the only chance we have, the discussion should be admissible.

The new architecture and the new city apply not only to houses but to every type of building for every need of man, each building according to its specific nature, and all according to the nature of man. The direct reference to houses is an allegory. It represents the creative activity of persons. Nothing is possible without that. There is a fond notion today that the state—or as we say "the government"—or industry—will do something. The exact opposite is true. Only persons do something. The state, if not actually exploitative, is timid, as Thoreau put it, "like an old woman with her silver spoons." The tough founding fathers who created the American republic did so in opposition to the English merchant state.

The ancient architectures were the expression of beliefs now outworn. With few exceptions these old expressions of architecture were dominated by the idea of man as mere creature, as supplicant on his knees. The temples were graven images, today perhaps only a few broken fragments overturned upon the sand, to mark the grand illusion of mankind, the ox skull of mind. All the while, then and now, there was the great reality of the universe, so vast it is merely printed on the cosmic bubble of space, some fifteen billion light years across. So now on midnight's promontory is written the awful truth of idolatrous man, pulling at strings to which nothing was attached.

Man does not easily lose his old habit of idolatry. The old idolatrous gods died and were reluctantly forsaken. But modern man has invented new idolatrous gods: money as idolatry, technology as idolatry, power as idolatry, war as idolatry.

It is these which dominate life today—not reason, not reality, not nature, but instead these bright new golden calves. Meanwhile man has learned a little, at least. The new idols are no longer quaint misunderstanding, like the rock which was Baal, the stone pillar which was Osiris. So the new idols are dangerous toys. There is a part of genuine knowledge in them. They actually can destroy the planet. That, in brief, is the situation today.

Notwithstanding, if we really wanted the good of man we could have a true architecture, an architecture based not upon idolatry in any form, but rather upon life, dominated by reason and reality, and the heart of man. Mass suicide in war is not a necessity. Life could go on.

Architecture is a shining tower in the distance. Architecture is a house reached on a tempestuous night. Architecture is a city for living with the endless white horses of Lake Michigan charging the shore.

On the Meaning of Mies (1986)

Ludwig Mies van der Rohe was a humanist in the age of science and technology. Just as civility is implicit in civilization—for that is the root meaning of the word—so humanism must be implicit in the values of science and in the use of technology. Without humanism, science is futile and technology is mere mechanics, leading to an existence of terrifying aridity.

When Mies came to America, fleeing Germany at the last hour, presumably a few steps ahead of the Nazis, he thought that his building days were over. The Nazis had already closed the Bauhaus, and no one could foretell what else they might do and to whom. So Mies was one of the illustrious of Europe, including scientists, writers, and scholars, discovering America, the country of refuge.

By the hundreds in haste and despair they came, walking down the gangplank from ships in New York harbor, each carrying a suitcase and very little else except what they had given to civilization. Mies, speaking of himself later in a laughing self-disparagement, said that he felt "like a flower out of water."

Named director of the department of architecture at the old Armour Institute in Chicago—subsequently renamed Illinois Institute of Technology—he was joined by L. K. Hilberseimer and Walter Peterhans, former colleagues at the Bauhaus. Shortly thereafter Mies was named architect for the new campus. So Mies picked up his old building problems once again—and in a strange land with a strange language, and finally in the midst of World War II. Looking back now, it seems incredible that so much was accomplished beginning with such forlorn possibilities.

Equally forlorn was the prevailing architecture of the time, as anyone can now determine by merely leafing through the architectural journals of that benighted period. Louis Sullivan had been dead fourteen years by the time Mies reached Chicago. The old Chicago school had been bankrupt and dishonored for at least ten years before Sullivan's death. Sullivan had eked out a gasping and precarious existence in rejection and frustration. Toward the very last he was a lonely figure writing late at night at a desk in the Cliff Dwellers Club, reduced to his *Autobiography of an Idea*—he of the mighty arm to build and the subtle and penetrating mind.

Frank Lloyd Wright, that great world figure in architecture, had been living out a self-imposed exile from Japan to Arizona, with a brief sanctuary in the warm Siberia of Los Angeles. He had been impoverished and literally without work for years on end, and a few chances to build again were just beginning to appear.

Modern architecture, considered a new fad, was a World's Fair flamboyance, or a version of strip windows, Lally columns, and plaster.

This in general was the situation. At that moment we were fascinated by the clarity of Mies's creations, as if looking in upon some prismatic otherworld. The space dissolved in a fantasy of reality. In that air benign something had changed.

As in the Barcelona Pavilion, there is a kind of magic. It is suddenly very still, like something enchanted. Paradoxically, there is something very ancient about it. There is a universal time about it. It has existed—or could exist—backward or forward thousands of years from this moment. Time is under a spell. The building exists in a region reached by no railroad lines.

Ugliness, vulgarity, meanness have disappeared—have somehow fallen asleep outside. Suddenly the world seems splendidly livable. This is the spell of harmony. The space is an icon, a symbol. This is architecture.

In this architecture, the bearing wall disappears completely, revealing at once that new and eloquent space beneath the sheltering roof and replacing the solid building walls with polished glass and marble.

By means of the steel frame construction, without hindrance of bearing-wall supports, it was possible to open what was necessary to open and to close what was necessary to close. In that constructive freedom buildings would become aerial, atmospheric. In that sense we stood on the threshold of the immaterial. Line replaced mass—taut black threads within a sunlit phantom.

This liberation of space from the archaic mass—so eloquently projected by Mies—may be historically considered as the second phase of a single great revolution of the Western mind.

The first phase occurred in the twelfth century with the development of rib vaulting. The old protoform of the Roman vault system—example, the Basilica of Maxentius was burdened with its enormous dead weight. It was therefore severely limited in span length, with its space held in the stone grip of its cavelike mass. This ancient building system was, by a series of brilliant innovations extending over less than a century, finally transformed into a light and elastic skeleton of piers and ribs. This was the definitive structure of the Gothic cathedral.

No eye was alien to that upward reach of space. The statical forces in the ribs, in restless quest of space, were gathered for the final leap across the aisle roof, to the flying buttress with its pinnacle, diagramming on the naked air a metaphysics of engineering. The space is that seeming nullity which is totality and which moves in irresistible fluxions through the great cathedrals, like the premonition of some irrational dimension.

The present moment, then, could be a new time, as it were, a second phase of the medieval development, and a time to go on without let or pause. It was like crossing a suspension bridge, cables drawn to a curve by gravity—perilous in sheer space, shrill wind upswing ballooning. It was as if, centuries hence, some figment race would unravel from the earth, like spider's filament, some longer span, anchoring in the bastions of unpeopled space.

Mies van der Rohe saw that steel would create a new structure, and that out of that structure must be created a new architecture. The architecture was implied in the structure. Concerning form, he had stated in 1923, and with a force which fairly rings now once again, "We refuse to recognize problems of form, but only problems of building. Form is not the aim of our work, but only the result. Form as an aim is formalism, and that we reject."

The architecture of the nineteenth century failed because it began not with the problem, but with a preconceived facade. A facade—to explain terms—is appearance made first, a building considered from the outside in, all show and nothing inside.

The school which Mies and his colleagues founded studied the great engineering works of structural science. Enlarged photographs were hung in the classrooms, showing in the classrooms the Gallery of Machines, the Crystal Palace, the great bridges over the Firth of Forth, and then Maillart's lithe spans. The curriculum was a silver symphony of rivets, grain elevators, a factory with its mile-long shell of glass, the beautiful visual force of derricks swung against the sky, high power transmission lines, farmers' barns, peasant houses, and old stone walls.

The school was one entirety from the beginning to the end. Thus the student was always working in the study of architecture in every year; and every year was related to every other year in a progression of studies. The courses differed one from the other only in their emphases. At the end the student understood every part of a building. He knew that structure is an idea of parts, leading to expression. He knew that expression wasn't something added, but something integral and innate. The truth flowered from within.

The teachers were devoted to the school, and by consequence the students were devoted. So naturally the students learned. Any student was at the end better than himself—the true and proper goal of education. Everything he worked on proceeded from principle and reason. The work was thorough, understandable, intelligent, useful. To a remarkable degree the student became the school. This was the school, excellent and memorable.

The tall buildings Mies built possess the same quality of knowledge and wisdom that Mies's school was meant to imply. The details of the buildings are superb in their knowing touch and clarity. Mies explained it—as if a craftsman working in a medieval cathedral—"God is in the details." The simplicity of the architecture has the splendor of a paradox. It is so forceful because, like the word unsaid, the act unacted, it leaves everything to the imagination. It takes the person into its confidence and so includes him. In its civility it refuses to exert its force, therefore it is never exhausted. In its candor it refuses to be impressive, therefore it impresses. Standing below and looking up, the mullions project to the sky. The construction simply stops at the top and disappears in thin air, an immediately understood abbreviation of infinity.

The very word infinity is a revelation of the meaning of Mies's sense of architectural space. Without that meaning the connotation of Mies is elusive to the last. Thus why the glass buildings at all? Why this prismatic transparency? Why the open plan? Why the free walls as planes in space? Why the collages— the elements themselves like moving planes, revealing the primordial depth beyond? Why the persistent lightness and sense of float in space? In the conté crayon drawings, the human figures, dematerialized like sprites, hover in a space beyond gravity. We ought not to be put off by Mies's urbane explanation that it is all made to be simple.

No, Mies is profound—and that is better than simple. This expression of space is profound because it is a part of the meaning of Western civilization. Western man's sense of space is the sense of infinite space. It is a space beyond space without end. That sense of space created the Gothic cathedral, with its mighty and irresistible fluxions outward and onward. In our own time, scientific explorations in space are of the same derivation; and there is no telling how far the mind of man may reach beyond this tiny planet.

We may say that the sense of space is the sense of human destiny. Space is extent. The where and how far is the definition of destiny. To the early Christian culture, at last centered in Byzantium, space was space within—thus the saying: "The kingdom of heaven is within." So all the architecture of this period is substantially the architecture of the interiors—the world within—the great domed basilicas.

Just so the ancient Greek Idea of the sublime body and the serenity of man created the Doric temple with its sublime bodylike proportions in space. Similarly, the ancient Egyptian idea of life eternal after death created the groovelike space vistas between the close-set columns of the gigantic temples—the one-directional tombward space between life and life eternal after death.

But Mies was not one to involve himself in explanations about his architecture. He built it, and that was the explanation.

His verbal explanations of anything were always concise, clear and exactly to the point. He said everything with the fewest words. He never said anything banal. His words had an intrinsic eloquence. The ludicrous in anything made him laugh, but there was never bitterness in it. He accepted persons for their good qualities and let the rest go. He was always human when he talked, and he was always considerate. Yet he was so modest, withdrawn, and unassuming that often—to some—it became a guessing game to actually know what he wanted. So the picture of Mies as a tyrant that today exists in some quarters is simply willful malice.

This, in brief, was the man who built the buildings. Just as he was always moderate in everything, so he was always moderate in discussing his buildings. If someone praised a building—say the Farnsworth house—Mies would reply: "You know, I think that is just a normal building. Something like that is what buildings should be in our time. We are just very careful and serious in our work. I never wanted to do anything to astound. I don't want to be interesting. I want to be good."

Once he said to this speaker: "I never wanted to build thousands of buildings. I only had in my life an idea that buildings ought to look like how they are actually built. And I wanted to try a few to see how it would be. Finally this is what I have done. In the process I had to build up an office. Now the persons in the office think that they would like to go on—which is natural. And I confess that, since the situation in architecture is so confused today, perhaps it would be good if we built a few more."

With his pervading sense of objectivity, Mies could see that the old sense of the special and specific functions of buildings had to be elastic. In this particular moment of history, with its characteristic changes, special uses and functions rapidly become obsolete. Therefore buildings should be built in such a way as to accommodate changes in function. Otherwise, when changes occur buildings would need to be torn down and rebuilt at prohibitive cost. This is the meaning of Mies's universal space.

Two examples should illustrate. The first, Crown Hall, 120 feet by 220 feet, is a clear open space without interior columns. Therefore it is entirely flexible in use. It could easily accommodate any changed function—almost at a moment's notice. As you may know, it once actually served for the evening as a superior ballroom with superior acoustics for the music. Crown Hall, besides being a school, is an exhibition hall. It is so continuously and flexibly used as such that it is taken as a matter of course and hardly anyone realizes its unique character.

So rational and clear is the structure that spans the 120 feet that the actual cost of the building, even with its elegant and aristocratic materials, was not much more per square foot than a factory building.

Crown Hall was placed on a raised platform which housed the unchanging functional requirements. Thus the clear span space was free under any circum-stances. Mies's Gallery of the Twentieth Century in Berlin was similarly planned. It was this method that accomplished the objective of the universal space.

In Mies's proposed convention hall for Chicago, the span of the building is 720 feet. With its vast accomplishment of a clear span of that dimension and area, it stands without equal. This is the universal space carried to the periphery of the possible. The trusses in the two directions are stiffened at the building edges by diagonal bracing, and there the loads are carried directly down to the columns. The very facts of the engineering become the architecture. It is not only without equal; it is without parallel.

The Chicago school, after a tragic lapse of twenty-five years, was continued in the work of Mies. It was not a conscious effort or an intention—quite on the contrary. However, that way of putting it is a fair approximation of what actually happened. If the Chicago school is anything, it is a part of Western man, and its roots go back many centuries to the Middle Ages and beyond. The Chicago school is not a geographical area or a corporate limit. It may be in London or Paris or Singapore. The one thing that the world is today, possessing as it does its awesome powers of self-destruction—the one thing that the world is today, if it is to survive, is one world. The one thing that it is not is provincial or nationalistic. So the name of the Chicago school is merely fortuitous.

Of all that has happened in architecture, since that moment of beginning again forty years ago, you yourselves must know. You yourselves must know it is very near impossible to build a large building today, other than the most trivial and saddest, that is not in some very important way influenced by the work of Mies. It is evident that he has left the architectural language immeasurably enriched.

Now the reason for that fact rests upon a very substantial foundation, laid down on the solid rock of reality. These methods of building initiated by Mies, and the rationality implied—to say nothing of the powerful expression in architecture—are so distinctly superior that it is virtually impossible not to use them.

It is the nature of man to strive for the superior artifact, whatever the artifact may be. Technic, upon which all of man's life on this planet has depended for the past million years at least, may be defined as maximum output for minimum input. If something now existing is more difficult and more expensive to produce, then in some vital respect it must be better in proportionate compensation. Otherwise that artifact is inferior. By the normal course of development it would be eliminated. This, in brief, is what is trying to happen today in nearly everything. The Mies influence, in developing a better way of building, is simply a very clear example.

Someone once asked Mies how he felt about others' drawing on his work. Did he resent it? He replied: "On the contrary, I think that this is why I work. I only hope that they understand and build a good building."

Now here we come to the critical point of the present situation in architecture. Mies's work was not a mannerism, nor can it be compared to a mannerism. It is a universal and objective principle. Whoever uses the principle properly is doing original work. Are surgeons unoriginal when they operate with sterilized instruments, thus following the findings of Pasteur? Are scientists, using the propositions developed by Einstein, therefore unoriginal? On that puerile basis, if every man would need to begin in the Stone Age the wheel would not yet be invented.

John Donne could say in the seventeenth century:

> No man is an island entire of itself; every man is a piece of a continent, a part of the main; if a clod be washed away by the sea, Europe is the less, as well as if a promontory were, or a manor of thy friends, or of thy own were; any man's death diminishes me, because I am involved in mankind; and therefore never send to know for whom the bell tolls; it tolls for thee.

Mies once said in conversation:

> If modern architecture is not a mere fashion but is instead a genuine historical development, comparable to the Doric temple of the Greeks and the Greek discovery of the individual, or to the Gothic cathedral and the religious epoch of the Middle Ages—certainly then men after us will go on. Each generation step by step would proceed as far as it dared.

So of course the matter is to go on. Man must go on; he cannot stand still, he cannot go back. It is too late.

That is why men such as Mies are so important. They give schematic directions. In very vigorous periods men are able to form a consensus and go on without wasting words. Weak periods are the Tower of Babel, and everything is brought down to destruction.

Mies thought of architecture as powerful, strong, clear expression. "Clear" became one of his great words. He thought about the masonry of the unknown medieval craftsmen. He thought about the wooden buildings of old, "where there was meaning in every stroke of the ax, expression in every bite of a chisel." He thought about Schinkel, Berlage, Van de Velde. He thought about Frank Lloyd Wright and the powerful expressions, like an ever repeated motif. He thought about the engineers of the tremendous long-span bridges of our time. Perhaps he is the beginning of a new age, unfolding out of the past, as must all ages.

Or perhaps he is the end of an age, an age that does not go on. In the screaming bedlam of this present moment in architecture, it is easy to believe that Mies is the last of the giants. But this cannot be true.

There is no finality in anything. The negative and the positive coexist in the same world. In fact every so-called good can lead to abuse—a frequent case. As well, every destruction prepares the ground for creation. The ridiculous and the sublime are both forever turned back into the primordial earth. The reality that once seemed hopeless becomes the renascence of tomorrow. Despair is maudlin.

Thus the world is imperfect and must remain so, because that is its nature. This basic imperfectability of the world is in actuality the reason for every creative act. That is its catalyst. Mankind has never arrived at any ultimate anything. Utopias are delusions. The true creator looks at his work quite otherwise. It was brief and fragmentary, and it tuned his soul. It was one triumphant moment out of the infinite imperfection, close under chaos.

And that is why man must always go on—out of the creative spirit, which is man, and in the world of his making, which is architecture.

Three Cantos on Color (1992)

1

Forever as a rainbow fades in color, the sun is all about. Not for an instant can we deny color. Our veins throb with rivers of color.

The blue spires of the larkspur flaunt the blue sky, while the golden bee swishes past the dappled door of the foxglove's lair. For color is the grass and every living thing.

In the very midst of the slums, girls go to work in gay-colored clothes. And young men in the very depth of the slums, and surrounded by smoke and urban filth, will go to their jobs wearing fresh clean shirts and colored neckties, as if the filthy slum was a disease and the clean shirt and the colored tie provided a kind of immunity to help survive the filth. The reason may be a variety of unconscious cunning. People today put up a hard fight against the leprosy-like filth of the American city. Fresh, clean color would not be the worst possible way to resist the American bubonic city. In this gray ugliness, is anyone truly happy? Perhaps only the young in their colored clothes.

Two men on the sidewalk talk about money. A line of mighty trucks speeds past, clattering within four feet of the two men. "For nothing like us ever was. We are the greatest nation that ever was." And this the capital of Philistia, and the city of gangsters. Where the police fished the dead men out of the river, or found them out in the lake bumping against the piers.

2

Chicago was also the city of great men, such as Louis Sullivan and Jens Jensen.

It was the city where Frank Lloyd Wright told Havelock Ellis, "I am the greatest architect existing in the world. I am the greatest architect who ever has existed in the world. I am the greatest architect who ever will exist in the world."

He set about to prove it, as a kind of one-man initiator of the world. Like Nietzsche, he saw the possibility of a new kind of humankind, wise and not ignorant, brave and not cowardly. He laughed at the impossible. To him it seemed the most natural thing in the world. He called on nature to prove the point. For nature was the ultimate reality. Nature was the truth. He called it organic architecture. Reality becomes expression. It isn't something passed on. He repudiated all forms of provincialism. What he made was "thought built," fresh and new. He eliminated all the platitudes of architecture. He built a bigger house for less money. His clients usually hired him solely for that reason. They could not afford the sentimental house they really preferred.

He put a red square on his stationery to show that he was the architect of the square deal. And the red square reminded him of the native lilies (*Lilium superbum*) that grew on the prairies when he was a child in Wisconsin. When the client could afford it, he made stained glass windows for the house—geometric lines of color, precise in statement, slim of line, like notes of music. The colors, precise and immaculate, are the lines and filaments of a new world, delineated by the bars of the flowerlike colors—and all of this in a few slim inches of space. If a thousand perfect persons were to appear, that would not amaze us. Beyond the stained glass windows would be the underside of the projecting roof, generally soft sand color. Beyond that were the trees and flowers of the garden.

Thus did Frank Lloyd Wright begin his great work in architecture. Today all over the planet the great idea and the great thoughts go on, in a vast multiplicity of expressions, in that furthest reach of the creative power of man.

Eventually clients of understanding and cultivation appeared. For these he constructed the first of the great houses. Among these was the Coonley house, where the very walls became a garden inside and out.

The Dana house was at Springfield, Illinois. Years later Wright recalled that Mrs. Dana expressed hope that in the future his work would be appreciated and understood. He replied that he hoped that day would never come because it would then prove that the architecture had failed. This was an assertion of an aristocratic ideal, which Wright was to maintain all of his life. Like Ortega y Gasset he hated the easy assurance of the mass man. He demanded life lived as a discipline. And that of course was the nature of the architecture. He loved and respected the geometric discipline of his buildings. He would extemporize on the piano before breakfast, as if expecting a joyous inspiration. He said he could have been a composer. When asked who, he said "Bach of course. Structure of course."

The dramatic interior height of the Larkin office building in Buffalo is repeated sixty years later for the Guggenheim building in New York City. Both illustrate a vertical space which astounds the prosaic, on the edge of the new world. It is as if a new race of man has suddenly appeared.

The very planet has changed. Homer and Walt Whitman walk on the meadow, stop to converse.

Lao-tsu explains the nature of space.

William Blake comes to dinner.

So he mused. Perhaps, like Alberti in the Renaissance, he would say, "Man can do things, if he only will."

In some such way he came to the idea of the mile-high skyscraper. He did not believe the Oswald Spengler estimate of Faustian man's ambition, which the devil had trapped into ruin. So he planned the mile-high skyscraper, the world. So miracles could happen and nobody knew they existed, and he understood that.

He disliked pretentious words.

Toward the end of his life, when he showed his sister the "new work" he said, "No, I am not a genius, so called: I just have longer antennae than others."

3

Once the earth was a teeming ball of fire. It cooled on the edges and lifted up the mountain floated on the molten magma. And the sun shined, and nothing lived—no least creature on the float of mountains. And the mountain crumbled at the edges and sloshed downward into the magma.

New mountains lifted and new crust floated on the seething magma. No frog croaked in puddles of molten magma. The world was dead, and no one can deny it. For some billion years it was dead. The flaky molten magma seethed in the shadow of a mountain. And the mountain itself would be folded back into the magma, into the fiery stuff of the earth. And the stars, wheeling into space, into this tiny star fragment, forlorn, trivial.

Nonetheless this planet, this tiny star fragment, survived.

Again and again crumpled-up mountains sank back into the magma, and new mountains and highlands arose, until finally the entire earth was a crust covering the planet.

Thus was the earth formed out of the stars, just an astronomical moment ago. And now we are in such a hurry, and where in the world are we going?

Mankind only came onto this planet in the last few astronomical hours or minutes. What could man actually accomplish?

Can man create a new type of man? We haven't the slightest idea. What there is against it, is a tenth-rate jeer. But human hope is the color of life. Everything else is ashes.

And lo the sun rises.

AUTOBIOGRAPHICAL MISCELLANEA

Alfred Caldwell's closest mentors were Jens Jensen and Ludwig Hilber-
seimer, and they often carried on their friendship through letters. The letters
included here from Caldwell to Jensen were written while Caldwell was
working for the Chicago Park District, and they are part of the Jens Jensen
Collection at the Morton Arboretum in Lisle, Illinois. In the late 1930s
Jensen was trying to keep his school alive at the Clearing in Ellison Bay,
Wisconsin. At the time of Jensen's death in 1951 no one was closer to him than
Caldwell, who gave his eulogy and recited Walt Whitman's "When Lilacs
Last in the Dooryard Bloom'd" as well as a poem of his own, though he can
no longer remember which one it was.

    The correspondence between Hilberseimer and Caldwell began
while Caldwell was away from Chicago building World War II military bases.
These letters are in the Hilberseimer Collection at the Burnham Library of
Architecture of the Art Institute of Chicago. During this time Caldwell also
was making drawings for Hilberseimer's book *The New City*. Hilberseimer
understood Caldwell's genius and got behind his causes, but in the end he
betrayed him.

Selected Letters to Jens Jensen (1937–41)

December 2, 1937
1953 Leland Ave.
Chicago, Illinois

Dear Mr. Jensen:

In line with your note: I will be waiting for you *"in the waiting room near the coffee shop entrance"* the Union Station on Dec. 8, 5:00 P.M.

Alfred Caldwell

Poor Finland—what have the world's peoples done to themselves to get such governments stark crazy? The peoples must be crazy. I do not think there are any natural and sane persons left in civilization, excepting peasants and exiles of one kind or another.

Poor Lincoln Park—it too is tragic—the ancient picnic grounds for Chicago's millions of poor—given over entirely now to the Buicks—to the city's prosperous mediocrity.

Alfred Caldwell

■ ■ ■

December 9, 1937
1953 Leland Ave.
Chicago, Illinois

Mr. Jens Jensen
The Clearing
Edison Bay, Wis.

Dear Mr. Jensen:

I've been wondering about your trip to Ames. I knew several fellows from that school and they had all the absurd notions.

This last snow I passed the red maples along Sheridan Rd. in Ravinia. You remember them: they are not big trees and only a few anyhow. They stand now grayer than a young beech and a little better I thought, seeming a little rarer. They weren't repeated, but just one along and a long way to the next, for that was sufficient; and the quality of the tree itself so slight and sufficient with just a few incredibly thin branches scratching the air. These trees had a manner with the world.

The trouble with people is they gang up. They stand repeated to the millionth time, and all their ways and motives are the same. They huddle in the great cities and they gang up in everything.

Alfred Caldwell

■ ■ ■

December 27, 1937
1953 Leland Ave.
Chicago, Illinois

Dear Mr. Jensen:

I'll be at the Wanheegan Hotel, Sheridan Road, Wanheegan, Monday, January 3, between 5 and 6 P.M. sometime. I don't know whether my wife can make it, but will try to get someone for the children. I am very happy at the prospect of seeing you.

I was happy to get your letter. Riding down to the administration building in the mornings and seeing all these thousands of native plants planted in the last year and still being planted, I can say to myself quietly, quietly "I am fine and have found an opening" for all these plants are a way to tell you Mr. Jensen that you were the best thing that ever happened to me. They are the only way I shall ever be able to tell you. Badly planted or how[ever], they are the only way.

All the snow here was gone by Christmas. But a few days before we'd driven out and remembered that red berries of rosa setigua in the know were red in the white snow, red in the white, were red tremendously thru deft down of new snow zoned on curved lair of the roses in the snow.

Alfred Caldwell

∎ ∎ ∎

December 30, 1937
1953 Leland Ave.
Chicago, Illinois

Dear Mr. Jensen:

I figured you meant the coming Monday. I received your note from Wanheegan yesterday. Your previous letter from Edison Bay didn't get here until Tuesday so I supposed you meant the next Monday.

I'm so sorry to have missed you. Will you let me know anytime you're coming in?

No money and I can't budge. My car isn't fit to run any distance and it's disheartening.

A good new year to you.

Alfred Caldwell

∎ ∎ ∎

August 6, 1938
1953 Leland Ave.
Chicago, Illinois

Dear Mr. Jensen:

Thanks for your letter. As to the proposed building in Humboldt Park, I can find nothing out about it at all. No one I know is working on anything to do with it. It would be kept secret as long as possible I presume. At least it isn't being discussed: I haven't heard a word. However I can try in what ways I can to discover anything and will keep you advised.

I will try to come up in the next few days or weeks. Naturally I am anxious to see your school.

By the way the Prairie Landscape got repudiated in the recent Civil Service Examinations. What I designed for the examination was the best work I ever did. The problem was a 60 acre park: it made a Prairie and a Prairie river. My mark was 36 the lowest grade of 18 applicants, many of them terribly inferior people like florists and foremen and such like. F. A. C. Smith with a presumably French design was the highest grade: 89. Mr. Otto Shaffer at the University of Illinois and Mr. Robert Moore were the experts selected to grade the papers.

The day the results were made known I sent the following telegram to Donoghue: "Civil Service list posted today makes me ineligible. You fellows have been signing my plans for 2 years. Native plants and Beachscapes and Prairies. Lincoln Park Extension, 55th St, Promontory, Your new boulevards, the Lily pool, the Riis park meadow, the biggest and the best things you have had. If I am incompetent a million dollars of landscape work is incompetent, most of it already planted, all of it approved. Do not fancy that Moore ever had anything to contribute to these plans but his name. Here is obvious fraud and sabotage of Civil Service and it happens to cast a very nasty slur indeed on my ability as a craftsman. If you are interested in investigating these antics I promise to come to you well heeled with evidence."

But no answer.

Why should a man have to stand such bastards just for the sake of doing a little work.

You mention writing a letter about Humboldt Park—say I can give you enough information about Lincoln Park alone for 10 letters and it ought to warrant a grand jury investigation. The citizen on foot is being disenfranchised, disinherited—to hell with the poor, to hell with picnics, to hell with landscape work.

ROADS ROADS ROADS ROADS ROADS

You see it is all for the rich of suburbs who drive to their businesses in the loop in the morning. Speed. Nothing is going to be left that could be termed a park. A man won't be able to walk over 300 or 400 feet without passing thru some stinking clammy concrete subway under some road or another.

Alfred Caldwell

I want to quit immediately but my wife is afraid.

■ ■ ■

September 6, 1938
1953 Leland Ave.
Chicago, Illinois

Dear Mr. Jensen,

Very sorry to have not driven up but supposed you were away.

I am anxious to see your building and the first chance I get now I will make it if only for a few hours.

I think I have a private job—a house—going to go ahead this fall. If it does I can at last be free of the parks and to go and come as I please.

I have been up to the clearing at Ravinia. The garden is pretty nice, lots of flowers, but the occupants have put a temporary shack right on the player's green. I sat in the council ring a while and looked down on the Ravine, the trees are big enough and the ravine deep enough and the ring like a high place, high enough to have just a little terror. That was what I came for—

Alfred Caldwell

■ ■ ■

February 25, 1939
1953 Leland Ave.
Chicago, Illinois

Dear Mr. Jensen,

I'll be glad when Spring comes all in all this winter hasn't been good—really a pain in the neck.

I meant to write you and tell you how much I enjoyed the visit to Ellison Bay but have been terribly discouraged about affairs here.

I did enjoy seeing you, and the building I still see. It is better than the little house that burned and as good as your last gardens. I am glad to have had the chance to see it. It is a thing to think of and I am glad.

Slim pickings here in the North Shore. Well anyhow, whatever work is given me to do I shall not play false. That, Sir, is a thought I can be frisky with.

Alfred Caldwell

■ ■ ■

March 2, 1939
1953 Leland Ave.
Chicago, Illinois

Dear Mr. Jensen,

Thanks very much for your letter. I have been sitting here thinking about

Planting plan, Lincoln Park extension, Chicago, Illinois, 1938. (Courtesy of Chicago Park District Special Collections)

some aspects of things you say: "a world in decay," "a few selfish fools who belong to an age gone by."

One summer afternoon, a sunday and my father was home, I was given a coin and told to go to the news stand to see if there were any papers out. I was 10 years old but I can still remember the faint familiar smells of the shops I walked by on the way. There were scarcely any automobiles in those days and sunday afternoons were quiet. I can remember the quietness of the street and the hot awnings all along, how sunless and hot it was under the awnings, and which awnings were low enough so you jumped to try to touch the fringe. I remember it was so quiet it didn't seem right to be jumping. Yes, there were news papers on the stand in front of the candy store at Wilson av. and Ravenswood. They were the first sunday afternoon papers I'd ever seen and they were real thin with great big words across the top: "EUROPE HURLED TO WAR" "GERMANY ON THE MARCH"

It seemed somehow to justify jumping at the fringes of all the awnings and running pell mell home with the paper and the exciting words on it. I felt so important to be bringing the thin news paper with the things it said.

I remember that I was in Pittsburgh in October 1929 and it was the day of the first world's series game between the cubs and Philadelphia. I remember I was out that day with two of Riis's park engineers setting some grades and we stopped at a farm house nearby to listen to the radio broadcast of the game. I remember how disappointed I was when Charley Root pitched a home run ball to Simonds. I had wanted the Cubs to win so badly. Later as we drove together back to Pittsburgh we passed a fine haw by the road I pointed it out and the one engineer said "that guy Jens Jensen who was here from Chicago told Riis to locate the end of the deep pool at one of those kind of trees growing up there in the park—nuts, if you ask me." I remember it depressed me because I didn't want to be in Pittsburgh and wanted to be back on a job for you. After a while we came into the city and the other fellow got out to get a paper with the baseball score. The headline of the paper wasn't about the game. The letters were 4 inches high: "STOCK MARKET CRASHES"

It's a cockeyed world to be sure. And to make the best of it becomes harder as we get along step by step from one insane catastrophe to another.

Alfred Caldwell

■ ■ ■

March 20, 1939
1953 Leland Ave.
Chicago, Illinois

Dear Mr. Jensen,

I have been told that the little pool for the memory of Mrs. Julius Rosenwald across from the Ravinia station is to be filled up with earth. This is Ravinia

Garden club doings. Naturally I supposed you would want to know about it and perhaps stop them.

I was your foreman there and I remember the work with some personal satisfaction. Quite aside from any higher value it may have, it cost money to build and oughtn't to be wasted.

The women say that there isn't any way to provide maintenance for it: the children throw in papers and rubbish.

I don't know any of the garden clubbers and this information is from an acquaintance in Winnetka.

Alfred Caldwell

I should like to come up to Ellison Bay for a day but my funds so low now I can't or haven't at all a right to. Next time you come into Chicago call me up (Ardmore 4982) if you have time and care to.

■ ■ ■

[May 1939]
1953 Leland Ave.
Chicago, Illinois

Dear Mr. Jensen,

The politicians finally kicked me out. Well, I am honored. The day may come when it will be considered a distinction to have been kicked out during this park administration.

Naturally I want to see you—not to talk about this park business, for I am sick of it—I want to see you because I am sicker than ever before of seeing stupid vapid weak persons. Never again shall I ever get myself in the position of having to associate with absurd persons and strutting knaves.

I shall probably try to get some landscape work around Chicago. And I hope my residence job gets ahead.

Alfred Caldwell

■ ■ ■

June 6, 1939
1953 Leland Ave.
Chicago Illinois

Dear Mr. Jensen,

Things are very bad with us. We have no food to eat and soon not even a place to sleep.

Can you suggest anyone who will give me work? Are all these years of earnestness and diligence worth nothing in the world? Please do not forsake me. If you have heard of anything, can suggest something—please do.

It is bad, very bad.

Alfred Caldwell

■ ■ ■

July 12, 1939
1953 Leland Ave.
Chicago Illinois

Dear Mr. Jensen,

At last I have discovered a prospect. Iowa State College, department of Landscape Architecture has a position open. I am today sending my application to professor Phillip H. Elwood.

Can you do something for me there? Could you write to Elwood of the department or whomever in my behalf.

I would deeply appreciate this—believe me.

We are still among the living. I do not know how but here nonetheless. But perhaps something good now. I do hope so. I could sing thinking how now I may finally get out.

Alfred Caldwell

■ ■ ■

July 14, 1939
1953 Leland Ave.
Chicago, Illinois

Dear Mr. Jensen,

Thanks so much for your letter and for your communication to Iowa about the job.

Landscape work is looked down upon because it all is sunk to the level of a man trying to make a living out of planting shrubs and trees or making plans for others to plant them. The landscaper is happy if he makes a living. That much makes him content. He is inferior and the whole profession so called is inferior: it is so considered. When [I] went to these towns in the middle west this spring trying to interest the park boards there I stopped calling myself a landscape architect. I would introduce myself as a park man and let it go at that. The first half dozen towns I'd called myself a landscape architect: at Davenport an old man, president of the board, had such uncivil things to say I changed.

Well, I like terratect as a name. Translated strictly it would mean technician of the earth. The man who lays out great rivers of travel for roads and plants them; parks and cities he would lay out; he would designate where the industries would be, the residences, the commercial areas; he would be a scientist as well as a gardener and he would know that human beings become twisted and diseased in the great metropolis, so there would be no metropolis: the largest town in the world would not exceed say 40 thousand people, and most settlements under 5 thousand. Human beings would have room to grow and live creative individual lives: the cities would be laid out by a master gardener: they would all be garden cities. No, and such a craftsman would never be too proud to plant just one tree or the smallest kitchen garden. Being a good gardener he would also be a good philosopher or good enough anyhow to realize the utter shallowness and triviality of being a big shot. The beauty of the green out of the brown earth: that would be the thing that possessed him. All the subtleties and the nuances of trees and herbs and all living things upon the earth, birds or airships above it or worms beneath it. His concern would be the earth—what Whitman called "the old brown Kronos."

That's a long way off from this and now.

Today, the only way one can exist even is to go along in the same rut of servility and stupidity. In public work (you have none) the only thing wanted is a superficial competence and a slavish willingness to be intimidated by power. All the landscapers give lip service. Just verbal ornament and meaningless and just to cover up the naked, the ugly. So I have found.

Pardon all this. I am not very happy. I am not. I wait for the mailman. Waiting for a miracle. I am down to miracles.

Alfred Caldwell

■ ■ ■

July 23, 1939
[No address]

Dear Mr. Jensen,

I was happy to get your last letter even if it was on the tough side—why be tough with me: I don't believe in dilettante conversation ("gas" as you call it—and properly so): I hate that as well as you do.

I am enclosing a letter from Iowa. That door is shut.

I have done the only thing I could do: I have gone back to the Chicago Park District. It was a thing I could do and I have done it. It seems to me not cowardly but really taking some little courage. Certainly I have wanted always to meet up with things face to face and not to flee from them. The necessity of providing shelter and a living for my family, that too, is a thing I do not want to flee from. If that obligation involves unpleasantness still it must be faced. I have had a hard choice to make between conflicting obligations. I realize that this looks danger-ously like compromise but it isn't. I know I have done what is for me the hardest thing to have done. How it will turn out I know not. It is so easy to convince oneself that running away from some situation too difficult to face is a fine proud nobility: I don't want to do that. If I am a real artist and not a sham or a weakling then no association with the corrupt and the stupid will ever anyplace really corrupt me and no tyranny will ever intimidate me.

May I see you next time you come to Chicago?

Thank you very very much for the counsel and aid you have given me always and cheerfully.

Alfred Caldwell

■ ■ ■

August 10, 1939
1953 Leland Ave.
Chicago Illinois

Dear Mr. Jensen,

You promised to call me up when you come into Chicago (on your way back from Culver in August you said). I have been waiting expecting you, for I would like to talk to you.

Your note to Elwood must have burned him. But that's the way they figure: education by tabulation, something like book-keeping.

About the parks. Not good naturally, but what to do in a world where some kind of job is a first need just to exist.

I wonder about your school and hope you get the students you want. There are such, not many but some. Well, I am a pessimist: it isn't a good world we live in. I think perhaps communism would be better. I cannot see how anything more than what we have can ever come out of our present system based on greed and the wilful exploitation of humans and the earth. Where the ideal of success is some species of getting ahead in business, that is, making money, mediocrity is the only outcome. By such a system any individuality or any energy spent in the cause of some genuine attainment is so much wasted. The person is penalized for it. I think students know this either by instinct or by reasoning and not many have the fortitude to do what they really would like to do. I know the students will come to you, but so slowly.

Do you think you could make it clear to those who are interested that there is a very real practical (job procuring and holding) advantage in being able to study under you? By learning from you they not only learn to appreciate the out of doors [but will] be able by that practical understanding of Nature to do work better and more thriftily than others with superficial education. The sword has two edges for you teach an appreciation and you also teach the practical by which the student is qualified beyond University students to earn a living.

Alfred Caldwell

I don't think there is anything miserable in this advantage, but rather just the opposite.

When I worked for you, you paid often on jobs "All the work I do is based on the practical." Once you said — "like a farmer." I always remembered it. It added a solidness to the making of landscapes — like a foundation.

Small council ring at the Clearing, Ellison Bay, Wisconsin, 1993. Jens Jensen, landscape architect. (Photo by Dennis Domer)

■ ■ ■

[No date]
1953 Leland Ave.
Chicago, Illinois

Dear Mr. Jensen:

I had gone up to Madison yesterday expecting to have a few words with you, but so many people were there I couldn't. I am most anxious to see you when you come into Chicago. Can you call me at my home at night (Ardmore 4982) or at my office number Harrison 5252 extension 335, during the day? If you call at the office I will have to speak carefully and not call your name for watchers observe things always.

I am getting to the end of my rope here. They ruin everything they touch. In the end I suppose I share the blame for countless things I have never had to do with, and for mutilation of what work I have worked on.

What you say about the progress of your school is quite a surprise to me. I am so happy to think that actually it is going ahead. I hadn't known at all that you'd got so far along. Naturally you plan a year round school as well as a summer school, and other subjects too besides landscaping, weaving, painting. What a school to ask Landburg to, Edna St. V. Millay, many. You do intend to have story telling and poetry part of it, don't you? When poetry stopped being oratory, that is became reading matter in books, it began to dry up and the poet lost his job with society. The radio might have given the troubadour his job back, but hasn't so far. Why not? I say that in the interval of the last few centuries poetry, being committed to paper, has become so complex in meaning that it would be unintelligible as a chant or oratory—it would have to be studied and the spoken word can't be, at least not to any great degree and the sequence of meaning maintained? The reader demands complexity—the listener, an uninvolved simplicity. What about it? You should be able to take it right in your stride, for you can really talk. Scarcely anyone I know, and not one person I grew up with has any ability to speak or to speak powerfully. This kind of vocal expression seems to be a quality dying out of the civilization we have. I think it is just because poetry degenerated into a written art. And we now are the nadir, the low ebb, not wholly in this regard but in all profound things, for indirect application of poetry really evolves from indirect application elsewhere, that is, in the large affair of life in the round. Surely we are altogether the stupidest. You should have a school to make amends, if you can, for the bad lot that we turned out to be. I say it is your generation that is at fault not us, for your neighbors and your friends were our school masters. Remember our school masters gave us a war for a text book, and a marvelous one it was too, and it isn't over yet. These school masters—any that I knew—thought poetry and such like was nonsense; they who gave us not the fallacy of words, that is verse, bestowed on us instead that malicious fallacy of prosperity; and they who scorned the despair in poems gave us the more genuine despair of a depression, and a marvelous one that was too—that isn't over yet.

I found a teacher who contradicted all the others—and that one was you, good things come together and I discovered Whitman and Frank Lloyd Wright. Thanks and Thanks.

Alfred Caldwell

■ ■ ■

October 18, 1939
1953 Leland Ave.
Chicago Illinois

Dear Mr. Jensen,

Thanks so much for your letter. I am not ashamed to confess that something very real is missing out of my life when I don't hear from you or see you. There are so few people in the world with elevation. It is a difficult thing to associate only with the tawdry, the sick, the absurd. Vitality is in what you say—it is good to listen to. There is nothing any better, any more necessary.

Sure, the cities are in decay: hopeless muddles of decay. 150,000 families on relief in Chicago. What of that economic gangrene?

Soon there will be trouble plenty. As long as they are fed it works along after a fashion. But how long can they feed them?

After this present war possibly not a single capitalist system will survive.

I am coming up as soon as I can—perhaps only for a few hours but come I will. There is nothing I want to do more. I am awfully sorry to have missed Mr. Olsen.

I am so glad you are getting your manuscript published. When? I haven't any idea what the book is about—except guessing of course.

The school you expected to take time. I wish you could get someone to pay the deficit incurred by opening with no matter how few students. Just to get started then many more will hear and come.

If I don't get up right away this fall to get the potatoes meantime there's no law against calling Ardmore 4982 next time you're in Chicago. But I'll be up somehow before winter.

Alfred Caldwell

Parks very bad.
very bad
very miserable working. They must change.

■ ■ ■

November 26, 1939
1953 Leland Ave.
Chicago Illinois

Dear Mr. Jensen,

Thanks for your recent letter. What you say about the color of your landscape makes me sick at heart. What to do to break the iron ring of economic necessity and to live in the countryside where life can have some satisfaction? I scarcely think now a days of anything else. I believe the city as a prison is the great dilemma of modern times. I cannot see how an intelligent person can have faith anymore in the city or anything dependent on the city: the city as it is. Chicago is land that will go back into prairie. A few more years I believe and it will be quite apparent to even those with real estate holdings who naturally enough have quite other hopes and wishes. What are the slums fit for but to go back into prairie? No, not parks—in that day when it comes there will not be money—of course you have always been predicting how there would not forever be the great sums for the politicians to handle for parks: so be it. But more, there may not even be money for bread.

History is the story of wars and of populations without money for bread and who are we to escape a condition that has been repeating itself on this planet for ten thousand years or more? Are we any wiser than those who were hungry in Assyria or Egypt? We may be stupider.

I hope a job will turn up soon—a park in a small town or a similar thing and then I shall be gone from here quickly.

You do not say anything in any detail about what you are doing except that you are busy. You don't say anything about your book. Perhaps I shall see you soon.

Alfred Caldwell

■ ■ ■

June 17, 1940
4651 N. Hermitage Ave.
Chicago Illinois

Dear Mr. Jensen,

Thanks very much for your letter.

Well, my boy friends kicked me out of the parks again. So I am on the street now. Gee, its funny after many years of having a little dignity, just a little, about one's calling in life to be pushed around like an inferior. It is something I'll have to get used to I suppose. There is no stability in this generation. There is trouble coming to America, very great trouble. I am sad thinking of the suffering ahead for so many and so soon. "Those whom the Gods would destroy they first make mad."

In your letter you dare me to repeat your comments about Grant Park. Speaking freely is one of my specialities: do you think I am disliked at the parks so much because my shoes aren't shined. Give the devil his due. I am much influenced by a certain man I worked for for 6 years who was very good at speaking freely. Perhaps you know him.

Whether the park action in firing me without any charges whatsoever is legal or not I do not know. I held the position of landscape designer by virtue of being first in a civil service examination with a grade of 86.7. I had been appointed 2 weeks. The reason given for letting me go was to save money, for now with the country on the brink of war and the closing up of W.P.A. in sight, the officials are frantic to get the highways at North avenue complete. Such is the story.

We talked the other night about the gardens around Buckingham fountain. It is very bad that Chicago fell for baroque gardening. I have seen photographs of Hitler city planning just as bad: long avenues just for parade purposes of the Nazi party—some way to plan cities. It is all the instability of our age. People want good things but they don't know how to get them and they are foolish and confused in what they make. The park district wants good things and they think highways in Lincoln Park are good. After they are built everyone will see how bad they are and in a few years they will be torn out. Millions wasted. There is no leadership. I asked Donoghue to get you a couple of years ago. The only result was resentment against me for suggesting it. Presumably everyone with any power was afraid he would have less to say. So colossal blunders. I want to do good things and I have spent my life learning how. I intend to keep on spending my life that way: learning and the doing in whatever way I can.

Alfred Caldwell

■ ■ ■

[July 19, 1941]
[No address]

Dear Mr. Jensen:

Thanks very much for your 2 letters. Needless to tell you I enjoyed reading the newspaper articles. Will give to Mr. Woodfill as you directed. Will return them to you then.

No need for you to visit the work for a while unless you have some special reason for coming. It all goes so slow (I have no control over those things you know) and consequently not much done in any period. The tractor has finally rough graded the tennis and badminton courts areas. I want to get the clay on this month but perhaps I won't be able to. I'll try but very slow, everything and everybody.

What you say about the Island is quite true. But then this little place is just the world in small. Chicago and Mackinac Island are the same—merely Chicago is larger. Our country is all middle class: what the French call petite bourgeoisie. And not only America but most of Europe is composed of the little business men, the bourgeoisie. That I think is what is so bad today. We need aristocrats and we need peasants. Or we need some order of some kind: something that will give to society the stability that the aristocrat and the peasant gave. The little dollar hunting businessmen can give nothing but mediocrity. They are the very soul of mediocrity. Therefore everything is bad today. We live under the rule of the shopkeeper. I think that perhaps this war will be the means to change things. I hope so. It is all $$$$$$$$$$$$$$ $$$$$$$$$$$$$$$$$$. But down underneath there are other forces at work in the world. Tremendous push to escape the tyranny of dollars, and to escape the tyrannical little men who spend their lives hunting dollars.

Alfred Caldwell

■ ■ ■

August 6, 1941
4651 North Hermitage Ave.
Chicago, Illinois

Dear Mr. Jensen:

Well, I finally got the plan off to you. If anything is done wrong or you would have anything otherwise send it back to me and I'll be glad to change it. You know

I had to use my judgement here and there and I wondered all along if that was the way you wanted it.

I showed no quantities, only the varieties and indicated as you showed them. Where you said such and such in groups along the border I showed the individual groups. Where you showed a general forest mixture of 2 or 3 plants in a large area, then I showed that, but no individual groups (excepting you noted them).

The quantities would not be practical to show anyhow where the work is to be done by collecting. The collected plants differ so much in size, some large and some small, that any definite estimate of the exact number required to properly fill in an area would apt to be misleading.

I hope I got the views right. The long view from the bowling green I made fairly large and then broke up with groups of sugar maples and other tall growing plants so that the view opening in the forest wouldn't look mechanical or like an allee. I judged that was the way you would do it. Look it over and if not right send it back to me and I will alter to your direction.

You had the large sing ring too far over and I changed it to the location you had shown me on the ground. I knew that you had only a very sketchy survey to make the plan from. The badminton and shuffleboard and horseshoes and quoits I had to shift considerably from what you showed with all of them on the tennis court axis. The existing forest of fine old cedars would have to be cut into more then you would do I'm sure in order to get all the games on the one axis. So I changed it.

The water line I showed and with the hydrants indicated, also the caliber of pipe for the different runs.

I showed the possible toilet building location and indicated the paths with dotted lines if such a building should be built. I do not know if that place is o.k. with you But I can change if not. Thanks for your letter and card today.

Alfred Caldwell

■ ■ ■

August 20, 1941
4651 North Hermitage Ave.
Chicago, Illinois

Dear Mr. Jensen:

Thanks for your letter. You mention that Mr. Perry said that I had said that there wasn't much to do and so he sent me home. At no time during the $2\frac{1}{2}$ months I was on Island was there much to do. I constantly referred to this fact. When one accepts wages he is under a certain obligation, he must do something for the wages—at least point out that he is willing to do something. That I did.

Mr. Perry called me into his office the morning of July 30. He asked me if I thought Mr. Rounds, the foreman, could build the tennis courts properly without me. Naturally I was very surprised at the question. If they were going to build the tennis courts then my services on the job were certainly justified. But I said nothing. How could I? I looked upon it as just a polite way of asking me to leave.

There hadn't been much activity simply because they hadn't let the work go ahead on the tennis courts. But the moment they decided to go ahead with the tennis courts they asked me to leave. It surprised and embarrassed me. Naturally I agreed to leave. By the next boat, in fact.

Mr. Perry asked me if I would send him instruction on how to make the courts, specifications to guide them in the work. I sent these instructions to Mr. Perry, with a little grading data, from Pittsburgh the next day. No word in reply.

I do not know why they asked me to go. While I was there I did everything possible to be of service. I went out of my way to be helpful. I kept my own counsel; whatever I have thought about these people on the Island I kept to myself.

Perhaps they thought that to lay me off for a month or so was the proper thing to do. That my services were comparable to a laborer's or a plumber's or bricklayer's. I do not know what they thought. I do know, however, that they have nearly a quarter of a million dollars and they didn't lay me off for lack of funds.

How are your buildings coming? I hope the means to finish them will be forthcoming. I happened to run into Sauers the other night and he wanted me to give you his regards. He spoke to me at great length about your work and how much he realized etc. etc. "It will last long after all of us" he said

Alfred Caldwell

■ ■ ■

[1937–1940?]

Dear Mr. Jensen

Thanks for your recent letter. I have inquired around here but so far have not uncovered an applicant for the gardener's job you mentioned.

Whenever I get a little interior quiet I can think about the plain white plaster and the tall slit of glass like a fabulous eye and the brute of the cliff in the distance, but not crouching there—not an animal—itself, and the green water mysteriously leading somewhere as if into another world. Like as not there are other worlds—worlds within worlds, worlds past worlds we never may reach. I think of it wanting to come up again just to look quick past the guardian cliff.

Alfred Caldwell

The cliff house at the Clearing, Ellison Bay, Wisconsin, 1993. Jens Jensen, landscape architect. (Photo by Dennis Domer)

Selected Letters to Ludwig Hilberseimer (1940–42)

November 17, 1940
P.O. Box #357
Tullahoma, Tennessee

Dear Professor Hilberseimer:

This is the sunny south on the edge of the Cumberlands but it gets very cold nonetheless. I live in a little mountain town of 1500 persons 11 miles from the job—there are no living quarters to be had much nearer.

I am a building inspector for the government. This is a construction project employing (so the newspapers say) about 10,000 men. It is all conventional wood frame construction and without ornaments. I think you would find much in the structures to approve of. Perhaps they are not at all architecture—not studied at all as architecture-but at least they are clear and understandable. Only the barns of farmers are as good. In the 600 mile drive from Chicago to Tennessee only the farmer's barns belonged to the landscape; the houses in towns along the way never.

The people hereabouts are very poor, certainly by city standards, and by any standards by my opinion. Wages ordinarily 50 to 60 cents a day. The farm land generally not suitable for crops. Perhaps it is suitable for forest growth only. One can buy a farm for 5 dollars an acre. But on such a farm one would starve.

I do not know how long I will be down here—probably not more than 6 weeks. It isn't necessary for me to tell you how sorely I miss the work in city planning and seeing you. But I'll be back if I may. I came down here expecting to do some writing in my off time but haven't done much: I am a very bad nomad—I get depressed and ambitionless away from home. Years ago when I traveled much for Mr. Jensen it was the same. I expect to be in Pittsburgh over Christmas and there they have a real smoke condition. The worst in U.S.A.

Alfred Caldwell

■ ■ ■

December 16, 1940
P.O. Box #357
Tullahoma, Tennessee

Dear Professor Hilberseimer:

I have been sick and consequently your letter has remained unanswered. I am sending a note to my friend Mr. George T. Donoghue, general superintendent of the Chicago Park District, and I am sure if Mr. Monson will call at Mr. Donoghue's office he will be directed to the men who have the material you need for your city planning. I am sure this way is the best. The man you referred to in your letter (whom you met at Mr. Kingery's office) Mr. Hazekamp, may not be in a position to get the material for you and you might just have more delay. I am enclosing a copy of the letter I am sending to Mr. Donoghue. If Mr. Monson will call at Mr. Donoghue's office a day or so after you get this letter Mr. Donoghue or his secretary will do what is necessary. Be sure to ask for the photographs you once mentioned. You remember you wanted to show tall buildings in the landscape. If Mr. Monson goes to the photographic department to see what is suitable have him ask for Gates Priest who knows all about you and your work from me (one of the poor souls I plague with talk about this fellow Hilberseimer). He will understand what you want. Get all you need.

I am very unhappy here and want only to get back, but leave I dare not until the work is finished. Much of it is boring and repetitions. Albeit, I am thankful for all I have learned about frame construction. I have had the day by day inspection of over 100 buildings of many different types and it is a wonderful discipline in wood architecture. For me anyhow. I feel I have so much I don't know. This camp of 1400 buildings is very much like a planned city and it is good and satisfying in a spatial sense. Many things are bad about it but it is better than any of the cities. I wish you might see it. You would laugh to think that a camp built to last 5 years is a pleasure to look at but it is. Cheap and clean and a pleasure too. Bad too. Too monotonous—nothing high (I know now in a very real way how right your schemes are with the tall buildings spaced thruout).

I want to get back and do some work with you. I want very much to get back. Have a good yule.

There are many things I want to talk with you about.

Alfred Caldwell

■ ■ ■

September 13, 1941
Alfred Caldwell
Landscape Architect
4651 North Hermitage Avenue
Chicago, Illinois

Dear Professor Hilberseimer:

I meant to tell you that I have been thinking of writing a paper on the "Chicago School" and to get your advice. But I'll see you soon.

Not only in architecture did these things happen at that time. Wright and Sullivan were not the only ones. Between 1890 and say 1912 was the great park building era in Chicago. Here were conferences on parks and playgrounds that were later to influence planning and thought about parks for the whole country—and I believe to some extent Europe as well. I know that at about that time Jensen wrote for the German garden magazine Gartenkunst. The German garden gestalta (spelt wrong?) were greatly interested in Jensen's philosophy of native plants for landscape work—and are now, curiously blended of course with the Nazi nationalism. So much so that Jensen was invited as the one American delegate for the garden conferences held in Berlin in 1937 and to read the opening address. He didn't go but his paper was read by a friend.

What is good in parks (the parks and gardens that I see) is indebted to this early work of Jensen. The sane sense of space was in these early parks as in the buildings of Wright. In Columbus park an island of forest stands free in one end of the mass of trees. It is done in such a way that space is intercepted but continued in feeling or fantasy far beyond actual physical dimensions. It intrigues one mysteriously: like what was beyond was another world and that the little visible of it was merely the portal to it. So also in Wright's Coonley house space takes on lengthened dimensions, by architectural means but in spirit the same. One feels almost the premonition of some unrational dimension beyond height, breadth and depth.

I meant to speak to you about space in Mies van der Rohe's buildings and the landscape space in the cities you make. These have a profound relationship to Chicago. Chicago is in the middle of the country, on the tremendous flat prairies of America. These prairies are like the floor of the world with a sense of freedom and space without end.

Alfred Caldwell
P.O. Box 61
Sparta, Wisconsin

■ ■ ■

March 11, 1942
4651 North Hermitage Avenue
Chicago, Illinois

Dear Professor Hilberseimer:

It has occurred to me that it might be a good idea to show the F.H.A. men your article and diagrams about planning published in the Armour magazine. I think it would impress them—not that it was published but the substance of it. Will it seem too academic? Will you think it over and let me know when we meet. I'll have a copy with me in case you wish to show it. Your planning proposals are very big and these 2 drawings I have been making are quite slight in the application of these principles. Therefore, I thought that it would be good to show them how the same principles would apply to the largest problems.

In addition it might be wise (if you so consider) to show them not only the perspective sketch of the L shaped houses looking from above, but also the perspectives of the commercial areas and the perspective of the plan of Chicago. This would show them large schemes and open their eyes. Well, anyhow I'll have these with me and you can tell me when we meet if you want them shown.

Confirming our meeting. We meet Monday next, March 16, at the old post office Dearborn Street entrance at 2 P.M.

I trust you are feeling much better.

Alfred Caldwell

I am writing the A. W. Hastings & Co. of Boston as you suggested regarding availability of windows of type you want. Also I will ask them to recommend a dealer to whom I might write regarding wood gutters.

■ ■ ■

March 13, 1942
4651 North Hermitage Avenue
Chicago, Illinois

Dear Professor Hilberseimer:

Enclosed the letter from the American Institute of Architects. I appreciate very much your kindness in suggesting these means. I was tempted with the possibilities, but perhaps it is better this way. The work could be done without money help. Such things then are stronger.

I have no faith in men and their institutions. I wish to see everything disintegrated into anarchy out of which could come new growth. I should not then take favor or gift from what I wish destroyed.

So far the world and I stand even. I have repudiated it and it has repudiated me. You may smile—but this is a quarrel of long standing. Here are some poems written many years ago.

Alfred Caldwell

■ ■ ■

May 26, 1942
4651 North Hermitage Avenue
Chicago, Illinois

Dear Professor Hilberseimer:

This morning I went to see Mr. Loebl and have just returned. We talked for over an hour; he was very kind and considerate and I am most grateful. I need not remind you again that I am grateful to you for your interest in my difficulties. I will not speak about what I have learned from you—that is as a mountain. Quite aside from that and as a person, you are the best friend I have ever had. These matters or feelings entail responsibility. Therefore, I have come to a decision. I must trust myself in this decision, my instincts. But first let me mention the discussion with Mr. Loebl.

It is quite as bad or worse even than I suppose. "Everyone they wrote to sent unfavorable letters." I told Loebl that the kind of men who would write such letters wished me dead. I should have compared it to the primitive magic of making a small doll to symbolize someone hated and then sticking thorns or pins in it to bring about the person's real death—I forgot to mention this. But I did say that the praise from such people would constitute an insult really just as their condemnation constitutes absurdity. I told Loebl that the man from the Chicago Park District writing the letter might next week be appointed clerk of garbage collection. People like that exist in their jobs just by virtue of some tawdry little political adventure or other. They have no opinions really. They are men with jobs. Wages are their opinions, the beginning and the end of every consideration. Mr. Loebl thought that by diplomacy things could be otherwise. I told him I believed diplomacy ends and hypocrisy and dishonesty begin. We talked a long time and I cannot cover it all. Finally I told him that they said these things because they hated me and I told him the reasons. I have the impression it seemed a little incredible to him. I showed him the letters and showed him the letter referring to the sabotaged civil service examination. I told him about the cause. He spoke again about diplomacy. I told him that on account of these letters no government agency would hire me because they imagine I am dangerous to have around, but those bringing good letters of recommendation are the real danger. The little diplomats are the danger to society. I want to see a city planned by diplomats. I have seen buildings made by diplomats—I think it would have been much better to have had an architect instead. What would a city be, made by the same men sitting cautiously in their offices? I prefer Chicago. Mr. Loebl and I spoke pleasantly even when we were basically disagreed. All this now leads me to my decision.

I am going away. I will need something like 10 days to finish the house plans I am now working on and a few days extra for the specifications. Nothing can come between the finishing of that now and as quickly as I can. Then I shall find a job somewhere. I know some men who know me and what I can do and will gladly hire me if they are in a position to. I do not care how far away I go and that will help in getting something.

I do not wish my needs to perplex anybody or burden anybody. Now certainly no one must speak in my behalf. You must not and I will not be a party to it. With letters like the ones Mr. Loebl knows of it is unsafe for anybody to recommend me. For it would be very unwise. What kind of a man would I be to willingly place others in an oblique position?

This whole thing challenges my feeling of self-sufficiency. I am extremely disturbed and I must do something now.

When I finish the plans I will call you on the phone and we can meet.

This may be the best thing that could have happened. The exact opposite of a thing sometimes makes a matter possible that otherwise would have been impossible.

Alfred Caldwell

■ ■ ■

August 27, 1942
4651 North Hermitage Avenue
Chicago, Illinois

Dear Professor Hilberseimer:

I would be surprised if you could easily publish your book. To be American is to be what everyone else is. If you tried to publish it in Turkey, it would then be called Un-turkish. People imagine that their sameness is some special virtue possessed only by themselves, the inhabitants of a certain geographical area. People imagine that a different thing is only suitable to a different type of human being. A great criticism of Wright's early buildings was that they were "foreign looking."

I am working nights on my article about planning and your city. I am rewriting what I did and it's slow work. What I would give to write—not to say it twenty times wrong to the one right way.

I had lunch recently with Kincaid director of the plan of Chicago. Another time with a Mr. Blessing of the Chicago Plan Commission. He was interested in Hilberseimer's city—and it is more than barely possible that he wanted just to discuss it and we met just for that reason. He is a young person and I don't think his position is too important but he is intelligent and was moved and certainly impressed with the idea. He asked if I supposed Hilberseimer would speak with him and he said he wanted particularly to speak about the plan of Amsterdam.

About the plan of the house—I will gladly make the changes you suggest. I can be reached on the phone anytime after 6 at night.

I have been with the War Department in Chicago for nearly a month.

The work in Nebraska was very bad. I saw what was happening and left. No, you wouldn't believe it: a munitions dump by these architects designed in Colonial Architecture. War too can be pretty.

Alfred Caldwell

Eulogy for Jens Jensen (1951)

Mr. Jensen was a special kind of man. He recognized it, was proud of it, and frequently referred to it. However, the time in which we happen to live today deeply distrusts the special kind of man and tries in every situation to eliminate him.

As the most natural thing in the world, and without the slightest show of malice, he is excluded or cashiered the moment his true identity becomes known. All this is part, of course, of the great general technique of managing and controlling the masses, the now trebled population of the world. This process implies the final and triumphant standardization of the human species. Man, like machine parts, must be made to fit the requirements of government, industry, and business.

It is a frightening world—this standardized mass sense of the world— because any form of higher life seems to be impossible. The life of caring, which distinguished man from a mere thing, a machine of appetites, belongs to individuals only. That is the life of the spirit.

The artist is the one who demonstrates the significance of caring. As we are capable of understanding that art.

The caring life of the artist, however, goes on in a world of its own which is closed and separate, but which generates everything the man does. That is why copy work and disciple work is always meaningless work, empty. There is nothing behind it but borrowed techniques.

So little is this inside world of the true artist recognized that the world often

View from the Clearing, Ellison Bay, Wisconsin, 1993. (Photo by Dennis Domer)

sees only a man strangely following fugitive and skittish guides that seem to lead him far and wide; or a man rapturously and mysteriously enchanted with the very things others see as only the commonplace unremarkable.

Pursuant to these thoughts, and no more rash than usual, I will read you a poem I made last week in memory of Mr. Jensen. You may in fantasy consider it a statement by the man we would honor.

Shortly after Ludwig Mies van der Rohe arrived in Chicago, he met Alfred Caldwell while visiting the Lily Pool in Lincoln Park with Ludwig Hilberseimer and Walter Peterhans. Mies recognized Caldwell's talent and hired him in 1945. They were friends and colleagues for over twenty years. One of Mies's most problematic and famous projects was the Farnsworth house in Plano, Illinois. Caldwell worked on it one summer, and through discussions with Dr. Edith Farnsworth, Mies, Myron Goldsmith, and others, he learned the details of the disagreement between Mies and Dr. Farnsworth from both sides. Caldwell's deposition in 1951 for the impending lawsuit over costs is one of the most revealing documents about what really happened between Mies and Dr. Farnsworth. Behind the dispute there was a broken romance. The architectural press backed Mies; Dr. Farnsworth lost the case, and Mies was awarded $14,000. The deposition is on file in the private collection of Alfred Caldwell.

Deposition on the Farnsworth House (November 17, 1951)

My name is Alfred Caldwell. I'm a registered architect, and I teach architecture at the Illinois Institute of Technology. In 1945 in the month of October, shortly after I first came to teach at I.I.T., van der Rohe spoke to me about Dr. Farnsworth and told me that she wanted him to build a house for her near Plano, Illinois. He had been out to the site with her once before. Possibly he had been out there with her more than once. In any case, shortly thereafter I went out there with Mies van der Rohe and Dr. Farnsworth and two young men from his office, namely Duckett and Edward V. Olencki. There was conversation as to where the house should be put. Mr. van der Rohe said that it was the feature of the property and he would prefer to put it on the floodplain. There was no talk on this occasion, at least so far as I heard, as to the kind of house or its cost.

About two or three weeks later Mies showed me a sketch of the house, and a couple of weeks after that Mies told me that he had met Dr. Farnsworth at dinner and had talked about the house and that she was crazy to build a house as soon as possible.

I came into Mies's office in connection with landscaping the campus at I.I.T. While at his office, I learned through Mr. Bonnet that Dr. Farnsworth was concerned as to whether the state would build a dam on Fox River and as to how the building of such a dam would affect her site. Mies referred this problem to me through Mr. Bonnet. I then went to talk to state officials about it, in the Merchandise Mart, and they told me there were certain reference points on various bridges in the area. Then I went out to the site with Dr. Farnsworth one day in her car with Olencki and I brought a level with me, this was around December 1945. I set some grades which informed us that if the area was flooded, the water would reach certain designated points. Dr. Farnsworth talked a great deal, the substance of what she had to say was that she was very anxious to have the house built and she wanted to know about the water condition. She also said that she knew that Mies was most interested in big buildings and that he wasn't really interested in small houses, nor was he interested particularly in money.

On this occasion Dr. Farnsworth told me that she had gone to see another architect about building a house for her on this site but that he had not satisfied her with his answers. A friend of hers had told her about Mies, and she had then made arrangements to have somebody who knew him invite them both to a dinner party where she met him. She thought when she first saw him that he was just "a cigar-smoking German." He said nothing during the dinner. But afterward

The Farnsworth house under construction, Plano, Illinois, 1950. Ludwig Mies van der Rohe, architect. (Photo by John Sugden)

when the others left and they were alone she said to him that she would like to have him build a house for her. He replied "I would gladly build anything for you." Then she said she had arranged to meet him and go out to the site. She then arranged that they should go out to view the site together. They did. In that conversation she told Mies about her having gone to see another architect and having asked him about what would happen if she didn't like the house that he would build for her—the plans for the house, that is. She asked if she would be obliged to pay him for the plans and to build the house, and he said she would have to do so. This dissatisfied her. She asked Mies if that question existed between her and Mies; he replied that it did not, that he would build a house for her as he would build it for himself and that he could do no better than that. She thought this was a highly satisfactory answer. She had seen a sketch Mies had prepared and was delighted with it.

I remember Dr. Farnsworth discussing Mies personally at this time, and she said he was the most timid man that she ever knew. She asked him to her house to dinner, he sits through the whole dinner and eats his steak without asking for the salt, such things. She was entirely fascinated with Mies's personality.

Continuously from this time on, that is to say from December on to the spring of the next year, Mies worked on the house in his spare moments and talked a great deal about it, was extremely enthused about it and reported conversations with Dr. Farnsworth; the burden of every conversation was "when do we get started." In the spring Mies had a model or rather two scale models at ½" scale made of two possibilities of the structure, one with the beams over the top of the roof and one with the beams under. Goldsmith worked on details for the house at this time. I cannot remember anything much about the cost because no real bona fide estimates were taken and too much was uncertain. Besides all this Mies was so busy with other work; the truth is he didn't have the time to start work on the house, but he did just this much because the pressure of the interest was so great. I remember I went to Dr. Farnsworth's house with Mies after the commencement exercises in the school about the 5th of June or somewhere around there of that year—that would be 1946—and he said Dr. Farnsworth asked you to her house with me tonight, and we went and the model was there and she said she had to use all her influence to get it away from Mr. Duckett. We sat the whole evening talking till six o'clock in the morning about the house. To say she was interested would be understated fantastically. She was pleased, fascinated beyond pleasure. When Mies went out of the room one time during this evening she said to me "Caldwell, will you give me some advice, Mies has spent a great deal of money for wages for his boys working on this, I know that and I daren't ask him about reimbursing him. Have I really the right to ask him? Should I ask him how much I owe him? Or something like that, and what shall I say?" And I said, "don't say anything, Mies will tell you if you owe him something and he wants to charge you." From time to time I saw Dr. Farnsworth, not very often perhaps, every six months and saw Mies two or three times a month. Whenever I saw Dr. Farnsworth she talked about her house. I remember on one occasion she called me at my home to ask about planting certain trees or something like that, then she talked about the house and she said "you know last week the steel restrictions were released, and now we could get the steel. I'm just hoping Mies will really get to work on it now so we can get the house built." Whenever I saw Mies during this same period nearly always we talked about the house. That was of very great importance to him. At this time he had his exhibit in New York and the house was exhibited and a new model was made, there was the greatest possible interest and the house was published in the book written by Philip Johnson.

This may show something of the attitude of Dr. Farnsworth toward Mies in his work. She called me up one time and she said, "Oh, poor Mies has got this exhibit at the Museum of Modern Art and he has to get it ready in the next four weeks. He has to have a lot of trees made out of rubber sponge." She said, "He is beside himself with all he has to do, and I am wondering, could I make some of those little trees I saw you make and will it be possible for me to do this? Would

Alfred Caldwell and Myron Goldsmith, 1994. (Photo by Dennis Domer)

you come and show me how to do it? I would like to help Mies." And she said, "I feel so sorry for him because he has so much to do and that is so important for him to have that exhibit just right, as he always wants things." So I said, "I'll think about it." Then I saw Mies two or three weeks later and I told him about it, and he said "Oh, let women knit"; he said, "We could find ways to make the trees ourselves." He said, "That's very nice and thoughtful of her, but we don't have to have such things."

I would like to say that Dr. Farnsworth was in my opinion seeking Mies out to build a house. It was she who was taking the action. Mies is by nature very slow moving, and she was impatient to get started building the house; in many ways I got that impression.

Shortly after the exhibit in New York, which is arranged by Philip Johnson, and publishing of the book on Mies's architecture by Philip Johnson, Philip himself built a glass house patterned after Mies's house for Dr. Farnsworth. It was certainly far inferior and was certainly misunderstood, and Dr. Farnsworth was furious about it and thought that Mies had made this house for her and here Philip Johnson had scooped it. About that time I saw Mies one night socially and he said, "You know, Dr. Farnsworth is after me all the time to build this house, and I would like to do it because you know I am so interested in it, but there's no one in my office that I can spare to work on it. Of course I am working on the restaurant, Joe is working on the apartment building, and Duckett doesn't get much time on the others and they have all things to do, I just don't know what to do." He said, "Everything has been worked out, you know there's just a few lines to draw." And I wondered whether he meant that I volunteer to draw these few lines for him, as he put it. And so I did volunteer and at the close of school in June I asked him again if there was anything else he wanted of me that year, and he said, "Well you did promise that you would come up to my office and work on the Farnsworth house." So I came up to his office and worked five weeks, but I could accomplish very little because Mies didn't give it any time at all, he had so much pressure of work, he had a project in the office at that time of eight or ten big apartment buildings in a group, and he is not the kind of a man that can think of more than one thing at a time, and so as the result of that I just did very little work that was toward the building of the house, toward the making of the plans, practically useless. I gave it up and stopped coming, especially after a conversation at Mies's house, in which Mies said, "Every good idea doesn't have to be built." He said this to Dr. Farnsworth, by which I construed him to mean that if Dr. Farnsworth wanted it cheap he wouldn't want to build it. I thought myself the house would never be built because Mies would never consent to have it lower in quality.

I was very surprised to receive a phone call at my house from Mies in about June 1949, saying that they were finally going to go ahead and build the house, and Dr. Farnsworth had the money to build it and wanted to build it very badly and would I go out and look at the site with them. They thought I might like to come along because I had been interested in the house so much, so Dr. Farnsworth picked me up with Mies and we drove out. I remember particularly the conversation going out because I think it is significant in relation to this discussion about the cost. Mies said to me "You know Dr. Farnsworth now has some money and she thinks she wants to build a house for $55,000 or $60,000." He said "We are going to cut the size of the house down a little bit because it is a little tight for that money, and we think with the prices we have gotten, Goldsmith has gotten some prices, that would run a little smaller house, $57,000, 58,000 — something like that." He said "Remember, leave at least $1,000 for the curtains, at least, so that we have to have some sort of leeway, some cushion, we want to certainly keep under $60,000 if it is at all possible." She said, "Well now, Mies, you're going to make the house a little smaller, I don't want to ruin it you know. I would rather have it the other size, the larger size if that would hurt it." "No," Mies said, "I think that will be all right, we will see when the boys finish the model." She said to me, "You know Caldwell, I have a legacy, a small legacy from an aunt," or some relative and she said, "By the way, Mies, I am now asked to vote on these stocks — isn't that curious?" She knowing perhaps that I wanted to build my own house in the country. She said, "Maybe you'll have an aunt who will die and leave you $10,000." I saw Mies at his house a few days later and I said, "Mies, I just am so surprised that you're finally going to build the house, she is really a good sport, she is really a fine woman. That she will go with this idea and actually build it, which she should do." He said, "Yes, she is going to do it." He said, "She has some money. She has $60,000 and is willing to spend it. I think the house can be built for that." After the house had been started, that is to say about December, Dr. Farnsworth called me up on the phone in reference to some ditch that was to be dug, or something like that, out there and asked me my advice I didn't welcome such conversations because I thought it would put me in a precarious position with Mies, but I had to endure. Then she began talking about the construction of the house. She said that Goldsmith irritated her to no end, and she related an incident when Goldsmith had a conversation that she thought was too long with the contractor about whether crushed rocks should be used or gravel and that the contractor had supplied the gravel and the crushed rock could have been gotten used as well, Goldsmith thought. She said, "Here they are discussing this, and I am paying $2.50 an hour for each person," or something like this. She said, "I was furious." She said, "Caldwell, that is so unnecessary because we have absolutely perfect plans made. That is not necessary for Goldsmith to come out there and talk this way and spend time for that." I said, "Look, Gold-smith is the salt of the earth, you are lucky to have a man like that." She said, "I saw Mies and I told him about it, and I thought he had first agreed with me, and later I saw him and he said "Look, if we are to build a house for you, you must leave us to handle these details." He said, "Technical problems which you cannot cope with, we must handle them." She said, "We had the first real quarrel that you could say we ever had." "Oh," she said, "we are patched up all right now, but every time we still see each other we look at each other very sharp." I think what is significant about this is the fact that she said with such emphasis, "We have perfect plans, everything had been worked out, every single thing of the house had been worked out." Of course she doesn't understand that you cannot work out supervision ahead of time and that is only on the place.

The question arises how much did Dr. Farnsworth decide things or how closely did she follow the construction. Was it right for her, is it right for her, to say that she had no real knowledge of what was going on and so forth? I can answer about the travertine. She selected the travertine. Mies worked on several possibilities to use blue stone, to use red tiles, to use linoleum or other things, and then to use travertine, and he went with her where she could see travertine. She decided herself freely that that was the material she wanted for the house floors. Mies said at the time that I was out there before the house was built with her and they discussed the travertine. She said, "I am so happy, Mies, we have decided upon travertine. Even though it is so God-awful expensive, I think it is befitting to use," and Mies said, "Yes, you are quite right, especially in a house like this. What is there, there is only the floor, if that isn't fine material then there is nothing." Both Dr. Farnsworth and Mies told me, or indicated to me that they had gone together and selected the travertine. The conversation with Dr. Farnsworth in which the question of rock or gravel and Goldsmith came up was about December of 1949. I might have referred to something that happened let us say a month or two before. It was my impression from this conversation that I had with Dr. Farnsworth that Goldsmith led a dog's life because she concerned herself so much with all the details. I had such jobs in my own life experience and didn't like them very much; they are about the worst thing you can get. The proposition that she never knew what was going on and didn't concern herself with it I think doesn't hold water at all.

I remember that I had seen Dr. Farnsworth and Mies together at the site just before the house was built, the episode I related in which they had talked about the travertine and about the money, and then I was with Mies when he saw for the first time the frame-up and the same occasion I was asked to go out. We went out, the three of us together, and Mies was immensely pleased, Dr. Farnsworth was immensely pleased, everything was wonderful. She was beside herself with satisfaction and pleasure. This was about December or January—no, this was about December. I think this was before the conversation over the telephone, about the gravel and crushed rock. About December 1950, or it might have been in January of 1950, I don't know, of 1951, Dr. Farnsworth called me again at my house and talked about trees or something like this and then talked about the house and said that she was immensely pleased with the house, and everything was perfect, only she didn't like Mies's idea about putting in his two Barcelona chairs with leather covers, and she didn't like Mies's IDEA about the curtains. She was afraid, to use her expression, he would ruin this house that he had built so well for her. She also asked me if I would help her with her landscape work, and I said I would think about it, and she called me about a month later and asked me again and then a month after that asked me to come out to dinner to her new house, which I did, and she wanted me to do the landscape work, which I did not want to do because she related to me that she had great friction with Mies and I did not want to become involved in such problems. I omitted saying that in the conversation of December or January of 1950 or '51 that she had said, "You know, Caldwell, this house has cost me a lot of money." I said, "Well, you have to spend a lot of money for things that are good; you didn't waste your money." She said, "I know I didn't, and I am really happy that I have the house. Only that I have to be careful, that is all now."

Dr. Farnsworth and I met at her house about April 1951 to discuss the landscape work. As a matter of fact we didn't discuss much about the landscape work, but only about her estranged relations with Mies. She complained bitterly about some total of money spent, she said it was so very much and she did not quite realize when she had started it that it was going to be quite that much. She's worried about her health, she couldn't continue to practice as a physician, she would have troubles financially, and I said, "Well, you think the house is wonderful, don't you?" and she said, "Yes, you know I could never ever come to take any other kind of a house again by another architect. I just love this so much, that you could see out of the walls, see the landscaping, it is so beautiful in the mornings, so beautiful at night," and I said, "All right, now let us say this. You have only dreamed this experience, you never really built this house. Tomorrow morning when you wake up and you find out that this whole experience of spending this money and having this strange relationship with Mies was only a dream. Wouldn't you still immediately want to have the house anyhow?" She said, "Yes, I'm afraid I would."

Unless otherwise noted, the letters and unpublished manuscripts by Alfred Caldwell referred to in the notes are in Caldwell's private collections in Bristol, Wisconsin, and Baldwin, Kansas.

1. Two scholars outside Chicago who recognized Caldwell's importance were Richard Guy Wilson and Sidney K. Robinson in *The Prairie School in Iowa* (Ames: Iowa State University Press, 1977), 64–65. They noted that Eagle Point Park "is perhaps one of the most important and yet unknown examples of Prairie School work in the 1930s." Wilson addressed Caldwell again in that same year with "An Artist and a Poet, Alfred Caldwell Illuminates Nature's Ways," *Landscape Architecture*, September 1977, 407–12. Werner Blaser published *Architecture and Nature: The Work of Alfred Caldwell* (Basel: Birkhäuser, 1984). Richard Guy Wilson gave considerable space to Caldwell's work in "Themes of Continuity: The Prairie School in the 1920s and 1930s," in *Modern Architecture in America*, ed. Richard Guy Wilson and Sidney K. Robinson (Ames: Iowa State University Press, 1991), 185–212. Robert E. Grese, in *Jens Jensen: Maker of Natural Parks and Gardens* (Baltimore: Johns Hopkins University Press, 1992), begins his discussion of Jens Jensen with Alfred Caldwell. Eli Bornstein, editor of the *Structurist* (Saskatchewan), began to publish Caldwell's essays in 1967, and with the 1993–94 edition he has now published seventeen.

2. Richard Guy Wilson attributes the demise of the early prairie school to a number of human factors, including death or retirement of its proponents, the loss of Wright's personal reputation, the renewal of revival styles, and the loss of interested publishers. See "The Early Prairie School, 1900–1930," in Wilson and Robinson, *Prairie School*, 26–27.

3. Shadow figures have probably always existed in architecture, and Ludwig Hilberseimer, ironically, was such a figure himself. See Richard Pommer, David Spaeth, and

Kevin Harrington, *In the Shadow of Mies: Ludwig Hilberseimer, Architect, Educator, and Urban Planner* (Chicago: Art Institute of Chicago, 1988). This book about Hilberseimer unwittingly contributes to Caldwell's place in the background in that it attributes the drawings for the proposed residence for Mr. S. Risch to Hilberseimer with Alfred Caldwell. When one looks at the drawing and the lettering, one sees that they were without doubt drawn wholly by Caldwell. Unfortunately, such misattributions consign important individuals to the shadows.

4. Carl W. Condit, *The Chicago School of Architecture: A History of Commercial and Public Building in the Chicago Area, 1875–1925* (Chicago: University of Chicago Press, 1964), 214. See also Condit's *Chicago, 1910–29: Building, Planning, and Urban Technology* (Chicago: University of Chicago Press, 1973), 208, in which he says of Caldwell's Lily Pool, sometimes called the Rookery, "the handsomest and possibly unique feature of the zoo is the Zoo Rookery" with its "little pavilion in the form of an open timber framework whose design places it exactly in the Wrightian-Prairie mode."

5. The Chicago Park District has many drawings from 1936 to 1939. The Canadian Centre for Architecture in Montreal has numerous drawings completed between 1946 and 1978. The Chicago Art Institute also has a few from the 1950s as well as several done for Hilberseimer's books.

6. Gerald R. McSheffrey and Dennis Domer, "Alfred Caldwell—Artist and Poet," unpublished manuscript, 1992, private collection of Alfred Caldwell, 1.

7. This text of 197 pages and 157 illustrations came for the most part from Caldwell's master's thesis at Illinois Institute of Technology and was based originally on a drawing by the same name that he had submitted to the 1942 *Herald American* competition to improve Chicago. In an interview in 1987 Caldwell said he wrote most of the text from 1929 to 1930. See Betty Blum, *Oral History of Alfred Caldwell* (Chicago: Art Institute of Chicago, 1987), 101–2. In 1989 he said he wrote most of it during World War II while working as a civil engineer, for "solace during that seemingly interminable combat of war afar." In about 1945 he presented it as a master's thesis, making a blustering defense when a business faculty member challenged it. Mies said later at a party that Caldwell's thesis was challenged because it was leftist. Caldwell reported that Mies "laughed and laughed and beat his hands" (Blum, 142–43). The thesis was announced as a forthcoming book on the cover of Ludwig Hilberseimer's *The New City* (Chicago: Paul Theobald, 1944), but it never appeared. Instead it was mysteriously lost. In 1987 Caldwell said Horizon Press lost the manuscript and all the illustrations, he believes for political reasons (Blum, 198); see also Malcolm Collier, "Interviews with Alfred Caldwell," eight tapes, Jens Jensen Archive, Morton Arboretum, Chicago, 1979, tape 1, p. 2. But Caldwell had a copy of the manuscript all along, though not the illustrations. Something stalled the project for years. In 1989 Caldwell edited the manuscript and provided a list of 157 illustrations. Its eighteen chapters outline his view of cities and his plan for decentralizing them by integrating them into the natural environment to produce a living landscape. This idea got him into trouble shortly after his appointment to the faculty of architecture at IIT. Now, more than fifty years after the original text was written, much of it is dated, though it is often passionate, poetic, and compelling.

8. McSheffrey and Domer, "Alfred Caldwell—Artist and Poet," 1.

9. Caldwell was born to Joseph Caldwell and Emma "Kitty" Davis Caldwell. His five sisters and brothers were Virginia, Kathryn, Isabelle, Teddy, and Joseph.

10. McSheffrey and Domer, "Alfred Caldwell—Artist and Poet," 2.

11. Ibid. In a shelflist of Caldwell's books at his Bristol home, I found three books of poetry Caldwell received from his mother for birthdays during his teenage years: by Ralph Waldo Emerson, by John Keats, and by Alfred, Lord Tennyson.

12. One of the books that most influenced Caldwell was H. S. Pepoon's *An Annotated Flora of the Chicago Area*, Chicago Academy of Sciences Bulletin 8, Nature History Survey (Chicago: Lakeside Press, 1927). Interview with Dennis Domer and Gerald McSheffrey, Bristol, Wisconsin, April 13, 1991. I taped twelve hours of interviews with Caldwell between 1991 and 1993 and spent many hours in discussion with him between 1980 and 1996. The interview transcripts are in Caldwell's private collection. From this point forward in this short biography, all direct quotations from Caldwell, unless otherwise noted, stem from these interviews. Other people have also done interviews with Alfred Caldwell, including Betty Blum, Gerald McSheffrey, Richard Guy Wilson, and Malcolm Collier.

13. Terrel, a landscape architect who worked for Jens Jensen, married into Caldwell's family. Caldwell idolized Terrel and still reminisces about him in glowing terms.

14. Wright lectured at Lawrence College on November 18, 1943.

15. Alfred Caldwell, "Atlantis and Return," unpublished manuscript, ca. 1974–80, Canadian Centre for Architecture, Montreal, 13.

16. Virginia Pullen, "Geda" (April 9, 1905, to September 2, 1988), was his fourth cousin. Geda's mother, Edith Davis Pullen, was a cousin of Emma Davis Caldwell, his mother. He and Geda eloped in 1923; they met at the Old Stone Church in downtown Cleveland and were married there. Geda got a new nightgown and a ring as wedding presents.

17. The 1924 date is earlier than previously thought. In a list he drew up in 1939 of his work with Jensen, however, Caldwell states that his first project with Jensen was in 1924 on the estate of Mrs. O. C. Barber in Akron, Ohio.

18. Carol Doty, "Ecology, Community, and the Prairie Spirit," in *Prairie in the City: Naturalism in Chicago's Parks, 1870–1940*, exhibition catalog (Chicago: Chicago Historical Society, 1991), 9.

19. Wilhelm Miller, "The Prairie Style of Landscape Architecture," *Architectural Record* 40 (December): 590–92.

20. Grese, *Jens Jensen*, 46–47.

21. For additional information on Jensen, see Julia Sniderman's "Bringing the Prairie Vision into Focus," in *Prairie in the City*, 19–31, and in that same volume Wim de Wit and William W. Tippens's "Prairie School in the Parks." Robert Grese provides a thorough discussion of Jensen's design career in his recent book *Jens Jensen: Maker of Natural Parks and Gardens*. An earlier work is Leonard K. Eaton's *Landscape Artist in America: The Life and Work of Jens Jensen* (Chicago: University of Chicago Press, 1964). Jensen himself wrote extensively, including *Siftings* (Chicago: Ralph Fletcher Seymour, 1939), *The Voice of the Clearing* (Ellison Bay, Wis.: Clearing, n.d.), and numerous articles on landscape and gardens. Grese provides a complete list of Jensen's landscape work and writing.

22. Jeremiads were a traditional part of American life from the Puritans to the moderns. Jensen and Caldwell were particularly influenced by the American transcendentalists, Ralph Waldo Emerson, Henry David Thoreau, Walt Whitman, and Herman Melville. In much of their writing they used the jeremiad as a rhetorical device. See Sacvan Bercovitch, *The American Jeremiad* (Madison: University of Wisconsin Press, 1978), 182–210. For an extended version of Jensen's jeremiad, see Grese, *Jens Jensen*, 1–2.

23. The Harley L. Clarke house was done in conjunction with the architect Richard Powers from 1926 to 1928. See Grese, *Jens Jensen*, 201.

24. Alfred Caldwell, "Experiential Qualifications," unpublished manuscript, October 11, 1939, Ryerson and Burnham Archives, Art Institute of Chicago Libraries. In this manuscript Caldwell says he began work with Jensen in 1924, a date somewhat earlier than previously believed. He says he worked five and one-half years with Jensen, and he listed as his last project for him a fountain and stonework in 1928 for the Mrs. Julius Rosenwald memorial in Ravinia, Illinois.

25. Alfred Caldwell, "Executed Work," October 11, 1939. See Grese's list and dates, *Jens Jensen*, 199–220.

26. Here Caldwell's memory has slipped. In a letter to Jensen on August 6, 1941, Caldwell wrote extensively about a drawing he had just finished for Jensen. Caldwell drew other landscape plans, and at least once Jensen drew a sketch of a pool for Caldwell to turn into a landscape plan. In a note with that pool sketch, Jensen refers to other plans: "Send me measurements of that land at the School for a sculpture court. Also measurement of the . . . golf course including the . . . pond." Caldwell still has this sketch, in black crayon and pencil on tracing paper, 16.5 by 17.25 inches. There was more discussion than drawing when these two worked together, but when a drawing was needed, Jensen knew Caldwell could easily make one.

27. The heady days of building Chicago, from about 1884 when Jensen came to the early 1930s, are well illustrated by Harold M. Mayer and Richard C. Wade, *Chicago: Growth of a Metropolis* (Chicago: University of Chicago Press, 1969), 283–374.

28. From 1912 to 1930 much more was written about Wright in German than in English. Significant works published in German during that period that Caldwell probably had access to in Wright's library included writings by Heinrich de Fries, Werner Hegemann, Fiske Kimball, Werner Moser, Henricus Th. Wijdeveld, Richard Neutra, Bruno Taut, and Gustav Platz. In addition, thirty-three articles on Wright were published in German during this eighteen-year period. For an excellent published dissertation on Wright's influence in Germany, see Heidi Kief-Niederwöhrmeier, *Frank Lloyd Wright und Europa* (Stuttgart: Karl Krämer, 1983).

29. Grese, *Jens Jensen*, 47–48.

30. Blum, *Oral History*, 49. Caldwell described Jensen as a "showbird." See Collier, "Interviews," tape 1, p. 4.

31. Interview with Dennis Domer, 1991, transcript A, 5.

32. Ibid., 4.

33. This letter is now in Special Collections at the Getty Center in California. I am grateful to Carol Caldwell Dooley, to Indira Berndtson of the Frank Lloyd Wright Archives, and to Brent Sverdloff at the Getty Center for making it available to me.

34. Eaton, *Landscape Artist*, 12–13.

35. George T. Donoghue or one of his relatives held powerful positions in one of the Chicago park organizations for over half a century. In the 1920s Donoghue was on the Lincoln Park Commission, which eventually fired him. He was out of work for a short time, then he was able to get J. Frank Foster fired from the South Park District and himself appointed. As superintendent of South Park, he managed to become superintendent of the newly consolidated Chicago Park District in 1934, a post he held until his nephew, Edward Kelly, succeeded him in the 1950s. Kelley held the post until the mid-1980s.

36. George T. Donoghue to Charles T. Landon, January 26, 1934, Dubuque Historical Society.

37. Jens Jensen to Charles T. Landon, n.d.

38. Alfred Caldwell to Charles T. Landon, January 24, 1934.

39. Helen H. Henschel to Dennis Domer, April 7, 1989. Mrs. Henschel was secretary to Glenn Brown while he was chairman of the Dubuque park board.

40. Charles T. Landon to Alfred Caldwell, February 22, 1934.

41. Carol Chalfant Caldwell was born on January 25, 1931, and James Allen Caldwell on December 12, 1933, both in Chicago.

42. *Dubuque Telegraph Herald and Times Journal*, n.d., Dubuque park board.

43. Alfred Caldwell to Charles T. Landon, February 2, 1934, Dubuque park board.

44. Wilson, "Themes of Continuity," 203.

45. Wilson, "Artist and Poet," 409.

46. *Dubuque Telegraph Herald*, January 14, 1936, 2.

47. Ibid., 2.

48. Julia Sniderman, "The Historic Resources of the Chicago Park District," National Register of Historic Places Multiple Property Documentation Form (March 22, 1990), section F, 19, Chicago Parks District.

49. Julia Sniderman, "Lincoln Park," National Register of Historic Places Registration Form, n.d., section 8, 78, Chicago Park District.

50. Interview with Luke Cosme, July 5, 1994. Cosme worked in the Chicago Park District from September 1935 to 1993, when he retired as engineer of design and contracts.

51. *Third Annual Report, Chicago Park District* (Chicago: Ringley, 1937), 131–38.

52. The Morton Arboretum's archive of Jens Jensen material has 24 letters Caldwell wrote to Jensen from 1936 to 1941. Caldwell has 64 letters Jensen wrote to him during that same period and a total of 139 letters from Jensen from 1933 to 1946.

53. Interview with Luke Cosme, July 5, 1994.

54. For further details on the Dill Pickle Club see Julia Sniderman, National Register of Historic Places Nomination Form for Washington Square, U.S. Department of Interior, National Park Service, 1991.

55. Alfred Caldwell, unpublished engineering notes, 1939–40.

56. Alfred Caldwell to J. T. Rettaliata, President, Illinois Institute of Technology, January 29, 1960; J. T. Rettaliata to Alfred Caldwell, March 1, 1960.

57. This was "The Living Landscape."

58. Ludwig Hilberseimer to Alfred Caldwell, June 9, 1941.

59. Richard Pommer disputes this in "More a Necropolis Than a Metropolis," in

Pommer, Spaeth, and Harrington, *In the Shadow of Mies*, 21. Pommer states that Hilberseimer was "unlike his contemporary Walter Gropius, whose work was shaped by his inability to draw."

60. Ludwig Hilberseimer to Alfred Caldwell, June 9, 1941.

61. Alfred Willis, "A Proposal for Replanning the Chicago Region 1942," unpublished report of the Canadian Centre for Architecture, May 1987.

62. Alfred Caldwell, "A Proposed Plan for Chicago, 1942," in Blaser, *Architecture and Nature*, 48.

63. Willis, "Proposal," 2.

64. Caldwell made documented lecture appearances at the University of Chicago in 1944, Rosary College in 1945, the University of Chicago again in 1947, and the City Club of Chicago in 1947. See the Ludwig Hilberseimer Papers, series 4:2, box 2, in the Ryerson and Burnham Archives, Art Institute of Chicago, and Caldwell's own archives. Among these papers there are short essays, usually dated, that are speeches Caldwell probably gave for Hilberseimer or Mies. Some, especially those given after 1945, may be ones he wrote on his own. No matter whom they were given for, Caldwell always lent the essays his poetic style even though he did not have complete authority over their content. They include "The Great City of Today" (October 8, 1946), "City Planning: City in the Landscape" (1944–45), a lecture on Mies (May 16, 1947), "Planning and Housing" (December 30, 1943), "Cities for Living" (February 19, 1943), "The New City" (1944), "The Great Industrial City Is a New Thing in the World," and "New Cities for Old" in the archives of the Art Institute of Chicago. In Caldwell's private archives are speeches titled "Balderdash in the Universities," "Be Your Own Man," "The Chicago School and the Lost Cause," "Fantasy and Play," "This Bridge Seems Alive, Springing thru Space," "Nature's Great Plan," "Structure: Principle and Ikon" (1964), and "Quod Semper, Quod Ubiquas, Quod ad Omnibus: This Applies Everywhere and to Everyone."

65. Alfred Caldwell and Ludwig Hilberseimer, "Design to Fit the Human Spirit: The Evolution of City Plans," unpublished manuscript, November 7, 1944, 1.

66. Alfred Caldwell, "Lincoln Park and the People," *Chicago Daily News*, January 20, 1942. In this short article Caldwell criticized "the multitudinous drives and the curiously irrational parking lots" that cut Lincoln Park into small, isolated plots. He believed the roads were made for the upper classes, leaving poor people in the slums without a park to picnic in. Jens Jensen was among the many who contributed to the correspondence in reaction to this article. He argued that "those who built these speedways thought of one class only. This is far from the democratic way of life." Caldwell continued his attack on roads in the parks in his article in the *Chicago Daily News* on April 24, 1942, "Spring in Grant Park." He said that "this park is a deserted wasteland of streets, automobiles, and monumental buildings." He accused the Park District of employing Nazi planning principles and called Grant Park "fit for nothing so much as the imperial parades of some future fascism." These were fighting words in 1942.

67. Alfred Caldwell to Ludwig Hilberseimer, November 17, 1940.

68. Information on Camp Forrest can be obtained from the Department of the Air Force, Arnold Air Force Base, Tennessee: see the short history "Camp Forrest Tullahoma, Tennessee 1941–1946," n.d., and Michael Bradley's *Reveille to Taps*, 1994, an unpublished

manuscript on the history of Camp Forrest. Bradley's chapter "Boom Times in Tul-lahoma" details the circumstances surrounding the building of this gigantic camp.

69. Alfred Caldwell to Ludwig Hilberseimer, November 17, 1940.

70. Ludwig Hilberseimer to Alfred Caldwell, November 27, 1940. He explains this reply by stating that "only farmer barns belong to the landscape because they do not pretend to be architecture. If a building pretends to be architecture, then in 999,999 cases of 1,000,000 it is very bad."

71. Alfred Caldwell to Ludwig Hilberseimer, December 16, 1940.

72. Robert B. Roberts, *Encyclopedia of Historic Forts: The Military, Pioneer, and Trading Posts of the United States* (New York: Macmillan, 1988), 852.

73. Alfred Caldwell to Ludwig Hilberseimer, August 27, 1942.

74. Alfred Caldwell, "A Job for Durga and Shiva," *Structurist*, no. 7 (1967): 7–12.

75. Ludwig Hilberseimer to Alfred Caldwell, November 27, 1940.

76. Alfred Caldwell, "Columbus Park," *Parks and Recreation* 25 (April 1942): 296.

77. Blum, *Oral History*, 84.

78. Caldwell, "Columbus Park," 296.

79. For a review of the contributions of Walter Peterhans to IIT, see Dennis Domer, "Walter Peterhans and the Legacy of Visual Training," *Structurist*, nos. 31–32 (1991–92): 44–51; Dennis Domer, "Walter Peterhans and Visual Training at Illinois Institute of Technology," *Reflections: The Journal of the School of Architecture* (University of Illinois at Urbana Champaign), no. 5 (fall 1987): 18–27; Inka Graeve, "Vom Wesen der Dinge zu Leben und Werk Walter Peterhans'," in *Walter Peterhans Fotografien, 1927–38* (Essen: Museum Folkwang, 1993), 6–20.

80. *Mies van der Rohe: Architect as Educator*, exhibition catalog, June 6–July 12 (Chicago: Illinois Institute of Technology, 1986), 155.

81. Jens Jensen to P. H. Elwood, July 13, 1939. P. H. Elwood to Alfred Caldwell, July 18, 1939.

82. Alfred Caldwell to Ludwig Hilberseimer, May 26, 1942. Referring to a discussion Caldwell had with Jerry Loebl only three years earlier, possibly about teaching at the Armour Institute, Caldwell wrote that Loebl told him, "Everyone they wrote to sent unfavorable letters." In this letter to Hilberseimer Caldwell explained the main problem from Loebl's point of view: "They are men with jobs. Wages are their opinions, the beginning and the end of every consideration. Mr. Loebl thought that by diplomacy things could be otherwise. I told him I believed in diplomacy; but it is only a word, and there is a place in affairs where diplomacy ends and hypocrisy and dishonesty begin. We talked a long time and I cannot cover it all. Finally I told him that they said these things because they hated me and I told him the reasons. I have the impression it seemed a little incredible to him. I showed him the letters and showed him the letter referring to the sabotaged civil service examination. I told him about the cause. We spoke again about diplomacy. I told him that on account of these letters no government agency would hire me because they imagine I am dangerous to have around, but those bringing good letters of recommendation are the real danger. The little diplomats are the danger to society. I want to see a city planned by diplomats. I have seen buildings made by diplomats—I think it would have been much better to have had an architect instead. What would a city be,

made by the same men sitting cautiously in their offices? I prefer Chicago. Mr. Loebl and I spoke pleasantly even when we were basically disagreed."

83. Ludwig Mies van der Rohe, "Lecture," in Fritz Neumeyer, *The Artless Word: Mies van der Rohe on the Building Art* (Cambridge: MIT Press, 1991), 325.

84. "Education and Architecture," Chicago Chapter *Bulletin of the AIA* 4 (June 1957): 46. Caldwell is pictured in the midst of his students on the front page of this bulletin.

85. Kevin Harrington, "Order, Space, Proportion—Mies's Curriculum at IIT," in *Mies van der Rohe: Architect as Educator*, 64.

86. Memo from Arthur Takeuchi, Paul Thomas, and San Utsunomiya to Dean Geoffrey T. Higgins and Professor Meyer Feldberg, December 14, 1987, private collection of Alfred Caldwell. Caldwell was named a distinguished professor of the Associated Collegiate Schools of Architecture in 1985, received the Distinguished Educator Award from the Chicago chapter of the American Institute of Architects in 1980, and was awarded a doctorate of humane letters and science by Illinois Institute of Technology in 1987.

87. Blum, *Oral History*, 118.

88. Alfred Caldwell interview with Gerald McSheffrey and Dennis Domer, July 1991.

89. Alfred Caldwell, "Brickwork," in *Encyclopaedia Britannica*, 1959 ed., 4:117–22.

90. Herrington, "Order, Space, Proportion," 64.

91. Paul Thomas, undelivered introduction to Alfred Caldwell on his receipt of an honorary doctorate at IIT, 1987, private collection of Alfred Caldwell.

92. "We learned brickwork. Mr. Caldwell said that even if he were teaching law students, he would have them learn about how to properly lay up bricks." Letter from Dennis DePietro, one of Caldwell's students from the California period, to Dennis Domer, October 3, 1994.

93. Caldwell, "Brickwork," 117.

94. Herrington, "Order, Space, Proportion," 64.

95. DePietro to Domer, October 3, 1994.

96. Blum, *Oral History*, 123.

97. Dan Lawrence interview, July 24, 1994. Lawrence teaches architecture at the Pasadena Arts Center.

98. Alfred Caldwell, lecture at IIT. n.d.

99. Werner Jaeger, *Paideia: The Ideals of Greek Culture* (New York: Oxford University Press, 1945), 1:xxii. See also Blum, *Oral History*, 146–47.

100. Jaeger, *Paideia*, 1:xxiii.

101. Dan Lawrence interview, July 24, 1994, 13.

102. Ibid., 11.

103. The most complete notebook extant belongs to Gerald Estes, who took Caldwell's sophomore and junior construction courses and his history courses from 1957 to 1959. There is nothing sloppy about these notebooks. They are typed or hand printed, with pen-and-ink drawings of buildings, landscapes, brick and wood, concrete and steel, and details of all sorts. Estes's notebooks are the best documentation of Caldwell's teaching.

104. For a history of IIT, see Irene Macauley, *The Heritage of IIT* (Chicago: Illinois Institute of Technology, 1978).

105. Alfred Caldwell, "Atomic Bombs and City Planning," *Journal of the American Institute of Architects* 4 (December 1945): 298–99.

106. Blum, *Oral History*, 140.

107. Alfred Caldwell, letter to the editor, *Chicago Sun*, May 23, 1946.

108. Ibid.

109. This letter was in response to a review by Norman Cousins and Thomas K. Finletter of "A Report on the International Control of Atomic Energy," *Saturday Review of Literature*, June 15, 1946. n.d.

110. See Blum, *Oral History*, 139–42.

111. For a review of President Heald's role and the place of IIT in the redevelopment of the downtown and particularly the South Side of Chicago, see Arnold R. Hirsch, *Making the Second Ghetto: Race and Housing in Chicago, 1940–1960* (Cambridge: Cambridge University Press, 1983), 102–4, 116, 253, 268.

112. Blum, *Oral History*, 143. Alfred Caldwell, "The City in the Landscape: A Preface for Planning" (master's thesis, Illinois Institute of Technology, 1948), ninety-nine pages and two drawings: "Plan of Chicago" and "The City in the Landscape."

113. Caldwell, "City in the Landscape: A Preface for Planning," 86. See also Alfred Caldwell, "The City in the Landscape," *Parks and Recreation* 18 (March–April 1945): 59–64. Caldwell published four of his drawings in this article: "The City in the Landscape," "The Landscape in the City," "Commerical Area," and "The Entire City a Park—the Park the Entire City."

114. Alfred Caldwell, "The Living Landscape," unpublished manuscript, 1943–54. This manuscript was announced as forthcoming on the cover of Hilberseimer's *The New City* in 1944 along with a book Mies was going to publish at the Theobald Publishing House. The atomic bomb article may have squelched it. Caldwell continued to work on it on and off for twenty years. The latest manuscript is identical to his thesis except for four chapters he added at the end titled "Decentralization, Strategy for Peace," "Landscape Making—Definition and History," "Landscape Making—Sense and Procedure," and "The Loaves and the Fishes." Caldwell sent it to Horizon Press in 1964, but in 1965 the editor declined to publish it.

115. Blum, *Oral History*, 121.

116. Harrington, "Order, Space, Proportion," 64.

117. Ibid., 64.

118. One of Caldwell's most inspired students was Richard Nickel, who led the movement to save Louis Sullivan's buildings in Chicago. Caldwell participated in this movement, but it was largely a failure. He gave a rousing speech in an effort to save the Garrick Theater. Nickel was an excellent photographer and photographed many drawings and models made by students in Caldwell's classes. While trying to photograph and save parts of Sullivan's Stock Exchange building in 1972, he fell through a floor, was covered by debris, and died. His body was found several weeks later. See Richard Cahan, *They All Fall Down: Richard Nickel's Struggle to Save America's Architecture* (Washington, D.C.: Preservation Press, 1994). See also Richard Cahan, "Death in the Ruins," *Inland Architect* 38 (November–December 1994): 5–13.

119. Blum, *Oral History*, 122.

120. Ibid., 123.

121. Caldwell resigned on April 2, 1958, in a letter to Dr. J. T. Rettaliata; Ryerson and Burnham Archives, Art Institute of Chicago Libraries.

122. Alfred Caldwell to Dr. Rettaliata, January 29, 1960. Rettaliata accepted his resignation "with regret" in a letter to Caldwell, March 1, 1960. Caldwell explained the reasons for his resignation in a letter to George Danforth, July 13, 1960, with copies to Mies and to Hilberseimer. In this letter he also said he was willing to return, on the urging of Hilberseimer and Reginald Malcolmson, but Rettaliata did not accept.

123. Franz Schultz, *Mies van der Rohe: A Critical Biography* (Chicago: University of Chicago Press, 1985), 287.

124. Interview with Myron Goldsmith and John Vinci, September 18, 1994.

125. Schultz, *Mies van der Rohe*, 286–87. See letter from Mies to Bunshaft, September 2, 1958.

126. In an August 5, 1958, memorandum of a meeting between Joe Fujikawa, one of Mies's employees, and R. J. Spaeth, Fujikawa lists Spaeth's five reasons for "going to other architects for the design of the new campus buildings. These reasons include not doing work fast enough, Mies's lack of interest in the campus, the overriding role of associate architects, mechanical problems and leaks in buildings, and the battle to get something practical and functional in the designs." Further, the board of trustees believed that "they were not building a monument to Mies on campus." Spaeth did have to battle Mies's office for work. There is a series of letters from June 4, 1956, to July 24, 1958, to Mies and others about the need for Mies to provide a new model of the campus. The model was never done.

127. Alfred Caldwell to George Danforth, July 13, 1960. In this letter Caldwell declined to respond to Danforth's request to suggest and train a replacement.

128. Caldwell to Ruth Roberg, October 11, 1960. Leo and Ruth Roberg were close friends who lent the Caldwell family money to tide them over until Caldwell got a new job. "The trouble has been," Caldwell wrote in a letter of appreciation, "that this particular situation came about at a time when every last dollar I had was put into the house completion." The house Caldwell was referring to was the one he designed in Deerfield, Illinois.

129. Ludwig Mies van der Rohe to J. C. Warner, October 3, 1960.

130. Ludwig Mies van der Rohe to Frank Montana, November 23, 1960.

131. In an interview with Myron Goldsmith, John Vinci, and Alfred Caldwell, September 18, 1994, Goldsmith remembered that Caldwell designed some details for the Farnsworth house near Plano, Illinois, that were never used. Caldwell was involved in the project as early as October 1945, according to Caldwell's fifteen-page deposition dated November 17, 1951, which presumably was used in court proceedings between Dr. Farnsworth and Mies.

132. Caldwell, "Nature and Architecture," 70. See also Alfred Caldwell, "Zoological Gardens," *Arts and Architecture* 77 (February 1960): 20–23.

133. Caldwell, in Blaser, *Architecture and Nature*, 74. See also Caldwell, "Zoological Gardens," 20–23. Both of these projects were influenced by a tour of thirteen European zoos he and Geda made during the summer of 1954. According to Caldwell's notes, the

Hamburg and Frankfurt zoos were the most impressive because they avoided artificiality and integrated animals into a natural setting. They also visited Regent's Park zoo and the Whipnard zoological garden in Great Britain, the Paris zoological garden at Vincennes, the Antwerp zoological garden, the Amsterdam zoo, the Copenhagen zoo, the Cologne zoo, the Munich zoo, the Milan zoo, the Rome zoological garden, and the Madrid zoo.

134. See David Spaeth, *Mies van der Rohe* (New York: Rizzoli, 1985), 134–39; Schultz, *Mies van der Rohe*, 293–96; and Caldwell, in Blaser, *Nature and Architecture*, 92–95.

135. David Spaeth, "Ludwig Hilberseimer's Settlement Unit: Origins and Applications," in *In the Shadow of Mies: Ludwig Hilberseimer, Architect, Educator, and Urban Planner* (Chicago: Art Institute of Chicago, 1988), 64.

136. Caldwell, in Blaser, *Nature and Architecture*, 50–51, 80–83.

137. Information about the human side of the special projects department as well as the projects completed there during Caldwell's tenure comes especially from Gerald Estes, who has cataloged and copied all the work from Caldwell's think tank. Estes also provided considerable information in a letter to Gerald McSheffrey, September 15, 1991, an interview on July 5, 1994, and a letter to Dennis Domer, October 12, 1994, as well as black-and-white photos of the think tank's most important projects. David Swan, who photographed most of the design work for presentation, also gave valuable information in an interview on September 18, 1994.

138. Alfred Caldwell, "Order and Beauty," unpublished manuscript, n.d., Chicago Department of City Planning, 2.

139. Ibid., 4.

140. Ibid., 8.

141. Ibid., 6.

142. Ibid., 10.

143. Ibid.

144. Percy Bysshe Shelley, *Prometheus Unbound: A Lyrical Drama in Four Acts* (1818).

145. Gerald Estes to Gerald McSheffrey, September 15, 1991, 2.

146. The Committee of Seventy-six was established in 1954 by John E. Stipp, Gerald F. Fitzgerald, Willard K. Jaques, Samuel H. Young, and Richard J. Nelson. In 1963 Samuel H. Young was the president of the forty-six-member committee that accepted Caldwell's design. See Committee of Seventy-six, "World's Fair Chicago 1976 Proposed Bicentennial Exposition," January 1963, Chicago Department of City Planning, 4.

147. Seventy-second General Assembly of the Illinois Senate, bill no. 831 (1961), 22.

148. The 1893 fair attracted 21 million visitors, and the 1933–34 fair brought 30 million. Both of these fairs made a profit. See *Chicago Daily News*, March 16, 1963, 8; Mayer and Wade, *Chicago: Growth of a Metropolis*, 194–205, 360–64, and Committee of Seventy-six, "World's Fair Chicago 1976," 5.

149. Committee of Seventy-six, "World's Fair Chicago 1976," 8.

150. Ibid., 9.

151. Alfred Caldwell, "Preliminary General Report, Proposed Bicentennial Exposition 1976," unpublished manuscript, Chicago Department of City Planning, March 9, 1962, 1.

152. Ibid.

153. Ibid., 2.

154. *Progressive Architecture* 42 (September 1961): 208–9. See the letter from Burton H. Holmes, technical editor of *Progressive Architecture*, to Alfred Caldwell, September 8, 1961. This suspension structure was republished in Europe in *Bauen und Wohnen* in 1963. See the exchange of letters between Alfred Caldwell and Madeleine Benz of *Bauen und Wohnen*, December 16, 1962, July 8, 1963, and July 11, 1963.

155. *Progressive Architecture* 42 (September 1961): 209.

156. Committee of Seventy-six, "World's Fair Chicago 1976," 13.

157. Gerald Estes to Gerald McSheffrey, September 15, 1991, 3.

158. Unpublished report of the Chicago City Planning Department, May 31, 1962, 10–13.

159. Alfred Caldwell. "Lake Shore Proposals in Two Parts," unpublished report of the Chicago Department of City Planning, May 7, 1962.

160. "Daley Proposes 'City of Future' Lakefront Plan," *Chicago Sun-Times*, April 20, 1962, 3. See also *Plans and Progress* (Chicago Department of City Planning), 3 (April 1962), and Department of City Planning press release, April 19, 1962.

161. See memos from Ira J. Bach to Alfred Caldwell, *City Planner*, April 8 and April 13, 1964.

162. Interview with David Swan, September 18, 1994.

163. Gerald Estes, "Navy Pier" (program for the development of the pier as a marine recreation center), unpublished report of the Chicago Department of City Planning, April 24, 1964; David Swan, "Chicago Riverfront Study," unpublished report of the Chicago Department of City Planning, May 28, 1964.

164. Swan, "Chicago Riverfront Study," 50.

165. These schools included Cornell, Syracuse, Rice, Yale, Western Reserve, University of California at Berkeley, Virginia Polytechnic Institute, North Carolina State University, Notre Dame, University of Illinois at Chicago, University of Washington, University of Toronto, Iowa State University, and Massachusetts Institute of Technology. In 1963 Larry Reich wanted Caldwell to meet Leonard Currie, dean of the College of Architecture and Art at the University of Illinois at Chicago, and though they never got together, Currie wrote to Caldwell suggesting he get in touch with Charles Worley, head of the Department of Architecture at Virginia Polytechnic Institute, who was a friend of both and who needed someone to head the planning program there. See Leonard J. Currie to Alfred Caldwell, August 7, 1963. Caldwell accepted invitations to lecture in schools of architecture around the country, invitations he received because of his reputation as a passionate and practiced speaker. In his speeches he employed themes familiar from his fifteen years of teaching architectural history at IIT. For example, in a lecture at the University of Kentucky in 1964 titled "Structure: Principle and Ikon," he criticized contemporary architecture as a parade of fashions and pleaded for the return to construction "proceeding from inner principle." Caldwell cited the peasant house, a Doric temple, a twelfth-century cathedral, a suspension bridge, and Mies's buildings as examples of construction that resulted from "inevitable consequences." This unabashed modernism got an enthusiastic reception, and since the breadth of his experience was unequaled, his outlook for a job in academia was good.

166. Charles Worley studied at IIT from 1939 to 1941 and received a master of architecture degree there in 1941. See his graduate thesis, "A School for Art and Architecture," 1941, in *Mies van der Rohe: Architect as Educator*, 130.

167. Alfred Caldwell to Leo Dekovic, December 30, 1965.

168. For an outline of the complexities and expectations of the new curriculum at USC, see Konrad Wachsmann, "Education for Building Research," *Arts and Architecture*, May 1967, 28–29.

169. Interview with Crombie Taylor and Hope Taylor, July 23, 1994.

170. Crombie Taylor to Alfred Caldwell, July 8, 1965. Alfred Caldwell to Gerald Estes, January 24, 1966.

171. Caldwell to Leo Dekovic, December 30, 1965.

172. Konrad Wachsmann was a German architect who came to the United States in 1941. In 1949 he was appointed professor of design and director of the Department of Advanced Building Research of the Institute of Design at Illinois Institute of Technology. In 1964 he was appointed professor of architecture, chairman of the Graduate School of the Department of Architecture, and director of the Building Research Division of the University of Southern California.

173. Alfred Caldwell, "Be Your Own Man," unpublished and incomplete manuscript, May 1, 1965. Interview with Jim Kehr and Eric Katzmeier, July 22, 1994.

174. Caldwell was listed in the *Bulletin of the University of Southern California* from spring 1966 to spring 1972 as teaching Architectural Design III, Architectural Design IV, Research, and Thesis.

175. Dennis DePietro to Dennis Domer, October 3, 1994, 1.

176. Interview with Dan Lawrence, July 24, 1994, 9. Konrad Wachsmann had long given up attempts to teach a traditional architectural design studio, and by May of 1967 he advocated a "new order . . . an inter-disciplinary system without barriers of faculty specialization, exploding in universal, international and comprehensive planned research." See Konrad Wachsmann, "Research: The Mother of Invention," *Arts and Architecture*, May 1967, 30. For Wachsmann the architectural design studio's "sole remaining importance consists in its being a place for building models, models intended not so much for the purpose of checking proportions or judging the effect of a facade, as for studying functions of every kind." See Konrad Wachsmann, *The Turning Point of Building Structure and Design* (New York: Reinhold, 1961), 23. If the faculty taught architectural design, either they, like Wachsmann, preferred "complex solutions to simple problems" or they offered no solutions at all. They didn't know what to teach. DePietro to Domer, October 3, 1994. For a critique of architects such as Wachsmann who pursued the technical ideal, see Charles Jencks, *Modern Movements in Architecture* (Garden City, N.Y.: Anchor Books, 1973), 212–18.

177. Interview with Dan Lawrence, July 24, 1994, 8, 12.

178. DePietro to Domer, October 3, 1994, 2.

179. Alfred Caldwell, "Education," unpublished lecture given at University of Southern California, May 1969, 1.

180. DePietro to Domer, October 3, 1994, 2. Thirty years later Caldwell's talk to his former students on July 22, 1994, in Los Angeles must have sounded familiar, for he

repeated the essence of his "Be Your Own Man" lecture. "You are the reason of life. Today is the meaning of life. What are you going to do? To hell with what we did a long time ago. I want today. Act!"

181. David R. Kendall to Sam T. Hurst, 1972.

182. Lawrence interview, July 24, 1994, 10.

183. Ibid., 19.

184. DePietro to Domer, October 3, 1994, 2.

185. Lawrence interview, July 24, 1994, 33.

186. Robert E. Stewart, president of the Adronicus chapter of Alpha Rho Chi Fraternity, to Sam T. Hurst, March 29, 1971.

187. Michael Gould to John R. Hubbard, President, University of Southern California, April 15, 1971.

188. Marc Simon Glasser to Sam T. Hurst, March 29, 1971.

189. Stephen A. Woolley to Sam T. Hurst, March 31, 1971.

190. Roger Alan Schultz to Sam T. Hurst, March 28, 1971.

191. Rollin D. Foss to Sam T. Hurst, April 5, 1971.

192. Jeff Lundahl to Sam T. Hurst, April 6, 1971.

193. Lawrence interview, July 24, 1994, 37.

194. Craig Ellwood to Gerald McSheffrey, December 19, 1980.

195. On February 11, 1969, Ellwood gave Caldwell Esther McCoy's book, *Craig Ellwood: Architecture*, with an inscription: "Alfred: Architect-Poet-Philosopher-Teacher-Friend—. Craig."

196. Although he took the job, Ellwood often did not have the time to teach at USC because he was busy with clients.

197. Interview with James Tyler, August 15, 1994.

198. See John W. Sugden, "Ongoing Projects and Completed Buildings," *Utah Architect*, no. 54 (autumn 1973): 10–17. Sugden went to IIT from 1945 to 1952 and took Caldwell's sophomore and junior construction courses and his history courses. Sugden graduated from IIT with a bachelor of architecture degree in 1950 and a master of architecture degree in 1952. See *Mies van der Rohe: Architect as Educator*, 163.

199. Interview with James Tyler, August 15, 1994.

200. Besides Esther McCoy's book on Ellwood, see her *Modern California Houses: Case Study Houses, 1945–1962* (New York: Reinhold, 1962), and her *Case Study Houses: 1945–1962* (Los Angeles: Hennessey and Ingalls, 1977); see also her book *The Second Generation* (Salt Lake City: Bibbs M. Smith, 1984), and Paul Heyer's *Architects on Architecture* (New York: Walker, 1966). Ellwood's work was published at least seventeen times in journals during that period, including *Architectural Forum* (three times), *Interiors* (two times), *Lotus, Bauen und Wohnen* (three times), *Domus* (two times), a whole issue of *Japan Architect, Architecture Française, Progressive Architecture, Architecture Plus, Architectural Design,* and *Building Research.*

201. Peter Blake, foreword to Esther McCoy, *Craig Ellwood* (New York: Walker, 1968), 6.

202. Ben Shahn, "Bread and Butter to the Aspen Conference on Design," June 1966: "But I think it would be nice if we just made a pet of her [meaning chaos] and let her go

free from time to time to get a breath of fresh air and romp around a little bit among the Planned Society," Shahn concluded.

203. Craig Ellwood to Alfred Caldwell, January 31, 1967.

204. Craig Ellwood to Alfred Caldwell, June 12, 1967.

205. Reports of Caldwell's speech were carried in the *Denver Post*, June 20, 1967; *Aspen Times*, June 22, 1967; *San Bernardino Daily Sun*, June 22, 1967; *Boston Globe*, June 20, 1967; *Des Moines Tribune*, June 20, 1967; *Des Moines Register*, June 22, 1967; *Sarasota Herald Tribune*, June 21, 1967; *Rocky Mountain News*, June 20 and 21, 1967; *Springfield Union*, June 27, 1967; *Topeka State Journal*, June 27, 1967; *Richmond News Leader*, June 20, 1967; *Corona (California) Independent*, June 21, 1967; and *Christian Science Monitor*, June 23, 1967.

206. Craig Ellwood to Gerald McSheffrey, December 19, 1980.

207. Alfred Caldwell, "Balderdash in the Universities," unpublished manuscript, 1967.

208. DePietro to Domer, October 3, 1994, 6.

209. Sam T. Hurst to Stephen A. Woolley, June 17, 1971. The decision to retire Caldwell in 1971 resulted in a student uproar with a letter to the editor of the USC student newspaper and nineteen protest letters from students to either Sam Hurst or John Hubbard, the president of USC.

210. DePietro to Domer, October 3, 1994, 5.

211. Sam T. Hurst to James A. Hutton et al., petitioners on behalf of Alfred Caldwell, February 23, 1972.

212. Dennis DePietro to Henry Salvatori, April 10, 1972.

213. Jeff Lundahl to Dr. John R. Hubbard, May 19, 1972.

214. Alfred Caldwell to Gerald Estes, January 24, 1966.

215. In April 1991 Gerald McSheffrey and I listed about 550 books in Caldwell's library at home in Bristol, and he keeps about 200 more in his apartment in Chicago. He and Geda had broad interests, and though most of the collection represents American and European writers of poetry, fiction, philosophy, religion, psychology, and criticism, they also read Eastern philosophers and collected works on Japanese art and design.

216. Gerald McSheffrey, "Alfred Caldwell's Essays on Architecture," unpublished manuscript, n.d., private collection of Alfred Caldwell, 5.

217. Caldwell gave these poems to Hilberseimer, and they, along with "Poem on Peace" (1945), are in the Hilberseimer Papers at the Ryerson and Burnham Archives at the Art Institute of Chicago.

218. For the story of Samson, see Judges 14–16.

219. Blum, *Oral History*, 184–88.

220. For the complete story on Caldwell's return to IIT, see Gerald R. McSheffrey, "The Teacher: An Essay on Alfred Caldwell," *Structurist*, nos. 31–32 (1991–92): 12–15, and "Mies's Greatest Bequest," *Architectural Record*, no. 8 (August 1984): 47–49.

Unless otherwise noted, all unpublished manuscripts by Alfred Caldwell are in his private collection at Bristol, Wisconsin, and Baldwin, Kansas.

Works by Alfred Caldwell

"The Architect." *Structurist*, nos. 25–26 (1985–86): 128–32.

"Architecture: Vision of Structure." *Structurist*, nos. 17–18 (1977–78): 17–19.

"Architecture and Technology." *Structurist*, nos. 21–22 (1981–82): 51–56.

"Atlantis and Return." Unpublished manuscript, ca. 1974–80, Canadian Centre for Architecture, Montreal. Eighty-eight pages.

"Atomic Bombs and City Planning." *Journal of the American Institute of Architects* 4 (December 1945): 298–99.

"Balderdash in the Universities." Unpublished manuscript, 1967. Eight pages.

"Be Your Own Man." Unpublished manuscript, May 1, 1965. Two pages.

"Brickwork." *Encyclopaedia Britannica*, 1959 ed. 4:117–22.

"The Chicago School and the Lost Cause." Unpublished manuscript, n.d. Eight pages.

"The City in the Landscape." *Parks and Recreation* 18 (March–April 1945): 59–64.

"The City in the Landscape: A Preface for Planning." Master's thesis, Illinois Institute of Technology, 1948.

"Columbus Park." *Parks and Recreation* 25 (April 1942): 295–96.

"Design to Fit the Human Spirit: The Evolution of City Plans." With Ludwig Hilberseimer. Unpublished manuscript, November 7, 1944. Two pages.

"Education." Unpublished lecture given at University of Southern California, May 1969. Twelve pages.

"Eulogy for Jens Jensen." Unpublished manuscript, 1951. One page.

"Experiential Qualifications." Unpublished manuscript, October 11, 1939, Ryerson and
    Burnham Archives, Art Institute of Chicago Libraries. Five pages.

"Fantasy and Play." Unpublished manuscript, n.d. Two pages.

"Gothic Cathedral Compared to a Truss." Unpublished manuscript, n.d. Seven pages.

"The Hex of Harmony." *Structurist*, no. 8 (1968): 27–34.

"Highway in Lincoln Park." Unpublished manuscript, 1942. Five pages.

"In Defense of Animals." *Our Native Landscape* (newsletter of the Friends of Our Native
    Landscape), December 1931.

"Interview on the Farnsworth House." Unpublished manuscript, November 17, 1951.
    Fifteen pages.

"Jens Jensen: The Prairie Spirit." *Landscape Architecture* 51 (January 1961): 102–5.

"A Job for Durga and Shiva." *Structurist*, no. 7 (1967): 7–12.

"Lake Shore Proposals in Two Parts." Unpublished report of the Chicago Department of
    City Planning, May 7, 1962. Fifty pages.

"Landscape Architecture." Unpublished manuscript, June 1, 1955. Fifty-three pages.

"Language and the Grammar of Structure." *Structurist*, no. 12 (1972–73): 75–79.

"Light and the Conquest of Kitsch." *Structurist*, nos. 13–14 (1973–74): 7–17.

"The Lily Pool, Lincoln Park." Unpublished manuscript, March 30, 1942. Two pages.

"Lincoln Park and the People." *Chicago Daily News* (Views on Many Topics), January 20,
    1942.

"The Living Landscape." Unpublished manuscript, 1943–54. 197 pages, 157 illustrations.

"Lost Cities of America." *Structurist*, no. 10 (1970): 67–75.

"Louis Sullivan." *Dimension* (University of Michigan College of Architecture and De-
    sign), 2 (1956): 9–15.

"Method of Objectivity Strategy of Truth." Unpublished report of the Chicago Depart-
    ment of City Planning, n.d. One page.

"Nature and Architecture." *Structurist*, nos. 23–24 (1983–84): 34–39.

"The Nature of Order." Unpublished manuscript, 1967. Eleven pages.

"Nature's Great Plan." Unpublished manscript, n.d. Two pages.

"The New Cities." Unpublished manuscript, 1944. Twenty-three pages.

"Order and Beauty." Unpublished manuscript, n.d. Ten pages.

"Order and Disorder." Proceedings of the Seventeenth International Design Conference,
    Aspen, Colorado, June 19, 1967. Three pages.

"Preliminary General Report, Proposed Bicentennial Exposition 1976." Unpublished
    manuscript, Chicago Department of City Planning, March 9, 1962. Twenty-nine
    pages.

"Spring in Grant Park." *Chicago Daily News* (Views on Many Topics), April 24, 1942.

"Structure: Principle and Ikon." Unpublished manuscript, 1964. Fifteen pages.

"Structure as Creative Principle." *Structurist*, nos. 33–34 (1993–94): 35–38.

"Structure in Time and Space." *Structurist*, nos. 15–16 (1975–76): 13–26.

"Suspension Structure." *Progressive Architecture* 42 (September 1961). Republished in
    Bauen und Wohnen, September 1963.

"Three Cantos on Color." *Structurist*, nos. 31–32 (1991–92): 11–12.

"Transparency of Architecture and Man." *Structurist*, nos. 27–28 (1987–88): 66–70.

"Truth and Continuity in the Nature of Things." *Structurist*, nos. 29–30 (1989–90): 46–49.

"Truth in Architecture." *Structurist*, nos. 15–16 (1979–80): 31–38.

"Zoological Gardens." *Arts and Architecture* 77 (February 1960): 20–23.

Secondary Sources

Achilles, Rolf, Kevin Harrington, and Charlotte Myhrum, eds. *Mies van der Rohe: Architect as Educator.* Chicago: Illinois Institute of Technology, 1986.

Benkert, Kyle G., Gerald Estes, Alfred Caldwell, Richard A. Pavia, and William R. Marston. "Preliminary Development Plan over the Illinois Central Art Rights East of Michigan Avenue and North of Randolph Street. Unpublished report of the Chicago Department of City Planning," April 19, 1962.

Bercovitch, Sacvan. *The American Jeremiad.* Madison: University of Wisconsin Press, 1978.

Blaser, Werner. *Architecture and Nature: The Work of Alfred Caldwell.* Basel: Birkhäuser, 1984.

Blum, Betty. *Oral History of Alfred Caldwell.* Chicago: Art Institute of Chicago, 1987.

Brooks, H. Allen. *The Prairie School.* Toronto: University of Toronto Press, 1972.

Cahan, Richard. "Death in the Ruins." *Inland Architect* 38 (November–December 1994): 5–13.

———. *They All Fall Down: Richard Nickel's Struggle to Save America's Architecture.* Washington, D.C.: Preservation Press, 1994.

Collier, Malcolm. "Interviews with Alfred Caldwell." Eight tapes. Jens Jensen Archive, Morton Arboretum, Chicago, 1979.

Committee of Seventy-six. "World's Fair Chicago 1976 Proposed Bicentennial Exposition." Unpublished report of the Chicago Department of City Planning, January 1963.

Condit, Carl W. *Chicago, 1910–29: Building, Planning, and Urban Technology.* Chicago: University of Chicago Press, 1973.

———. *The Chicago School of Architecture: A History of Commercial and Public Building in the Chicago Area, 1875–1925.* Chicago: University of Chicago Press, 1964.

Domer, Dennis. "A Socratic Conversation with Alfred Caldwell." *Structurist*, nos. 31–32 (1991–92): 4–9.

———. "Walter Peterhans and the Legacy of Visual Training." *Structurist*, nos. 31–32 (1991–92): 44–51.

———. "Walter Peterhans and Visual Training at Illinois Institute of Technology." *Reflections: The Journal of Architecture* (School of Architecture, University of Illinois at Urbana Champagne), no. 5 (fall 1987): 18–27.

Doty, Carol. "Ecology, Community, and the Prairie Spirit." In *Prairie in the City: Naturalism in Chicago's Parks, 1870–1940*, 8–17. Exhibition catalog. Chicago: Chicago Historical Society, 1991.

Eaton, Leonard K. *Landscape Artist in America: The Life and Work of Jens Jensen*. Chicago: University of Chicago Press, 1964.

Estes, Gerald. "Navy Pier." (Program for the development of the pier as a marine recreation center.) Unpublished report of the Chicago Department of City Planning, April 24, 1964.

Grese, Robert E. *Jens Jensen: Maker of Natural Parks and Gardens*. Baltimore: Johns Hopkins University Press, 1992.

Heyer, Paul. *Architects on Architecture*. New York: Walker, 1966.

Hilberseimer, Ludwig. *Entfaltung einer Planungsidee*. Berlin: Ullstein, 1963.

———. *The Nature of Cities*. Chicago: Paul Theobald, 1955.

———. *The New City*. Chicago: Paul Theobald, 1944.

———. *The New Regional Pattern: Industries and Gardens, Workshops and Farms*. Chicago: Paul Theobald, 1949.

Hirsh, Arnold R. *Making the Second Ghetto: Race and Housing in Chicago, 1940–1960*. Cambridge: Cambridge University Press, 1983.

Jensen, Jens. *Siftings*. Chicago: Ralph Fletcher Seymour, 1939.

———. *The Voice of the Clearing*. Ellison Bay, Wis: Clearing, n.d.

"Konrad Wachsmann." *Arts and Architecture*, May 1967, 6–30.

Malcolmson, Reginald. "The School of Mies van der Rohe: A Philosophy of Architectural Education." Unpublished manuscript, 1986. Private collection of Alfred Caldwell.

Mayer, Harold M., and Richard C. Wade. *Chicago: Growth of a Metropolis*. Chicago: University of Chicago Press, 1969.

McCoy, Esther. *Case Study Houses: 1945–1962*. New York: Reinhold, 1962.

———. *Craig Ellwood: Architecture*. New York: Walker, 1968.

McSheffrey, Gerald R. "Alfred Caldwell's Essays on Architecture." Unpublished manuscript, n.d. Private collection of Alfred Caldwell.

———. "Mies's Greatest Bequest." *Architectural Record*, no. 8 (August 1984): 47–49.

———. "The Teacher: An Essay on Alfred Caldwell." *Structurist*, nos. 31–32 (1991–92): 12–15.

McSheffrey, Gerald R., and Dennis Domer. "Alfred Caldwell—Artist and Poet." Unpublished manuscript, 1992. Private collection of Alfred Caldwell.

Miller, Wilhelm. *The Prairie Spirit in Landscape Gardening*. Circular 184. Urbana: College of Agriculture, 1915.

———. "The Prairie Style of Landscape Architecture." *Architectural Record* 40 (December): 590–92.

Neumeyer, Fritz. *The Artless Word: Mies van der Rohe on the Building Art*. Cambridge: MIT Press, 1991.

Pepoon, H. S. *An Annotated Flora of the Chicago Area*. Chicago Academy of Sciences Bulletin 8, Nature History Survey. Chicago: Lakeside Press, 1927.

Pommer, Richard, David Spaeth, and Kevin Harrington. *In the Shadow of Mies: Ludwig Hilberseimer, Architect, Educator, and Urban Planner*. Chicago: Art Institute of Chicago, 1988.

Schulze, Franz. *Mies van der Rohe: A Critical Biography*. Chicago: University of Chicago Press, 1985.

Sniderman, Julia. "Bringing the Prairie Vision into Focus." In *Prairie in the City: Naturalism in Chicago's Parks, 1870–1940*, 19–31. Exhibition catalog. Chicago: Chicago Historical Society, 1991.

Spaeth, David. *Mies van der Rohe*. New York: Rizzoli, 1985.

Spengler, Oswald. *The Decline of the West*. New York: Alfred A. Knopf, 1926.

Swan, David. "Chicago Riverfront Study." Unpublished report of the Chicago Department of City Planning, May 28, 1964.

Wachsmann, Konrad. *Holzhausbau*. Berlin: Wasmuth, 1930.

_____. *The Turning Point of Building Structure and Design*. New York: Reinhold, 1961.

Wilson, Richard Guy. "An Artist and a Poet, Alfred Caldwell Illuminates Nature's Ways." *Landscape Architecture*, September 1977, 407–12.

_____. "Themes of Continuity: The Prairie School in the 1920s and 1930s." In *Modern Architecture in America*, ed. Richard Guy Wilson and Sidney K. Robinson, 185–212. Ames: Iowa State University Press, 1991.

Wilson, Richard Guy, and Sidney K. Robinson. *The Prairie School in Iowa*. Ames: Iowa State University Press, 1977.

Wit, Wim de, and William W. Tippens. "Prairie School in the Parks." In *Prairie in the City: Naturalism in Chicago's Parks, 1870–1940*, 33–41. Exhibition catalog. Chicago: Chicago Historical Society, 1991.

Library of Congress Cataloging-in-Publication Data

Alfred Caldwell : the life and work of a Prairie school landscape architect / edited
    by Dennis Domer.
        p.   cm.
    Includes bibliographical references (p.   ) and index.
    ISBN 0-8018-5551-9 (alk. paper)
    1. Caldwell, Alfred, 1903–   . 2. Landscape architects — United States —
Biography. 3. Landscape architecture — United States. 4. Prairie school
(Architecture)   I. Domer, Dennis E.
SB470.C33A78   1997
712'.092 — dc21   96-49076
                                                                      CIP